T0339439

PROPERTY TAX: AN INTERNATIONAL COMPARATIVE REVIEW

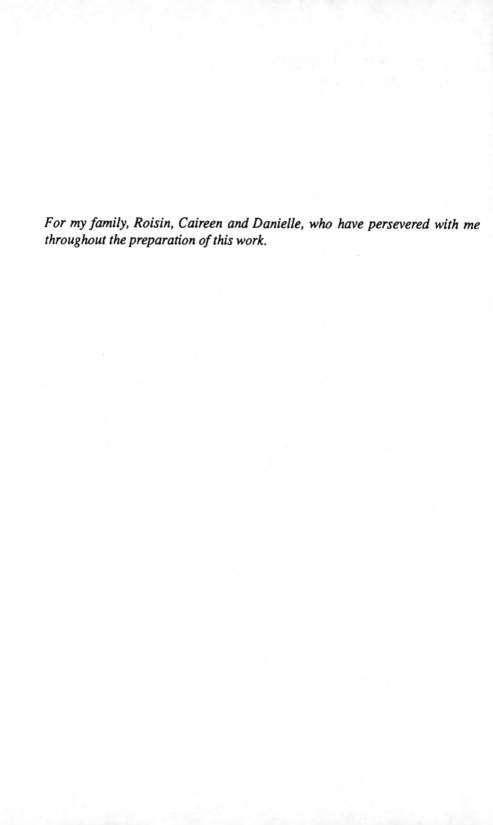

For my family, Roisin, Caireen and Danielle, who have persevered with me throughout the preparation of this work.

Property Tax: An International Comparative Review

Edited by
WILLIAM McCLUSKEY
School of the Built Environment
University of Ulster
Northern Ireland

Routledge
Taylor & Francis Group

LONDON AND NEW YORK

First published 1999 by Ashgate Publishing

Reissued 2018 by Routledge
2 Park Square, Milton Park, Abingdon, Oxon, OX14 4RN
52 Vanderbilt Avenue, New York, NY 10017

Routledge is an imprint of the Taylor & Francis Group, an informa business

A Library of Congress record exists under LC control number: 98074435

ISBN 13: 978-1-138-36277-2 (hbk)
ISBN 13: 978-1-138-36289-5 (pbk)
ISBN 13: 978-0-429-43184-5 (ebk)

Contents

Figures and tables

List of contributors

William McCluskey (editor) is Senior Lecturer in Real Estate at the University of Ulster, Northern Ireland and Visiting Professor of Real Estate at the University of Łódź, Poland. He has some 20 years practical and academic experience within the field of property taxation. He holds a undergraduate degree in estate management from the University of Ulster and a Postgraduate Diploma in Property Investment from the College of Estate Management. He is the author and editor of several books and has published extensively on property tax systems, computer assisted mass appraisal and geographic information systems.

Oscar Baraquero is the Provincial Assessor for the Province of Rizal, Philippines. He has been in the assessment service for 34 years and holds a bachelors degree and masters degree in Business Administration. In 1977, he was selected by the Department of Finance to undertake technical training in Real Property Tax Administration (RPTA), a program sponsored by the United States Agency for International Development (USAID) held at the University of Southern California. He has been the Executive Vice-President of the Philippine Association of Local Treasurers and Assessors.

Geoff Brakspear studied at the University of Reading and obtained a BSc in Estate Management in 1976. On his return to Zimbabwe in 1980 he was employed by Knight Frank, where he is now a partner in the Zimbabwe operations. In 1990/92 he was involved in the rating revaluation of the city of Harare and in 1992/94 in the revaluation of the city of Bulawayo. He is a past president of the Real Estate Institute of Zimbabwe and was conferred Honorary Life Membership for services to the Institute in 1995.

Jan Brzeski holds a doctorate in public finance and is currently the President of the Crakow Real Estate Institute. He has been in the forefront of Polish economic reform with particular interest in ad valorem property taxes. He has written widely on the subject and spoken at numerous conferences. He is presently senior advisor to the Deputy prime Minister in relation to real estate reform. He also lectures at the Jagiellonian University.

Claudia De Cesare has a MSc, Diploma in Real Estate Valuation and a BSc C.Eng. She currently works in the field of property taxation for the Porto Alegre City Council, Brazil. In addition, she is a part-time lecturer at the Department of Architecture and Urban Studies of the Ritter dos Reis Institute.

Garry Dowse is based in the Finance and Property Studies Department at Massey University's Palmerston North Campus. He is a lecturer in valuation, a registered valuer and has a number of years experience working with Valuation New Zealand as a rating valuer.

Riël Franzsen is Professor in the Department of Mercantile Law at the University of South Africa, lecturing primarily in tax law. He has contributed chapters to various books on mercantile law and also a number of articles on taxation to South African and international journals. He has presented papers on property taxation at conferences in South Africa, the United States, United Kingdom, Italy, Ireland and Denmark.

Stuart Gronow holds a MA and BSc and is Professor of Real Estate Appraisal at the University of Glamorgan. His research interests include residential property, information technology applications, education and training, urban regeneration and environmental issues.

Bob Hargreaves is based in the Finance and Property Studies Department at Massey University's Palmerston North campus. He holds the Chair in Property Studies and is a registered valuer and member of the Land Valuation Tribunal. He has published widely in the field of property taxation and delivered a number of papers at international conferences.

Bobby Hastings is a lecturer in the Department of Real Estate and Construction at the University of Hong Kong where, as part of a multi-disciplinary team, she lectures in the areas of real estate economics and management. Her research interests currently include property issues in relation to real estate management and urban renewal in Hong Kong and China.

Raja Hizam was previously a lecturer at Institut Teknologi Mara, Shah Alam, Selangor, Malaysia, when she undertook her MPhil research at the University of Glamorgan. She is currently director CDSB Culon Development (M) SDN.BHD, Kuala Lumpur.

David Hornby is currently a lecturer in real estate at the Canberra Institute of Technology. He is the author of a number of books on valuation and has written widely on the subject of property taxation. He has presented numerous papers at international conferences.

David Jenkins is Senior Researcher at the Centre for Research in the Built Environment at the University of Glamorgan. He is a Fellow of the Society of Valuers and Auctioneers and his research interests include new technologies for surveyors, knowledge strategy, valuation methodology and business ethics.

Simon Keith, a Chartered Surveyor in the Rural Practice Division, is presently Senior Officer in the Land Tenure Service of the Food & Agriculture Organization of the United Nations. He was previously Assistant Chief Valuer in the United Kingdom Valuation Office and subsequently Chief Executive of the Commonwealth Association of Surveying and Land Economy. He has been involved in the design of property tax systems and other land tenure matters in some 20 countries.

Nat Khublall is both a Chartered Surveyor and a Barrister and in 1997 has been awarded the higher doctorate degree (DSc) by the University of Reading. He has many years of professional and academic experience in the United Kingdom, Hong Kong, Guyana and Singapore. Until recently, he was an Associate Professor at the National University of Singapore. He has to his credit nine textbooks in real estate law and taxation.

Jan Paul Kruimel has been involved in local authority property taxation since 1976. He has been a consultant and in the 1980s worked for the Ministry of Internal Affairs and was responsible for drafting of legislation on provincial and municipal taxes. Currently he is a consultant on local taxes for several government agencies.

Mihály Lados is currently Deputy Director of the West Hungarian Research Institute of Centre for Regional Studies of the Hungarian Academy of Sciences, Győr. Previously he was a senior research fellow in the same organization with specific interests in public finance, local government finance, national and local tax systems and regional policy. He has a MSc in Economics from the University of Pecs, Hungary, a MSc in Urban Management from Erasmus University, the Netherlands and a PhD in Economics awarded by the Hungarian Academy of Sciences.

Suzanne Lyons is Assistant Commissioner with the Land Valuation and Estates Department, Jamaica. She holds a degree in Estate Management from the College of Estate Management, Reading and has considerable experience in land value based property tax systems.

Ngaka Monagen was a Senior Lands Officer in the Department of Lands responsible for assessment of properties in six rating authorities. Now Principal Lands Officer in charge of Rating and Estates Division in the Department. He completed a HND in Estate Management at the North East London Polytechnic in 1985, a BSc in Land Administration at the same Institution in 1988 and an MSc in Real Estate at Reading University in 1994. He is a member of the Real Estate Institute of Botswana.

Abdul Nawawi is a lecturer at the Department of Urban Estate Management, Institut Teknologi Mara, Shah Alam, Selangor, Malaysia, who undertook his PhD research at the University of Glamorgan into knowledge acquisition for rating valuation in Malaysia.

Washington Olima holds a Bachelor of Arts in Land Economics (Honours) degree and a Master of Arts in Housing Administration, both degrees from the University of Nairobi, Kenya, as well as a PhD in Spatial Planning from Dortmund University, Germany. He has been a lecturer in the Department of Land Development, in the University of Niarobi, Kenya, since 1988. He is a full member of the Institute of Surveyors of Kenya, Valuation and Estate Management Surveyors chapter. He has written several papers in refereed international journals, and has attended several local and international conferences, workshops and seminars.

Antonakis Panayi is the Valuation Officer in charge of the Lemesos (Limassol) District Land Office. He deals with all types of valuations, including valuations for acquisitions, taxation, sales at auction, leasehold etc. He is a member of the Society of Surveying Technicians (MSST) and has 25 years experience in property valuation in Cyprus.

Panayiotis Panayiotou is a Land Officer based at the Land Information Centre of the Lands and Surveys Department. His main duties include research for the development of Land Information Systems and the introduction of computerized methods and procedures in the Lands and Surveys Department. He is currently undertaking research into immovable property taxation and the application of an artificial neural network valuation system for residential properties for tax purposes in Cyprus.

Gábor Péteri is currently head of the International Bureau of the Council Associations. He has a PhD in public finance and has published extensively in local finance and municipal policy. He previously was employed by the Hungarian Institute of Public Administration.

Frances Plimmer is Reader in Real Estate Valuation at the School of the Built Environment at the University of Glamorgan. She is a Chartered Valuation Surveyor and researches into valuation for land taxation, professional qualifications for real estate professionals. She is the editor of 'Property Management' and is a member of committees of the Royal Institution of Chartered Surveyors dealing with research and both UK and international professional qualifications.

Alena Rohlícková is currently Director of the Property Taxes Department within the Ministry of Finance of the Czech Republic. Her primary responsibilities include the preparation of legislation on property tax, transfer taxes and local fees. She graduated from the Faculty of Law, Charles University in 1982, and was awarded a doctorate in legal and state sciences from Charles University in Prague in 1983.

Les Ruddock holds a PhD, CStat, MSc Econ., MSc, and BA. He is Director of International Activities at the Research Centre for the Built and Human Environment, University of Salford, UK. He has authored several books on the economics of the property market. As a Co-ordinator for the "Conseil International du Batiment pour la recherche l'Etude et la Documentation", he specialises in international comparisons of property market data.

Tambet Tiits is currently Director of a real estate consultancy organization with a particular interest in property tax matters. Previously he was Director of the National Cadastre at the Estonian National Land Survey. He presently holds a bachelor of science degree in land surveying and a masters degree in economics.

Aivar Tomson is presently Deputy Director of a private real estate consulting firm in Tallinn, Estonia. His previous work experience included land registration and valuation for property taxation at the Estonian National Land Board. He holds a bachelor of science degree in land surveying from the Estonian University of Agriculture.

Sakon Varanyuwatana is Assistant Professor of Economics at Thammasat University. He received his PhD from Maxwell School of Citizenship, Syracuse University, New York, United States. He has served on sub-committees with regard to budget reform and numerous government advisory boards. His main academic contributions have been in the area of economics and local public finance.

Megan Walters is Assistant Professor at the Hong Kong Polytechnic University lecturing on property management and corporate real estate issues. Prior to lecturing in Hong Kong she worked in both the public and private sectors in the United Kingdom. Her research interests include the use and management of property by organisations and the management of multiple ownership property in Hong Kong.

Brendan Williams is a lecturer in urban economics at the Dublin Institute of Technology (DIT), and Director of Research at the Consultancy and Research Unit for the Built Environment at DIT. His research and publications have centred on fiscal policies and urban property markets and specifically the role of fiscal interventions in urban development and regeneration.

Preface

The main purpose and goal of this book is to add to the existing body of knowledge with regard to the application of ad valorem property taxation in various countries. To this end the present volume has essentially focused on updating, revising and extending the coverage of material included in the earlier book, 'Comparative Property Tax Systems' (McCluskey, 1991).

Interest in property tax systems, particularly from the international community of assessors, politicians, economists, fiscal experts, has been steadily growing over the last 20 years. There are several reasons which might help to explain this. As Bahl and Linn (1992) commented, 'The property tax is the single most important local government tax in developing countries'. In fact, if sufficient empirical research was undertaken one might find that the recurrent property tax is of significant importance in most countries where it is employed. In terms of the lower tiers of government, the property tax is ideally suited as a source of tax revenue to fund local services. In all countries a considerable amount of wealth is tied up in real estate (land and buildings); rising property prices can in many instances be correlated to the efforts and expenditure in infrastructure by government, therefore a tax on property values can be looked upon as a form of wealth tax and a mechanism to tax the unearned increment. In developing countries the choice(s) of tax base can be somewhat limited, particularly from the perspective of accurately identifying the taxpayer, enforcing payments and collecting arrears. Reliance on the property tax in these countries has the advantage that the tax base is uniquely fixed, taxpayers in terms of owners or occupiers are readily identifiable and enforcement can easily be effected by placing a charge on the property or by forced sale.

Emphasis on property taxation is high on the agenda of many countries, none more so than the former soviet satellite republics of Central and Eastern Europe. In those countries even with a number of unique disadvantages not common to other countries, for example, limited private ownership of land, partial cadastres and rights of land restitution, the property tax is set to become an important revenue source particularly for the new tiers of local government created by the process of decentralization. Interest by international funding bodies such as the World Bank and USAID in relation to public finance systems attaches a significant degree of importance upon the strengthening and reform of existing property tax systems.

The decision criteria in terms of country selection for the present volume was essentially four-fold; firstly, to include several of the countries first described in the earlier book, in fact 13 countries were included in that book, eight of which have been incorporated within the present volume; secondly, to provide as wide a geographical spread as possible, which has resulted in the following continents being represented, South America, Europe, Africa, Asia and Australasia. There is however, one notable exception from this list, North America. My only defense for not including a chapter on either Canada or the United States is essentially based on the fact that there is already a wealth of published material on the North American property tax. Given that space within the current volume was at a premium I took the decision, rightly or wrongly, to exclude North America, therefore all responsibility for this lies with myself as the editor. Thirdly, to provide coverage of all the main property tax bases including improved capital value, unimproved capital value, annual rental value and area based systems; and finally, it was recognized as important to ensure that the countries included should, as far as possible, complement rather than duplicate other published material such as the 'International Survey of Taxes on Land and Buildings' (Youngman and Malme, 1994).

The current volume includes 21 countries, by far the largest coverage of comparative material in one publication. It has been the overriding aim of this volume to provide a concise and comprehensive exposition of each country and to this end the expert authors have to be commended in their diligence and respect of detail given the constraints placed upon them in terms of both time and space. The material collected will enable a comparison of different tax systems, policy criteria and critical analysis to be undertaken. Notwithstanding that the country reviews are in essence a distillation of each system as it is applied in different countries, they do form the basis for identifying common approaches, including specific system adjustments to reflect cultural, historic, tenure and social differences.

A property tax system is essentially an amalgam of important factors all of which have their part to play in the effective and efficient operation of the tax. The main features would include the basis of the tax, its role within local, state and national fiscal systems, assessment techniques, incidence of the tax, breadth of the tax base, exemptions and reliefs, collection procedures and enforcement mechanisms. Each can be examined and analysed independently of the rest, however, it is the overall integration which is significant. In addition to the actual mechanics of the tax, other issues such as transparency, acceptability, equity and fairness are of equal importance. Therefore, the analysis of a property tax system must take cognisance of the political environment, the social and economic objectives of the tax and the cultural background.

This book demonstrates the variety of techniques, processes and procedures with regard to property tax implementation. It highlights the weaknesses and strengths of systems and the continuing need for systems to evolve to address these. One of the underlying themes among most, if not all, of the countries surveyed is the relative importance of the property tax as a revenue source for local government. Several countries are able to maximize revenue generation, in other countries the application of the property tax is constrained and adversely affected by attempting to achieve other economic and political goals.

Finally, it is my hope that this volume of internationally based property tax systems will continue to focus the debate and interest in what is an unique form of public finance.

William McCluskey

Acknowledgements

It goes without saying that the eventual completion of this book was more the result of a team effort than a solo endeavour. Assistance over the time it took to complete this venture took many forms including help with editing, proof reading, graphics and general encouragement. Special thanks must therefore go to Rosemary Clelland for the preparation of the graphics contained in the book. And finally, deepest appreciation to Roisin McCluskey (my wife) for her patience and tremendous support.

1 Introduction: a comparative evaluation

William McCluskey and Brendan Williams

Introduction

The main purpose of this chapter is to compare and contrast several of the principle elements relating to ad valorem property tax systems. What is clear from the findings presented in this book are both the broad similarities and the significant differences between countries' systems. This dichotomy is however, more apparent than real as each tier of government with an interest in property taxation is essentially trying to achieve one specific goal, that of revenue generation. In some instances the subsidiary issues of land policy, land development, environmental aspects and income redistribution can also be influenced to varying degrees through the implementation of local property taxes.

This chapter by its very nature can only hope to provide a macro-level analysis, but it does provide and permit a robust comparison of some of the essential features of the real property tax. For a more in-depth study the chapter reviews provide a wealth of information based on local expert knowledge.

Local fiscal autonomy

In terms of a local financial system it has to be recognized that no single set of financial circumstances will serve all purposes (Layfield, 1976). The first and most vital component is local accountability, meaning that the government, whether central or local, should be accountable to the electorate. The issues of local autonomy and local accountability are closely related, in that one of the principal reasons for giving local government a measure of fiscal discretion is to improve or encourage local accountability (Owens, 1992). This results in the local electorates being empowered in terms of influencing the mix of available taxes, fees and charges, thereby encouraging and promoting a more efficient allocation of resources at the local level. It could be argued that local accountability and locally determined expenditure should be passed on to those residing in a local authority and availing of local services either through property taxes or service charges. It is clear, therefore, that this can best be effected if local authorities have their own tax resources. It tends to follow then, that there is a case to meet the cost of local services primarily through locally based revenue, as opposed to central funding such as grants, etc. It can of course also be argued that central government grants can be essential in terms of equalization to ensure that there is parity of services delivered between different jurisdictions. Service charges and fees have the attraction of 'let the user pay', therefore the benefit is directly related to the charge, notwithstanding that user charges tend to be insufficient to cover the full economic cost of the services provided.

Range of local taxes

In essence to give a measure of credibility to their status as autonomous entities and to enhance local accountability local governments need to have a strong source of own fiscal revenues. Most countries would tend to have only one or two major local taxes even though others could be incorporated within the fiscal package. There are essentially four main tax options for local government, namely:

1   an increase in existing local taxes such as tourist taxes or dog licensing taxes;

2   an assignment of a central tax such as income tax to the local level;

3   introducing a local sales tax such as VAT; and

4   either the introduction or extension of an ad valorem tax.

Table 1.1 gives a brief summary comparing the likely impact of the range of taxes across a specified set of criteria.

Principles of a good local tax

The canons of taxation were initially formulated by Adam Smith and published in his book 'Wealth of Nations'. These principles or maxims postulate that:

•   'The subjects of every state ought to contribute to the support of the government, as nearly as possible in proportion to their respective abilities.'

Table 1.1
Evaluative characteristics of local government taxes

Criteria	Income Tax	Sales Tax	Property Tax	Tourist Tax
Yield	H	H	H	H
Fairness	H	H	H/M	M
Accountability	M	M	H	L
Administration Costs	H	H	L	M
Equity	H	M/H	M/H	L
Efficiency	H	M	H	L
Avoidance	H	L	L	M/H

H = high; M = medium; L = low

In terms of equity this would imply that people should contribute to the finance of the state or jurisdiction according to their means. Whereas income is indicative of ability to pay, the ownership of real property may not be, unless it is held as an investment and generates an annual income.

• 'The tax which each individual is bound to pay ought to be certain and not arbitrary. The time of payment, the quantity to be paid, ought to be clear and plain to the contributor, and to every other person.' To a large extent both personal income tax and property taxes would comply with this canon.

• 'Every tax ought to be levied at the time or in the manner, in which it is the most convenient for the contributor to pay it.'

• 'Every tax ought to be so contrived as both to take out and to keep out of the pockets of the people as little as possible over and above what it brings into the public treasury of the state.'

In addition, the following new principles are particularly important with regard to local taxes.

• Taxes should be difficult to avoid and evade. Property taxes score particularly well here as the basis of the tax is immoveable property which is fixed in location.

- They should be local in nature with local authorities being able to vary the rate of tax. Obviously linked to this is that the tax base should be readily identifiable with the local authority area.

- Local taxation should have a clear identity and be perceptible to local taxpayers. That is to say, they should be aware they are paying the tax, of its amount, to whom it is payable and the purposes to which the revenue collected is put.

- The basis upon which the tax is assessed should be applied uniformly and the assessments should be comprehensible to the taxable.

- The revenue from the local tax should be predictable and substantial to the budgetary and financial planning processes of local authorities. In addition, the revenue yield should be stable and not prone to severe fluctuations and variability.

- The local tax should be a practical tax and not unduly complex in nature or application. This would include ensuring that the methods of assessment are transparent and the appeals process at the first instance is accessible, inexpensive and informal.

- The tax should be fair in terms of definition but also in application. In relation to the meaning of fair the objective would seem to be to ensure that the tax is applied fairly across all taxpayers within a specific jurisdiction.

- The tax should be administratively efficient to assess and collect. It is important to ensure that the costs of the administrative system should be minimized whilst maximizing the collectable amount. Monitoring of arrears and instituting procedures to enforce its collection play an important role within the overall process.

- The tax should be easily understood. Simplicity is an essential concept, given that taxpayer understanding is essential if support for the system is to be maintained.

- The tax should be sustainable. This is an important aspect relating to its long term application and degree of permanence.

Rationale of the property tax

The property tax is clearly a fiscal tool aimed primarily at the raising of sustainable revenue to meet a range of specific expenditures. In many ways this purist rationale becomes diluted when the property tax is also considered as a mechanism to solve a multiplicity of economic, political and social problems. The two rationales are not essentially compatible, because in achieving the latter, revenue potential is compromised. Tax bases are narrowed through generous exemptions and reliefs, coverage becomes inequitable, inadequate sanctions and penalties lead to unfairness and low compliance.

The property tax essentially provides for an element of balance and equity within the total tax system, by taxing one component of ability to pay which tends to be exempt from general taxation. Therefore, the property tax allocates the cost of services, whether provided by the local, state or central tier of government according to ability to pay as measured by real property wealth.

One of the main disadvantages associated with property tax is that the tax is based on unrealized values, with the exception of income producing investment property, for example, owner occupied property, vacant or undeveloped property. There is often a misunderstanding by taxpayers as to the relationship between assessed value and tax liability. A reassessment does not always result in an increase in tax liability, but rather a redistribution of the tax revenues. A further problem relates to the linkages between the property tax and the services it is supposed to cover, with some services only being indirectly related to property ownership or occupation.

The property tax is a unique mechanism for local revenue generation. The primary store of accumulated wealth in both developed and developing countries is in real estate. Such property is visible, immobile and a clear indication of one form of wealth. The property tax is thus difficult to avoid and if well administered can represent a non-distortionary and highly efficient fiscal tool.

Theories of taxation

Currently the two main theories of taxation as they are relevant to property taxation are the 'benefit theory' and the 'ability to pay' theory. Whilst their origins go back over several centuries the basic concepts underlying them have remained the same.

Benefit theory

The underlying rationale of this theory is that all should contribute to the cost of services in relation to the benefits they receive. In essence, the benefit principle rests on the commercial foundation that it is only fair to pay for what you receive in terms of services. When someone receives a direct and measurable benefit from a government activity it would seem logical that they should pay for it. However, one of the basic problems with this approach is that there is, in general, no precise way in which policy makers can determine individual evaluations of public services. The lumpiness or indivisible nature of many public services, makes the task of determining the marginal benefits received by particular individuals an almost impossible task. The major application of the benefit principle in practice has traditionally been to justify differential taxation on those individuals or groups that are considered to specifically benefit from a service, for example motor fuel taxes, water charges and special assessments levied to finance urban capital improvements. As an argument, if a person owns property worth twice that of someone else, then their contribution for protection should be twice as much. From the benefit principle point of view it can be argued that the property tax used to meet expenditures such as fire protection, street cleaning, environmental improvements etc. are basically site orientated services, benefiting local property owners and thereby increasing the value of their properties. Support for this contention is provided by evidence of nearly full capitalization of service benefits into housing values (Bloom et al, 1983). In essence the property tax can be considered as the price to be paid for the particular bundle of services supplied by the appropriate tier of government.

One of the criticisms of this theory, is that it requires measurement of what is effectively immeasurable. However, there is a direct link between the fiscal system and the perceived benefits to be derived, people will not tolerate for long a system from which they do not benefit. A willingness to pay specific taxes for specific benefits is an indication of a person's or society's preference which can be used as the basis for public expenditure decision making.

Ability to pay

This theory is based on the proposition that, on the grounds of equity, people should contribute to the finance of the state in accordance to their means. Income is traditionally taken as a direct indicator of taxable capacity, whereas, the ownership of real property may not be, unless the property is let and generating an income. Clearly then, ability to pay must be related to individual circumstances and reflect all potential sources of income and wealth.

Equality of sacrifice is often suggested as being an important component within a local tax system. What is generally agreed, is that the payment of taxes involves sacrifice. An equitable tax system should therefore aim to ensure that all taxpayers should make an equal sacrifice. There have been few attempts to quantify the expression 'equal sacrifice', as much depends on individual material circumstances. Equity is an essential quality of any tax system including property taxes. One can distinguish between the two dimensions of horizontal and vertical equity; horizontal equity requires the same treatment for tax purposes of people in the same economic circumstances, vertical equity on the other hand implies that taxpayers having different economic circumstances should have different tax liabilities. Many of the most difficult questions relating to tax policy stem from the practical difficulties of determining economic well-being and how best to measure that in terms of the most appropriate tax base. In any event equity should also be considered from the perspective of tax neutrality. In this context neutrality is taken to mean that the tax system should not influence economic or behavioural decisions of taxpayers.

It can be argued that the property tax is consistent with both the ability to pay and benefits principles of taxation. From the viewpoint of ability to pay, the property tax can in certain cases compensate for the imperfections within the taxation of incomes. The preferred measures of income should in an ideal situation be a comprehensive one, in that being comprehensive, tax neutrality or economic efficiency can be achieved. This would require that all additions to wealth whether in the form of money income, savings, stocks, bonds, real estate etc. should form part of the tax equation. However, in reality due to both practical issues and complexities this is not the case. In practical terms most countries tend to combine elements related to both ability to pay and benefit principles by incorporating a range of taxes, fees and charges.

Relative importance of the property tax

Table 1.2 shows the relative importance of property tax as a percentage of total revenue to both state and local tiers of government. The figures give a broad indication of the relative changes in importance over a 19 year period. The information is based on a number of Organization of European Cooperation and Development (OECD) countries under the heading of recurrent taxes on immovable property. Covered under this heading are taxes levied regularly in respect of the use or ownership of immoveable property. These taxes are levied on land and buildings, in the form of a percentage of an assessed property value based on rental income, sales price or capitalized yield; or in terms of other characteristics of real property, such as size and location from which are derived a presumed rental or capital value. Unlike taxes on net wealth, debts are not taken into account in their assessment.

Table 1.2
Property taxes as a percentage of total tax revenue of local or state government in selected OECD countries

	1975	1985	1994	% Change
Australia				
State	26.6	25.7	29.4	+1.1
Local	100.0	99.6	99.6	-
Canada				
State	2.3	4.0	7.3	+217.0
Local	88.3	84.8	85.3	-3.3
United States				
State	4.1	3.7	4.3	-
Local	81.9	74.2	75.8	-7.4
Czech Republic	-	-	0.4	-
Denmark	13.2	6.4	7.1	-46.2
New Zealand	89.1	93.0	90.2	+1.2
France	19.1	25.2	26.0	+36.1
Hungary	-	-	9.7	-
Ireland	100.0	100.0	100.0	-
Italy	17.5	-	42.1	+140.6
Netherlands	54.2	75.2	66.9	+23.4
Poland	-	-	36.5	-
United Kingdom	100.0	100.0	100.0	-

Source: Revenue Statistics of OECD Member Countries, 1965-1995

In relation to Table 1.3 the categories chosen are fairly robust and relate to how important the property tax is as a percentage of total local government revenue. The following therefore apply; marginally significant - less than 30 per cent; significant - greater than 30 but less than 50 per cent; and very significant - greater than 50 per cent.

Table 1.3
Significance of the property tax to local government

Country	Marginally significant	Significant	Very significant
Australia			*
Botswana		*	
Brazil		*	
Cyprus		*	
Czech Republic	*		
Estonia			*
Hong Kong[1]			*
Hungary	*		
Ireland	*		
Jamaica			*
Kenya			*
Malaysia			*
Netherlands			*
New Zealand			*
Pakistan	*		
Philippines		*	
Poland		*	
Singapore[2]			
South Africa		*	
Thailand			*
Zimbabwe			*

1   *Whilst the revenue from the property tax is primarily a central tax, a refund is made to the two municipal councils representing their major source of revenue.*
2   *The property tax in Singapore is a central tax only.*

Reassessment cycle

One of the most important structural features of the ad valorem property tax is the reassessment or revaluation cycle. It represents an important determinant related to the accuracy of assessed values and revenue productivity (Bahl and Linn, 1992). Essentially revaluations occur in an attempt to realign property tax liabilities among properties in proportion to the assessed value of the property. As the tax is a function of the market value of the property, it is imperative that similar property should have similar values. In other words the principle of horizontal equity should be adhered to. Just as the tax liability is a function of the value of property, the value of property is also a function of the market. Given the imperfections of the real estate market it is a realistic assumption that over a given period of time the market value of different property types will tend to move at different rates, and in addition, the values of similar property can vary according to location and neighbourhood attributes. To maintain equity and fairness within the ad valorem system it is important to recognize the impact of differential changes in property values and to implement revaluations to account for them. The effect of the tax is to distribute the cost of services between the owners/occupiers of real property pro rata to the values recorded in the valuation list/roll. The correctness of the values is crucial to the proper operation of the system. Without frequent and regular revaluations, no property tax can be fairly applied.

Having irregular revaluation cycles creates the problem of low levels of buoyancy in property tax revenues, since the only manner in which the property tax base can grow is by new properties being added to the valuation list/roll. In the presence of inflation, assessed values are eroded in real terms which creates significant increases in relative tax burdens when a reassessment eventually does occur. In the absence of revaluations one possible alternative is the use of indexation, where property values are increased at least by the prevailing rate of inflation. In Brazil, municipalities are permitted to make increases in the assessed values providing they do not exceed the general inflation rate.

As far as the authors are aware no empirical research has been undertaken into determining an objective basis for establishing the most effective revaluation cycle. In most countries the requirement to undertake revaluations is normally prescribed by legislation, inclusive of the proviso to postpone or cancel if necessary. Because of the scarcity of assessors and other factors directly related to frequent reassessment, the cycle tends to be extended, in many cases in excess of 10 years. In contrast to having rigid and pre-determined cycles, the alternative option is to have a market led approach of revaluations. This would suggest that the revaluation should be in response to market changes and based upon objective market research. Table 1.4 illustrates the frequency of the revaluation cycles for the survey countries.

From an international perspective there is still an over reliance placed on statutory prescribed cycles; alternatively, if not a legislative requirement revaluations tend to be scheduled on the basis of ad hoc local authority decisions. Clearly, the former while not totally satisfactory, is much more preferable than the latter option. In a number of Australian states recognition is made of the fact

10

Table 1.4

Frequency of revaluation cycles

Country	Revaluation Cycle
Australia	Annually for the large urbanized areas and 3 - yearly for smaller local authorities
Botswana	5 - yearly
Brazil[1]	No legal requirement
Cyprus	Last revaluation in 1980
Czech Republic	Not applicable
Estonia	No frequency for revaluations stated, likely to follow a 3-yearly cycle
Hong Kong	3 - yearly
Hungary	Not applicable
Ireland	Last revaluation 1914
Jamaica	5 - yearly
Kenya	At discretion of municipalities, normally 10 - yearly
Malaysia	5 - yearly
Netherlands	At discretion of municipalities, normally 4 - yearly
New Zealand	3 - yearly
Pakistan	5 - yearly
Philippines[2]	3 - yearly
Poland	Not applicable
Singapore	Annually
South Africa	4 - yearly
Thailand	4 - yearly
Zimbabwe	To be undertaken not less than every 3 years nor more than every 10 years

1   *In Brazil local municipalities can implement annual indexation at the rate of inflation.*
2   *A system of indexing applies between revaluations.*

that particular urbanized local government areas have quite volatile property markets and to reflect this, revaluations are conducted annually (e.g. Brisbane, Perth, Sydney and Melbourne). Revaluations for the remaining local authorities are determined by reference to property price movements but still adhering to a three year cycle. In New Zealand, Wellington is the only city to have an annual revaluation cycle while the remaining local authorities tend to be revalued every three years.

The Institute of Revenues Rating and Valuation (IRRV) (1997) identified a number of reasons for regular revaluations including: the failure to revalue leads to inequity between taxpayers; it results in inequity between local authorities or municipalities; and as property prices move away from their base date values, confidence in the system is undermined.

The tax base

The basis of the tax is normally established by the laws of the respective countries. In some instances the basis is prescriptive and must be adhered to, whilst in other cases, the municipality or state has a choice of several options (New Zealand, Malaysia, South Africa). There is a great variety in the international practice with regard to the approaches employed in ad valorem property taxation. There are essentially three basic forms of ad valorem property taxation; the tax may be levied on the annual or rental value of the property, the improved capital value, or the site value of the land excluding improvements. This classification, whilst sufficient at a general level does disguise the application of hybrid approaches and system refinements to reflect particular social, economic, cultural and fiscal characteristics. In essence, each country implants its own style, cultural values and political considerations on the format of the property tax. The choice between the particular bases according to Youngman and Malme (1994) tends to relate more to social and political concerns. They contend that the primary distinction between annual and capital values lies in the recognition of potential future gains. However, it can also be argued that this somewhat over simplifies what is a very complex matrix inherent within the choice and selection of a particular system.

Table 1.5 shows the use of the various bases amongst the surveyed countries. From a total of 21 countries the split in terms of base usage is: 9 countries employ improved capital values, 3 unimproved values, 4 annual rental values and 3 on an area basis whilst the remaining 6 have employed a combination of bases. However, some caution should be placed on this rather robust analysis, since the countries researched in this book were pre-selected and would therefore in a statistical sense not be representative of the whole population of countries.

In South Africa and Zimbabwe the valuation rolls must show the values of both the unimproved land and the value of the improvements to enable differential rates to be applied. In New Zealand municipalities can select between annual rental value, improved and unimproved bases. Interestingly, in that country there has been a tendency to shift from unimproved value systems to ones based on improved values. In Botswana, which applies an improved capital approach, a proposal is currently being considered which would result in commercial

12

property being valued on annual rental values. In some Australian states (Western Australia and New South Wales) unimproved values and annual rental values are simultaneously provided with each having a particular role in relation to financing certain services.

Table 1.5
Basis of tax

Country	Capital Improved	Capital Unimproved	Annual Rental Value	Area Basis
Australia		*	*	
Botswana	*[1]			
Brazil	*			
Cyprus	*			
Czech Republic				*
Estonia		*		
Hong Kong			*	
Hungary				*
Ireland			*	
Jamaica		*		
Kenya		*		
Malaysia	*		*	
Netherlands	*			
New Zealand[2]	*	*	*	
Pakistan			*	
Philippines	*			
Poland				*
Singapore			*	
South Africa	*	*		
Thailand		*	*	
Zimbabwe	*	*		

1   Land and buildings are valued separately, the arithmetic sum of both equalling the assessed value.
2   Auckland applies the annual rental value system.

Annual rental values, which have as their origins the colonizing influence of the British Empire, are still widely used by former colonies. The basis of the system is defined as the notional or expected rental value of the subject property. Whilst rental value is the basis, the question of whether the rents are gross or net of outgoings (normally maintenance and insurance costs) often arises. Gross rents have been used in England and Wales for both domestic and commercial property (prior to 1990) whilst in Northern Ireland net rents have been applied. Most countries which apply this basis tend to adopt rentals based on current use as opposed to highest and best use. As an example, the United Kingdom property tax (Rates) is regarded as a tax on actual occupation rather than ownership, therefore in terms of fairness, it would seem more appropriate to base the tax liability on the actual use being made of the property. This would imply that the rent to be adopted for tax purposes should represent current use value as opposed to open market value. Therefore, property which is under-utilized or ripe for development would tend to have assessed values lower than potential market values. However, instances such as those would tend to be the exception and would only ever represent a small percentage of the total tax base. The vast majority of properties, particularly commercial property, would be let at its full market value representing the most profitable use of the land and buildings. Where there is no current use, i.e. when the property is vacant and not producing a rent, it could be argued that as there is no actual occupation, no liability should attract (Northern Ireland), however, irrespective of whether the property is used, an assessment can be applied and a policy decision taken as to whether the owner should be taxed.

Rental value based systems do have one particular disadvantage which is not common to the other bases, that is the effect of rent control. The rationale for having rent control provisions is largely to protect a group of society from the ravages of open market competition. The tendency is for residential property or dwellings occupied by low income families to attract this form of protection or to have subsidies for the occupation of local authority housing. Clearly then, controlled or subsidized rents cannot be directly used to assess market rents unless the majority of properties are equally affected. This creates a significant problem in terms of the reliability and quantity of market based evidence (Pakistan). This was a problem recognized in Great Britain at the time of the 1973 general revaluation when there was an extreme shortage of openly negotiated residential rents, exacerbated by the fact that levels of owner occupation were increasing dramatically. Since 1993, domestic property tax in Great Britain has since been based on capital values. From an assessment point of view, as the property tax is an ad valorem tax, it is important that there is sufficient data upon which the assessments can be derived and defended in terms of taxpayer appeals.

A further problem associated with this approach relates to difficulties in determining the annual rental value of 'unique' properties, which by their nature are not let on the open market and in reality would only have one possible user. Typical examples would be properties associated with the petroleum and chemical industry, sewerage and water treatment plants and public utilities. The approach adopted is to calculate the effective cost of constructing the buildings less depreciation and then to apply a discount rate to determine the notional rental value.

Improved capital value basis

The tax base can be defined as the assessed value of land and improvements, as with the approach adopted in the annual rental value, the tax is based on the total value of the property. However, a differentiated approach is adopted in some countries where separate values for the land and buildings are provided to enable a different rate structure to be applied to each (Zimbabwe, South Africa).

In theory, the tax base is normally defined within the legislation as being equivalent to full market value, that is, the value freely negotiated between a willing seller and a willing buyer. The adoption of market value as the standard introduces the concept of highest and best use; in other words the value of the property is maximized reflecting any possible development potential. In most cases the property or land will be used to its optimum, but instances do arise where the existing use of a property is not its most valuable, e.g. agricultural land on the periphery of urban areas. The capital value approach does capture the true value of the property, and on this basis is more in line with ability to pay.

Generally from the international perspective, the capital value base is tending to become the most widely used system. In New Zealand where local authorities have the option to choose between the three bases there is currently a slight bias towards improved capital values at the expense of unimproved values. Domestic property in England, Scotland and Wales previously valued on annual rental values is now assessed on capital values (Council Tax). The reasons for this change to improved capital values include a greater volume of transaction evidence, more easily understood by the taxpayer and more abundant statistical data on property price movements.

Associated with the capital value base are a number of problems. Reliability and currency of sales information is a feature of some property market systems (Pakistan). This is to some extent related to the professional and ethical standards of the assessors/valuers and their academic and practical qualifications. In a

15

number of countries there is a quite severe shortage of qualified staff which has the adverse effect of not only being unable to maintain the assessed values but also the inability to undertake regular revaluations. A further problem which closely impacts on the performance relates to the high level of transfer taxes, which encourages under-reporting of transaction prices.

The provision of a separate valuation for land and buildings provides the taxing authorities with greater flexibility in inducing allocative effects, however, there are associated costs. These relate primarily to the assessment function and the resources available to undertake separate assessments for each property. The desired balance must be between the perceived need to apply differential taxation and the ability of the assessment department to provide accurate assessments of land and buildings.

Unimproved (site/land) value

The unimproved value system is a form of capital value taxation in which improvements to the land are exempt. Site and land value systems differ in respect whether or not improvements such as clearing, draining, levelling and the surrounding infrastructure are reflected in the property's value.

This particular approach is of particular interest because of its potential in improving the efficiency of urban land use (Bahl and Linn, 1992). The argument suggested is that since only land is taxed, the owner will have an incentive to develop the land to its most efficient use. As the tax is based on the immobile factor of production it thus reduces economic distortions and encourages intensive use of land (O'Sullivan et al, 1995). Whilst this is the theoretical rationale, the results are inconclusive on whether this form of property taxation leads to a more intensified use of urban land.

One of the disadvantages of the approach relates to the valuation of unimproved land within an environment characterized by a low transaction base. The paucity of evidence, especially in urban areas, creates the assessment problem of having to extract the value of the land from improved value sales. This approach of deducting the value of the improvements makes site valuation less objective than improved property valuation. However, from the experiences of those countries which apply the approach, the perceived lack of market evidence on land sales does not create insurmountable difficulties. A further disadvantage is that unimproved value provides a restricted tax base, and can only produce sufficient revenue at high tax rates. A substantial degree of wealth within a community is effectively untaxed with the incidence of the tax being firmly on the owner of land resulting in a more progressive tax.

An important advantage of unimproved value taxation also relates to the assessment function. By excluding all improvements the assessment process is

16

less constrained by having to regularly inspect properties to record building alterations and therefore the process is much less demanding and can be completed more cost effectively. In theory at least, revaluations should be less problematical and undertaken with shorter revaluation cycles. But this does not always translate into practice given that in Jamaica revaluations are on a 10 - year cycle, however, in Australia and New Zealand many of the large cities are on annual revaluations. This could be explained, more by reference to the level of computerization and the number of qualified and experienced staff rather than the tax system employed.

Area based systems

The alternative to ad valorem based systems is to base the tax on the physical area of the land and buildings. An area based tax was used in the Netherlands however, since 1997 it has been replaced by one based on market values. Several of the emerging democracies of central and eastern Europe have been investigating the potential role of property taxation within their newly designed fiscal systems. The Czech Republic, Hungary and Poland, whilst investigating the possible inclusion of value based property taxes, have in the interim introduced local taxes based on area. These systems have the advantage of being relatively simple to administer, enabling municipalities to establish fiscal cadastres, identify owners and occupiers, provide details on land and buildings, in essence, essential information which would be required for a value based system.

Remarks

The choice of which property tax base is optimal depends upon a number of factors, which are unique to the particular country in question. The influence of social, cultural, economic, political and historic issues, land tenure, land use, transaction evidence, staff resources and experience amongst many others contribute to the successful working of a property tax system. International experience demonstrates that most countries tend to rely on applying one system universally across all properties. There are exceptions to this, in New Zealand all three value based approaches are currently being used, most states in Australia apply unimproved values and annual rental values, Kenya can apply both capital value approaches. The use of mixed or hybrid approaches, though not widespread, does incorporate a flexibility of approach and a recognition that systems are not rigid, but dynamic and need to evolve to reflect changes within particular countries.

Responsibility for assessments

Responsibility for the assessment function can normally be classified into three broad groups. Firstly, a centralized state or nationwide valuation department secondly, each individual local authority, municipality or city undertaking the assessment function and finally the use of private firms to either assist in the process or to provide a complete service (see Table 1.6). Whilst this broad classification will cover most situations it is possible to find a combination of approaches.

Table 1.6
Responsibility for the assessment function

Country	Centralized Country/State	Municipality	Private Firms
Australia	*		
Botswana		*	*
Brazil		*	
Cyprus	*		
Czech Republic		*	
Estonia	*		
Hong Kong	*		
Hungary		*	
Ireland	*		
Jamaica	*		
Kenya		*	*
Malaysia[1]		*	
Netherlands		*	*
New Zealand[2]	*		
Pakistan	*		
Philippines		*	
Poland		*	
Singapore	*		
South Africa		*	*
Thailand		*	
Zimbabwe		*	

1   *Assessment is a municipal function however due to the lack of resources at the municipal level the central valuation authority undertakes the provision of assessments for the majority of the smaller jurisdictions.*

2   *The city of Auckland employs its own valuation staff to prepare the annual rental values.*

State or national valuation departments tend to utilize satellite sub-offices located throughout the country which provide a number of important advantages. These include economies of scale in terms of the application of information technology such as computerized administrative systems, mass appraisal and the use of geographic information systems (GIS). Smaller jurisdictions on the other hand would find the initial capital outlay on this information technology substantial and possibly prohibitive. Research and development can be undertaken more cost effectively with staff being specifically allocated to this increasingly important and supporting function. The development of uniform practices across an entire country can lead to enhanced valuation uniformity, standardized procedures and ultimately, greater efficiency. The question of data quality and quantity are important issues, obviously less of a problem for those large jurisdictions which can have several hundred thousand parcels than for areas with only a few thousand properties. A possible disadvantage would be from the perspective of the local authority which would have no real effective control on the assessment process, timing of revaluations, treatment of exempt property, etc.

There are instances where there are state/country valuation departments in addition to similar departments at the local level. In these cases the functions between the two levels of assessment organization need to be clearly defined. The State can have a strong role in promoting application of tax laws, undertaking the assessment of cross jurisdictional property such as power lines, railroads, waterways and other public utilities.

Having the assessment function controlled at the municipal level brings with it a range of issues which are largely dependant upon the size of the jurisdiction. Some large municipalities can have more parcels of real estate than some countries. The larger municipalities again can benefit from economies related to the scale of the assessment task. The smaller authorities can experience extreme difficulty in undertaking the assessment task and particularly revaluations. To resolve the problem, the larger jurisdictions, state or government valuation department can provide valuations services (as in Botswana) or alternatively private sector valuers are employed. In Malaysia 70 out of a total of 99 local authorities have to utilize the services of the Federal Valuation and Property Services Department for property tax assessment.

The use of the private sector to undertake the assessments is becoming more widespread (Pakistan, South Africa). Traditionally, there have always been situations where private valuers have assisted municipalities in the assessment process however, with the growth in competitive tendering, formerly sacrosanct public sector responsibilities are now going out to private tender. For example, in New Zealand the provision of property tax assessment is being radically reorganized. Local authorities will be able to seek tenders from the previous

19

government valuation service (Valuation New Zealand) and appropriate private firms to provide a property tax valuation service.

The sole use or indeed a partial use of the private sector brings with it certain difficulties. For example data confidentiality, conflict of interests, quality control measures and levels of post-valuation support. With regard to the latter point arrangements need to be considered in respect of the appeal procedures. Does this become the responsibility of municipal staff or retained by the private firm? This can be partially addressed by limiting the period of time allowed for objections to the new assessments.

Qualifications of assessors

Academic qualifications and relevant practical knowledge of the assessment process tends to vary considerably between countries. In some countries it is mandatory that valuers have cognate university/college degrees in typical land economy or estate management disciplines. In certain countries, the educational sector may not cater for real estate courses resulting in the valuations being undertaken by a range of other professionals such as architects, engineers and lawyers (Brazil, Pakistan). However, there is a clear trend in most countries to ensure that those undertaking the assessment function are properly qualified. Professional assessment associations are becoming more proactive in terms of training and academic accreditation such as the International Association of Assessing Officers and the International Property Tax Institute.

Responsibility for payment of the property tax

The onus in terms of the legal responsibility for payment of the property tax is normally that of the owner, occupier or in some instances both. There is a broad correlation between liability and the basis of the property tax. Generally speaking, systems based on capital values, whether improved or unimproved, tend to make the owner primarily property liable, whereas, under annual rental value systems, the occupier would be liable. Table 1.7 illustrates the spread in terms of legal liability. In the Netherlands the property tax is paid by both the owner and the user, i.e. two separate and distinct taxes targeted at each group. In Estonia and the Czech Republic the person primarily responsible for payment is the owner, however recognition is made to reflect the previous land tenure system (state ownership) by making occupiers of government owned land also liable.

Table 1.7
Person liable for payment of property tax

Country	Owner	Occupier	Both
Australia	*		
Botswana		*	*[1]
Brazil	*	*	
Cyprus	*		
Czech Republic[2]	*	*	
Estonia	*	*	
Hong Kong	*		
Hungary			
Ireland	*		
Jamaica	*		
Kenya	*		
Malaysia	*		
Netherlands			*
New Zealand		*	
Pakistan	*		
Philippines	*		
Poland	*	*	
Singapore	*		
South Africa	*		
Thailand	*		
Zimbabwe	*		

1   *If the owner defaults on payment the tax can be demanded from the occupier.*
2   *The owner is primarily liable however, in the case of state owned land, the occupier is responsible for the tax.*

Enforcement

The range of enforcement procedures tend to be fairly standard across most of the countries. Unpaid taxes normally become a first charge or lien against the property. Where the property tax payments are in arrears, the debt outstanding accrues a penalty based on either a fixed monthly rate or on a sliding scale relative to the length of time the tax has remained unpaid. In Kenya the penalty rate is 2 per cent per month, whereas in Singapore it is 5 per cent of the total debt. Legislation in most countries tends to permit the seizure and sale of goods and chattels belonging to the taxpayer; in addition the subject property can be seized and sold at public auction (Malaysia, Netherlands and Singapore), although, this action is normally one of last resort. In New Zealand whilst the occupier is primarily liable, in the instance of occupier default an authority may ultimately sue the owner or any party holding an interest in the property for the recovery of arrears. Other mechanisms to recoup delinquent taxes can involve the attachment of wages and salaries or property rents payable to the defaulter. It is quite common that, prior to the sale or transfer of real property, a clearance certificate must be obtained which declares that all outstanding tax debts have been settled (Cyprus, South Africa, Zimbabwe). In addition, the delinquent taxes may be deducted from the purchase price.

In Thailand the new owner of a property is jointly liable with the previous owner for land tax arrears extending over the previous five years. Tax arrears in excess of five years remain the responsibility of the previous owner.

Collection

The two essential components of a properly constituted property tax system are assessment and collection. Which should be given precedence is something of a moot point, or indeed, should both not be of equal importance? In some countries however, there is a tendency to emphasis one aspect, for example the system would be either collection led or valuation pushed. The assessment component is essential in terms of promoting fairness and equity within the system. The assessed values provide the basis upon which the tax is levied therefore, it is important to develop valuation methodologies which are robust, cost effective and transparent. The collection system attempts to ensure that the tax levied is actually paid with the dual objectives of maximizing prompt payment and minimizing delinquency and arrears. It could be argued that the assessment system may be state of the art, but if the tax is not, or cannot be efficiently collected then the sustainability of the system is in doubt. Hence, the case for emphasising collection, with a view to engendering an ethos of payment.

Practical experience shows that a comprehensive system of collection and enforcement relies on a range of incentives, sanctions and penalties, or a combination. Incentives can take essentially two forms firstly, a financial inducement to attempt to maximize compliance and secondly persuade taxpayers through education and media of the links between tax revenue and improved local government services. When there are problems with voluntary compliance the government must have a series of penalties to enforce payment. The sanctions could include the withholding of certain services e.g. water. Finally, if sanctions are not effective a further range of more severe penalties need to be applied such as fines, liens, seizure of personal property and eventually forced sale of the real property.

Problems associated with the collection system tend to centre around the inadequacies of the collection procedures including, the actual structure of the tax, inadequate penalties to enforce the payment and weak inducements necessary to stimulate prompt payment. Within most countries surveyed collection rates or levels of delinquency tend to be generally low. However, Botswana, Kenya, Malaysia and Jamaica are experiencing significant problems in relation to collection, with annual levels tending to be around only 60 per cent and arrears on an upward spiral. A number of reasons can account for this including inefficient administrative processes, the reticence of government to vigorously exercise their powers to impose heavy penalties, the inability to actually implement basic enforcement procedures and the failure of maintaining up-to-date records of taxpayers. In the Philippines unpaid taxes remain collectable for a period of five years, this period is extended to 10 years if fraud is proven. Another issue is related to the recipient of property tax revenue. Normally, if property tax revenue is a municipality's primary source of revenue there is a greater incentive to ensure compliance.

Table 1.8 illustrates whether the collection is undertaken as a local function or by a centralized government department. In Singapore all property tax revenue is allocated to the Consolidated Fund, whereas in other countries where the collection is centralized the revenue collected is redistributed back to the municipalities.

Hardship relief

The relief of hardship and measures to protect those on low incomes are normally provided for within the legislation. The range of mechanisms used include tax deferral programmes, where the tax is settled either on the sale of the property or on the death of the owner. In order to protect agricultural land and in particular, land at the periphery of urban areas, current use values are applied as opposed to full market value, therefore the speculative element is excluded (Jamaica, New Zealand). This can also apply to residential property located in an area which has over time changed its character from residential to commercial (Jamaica). In Singapore there is a special form of remission to commercial/industrial property owners to reflect economic recessions. Tax rebate schemes aimed at low income groups and pensioner reliefs for the elderly are also quite widely applied. In Malaysia, vacant buildings which meet specified criteria can obtain a remission on the amounts already paid. In Thailand a similar relief is also available which is currently creating administrative problems in terms of identifying whether the property is actually vacant.

Table 1.8
Responsibility for collection

Country	Local	Centralized
Australia	*	
Botswana	*	
Brazil	*	
Cyprus		*
Czech Republic		*
Estonia		*
Hong Kong		*
Hungary	*	
Ireland	*	
Jamaica		*
Kenya	*	
Malaysia	*	
Netherlands	*	
New Zealand	*	
Pakistan		*
Philippines	*	
Poland	*[1]	
Singapore		*
South Africa	*	
Thailand	*	
Zimbabwe	*	

1   In Poland the State Tax Office undertakes the collection for the smaller jurisdictions.

Exemptions

The exemption of land and buildings or both to the property tax is normally prescribed by statute or within municipal byelaws. Generally exemptions tend to fall into two categories: those based on ownership, for example state or government owned property, or those based on the use of the property such as religious or charitable purposes. It can be expressed as 'one man's exemption is another man's burden'. The level and breadth of exempt property can have an important effect on the property tax in terms of both taxpayer equity and potential loss of revenue. In Thailand, due to the exemption of owner occupied dwellings, a significant source of revenue is lost, particularly in those areas where residential property values are high. Therefore, property tax policy should ideally attempt to maximize social issues whilst minimizing the decline in the property tax base.

Government owned property

Generally speaking government owned property (including Crown land) whether it be municipal, state or central government tends to be given full exemption from property taxes. Though in the Philippines government owned or controlled property is fully taxable. There are instances where the various tiers of government who own or occupy property voluntarily make a contribution in lieu of property taxes in recognition of the fact that public buildings still require certain services which have to be paid for (Malaysia). The situation in Botswana is that the government makes an advance payment equal to approximately 90 per cent of the rates at the beginning of the financial year with the balance at the end of the year. Whether such a payment is made largely depends on the beneficiary of the property tax, if it is central government then from a practical perspective there would be little to be gained from making itself liable. However, taking the case where the beneficiary is the municipality, there is the very real scenario where within a particular municipal area there are many public buildings which could create a considerable loss of revenue (Australia).

It is normal to find that property belonging to foreign governments such as embassies, high commissions, etc. are exempt from property tax.

Agricultural and forestry land

The treatment of agricultural and forestry land varies considerably, with some countries giving full exemption (Cyprus, Ireland), some awarding partial relief (Jamaica, Netherlands), whilst others offering no relief or exemption whatsoever (Australia, New Zealand). Where agricultural land is taxable it is common to find that it is valued at its current use value as opposed to market value which could include hope or potential development value (New Zealand). In New Zealand, if agricultural land is deemed to have a value in excess of its current use, then two values are provided, one for the existing use and the other for the highest and best use. The difference between the rates as assessed on the two values may be postponed until the land is sold, or it ceases to be used for farming. The postponed rates can be written off at 5-yearly intervals. In countries which would be predominantly rural or have a propensity to have large rural municipalities, it is important for those communities to have a tax base from which to raise revenue. In those cases agricultural land would be included within the base as a matter of fiscal necessity.

Educational, charitable and welfare property

It is common in most countries to exempt property used for educational and charitable purposes. In addition, property used for health and welfare purposes are normally exempt however, profit making privately run clinics would not be so entitled. The occupation of cultural buildings such as museums, art galleries and theatres would be entitled to exemption; listed historical buildings depending on the proposes of the occupier and its use may also be exempt.

Vacant land and buildings

In some cases vacant land and/or buildings are either not taxed or indeed taxed at rates higher than those applied to occupied properties. In Botswana vacant land is taxed at a rate which is four times higher than that for developed land; and in the Philippines a 5 per cent surcharge is applied. Under unimproved value systems unused or under-utilized land/buildings would be valued at market values assuming most profitable use resulting in a penalty to the owner and an incentive to either redevelop or sell for someone else to develop. The situation under annual value systems is somewhat different. As the person primarily responsible for payment is the occupier and as the tax is based upon occupation, then if there is no occupation no liability to tax should arise.

Tax rates

Tax rates may be prescribed by law or alternatively determined by the level of expenditure which must be met by property taxation. Normally the basis of the tax is a fixed percentage of the assessed value which is set annually. Where the tax rates are set by municipal authorities there are instances where central government limit the maximum level of the tax rates, essentially a form of rate capping (Botswana, Estonia, Hungary). In relation to local autonomy, there is a general acceptance that each local municipality should have discretion in terms of determining their own rates as opposed to a uniform national rate.

Tax rates can either be proportional or progressive. With regard to the latter it can be argued that progressive rates more effectively target expensive property and therefore is a better reflection of ability to pay (Brazil, Pakistan). For a comparison of tax rates either nominal or effective among countries to be meaningful, an in-depth analysis encompassing reliefs, concessions, discounts and basis of the assessed value would need to be undertaken.

Differential tax rates

Differential tax rates can be applied to property according to the use and location and between land and improvements. It is somewhat uncertain as to the economic, social or fiscal rationale for adopting a differential rate structure, though two examples might help to illustrate the application. Lower rates on improvements are justified as providing an investment incentive; higher rates on improvements are justified on the grounds that improvements reflect ability to pay and thus higher improvement rates are beneficial on equity grounds. It could be argued that it is a mechanism to target a form of relief to, say, residential property as opposed to other commercial and industrial uses (New Zealand). The latter may represent a greater expenditure liability and therefore should contribute a larger amount. In Malaysia the rate structure is between 4-13 per cent depending on the actual use. In Kenya there is a mechanism to discriminate among properties according to both use and location, especially in urban situations.

Computerization

Property tax administration, i.e. collection and assessment, lends itself to highly automated computerized systems. In fact, it is almost essential to have such systems if the property tax is to be administered efficiently, as the large number of properties and taxpayers create problems of scale which can more readily be handled by the processing capacity of computers.

It is clearly evident from most of the countries surveyed that administration components are, by in large, computerized. However, several countries have yet to embrace the real advantages and economies to be derived from utilizing computer assisted mass appraisal systems (CAMA). When dealing with hundreds of thousands or million+ properties the reality of undertaking a manually based approach of assessment is manifested in the length of time to undertake the project. By employing such techniques as multiple regression analysis, comparable sales analysis and adaptive estimation procedure (feedback) mass appraisal is well within the capabilities of all sizes of jurisdictions. Australia, New Zealand, Hong Kong, Singapore provide excellent examples of efficient application of CAMA systems. Other countries such as Kenya, Zimbabwe, Malaysia, Poland and Estonia are at various stages in developing mass appraisal methodologies.

Appeals procedures

The appeal system normally comprises two distinct elements. Firstly, appeals can be made against a new valuation list/roll prior to its coming into effect and secondly, appeals against revised assessments made during the currency of the valuation list/roll.

After the preparation of a new valuation list, it is normal that a period of time is given to enable taxpayers to review their new assessments and to lodge appeals if necessary. This period of time varies in most countries, however, the norm would tend to be between one and six months. On the expiry of the appeal time limit an independent body or review committee (valuation tribunal, valuation court, etc.) comprising members drawn from the legal and assessment professions sit to consider the objections. After all the objections have been heard, the review body will normally confirm the list subject to any revisions. It would be extremely rare for the list to be completely set aside given the implications of such a recommendation. The approved list will remain in force until a new list has ben prepared.

During the currency of the list, taxpayers may be able to lodge appeals, but normally only to reflect specific criteria such as, revised assessments due to alterations to the property or change in ownership. In these cases annual supplementary lists are prepared which would become effective from the next financial year subject to any backdating provisions. Objections would generally be heard before the same body which reviews new lists. Given the expert nature of these bodies it is usual that they are the final arbitrator on matters of fact and valuation however, further appeals can be made to the courts on matters pertaining to points of law.

The payment by the appellant of a lump sum in advance of the appeal or objection being heard is operated in Estonia and several Australian states. The rationale of this is to discourage frivolous appeals; well founded appeals are entitled to a full refund of the lump sum.

Valuation date

Establishing an operative date of valuation is an important component of the property tax system, as it is designed to promote equity and fairness. The aim is to assess all property to values prevailing at a specific point in time. The operative date of a valuation list is therefore fixed until a new list comes into operation. New properties or existing properties requiring revised assessments should be valued relative to values at the operative date notwithstanding general increases or decreases in property values since the operative date. Hong Kong and Malaysia apply was has become known as 'tone of the list' to revised assessments made during the currency of the list. Singapore is, however, an exception where new or altered properties are reassessed to current values.

Assessment performance

The testing of assessments for accuracy, equity and uniformity by the application of standard statistical measures such as ratio studies, including coefficient of dispersion and coefficient of variation, is becoming essential. A ratio study is used as a generic term designed to evaluate assessment performance through a comparison of assessed values with market values or sale prices (IAAO, 1998).

Mechanisms to measure assessment performance particularly following a revaluation, are not widely used although a number of countries are presently investigating the application of performance standards or benchmarks as an integral part of the assessment function. In many ways the ability to undertake such an analysis is linked to the level of computerization of the country in question and specifically to the application of mass appraisal techniques.

Conclusions

From this brief comparative analysis a number of emerging themes are clearly evident. The last two decades have witnessed an increasing interest in the property tax primarily due to the need to establish decentralization programmes from the centre to local tiers of government. The basis of the interest suggests that local government can provide certain public services more effectively. This requires devolution of both revenue and expenditure functions and has created the framework for major reforms in local government finance. In support of this view, one has only to examine the changes occurring in the new democracies of central and eastern Europe and the renewed emphasis being placed on local forms of taxation.

A further issue relates to the importance of ad valorem property taxes. However, the term 'importance' depends upon the perspective taken and the comparative statistics being used to quantify it. Two of the most often used measures are the percentage of property tax on gross domestic product (GDP) of the country and property tax as a share of total tax revenues. When measured against either of these, the property tax does not appear to be significant or important. They tend to represent less than 1 per cent of GDP and around 1.7 per cent of total taxes raised (IMF, 1996; OECD, 1995). This macro-economic importance of the property tax is only one view, a more micro analysis at local government level provides a significantly different picture. In this respect reliance on property tax revenue is significant in just over 50 per cent of the surveyed countries.

One of the fundamentals of the property tax relates to the tax basis. There is a clear emphasis on or possibly a slight shift towards improved capital value systems. Notwithstanding that, those countries which choose to use other approaches have developed, by in large, successful systems. However property tax reform tends to always be on the political agenda in terms of its transparency, acceptability and fiscal functions.

As this volume builds upon the earlier book (Comparative Property Tax Systems, 1991) it is hoped that this and other relevant published material will create an informed source of information on the international aspects of property taxation. Much can be learned from the experiences and programmes of other countries, the difficulty has always been the accessibility of information.

References

Bahl, R.W. and Linn, J.F. (1992), *Public Finance in Developing Countries*, Oxford University Press, Oxford.

Foster, C.D., Jackman, R.A. and Perlman, M. (1980), *Local Government Finance in a Unitary State*, George Allen and Unwin, London.

Institute of Revenues Rating and Valuation, (1997), *Principles for Local Government Finance*, IRRV, London.

International Association of Assessing Officers (1998), *Standard on Ratio Studies*, IAAO, Chicago.

International Monetary Fund, (1996), *Government Finance Statistics Yearbook*, International Monetary Fund, Washington DC.

Layfield Committee, (1976), *Report of the Committee of Inquiry into Local Government Finance*, HMSO, Cmnd 6453, London.

McCluskey, W.J. (1991), *Comparative Property Tax Systems*, Gower Publishing Company, England.

O'Sullivan, A., Sexton, T.A. and Sheffrin, S.M. (1995), *Property Taxes and Tax Revolts: The Legacy of Proposition 13*, Cambridge University Press, Cambridge.

Organisation for Economic Cooperation and Development, (1995), *Revenue Statistics of OECD Member Countries 1965-1995*, OECD, Paris.

Owens, J (1992), Financing Local Government: An International Perspective with Particular Reference to Local Taxation in King, D. (ed.), *Local Government Economics: Theory and Practice*, Routledge, London.

Smith, A. (1776), *The Wealth of Nations*, London.

Trotman-Dickenson, D.I. (1996), *Economics of the Public Sector*, Macmillan, London.

Youngman, J.M. and Malme, J.H. (1994), *An International Survey of Taxes on Land and Buildings*, Kluwer Law and Taxation Publishers, Netherlands.

2 Singapore property tax system

Nat Khublall

General introduction to the property tax system

Property tax in Singapore is an unavoidable tax which is levied on immovable property. This is a relatively simple tax in concept but, like most taxes, its administration is somewhat complex and occasionally controversial in operation. Property tax is a major revenue earner for the government; it is second[1] to income tax and is paid directly into the Consolidated Fund as general revenue, unlike the position in other countries where generally, the tax is levied and tied to the provision of local services. This being the case, the tax can be used as an instrument of economic policy as indeed it has been used in the 1980s to mitigate the adverse effect of the then recession in the business and property development sectors.

Taxation of immovable property goes far back into history, and it has been favoured because the quantum is predictable and difficult if not impossible to evade. The rationale for this tax is that possession of wealth in the form of land and/or buildings is generally an indication of one's ability to pay. This rationale, however, can be criticized in that a great deal of wealth today can be held in other forms. The accepted criteria for the taxation of property are set out in the British Government Green Paper 'Alternatives to Domestic Rates'.[2] These criteria are the need for a predictable yield, ease of collection at low cost, difficulty in avoidance and evasion, capacity to provide local identity and acceptability, equity in terms of ability to pay and the need for easy understanding of the tax. The property tax in Singapore is capable of accommodating all these criteria, albeit with the need for minor legislative amendments in certain areas.

The intention of this chapter is to present a concise account of the Singapore property tax system and to highlight and comment on certain issues which are of some importance and perhaps may initiate a move for some further reform.

Historical background

The historical background of the property tax system in Singapore is briefly set out in the Table 2.1.

Singapore property tax is based on the rating system introduced in England under the Poor Relief Act 1601 as subsequently amended. Thus, British rates can be regarded as the ancestor of the property tax now in force in Singapore. The precursor to the present tax was a tax levied on land and buildings for the provision of local services as is the present position in England. By reason of certain political and administrative developments[3] in 1961, property tax was introduced in lieu of rates. In substance, the tax remains the same apart from one fiscal change; it is levied on the ownership of immovable property, rather than on beneficial use and occupation of such property. Table 2.1 gives the sequence of events in respect of the background to the property tax system in Singapore.

Tax rates

Until recently a multiplicity of tax rates existed in Singapore, not only during the period prior to 1961 but also up to the year 1983. This multiplicity of rates was due to a number of factors such as the number and level of services provided, particularly in the early years. The multi-tier structure of tax rates continued under the new system by virtue of an Ordinance passed in 1960 which empowered the Government to lower the rates for certain areas or types of properties. Also, various concessions relating to the encouragement of development and urban renewal were introduced in 1967 but have since expired.

In order to encourage the population to become a nation of property owners and to revitalize the city areas, the government in 1978 decided to rationalize the multi-tier structure of rates between 1979 and 1983, whereby a uniform rate of 23 per cent was introduced. However, tax rates have now been substantially reduced and a rate of 4 per cent is levied in respect of owner occupied residential properties. As regards all other properties, the rate was fixed at 16 per cent in 1990 but with the recent introduction of the Goods and Services Tax this rate has been reduced gradually and it now stands at 12 per cent.[4]

Statistics on the size of the tax base and the tax

The number of properties subject to property tax in 1994/95 was 782,838. Table 2.2 shows a breakdown in terms of uses.

Table 2.1
Historical background to the Singapore property tax

1820	Taxes were levied on opium and liquor to finance police costs, while gaming revenue was used to keep the streets clean.
1825	Houses were assessed for the first time to support the inadequate revenue from the above sources and to defray the cost of sundry municipal works.
1832	A rate of 5 per cent was levied on all houses within the town.
1840	The rate was increased to 8.5 per cent on all houses within the town. A new levy was imposed on all houses outside the town.
1848	Rates of 10 and 5 per cent were levied on town and country houses respectively.
1856	A municipality or local government body was established to provide better services.
1935	A rural board was established to cover the greater part of the territory.
1950s	Further refinements to local government administration were made.
1951	The municipality was incorporated as the City Council by Royal Charter.
1954	The Rendal Commission recommended the integration of the City Council and the Rural Board into a city and island council.
1956	A new government appointed a committee on local government to consider the desirability of decentralizing the powers and functions of the City Council and the Rural Board.
1957	The Local Government Ordinance was enacted, which is now the Property Tax Act (Cap 254 - the 1985 Edition). The administrative integration of the department of local authorities was accomplished.
1961	The City Council Assessment and Estates Department, the valuation staff of the Land Office and the Rural Board were integrated with the Inland Revenue Department (IRD) to become the Property Tax Division of the IRD.
1992	The Inland Revenue Department was made a statutory board and is known as the Inland Revenue Authority of Singapore (IRAS) to which the Property Valuation and Assessment Division is attached.

Table 2.2
Breakdown percentages according to use

Uses	Percentage
Commercial/industrial	6.0%
Private residential	17.3%
HDB*	75.6%
Others	1.2%

*   *These are properties developed by the Housing and Development Board (HDB) and
include public housing and other properties.*

Source: IRAS Annual Report 1994

Property tax imposition and performance

Property tax in Singapore is levied at 'the rate or rates ... for each year upon the
annual value of all houses, buildings, lands and tenements' by virtue of section
6(1) of the Property Tax Act.[5] Industrial plant and machinery are specifically
excluded under section 2(a).

Imposition of the tax

The owner of a property is primarily liable to pay the tax, unlike the position in
England where the liability is generally on the occupier. The term 'owner' is
taken to mean the person for the time being receiving the rent of the subject
property or the person whose name is entered in the valuation list. Thus, agents
and receivers who are not normally regarded as owners legally or beneficially
may be liable for the property tax.

There is a statutory requirement to give notice to the Chief Assessor of any
change of ownership. This requirement is not only for the purpose of tax
collection, but perhaps most importantly for the purpose of reassessment as
change of ownership may give rise to a reassessment, especially if the assessed
value is very low.

Property tax surcharge

A peculiarity in the property tax system in Singapore is the 10 per cent surcharge,
in addition to the normal property tax, which is levied on foreign owners of
residential properties or vacant land. This was introduced in 1974 to ensure that
residential property prices are kept within reasonable limits.

There are certain exemptions from the surcharge conferred by the Property Tax (Surcharge) Rules 1974. Among the persons and bodies entitled to the exemption are citizens, permanent residents, persons approved by the government and foreign companies registered locally for the purpose of carrying on business in Singapore.

Property tax performance

Rates and contributions in lieu of rates were the most important component of the revenue of the Consolidated Fund for the whole of the period 1946 to 1955. For the years 1964 to 1970 the annual percentage increase for property tax revenue and annual value were 10.8 per cent and 9.1 per cent respectively.

Between 1970 and 1979 the increase in revenue from property tax was almost fivefold, and between 1979 and 1985 the increase was just half the previous period. In 1986 there was a significant decrease in property tax revenue, with a smaller decrease in 1987. This decrease was due to property tax concessions given to cushion the effect of the economic recession in those years. Today, property tax is the second major revenue earner for the government after income tax. However, it is likely that the revenue from the Goods and Services Tax will surpass that from property in a year's time, having regard to the reduction in the rate from 16 per cent to 12 per cent and the wider scope of the Goods and Services Tax.

Cost of administration

The cost of property tax administration, assessment and collection for the year 1985 was 0.54 per cent of the amount of property tax revenue collected, while in 1984 and 1983 the corresponding figures were 0.55 per cent and 0.63 per cent. The trend is definitely downward, and this can be regarded as a remarkable achievement when compared with the costs involved in the administration and collection of other taxes. The cost of collection for the year 1986 was around 1 per cent.[6]

Total revenue raised

The revenue from property tax has increased significantly over the last six years as can be seen from Table 2.3. The increase in 1994/95 over the previous financial year is over 10 per cent. The increase for income tax over the same period is just over 5 per cent, presumably due to an overall reduction in income tax rates and rebates given to all taxpayers.

Comparison with other taxes

As can be seen from Table 2.3, the revenue figures for 1995/96 increased substantially. For income tax, property tax, GST and stamp duties, the figures in billion were $8.1 (56%), $1.9 (13%), $1.8 (12%) and $1.6 (11%) respectively. What is significant here is that the figure for GST is a mere $100 million behind that for property tax. It is likely that within a short time the revenue from property tax will be relegated to third position after that from GST.

Table 2.3
Property tax revenue compared with other taxes

Taxes	1990 $'000	1992/93 $'000	1993/94 $'000	1994/95 $'000
Income Tax	4,415,050	6,439,640	7,308,523	7,693,399
Property Tax (inc. surcharge)	1,064,975	1,476,702	1,615,172	1,788,517
Goods and Services Tax	-	-	-	1,522,729
Stamp Duties	644,214	675,515	1,109,066	1,390,356
Duty on Betting	443,664	623,208	723,690	774,447
Duty on Pte Lotteries	70,396	98,544	118,240	143,346
Estate Duty	45,997	21,954	42,842	46,138
Others	1,308	1,687	1	-
Total	6,685,604	9,337,250	10,917,534	13,358,932

Source: *Inland Revenue Authority of Singapore (IRAS) Annual Reports for the relevant years*

Whereas Table 2.3 provides information on various taxes for a number of years, Table 2.4 provides a comparison of property tax with total revenue and the GDP for the year 1994/95.

Table 2.4
Property tax compared with total revenue and GDP

Particulars	1994/95
Total revenue	$13.3593 billion
Revenue from property tax	$ 1.7901 billion
Property tax as a percentage of GDP	1.74%
All taxes as a percentage of GDP	13.00%

Source: *IRAS Annual Report for 1994*

Purpose of the tax

Unlike the position in many countries, the revenue raised from property tax is not tied to the provision of local services but is paid directly into the Consolidated Fund. Of the total revenue received from all sources (including development charge and other sources), a significant proportion is put into reserve. The revenue surplus in Singapore for 1994/95 was some $4.81 billion and is expected to be higher by $1.6 billion for 1995/96.

Level of government for whom the tax is a revenue source

There is a single tier government in Singapore as can be seen from Table 2.1, local authorities were abolished in 1961. No revenue from any tax source is earmarked for any special purpose. Thus, the revenue from property tax, like others, is paid into the Consolidated Fund.

Importance of the tax

The importance of property tax can be seen from its ranking with revenue receipts from other taxes. For many years, the revenue from property tax has been ranked second to income tax. However, it seems very likely that it will be relegated to third position within a year or two after the revenue from GST. Also, the receipt from stamp duties is trailing close behind. Whether or not the receipt from property tax will be relegated to fourth position will depend on a number of factors, such as the updating of annual values of properties, future tax rates and the continued escalation in property values. An escalation in property values will affect both taxes in the same direction. But the increase in stamp duties will be greater as stamp duties are based on the total consideration paid, whereas property tax is a product of the annual value and the applicable rate.

Property tax basis and valuation

In addition to the concept of annual value, this part of the chapter deals with the principles of assessment and the methods of valuation.

Annual value

The basis of property tax is the annual value of a taxable unit. The annual value is the gross rent at which the unit could be expected to be let from year to year, the landlord paying the expenses of repair, insurance, maintenance or upkeep and all taxes. As mentioned earlier, the rent is a gross rent[7] with no deduction to arrive at a net figure as is the case in some countries. However, in the case of marine structures the annual value reflects the net rent plus the property tax payable. Thus, the annual value of a property (of whatever type) will include an element for the tax itself.[8]

The hypothetical concept of rent

The rent, as under the rating system in England, is a hypothetical rent.[9] Even where the property is owner occupied a hypothetical landlord-tenant situation is assumed. But this does not apply to rent-controlled premises as the actual rent payable for such premises is taken in determining the annual value thereof. However, once a property becomes vacant, it is no longer subject to control and the property can be assessed by reference to the definition of annual value.

Provisos to the definition of annual value

There are seven provisos to the definition of annual value, and of these, four are usually labelled in practice as secondary definitions. For various reasons, the Chief Assessor is empowered to determine the annual value of a property by reference to:

1   5 per cent of the estimated value of the land and buildings (proviso (b));

2   the annual equivalent of the gross rent at which the property is let, and in such a case he may have regard to any capital or periodical sums or other consideration given (proviso (c));

3   5 per cent of the estimated value of any land occupied as appurtenant to any house or building which is considered to be in excess of the quantity fixed by the Comptroller and sanctioned by the Minister (such land shall be deemed to be vacant) and shall be assessed separately from the property to which it is appurtenant (proviso (d)); and

4   the gross receipts of certain tourist hotels (proviso (g)).[10]

The other three provisos should be taken into account, where appropriate, in determining annual values in accordance with the primary definition. They are as follows:

5   the first of the other three is proviso (a) which excludes from assessment any machinery which is used for industrial purposes;

6   subsidiary proprietors, i.e., owners of units in a subdivided multistorey building, are to be regarded as owners for property tax purposes and that there shall be no separate assessment for the land on which such a building is erected (proviso (e)); and

7   the grantee of a lease in respect of state land shall be regarded under proviso (f) as owner of a freehold for property tax purposes, and no deduction shall be made in respect of any premium or rent payable.

Principles of assessment

Subject to the foregoing, the principles and methods of assessment are the same as in England. A hypothetical landlord-tenant relationship is assumed and the rental comparison method of assessment is preferred to the other methods. However, this is subject to certain statutory provisions under which this hypothetical relationship can be ignored.[11]

Vacant and to let

This concept is applied along the same lines as in England, except that it does not apply to rent controlled premises[12] and where the Chief Assessor exercises his power or is required to value a property in accordance with certain statutory provisions.[13]

Rebus sic stantibus

In addition, the principle of *rebus sic stantibus* is incorporated into the property tax system; a property is to be assessed as it stands and as used and occupied at the date of assessment. The use of the property need not be in conformity with the zoning.[14] In *Southern Wood Products (Pte) Ltd v Chief Assessor*,[15] it seems that the Valuation Review Board was of the view that the actual use was not important if the building was not built or converted for that purpose. If this view is correct, it remains to be seen whether judicial approval will be given to it on an appeal.

Restrictions

Restrictions are of two types: general and special. Any statutory restriction of a general nature affecting the value of a property must be taken into account. An example of a special statutory restriction is the Control of Rent Act,[16] the effect of which is to restrict the rent of premises built on or before 7 September 1947. As mentioned earlier, the rent could be very low when compared with market rents for similar premises built after this date. The other restriction relates to environmental factors. Unless common to the entire locality, environmental factors are to be taken into account in assessing the value of a property. This is particularly important where an environmental factor affects the subject property to a greater extent than comparables used to assess it.

Valuation date

The Chief Assessor of Singapore is not constrained by any statutory or case law requirement that a property must be assessed for property tax purposes by reference to values prevailing at a particular date, as is the practice in England,[17] Hong Kong[18] and certain other countries. The usual date on which values are taken is the date of the assessment of a particular property regardless of any disparity which this policy may cause in relation to the assessed value of other properties in the locality.

Valuation methods

There are three methods of assessing annual values of properties in Singapore. They are the rental comparison method, the contractor's basis and the profits test. In addition to these, as mentioned earlier, the Chief Assessor may resort to other means as he is empowered to do under section 2 of the Act.[19] Indeed, in the case of certain gazetted hotels, a prescribed formula[20] requires 15 per cent of the gross receipts from guest rooms and 5 per cent of gross takings from restaurants and bars to be added to the rent received from lettable parts for the purpose of determining the annual values of such hotels.

Excess land

Under proviso (d) to section 2, land which is in excess of what is reasonably required for the enjoyment of a property may be treated as excess land for the purpose of a separate assessment. Where this is the case the land will be demarcated by the Comptroller of Property Tax with the approval of the Minister.

Tax base

The Property Tax Act provides for the levy of a tax on the owners of immovable property. The term 'immovable property' is defined in section 2 of the Interpretation Act[21] to include land, benefits arising out of land, and things attached to the earth or permanently fastened to anything attached to the earth. While from this it follows that fixtures are included in the definition, plant and machinery are excluded by virtue of section 2(a) of the Act.

The property tax as it stands today was imposed on 1 January 1961 at the specified rate or rates on a yearly basis 'upon the annual value of all houses, buildings, lands and tenements whatsoever' as included in the valuation list.

Land, buildings and improvements

An assessable unit could be land, land and buildings (including other improvements) or a part of a building. Vacant land is subject to property tax as are buildings sites under construction.[22] In *Intercontinental Properties (Pte) Ltd & Ors v Chief Assessor*,[23] Chua J. held, *inter alia*, that each unit within a building is deemed to be a 'building' by virtue of section 10(3) of the Act. Also, each occupied unit in a partially completed building is deemed to be a building.[24] Indeed, this is in compliance with section 10(4) of the Act. Where many units in a building are owned by one person, each is given an annual value and taken as a separate 'tenement' for property tax purposes.[25]

Responsibility for making the assessments

The Chief Assessor of the Valuation and Assessment Division of the Inland Revenue Authority of Singapore (IRAS) is responsible for the assessment of properties for property tax purposes, while collection of the tax is the function of the Comptroller of Property Tax. The duties of the Chief Assessor are set out in section 4(2) of the Property Tax Act. These duties are:

1   the preparation of the valuation list;

2   matters relating to objections and appeals; and

3   the alteration and authentication of the valuation list.

The Chief Assessor is assisted by a number of in-house valuers and other supporting staff. All professional staff are qualified in estate management or other relevant discipline. A data bank has been established on computer and, although it is ideally suitable for mass assessments for property tax purposes, only about 50 per cent of properties are valued with the aid of the computer under the computer assisted mass appraisal (CAMA) system introduced a few years ago.

The other important functionary in the Property Tax Division is the Comptroller of Property Tax. Under section 4(1) of the Property Tax Act the Comptroller shall be responsible generally for the following:

1   the carrying out of the provisions of the Act;

2   the collection of property tax; and

3   the payment of all sums so collected into the Consolidated Fund.

The Comptroller is constrained by section 4(3) to amend or otherwise vary the annual value ascribed to any property by the Chief Assessor. However, with regard to the collection of 'back taxes', the Comptroller is empowered under section 21(6) to serve a notice on any person to require within 21 days a return containing such particulars as may be required for determining the tax payable in respect of a new building or where a property has ceased to be owner occupied or where the rent has been increased and for some reason the valuation list for the period in question was not amended.

The valuation list

The Act provides for a new valuation list to be prepared every year. However, until recently this was not undertaken, but the list was amended and adopted for the ensuing year.

Frequency of revaluation

In the past, revaluation was done on a piecemeal basis over a period of nine to ten years reflecting values as at the date of the assessment. As Lai Kew Chai J. observed:[26]

> ...it was decided by the Chief Assessor as a matter of administrative policy and practice that with regard only to owner occupied properties in Singapore, there would only be a 'general assessment' of the annual values once in every 9 or 10 years, unless such owners carried out renovations or unless such owners has ceased to occupy their properties and had let them out.

This inevitably meant that annual values of properties which were assessed earlier were much lower than those that were assessed towards the end of the ninth or tenth year. This problem was compounded by section 20(9) under which ad hoc assessments could be carried out not only for physical changes but also for non-physical changes, such as an increase in the rent, a change of occupancy or ownership.[27] The relevance of non-physical changes has been given statutory force under section 20(9) as a direct response to the decision in *Town and City Properties Ltd v Chief Assessor*[28] in which the Valuation Review Board held that only physical factors could be taken into account.

The magnitude of the problem as prevailed in the past has been reduced in view of the yearly revaluation of about 70 to 80 per cent of all properties in the valuation list. This is assisted to a large extent by the use of computers to assess hereditaments of the same type, such as flats in high rise buildings.

The declared intention of the IRAS a few years ago was to achieve a 100 per cent yearly revaluation by 1995. Out of a total of some 800,000 properties in the valuation list, about 600,000 are reassessed every year.[29]

Reassessment between general revaluations

The need for a reassessment may arise where a property is transferred, the owner dies, a building is physically altered or demolished, there is an increase/decrease in the rent, or there is a change of occupancy. Further, section 20(9) specifically states that the list is deemed to be inaccurate in the following circumstances:

1   where the annual value of a property in the list does not correctly represent the annual value, having regard to:

   (a)   the rent obtained from a tenant of a property which was previously occupied by its owner;

44

(b)   the rent which can be obtained for that or a similar property; or

(c)   the consideration paid on a sale or transfer of the property or similar property;

2   where the rent payable is less than what is considered to be a reasonable rent;

3   where a new building is erected or any existing building is rebuilt, enlarged, altered, improved or demolished; and

4   where a property which is not exempted has not been included in the list.

Section 20(9) has been introduced as an amendment to the section following the decision in *Town and City Properties Ltd v Chief Assessor.*[30] The main purpose of the amendment is to widen the circumstances, including non-physical changes, under which the current valuation list can be amended.

In the light of the above, the annual value of a property may be subject to reassessment by virtue of one or more of the above events taking place, which resulted in a disproportionate increase (or decrease) in the property tax payable. This is quite different from the position in England and many other countries, where the assessed value does not normally alter following, for example, a transfer[31] of the property, a change of occupancy or a variation of the rent.

Assessment department

All functions relating to assessment of properties, imposition and collection of property tax are carried out by the Property Valuation and Assessment Division of the Inland Revenue Authority of Singapore (IRAS). This body was created in 1992 and operates as a statutory board. Hitherto, the IRAS was a department within the Ministry of Finance. The move was presumably for more efficient administration and the recruitment of suitable staff.

Qualification of the assessors

Assessors within the Property Valuation and Assessment Division of the IRAS are graduates in estate management from both the local and overseas universities. They are assisted by valuation officers who hold polytechnic[32] diplomas in estate management, building or management.

Notification of assessed value, valuation list

Section 12 of the Act requires the Chief Assessor to publish a public notice in the *Gazette* and other places in the month of August of each year to enable the valuation list for the ensuing year to be inspected over a period of 28 days. This period commences on the day of the notice. In addition, the Chief Assessor is required within 14 days of the said notice to serve on every owner whose property has been included in the list for the first time or where the annual value has been increased, a notice with relevant particulars.

Appeal procedures

Matters concerning objections are dealt with by the Chief Assessor or the Comptroller of Property Tax, depending on the nature of the objection. An owner who is not satisfied with the decision following an objection may appeal to the Valuation Review Board.

Objections

The Property Tax Act provides for the redress of any grievance resulting from any matter contained in the valuation list. An objection must be lodged with the Chief Assessor or the Comptroller of Property Tax, as the case may be, within a certain time limit and if the grievance is not resolved an appeal to the Valuation Review Board may be made. The circumstances in which objections may be made are given below:

1   an owner who is dissatisfied with the annual value ascribed to his property in the list for the ensuing year may lodge an objection in the prescribed form as required by section 14;[33]

2   where the Chief Assessor proposes to amend the current valuation list he must give notice to the owner who, if aggrieved by the proposal, may lodge an objection within 21 days of the notice under section 20(3) stating precisely the grounds of his objection. An objection under section 20(2) may be triggered by reason of the Chief Assessor acting under section 20(9) referred to earlier; and

3   for a number of reasons the Comptroller may serve a notice under section 22(1) to backdate the recovery of tax (beyond the current year). An owner who is aggrieved by such a notice may lodge under section 22(2) an objection within 21 days of the notice.

In these situations the Chief Assessor or the Comptroller, as the case may be, has to look into the objection and in due course notify the owner as to his decision. An aggrieved owner who is still not satisfied after a decision has been made following his objection may appeal within 21 days against the decision to the Valuation Review Board. A notice of appeal is required under section 29 and after some prior investigation by the Chief Assessor or Comptroller, who is required to submit a report to the Board, the hearing will be held. The appellant may be required to furnish a statement from which he cannot depart at the hearing.

Alteration of assessments

An alteration to the valuation list following a revaluation exercise may be made by the Chief Assessor under section 14(3). This applies where an owner makes an objection to a matter contained in the valuation list. The Chief Assessor under section 20 may amend the current list where it has become inaccurate in any material particular.

By virtue of sections 21 and 22, the Comptroller may recover property tax in respect of a property which has been altered in some manner or there has been non-physical changes as to warrant an amendment of the annual value but at the relevant time no such amendment was made to the valuation list. In this regard, the Comptroller may consider a valuation list which, in so far as the Chief Assessor is concerned, has ceased to be effective.[34]

Appeal system

Any appeal on a decision following an objection relating to an entry in the valuation list, an amendment of the list or tax on new buildings, etc. (regarding a previous list) shall be made to the Valuation Review Board.

Valuation Review Board

An appeal following a decision of the Chief Assessor or the Comptroller is made to the Valuation Review Board. The Board's jurisdiction is confined to appeals on the decisions of either:

1   the Chief Assessor, who has served notice as to his decision under section 14 or 20; or

2   the Comptroller of Property Tax, who has served notice as to his decision under section 22.

The Board consists of a Chairman and not more than nine other members, all of whom are appointed by the Minister. No person shall be appointed or remain appointed who is a Member of Parliament, is an undischarged bankrupt, has been sentenced to a term of imprisonment exceeding six months or is of unsound mind. A clerk to the Board and other officers and servants as may be necessary are also appointed.

The proceedings before the Board are less formal than in the courts and the parties are usually heard through their representatives. At the conclusion of the hearing, the Board may dismiss the appeal or increase or decrease the annual value and vary the effective date. There is provision for either party to appeal to the High Court and, thereafter to the Court of Appeal, which is now the final court of appeal.[35]

Methods of assessment

In assessing properties under the Act, there are three valuation methods which are employed. In addition, where appropriate, the Act empowers the Chief Assessor to assess by reference to certain formulas as set out in section 2 in relation to the definition of annual value.[36]

Market comparison method

This method is the most suitable, having regard to the definition of annual value which is given in terms of the rent the property could fetch in the market. Where a property is let at a rent, this rent could be used. However, for obvious reasons the rent passing is not necessarily conclusive in determining the annual value of a property. Therefore, the rent obtained for similar properties is usually taken into account. The rental comparison method is applicable to houses, flats, factories, shops, offices and other properties for which there is an abundance of rental evidence.

It is necessary to ensure that the rental evidence available is adjusted, if necessary, to conform to the statutory definition of annual value. Since the annual value in general is based on a gross rent plus the property tax, the rent must reflect an element for repairs, insurance, maintenance or upkeep and the property tax. Where the rent is inclusive of an amount for service charge or in respect of furniture and other items supplied by the landlord, that amount must be deducted.

Contractor's test

This method may be used to determine the annual value of a property in the absence of rental evidence. This is a well recognized method of valuation and, though similar, should not be confused with the formula prescribed under section 2(b) in relation to the definition of annual value.[37] This method looks at values from the angle of cost and, therefore, cannot be a primary indicator of rental values. It involves a five stage process in which a rate percent is applied to the capital sum required to acquire the land and to erect the building.[38] The resultant sum is adjusted upwards to take account of the cost of repairs, insurance, maintenance or upkeep and the property tax payable. The figure arrived at is taken as the annual value.[39]

The contractor's basis is usually applied in the assessment of purpose-built factories as a rough check after an assessment is made by the rental comparison method. In some situations, the method is used as a last resort because no other method is suitable, as in the valuation of a shipyard in *Chief Assessor v National Shipbreakers Pte Ltd*.[40] This method is also used in Singapore to assess petrol filling stations, presumably because of the substantial variations of assessments which could result from the quasi-profits test, i.e., the 'throughput' method based on petrol sales.

For a recent case relating to the contractor's test refer to *Chief Assessor & Comptroller of Property Tax v Keppel Corp Ltd*.[41] In applying the contractor's test, the rate of 6 per cent was used, but the High Court held that in the light of market conditions at the relevant time the annual value arrived at was too high.

Profits test

In the absence of rental evidence and where the contractor's basis is inapplicable, the profits test (or accounts method) can be used to assess the annual value of a property. It can be used to determine the annual value of a property where there is a sufficient element of a legal or factual monopoly and the valuer is of the opinion that the accounts of the occupier of the premises provide a reasonable guide. Like the contractor's basis, this test is only an aid in determining the rental value of the property.

The principle of the profits test derives from the ability of the property to produce an income to the occupier, tenant or owner and which will compensate him sufficiently for operating the concern and, in addition, provide a surplus to remunerate the capital invested. The principle involves the ascertainment of the gross receipts of the enterprise from which purchases (as adjusted) and working expenses are deducted from the gross profits. The residue is known as the divisible balance to be shared between the operator and the landlord. The

49

landlord's share is the rent for the premises and is taken as the annual value on which the tax is calculated. There is no further addition.

Formula

Mention has been already made that the Chief Assessor has the option of determining the annual value of a property by taking 5 per cent of the estimated capital cost of the land and building.[42] Another formula of relatively recent origin is that applicable to certain gazetted hotels by virtue of proviso (g) to the definition of annual value. The annual value of such a hotel is derived by reference to 15 per cent of the gross receipts from guest rooms and 5 per cent of gross receipts in respect of food and beverage outlets. For these parts of a hotel the annual value will reflect more accurately the actual tariff and occupancy rate of the hotel. The ancillary parts of a hotel, such as offices, shopping space, etc. will continue to be assessed in the usual manner, i.e., by reference to rental evidence where appropriate. An example of this approach is given below.

Example of a typical hotel assessment

Gross takings from guest rooms	$3,000,000
Gross takings from restaurants and bars	$1,500,000
Gross rents from shopping area and offices	$ 200,000

Assessment

Receipts from various sources:		
Guest rooms	$3,000,000	
@ 15%		$ 450,000
Restaurants & bars	$1,500,000	
@ 5%		$ 75,000
Rents	$ 200,000	
Less 33.33%	66,660	$ 133,340
		$ 658,340

As there has been no change with regard to the assessment of ancillary accommodation, the previous practice will continue. Thus a deduction of 33.33 per cent for service charge is allowed.

Use of mass appraisal techniques

The problem of not being able to value all properties in a revaluation exercise within a reasonable time can be largely solved by the use of computers, given that Singapore is a very small country with similar units in many of the developments. The multiple regression technique is particularly suitable for the mass valuation that is required in a revaluation exercise. In addition to the use of computers, a base date should be chosen by reference to which all values are taken regardless of the actual date the assessment is carried out. In some countries, computers have been introduced to assist in mass valuation for property tax purposes since the early 1970s if not earlier.

System in use in Singapore

The Computer Assisted Mass Appraisal (CAMA) system that has been adopted in Singapore since 1992 is intended to replace to some extent the human element and to increase productivity. This is estimated to be as much as three times more than the conventional assessment process.[43] About 45 per cent of all properties in the valuation list are assessed by the CAMA system, and the intention is to increase it to about 55 per cent in due course.

Other properties are assessed by the conventional method, in which the human element plays a great part. Many of these properties are dissimilar in characteristics for a number of reasons. Thus their annual values are likely to differ substantially, partly attributable to different characteristics in respect of physical factors and partly due to non-physical factors as discussed under section 20(9) of the Property Tax Act. Such non-physical factors could cause a disparity of annual values for similar properties. Further, a disparity is likely to arise in respect of those properties comprising about 20 per cent or so which were not reassessed in the last revaluation exercise. The target as disclosed a few years ago is to assess all properties on a yearly basis.

Exemptions, reliefs and concessions

There are four aspects to consider under this part of the chapter; they are exemptions, refunds, concessions and remissions.

Exemptions

Certain properties are exempt from property tax because of their nature or use. Under section 6(5) of the Act, exemption is given to the following:

1   places of public religious worship;

2   buildings used for public schools which are in receipt of grants-in-aid from the government;[44]

3   buildings which are used for public charitable purposes;[45] and

4   buildings which are used for purposes conducive to social development.

The exemption under section 6(5) is not automatic; an application must be made for it. Where only a part of a building is used for any of the above purposes, the remainder will not be exempt.

During the last economic recession, land under development with effect from 1 July 1986 was exempt from the tax. The exemption was for up to five years. However, this exemption has since been withdrawn, presumably because the economy is growing at the rate of about 8 per cent per annum.

Refunds

A major relief from property tax takes the form of a refund of the tax paid where the property has been unoccupied for at least 30 days or one calendar month. The relief takes the form of a refund because the tax has to be paid half-yearly in advance in January and July. Where the property is vacant for the minimum period, notice must be served within 14 days of the commencement of the vacancy period for the purpose of obtaining a full refund in due course. The owner is required to satisfy the following conditions:

1   that the building in respect of which a refund is claimed is in good repair and fit for occupation;

2   that he has made a reasonable effort to obtain a tenant;

3   that the rent demanded is reasonable; and

4   that the building has been vacant for the entire period during which a refund is claimed.

Owner occupier's concession

This concession is given in respect of owner occupied residential properties. With effect from 1 July 1996, the general tax rate is 12 per cent but the rate is 4 per cent for owner occupied residential properties. The 4 per cent is to encourage home ownership.

Urban renewal concession

This type of concession was given between 1967 and 1974 to encourage redevelopment of the business district. The concession took the form of a substantially reduced tax rate for 20 years. In the not too distant past the rate was about 23 per cent if not higher. Much earlier it was 36 per cent. However, this exemption was withdrawn in 1974 in respect of new projects.

Remissions

From time to time remissions are given particularly with regard to commercial and industrial premises as a fiscal measure. All those that were granted during the last economic recession have since been withdrawn.

In the case of decontrolled premises,[46] some concession is given for the first and second years following the reassessment of such properties. In the first year, the concession is two-thirds of the additional tax and is reduced to one-third for the second year. The full tax is payable from the third year.

Collection procedures

Sections 36 to 48 of the Act deal with collection and recovery of the tax. The tax is payable half-yearly in advance in January and July without demand.[47] However, in the event an owner of a property is liable to a surcharge, the entire surcharge for the year is payable in January. Despite the provision in the Act as to half-yearly payment of the tax, the Comptroller may, at his discretion, permit payment by way of instalments. In such a case, he may charge interest which shall not exceed 10 per cent per annum. An application to pay by instalments should be made in good time, at least before enforcement proceedings are taken, i.e., before any warrant of attachment is issued.

Liability for and computation of the tax

Unlike the position in England, the owner is liable to pay the tax in Singapore. The tax is computed by applying the appropriate tax rate to the annual value as assessed by the Chief Assessor.

Enforcement procedures

Property tax is a first charge on the property concerned and, if it is not paid within the period allowed, proceedings can be taken under section 6(3) for its recovery. A period of one month is allowed for payment, and on default a notice of demand together with the requirement to pay a fee of $1 will be served on the owner. The owner is given a period of 15 days to pay the tax. If the tax is still unpaid within this 15-day period or any further period that is allowed, the tax will be deemed to be in arrears and is recoverable by means of a warrant of attachment under section 39(1). In such a case, the owner will be required to pay a warrant fee of $5 and a penalty not exceeding 5 per cent of the outstanding tax.

As a last resort, the Comptroller may exercise successively or concurrently either or both of the following:

1   seize and sell any movable property or crops of any person found on the property in respect of which the arrears are due; and

2   serve a public notice of sale in the prescribed manner indicating his intention of selling the property for which the tax is due and if the tax is not paid within three months the whole or a part of the property may be sold by public auction.[48]

Back year tax and tax on new buildings

There may be a need in some cases to collect back taxes. This may arise, for example, where a property is let for the first time or a rent is revised but there was no immediate reassessment. In some cases a problem may arise regarding the taxation of a new building.

Back year tax

As mentioned earlier, the liability for payment of property tax is on the owner at the relevant time, but where a previous owner failed to serve a section 19 notice as to one or more of the events which could have given rise to a reassessment, e.g., a rent increase, an assessment relating thereto may result in the new owner having to pay 'back tax'. Although the previous owner is primarily liable for the tax, the subject property could be sold eventually for the recovery of the tax.

The problem of back tax, though not widespread, recurs from time to time, and there is no effective solution under the existing law. Therefore, a prospective purchaser should make investigation as to whether or not the property could be subject to back tax. A very low current assessment, when the property at the same time is producing a rent which is substantially higher than the annual value as in the list, could be indicative of a failure to serve the section 19 notice. In this regard it should be noted that a favourable reply to a property tax requisition will not prevent the Comptroller of Property Tax from recovering any back tax.

Tax on new buildings

The imposition of property tax on new buildings is an area which has been prone to litigation. Whether or not an annual value has been ascribed to a building in the valuation list the owner is nevertheless liable under section 21 to pay tax in respect of that building. The date of completion of a building is usually taken as the date of issue of the Temporary Occupation Permit by the Building Control Division. However, where a building is occupied before the date of issue, the date of occupation will be taken as the date of completion as was held in the case, *Yap Swee Hoo v Chief Assessor.*[49]

An illegal building or structure is subject to property tax. In this regard Chua J. said that the Property Tax Act 'is not concerned with whether a building has been built in accordance with approved plans. An unauthorized building can be entered in the Valuation List and be liable to property tax so long as the work of erecting that unauthorized building is completed'.[50]

Building under construction

Tax can be levied in respect of a part of a building which is still under construction. Liability to tax is authorized by section 21(2) from the date of commencement of the use of that part notwithstanding that the valuation list has not been amended under section 20, and shall be calculated on the basis of the annual value or revised annual value, as the case may be, subsequently ascribed to that part.

Critical aspects of the tax system

Singapore is a small city-state with a small land area supporting a resident population of about three million. In general Singapore is ahead of many countries in economic development. Important decisions are implemented very quickly and efficiently. In view of this, the government had made great strides over the last three decades in several major areas of social and economic development. However, the area in which lip service was given is in respect of property tax. But in recent years some changes have been introduced with regard to updating the valuation list, and the objective is to achieve 100 per cent reassessment every year. The aim of this part of the chapter is to discuss this and a number of critical issues.

Definition of annual value

The concept of annual value in Singapore is generally the same as the concept of 'gross value' which has been replaced in England.[51] One major difference is that the definition of annual value in Singapore is subject to a number of provisos. Also, annual value as defined in section 2 of the local Act is inclusive of the property tax as well, in addition to the cost of repairs, insurance and maintenance. In view of this, the tax is paid in respect of outgoings as well. This is not usually the position in other countries.

The definition is subject to certain provisos some of which relate to what a valuer takes into account in appropriate circumstances. One is similar to the contractor's basis of valuation. Under another, the Chief Assessor may take into account the annual equivalent of any capital sum paid by a tenant. Again, proviso (e) prevents any separate annual value of the land where a property comprises a lot, the title of which is issued under the Land Titles (Strata) Act. As these matters are taken care of in valuation practice, there is no need to legislate for them.

The question that can be posed is whether the time is ripe to replace some of the provisos and to redefine the concept of annual value with a view to simplifying the definition in terms of a net rather than a gross rent.

Rent controlled premises

A hitherto important anomaly in the property tax system was in respect of the basis of assessing rent controlled premises. The present method, which is based on the controlled rent, is illogical since property is assumed to be vacant. Although the number of such properties is diminishing, this is no reason for the continuation of such an anomaly in the tax system. Hong Kong has removed this anomaly but Singapore lags behind despite its spectacular achievements in many areas of social and economic development.

Disparity under the valuation list

The fact that most properties are now reassessed on a yearly basis has removed to a large extent a blatant anomaly in the property tax system. However, until such time as all properties are reassessed by reference to values prevailing at a particular point in time, this anomaly cannot be completely removed. The paragraph immediately below further amplifies the nature of the disparity.

Absence of the tone of the list

In the absence of any statutory provision to require assessments to be carried out in accordance with the 'tone of the list' as is the position in England and Hong Kong (among other countries), the Chief Assessor may ascribe an annual value to a property according to the circumstances of the case. More specifically, the practice in Singapore is that values prevailing at the date of the assessment or the relevant event giving rise to the assessment are taken into account. The Chief Assessor has the power under section 20(9) to adopt this approach. Thus, the adoption of current values cannot be challenged on the ground that they do not accord with the 'tone of the list', i.e., annual values arrived at during the previous revaluation exercise. It is submitted that the 'tone of the list' should be mandatory in Singapore. This would necessitate an amendment to the Act. In England, the tone of the list concept was adopted before legislative intervention despite the decision in the *Ladies Hosiery* case which was largely ignored.

Collection of back taxes

The crux of the problem relating to the recovery of 'back tax' is in relation to its enforcement against the property and hence the present owner when in fact it was the previous owner who was at fault for not serving the relevant section 19 notice. After a change of ownership, the vendor or transferor is required to serve a notice under section 19(1) to the Chief Assessor. Such a notice could give rise to a reassessment of the property. Obviously any relevant event which occurred in the past but was not reported would be taken into account if it is material enough to effect a change in the assessment. Although it is the previous owner who is primarily liable for any retrospective increase up to the date of the transfer of the property, it may be prudent for the present owner to pay the tax to avoid any enforcement proceedings against the property. The recovery of back tax does not appear to be a widespread problem though an innocent purchaser may be unduly penalized.

Conclusion

Singapore property tax, which is based on the English system, serves an entirely different function: whereas in England rates and Council Tax are tied to the provision of local services, property tax in Singapore is paid directly into the Consolidated Fund. As such, the property tax system can be, and sometimes is, used as an instrument of economic policy. As an economic tool, the tax rate has been amended from time to time and during a recession certain exemptions and remissions are given.

It has been seen from the discussion that while a great deal of concepts and principles as developed and practised in England were adopted in Singapore, certain new ideas were also introduced under the local property tax system. For example, while the basic concept of annual value is similar to the English definition of 'gross value' (now no longer applicable in England), the provisos

57

added to the local definition of annual value are generally of local origin. Another significant difference between the two systems is that while there was a positive effort made towards improving the English system, especially in terms of fairness, Singapore continues to have a property tax system in which the tone of the list is absent. In the interest of fairness among taxpayers, all properties should be assessed by reference to values prevailing at a particular point in time.

Although it may be argued that there is no tax system which is completely devoid of anomalies and inequities,[52] it should be possible to give some consideration to the apparent anomalies in the system with a view to ensuring greater fairness and equity among taxpayers. In the light of the unparalleled strides Singapore has made over the previous 30 years in major areas of economic development, there is still scope for improving the property tax system. The yearly revaluation in which most properties are reassessed has the effect of reducing the disparity in assessments, but there is no need for such frequent revaluations if the tone of the list concept is adopted.

Notes

1   Property tax is likely to be overtaken by the recently introduced Goods and Services Tax (GST), which is very broadly based. In the first year 1994/95, the revenue from GST was $1.5 billion, close behind that for property tax which was just under $1.8 billion.

2   Cmnd Paper No 8449 of 1981 HMSO, London.

3   A single tier central government replaced the municipalities in 1961.

4   As announced in the 1996 Budget (see *Straits Times Budget 1996 Special*, 29 February 1996, p. 4).

5   Cap 254, Revised Edition 1985.

6   No up-to-date information is available.

7   Except that in the case of marine structures, the rent is exclusive of the cost of repairs, insurance, maintenance or upkeep but includes the property tax itself.

8   See section 2 of the Property Tax Act, Cap 254, Revised Edition 1985.

9   This no longer applies to residential properties in England. These properties are valued on the basis of bands of capital values for council tax purposes.

10   Property Tax (Valuation by Gross Receipts for Hotel Premises) Order 1987, S222/1987.

11   Refer in particular to the provisos to the definition of annual value under section 2 and section 20(9) regarding amendments to the valuation list.

12   This is not of much importance today as such premises are being phased out.

13 The relevant provisions are contained in certain provisos to the definition of annual value and section 20(9) of the Property Tax Act.

14 Khublall, N, (1993), *Taxation Relating to Investments in Real Property*, Longman, p. 134.

15 [1987] 2 MLJ ix.

16 Cap 58, Revised Edition 1985.

17 See section 121 of the Local Government Finance Act 1988 which provides for an antecedent date to ensure that a subsequent assessment of a property will reflect the 'tone of the list', i.e., values as established in the valuation list.

18 See sections 7 and 7A of the Rating Ordinance, Cap 116.

19 Refer to the four provisos labelled as secondary definitions of annual value mentioned earlier.

20 See the Property Tax (Valuation by Gross Receipts for Hotel Premises) Order 1987, S222/87.

21 Cap 1, Revised Edition 1985.

22 The exemption of building sites that was granted a few years ago has subsequently been withdrawn.

23 [1982] 1 MLJ 119.

24 *Sandilands Buttery & Co Ltd v Chief Assessor* [1966] VRB No. 294.

25 *Cho Chih Yee v Chief Assessor* [1969] 2 MLJ iii.

26 See *Howe Yoon Chong v Chief Assessor* [1985] 1 MLJ 82 at p 191.

27 See *Howe Yoon Chong v Chief Assessor* [1981] 1 MLJ 51 (PC).

28 Valuation Review Board Appeals Nos. 25-35, 37 and 38 of 1964.

29 As declared by the Commissioner of IRAS, Mr Koh Yong Guan, at the Sixth Conference of Heads of Commonwealth Valuation Departments.

30 VRB Appeal Nos. 25-35, 37 and 38 of 1964.

31 In California, USA, the consideration paid on a transfer will form the basis of the assessment, though it seems that the assessments of other properties will remain unaltered.

32 Singapore Polytechnic and Ngee Ann Polytechnic.

33 Section 14(1) requires any objection to be made within the period available for inspection of the valuation list. Under section 12(1) the period is 28 days usually within the month of August.

34 See *Ong Poh Tan v Comptroller of Property Tax* [1977] 1 MLJ xliii.

35 The right of appeal to the Judicial Committee of the Privy Council was abolished by the Judicial Committee (Repeal) Act 1994.

36 With regard to certain gazetted hotels, proviso (g) of section 2 is mandatory and the Chief Assessor does not have an option.

37 See *Chief Assessor v National Shipbreakers Pte Ltd* [1982] 1 MLJ 4 in which it was said that the contractor's method falls within the primary definition of annual value.

38   In the case of an older building, a deduction is allowed on the construction cost for age and obsolescence.

39   However, in some cases the assessment may be too high as was the position in *Chief Assessor & Comptroller of Property Tax v Keppel Corp Ltd* [1994] 2 SLR 100. This is especially so during a recession.

40   [1982] 1 MLJ 4.

41   [1994] 2 SLR 100.

42   See section 2(b) regarding the second proviso to the definition of annual value.

43   Lim Siew Leng, *Computer Assisted Mass Appraisal in IRAS*, Inland Authority of Singapore, p. 26.

44   Schools which are not in receipt of such grants but are run on a charitable basis may be exempt under (c).

45   The classic description of charities is contained in the judgment of Lord Macnaughten in *Income Tax Special Commissioners v Pemsel* [1891] AC 531. Trusts for the relief of poverty, advancement of education or religion and certain other purposes beneficial to the community are charitable trusts.

46   Subject to the Control of Rent Act, Cap 58, Revised Edition 1985. Only a small number of such premises remain as they are being phased out.

47   In spite of this, it is normal practice for the Comptroller to send out bills during the months of January and July each year.

48   In reality, it seems that some properties are sold by public auction some six or seven years later as reported in the *Straits Times*.

49   [1987] 2 MLJ vii.

50   *Intercontinental Properties (Pte) Ltd & Ors v Chief Assessor/Comptroller* [1982] 1 MLJ 119.

51   See the Local Government and Finance Act 1988.

52   Manning H. J., For How Much Longer Will Singapore Out-Moded Property Tax System Be Retained, *UNIBEAM*, 1976/79, p. 70, School of Building & Estate Management, National University of Singapore.

3   The property tax system in Hong Kong

Bobby Hastings and Megan Walters

Introduction

Hong Kong, with a GNP per capita in excess of US$24,500 - higher than the United Kingdom and many other European Community countries - is perhaps one of the most exciting and dynamic economies in the world. But the territory's total land mass is relatively small, covering an area of 1092 square kilometres, of which less than 16 per cent is actually developed (Table 3.1). However this area supports a population of over six million people and as Walker (1995) points out, real estate and construction form an important part of the economy - the value of the property stock is about HK$3,300 billion, excluding government buildings. Annual investment in property represents over 60 per cent of all capital investment and about 35 per cent of government expenditure is on property. So it is not surprising that the Hong Kong Government would choose to raise revenue by taxing real property.

A brief historical review of Hong Kong may help to explain the differences in the administration of property tax between the more developed areas of Hong Kong Island and the Kowloon peninsula and the traditionally rural districts of the New Territories. In 1841 Hong Kong Island was ceded to the British under the Convention of Chuenpi, ratified under the Treaty of Nanking in 1843 and Hong Kong was proclaimed a British colony. In 1860, after a further series of Anglo-Chinese wars, part of the Kowloon peninsula was also ceded in perpetuity. But the remainder of the Territory, which consists of the majority of the Kowloon peninsula and New Territories, was leased from the Chinese Government for 99 years from 1898. The difference between the land tenure structure in the ceded and the leased areas of the Territory and the acceptance of the role of Chinese law and custom in the New Territories, has resulted in slightly different treatments of property interests.

Table 3.1
Land use in Hong Kong as of 31 March 1995

Class	Approximate Area (km²)	Percentage of Total
A: Developed Land		
Commerical	2	0.2
Residential	55	5.0
Industrial	11	1.0
Open Space	16	1.5
Government, Institutional & Community (G/I/C)	18	1.6
Vacant Development Land	41	3.8
Infrastructure	27	2.5
Sub Total	**170**	**15.6**
B: Non Built-up Land		
Woodland/Grass/Shrub etc.	783	71.6
Arable, Farms, Fish Ponds	91	8.4
Reservoirs	26	2.4
Other Uses	22	2.0
Total	**1,092**	**100.0**

Source: *Hong Kong Annual Report 1966 (modified)*

Legislative powers in Hong Kong are derived from its status as a Crown Colony and Letters Patent. The Governor and Legislative Council are responsible for making the laws, which in Hong Kong are known as Ordinances. In certain cases an ordinance may delegate powers (usually to government bodies such as the Rating and Valuation Department) to implement specialized rules or regulations.

The taxation system in Hong Kong is relatively simple with few taxes or duties being imposed on real property. There are only two taxes, Property Tax and Rates and two duties, Estate Duty and Stamp Duty. Property tax is imposed under the Inland Revenue Ordinance No. 20 (1947) which, with its amendments, covers three separate taxes - profits tax, salaries tax and property tax - on profits and income derived in Hong Kong. Under the Ordinance (s5(1)):

> Property tax shall ... be charged for each year of assessment on every person being an owner of any land or buildings wherever situate in Hong Kong and shall be computed at a standard rate on the net assessable value of such land or buildings or land and buildings for each such year.

In practice owners of land or buildings in Hong Kong are charged property tax at a standard rate of 15 per cent of the actual rent received, less a statutory deduction of 20 per cent for repairs and maintenance. Properties owned by corporations are exempt from property tax, but profits derived from ownership of land and buildings are chargeable to profits tax.

Estate duty, which is the only form of direct taxation on capital in Hong Kong, is governed by the Estate Duty Ordinance (Cap 111) and is payable on the value of all property located in Hong Kong on the death of an individual. The duty is calculated on a sliding scale and is imposed on estates over a specified value. Estate Duty will affect land and buildings, since under s3 of the Ordinance the definition of property include immovable property.

Stamp Duty is impose by the Stamp Duty Ordinance (Cap 117). The duty is chargeable on all conveyances on sale or leases of immovable property in Hong Kong and is based on the value of the property being transacted. The rate is currently 2.75 per cent of the value for properties over HK$3 million with a reduced sliding scale for lower value properties.

The only separate system of tax levied on ownership and occupation of property in Hong Kong is known as Rating, the regulation for which is prescribed under Rating Ordinance Chapter 116 (together with various amendments made from time to time). The administration of the system is undertaken by different areas of government. The Commissioner of Rating, as the head of the Rating and Valuation Department, is responsible for all matters relating to the assessment of the rateable value. The actual rates are fixed by resolution of the Legislative Council, which is responsible for prescribing the percentage of the rateable value to be the rates for the year and the monies are collected by the Director of Accounting Services, as head of the Treasury.

The basic principles of the system are very similar to those in the United Kingdom. All rateable property, referred to in the Ordinance as a 'tenement', is assigned a rateable value, equal to the rent at which it might reasonably be expected to be let from year to year, subject to various term and conditions. The values for each property are kept on a valuation list and each year the government levies a tax based on a percentage of the dollar value assigned to the tenement.

Originally the revenue generated by the property rates was used to fund specific services, initially the Police force. Today it forms part of the general tax income for the Hong Kong government and is the major source of revenue for the Territory's two municipal councils, the Urban and the Regional Council. Details of the different categories of tax collected by central government and the amount of revenue collected in each, can be found in Tables 3.2 and 3.3.

Table 3.2
Government revenue (in HK$ 000,000)

	89/90	90/91	91/92	92/93	93/94	94/95	95/96
Duties	4,627.6	5,729.0	6,843.9	7,216.6	7,113.0	7,582.0	7,898.9
General Rates	1,662.7	3,038.9	3,493.6	4,423.5	4,461.0	5,156.0	5,805.0
Internal Revenue	45,596.3	50,139.5	63,958.8	79,098.0	96,645.0	98,956.0	102,187.0
Motor Vehicle Tax	1,735.0	2,053.0	3,437.0	4,939.9	4,171.0	4,662.0	2,879.0
Fines stc.	578.0	651.8	885.5	891.6	1,122.0	1,519.0	1,606.8
Royalties	954.0	952.4	1,188.0	1,135.7	1,378.0	2,286.0	1,773.0
Property	7,278.9	5,845.7	4,554.0	3,587.8	8,256.0	8,375.0	8,734.8
Land Transactions	211.9	241.0	412.0	266.9	264.0	393.0	412.0
Loans/reimbursement	1,730.0	2,412.8	2,863.0	4,032.0	3,843.0	4,166.0	4,811.0
Utilities	4,857.0	5,616.8	6,649.7	7,173.9	7.996.0	8,391.0	7,199.0
Fees and Charges	5,132.0	5,992.0	7,169.7	8,014.7	8,627.0	9,561.0	9,879.0
Total	74,366.4	82,672.9	101,455.2	120,780.6	143,896.0	151,047.0	153,185.5

Source: *Hong Kong Government Annual Statistics 1990-1996*

Table 3.3
Breakdown of internal revenue (in HK$ 000,000)

	89/90	90/91	91/92	92/93	93/94	94/95	95/96
Bets & Sweep Tax	4,829.0	5,884.0	7,109.9	7,818.0	10,082.0	9,351.0	11,051.0
Interest Tax	34.8	7.0	(8.0)	0.2	(0.1)	(0.7)	35.0
Profit Tax	21,231.0	21,241.0	25,203.0	32,248.0	39,857.8	47,430.0	46,706.0
Personal Assessment	879.0	846.9	1,027.0	1,308.6	1,565.0	1,758.0	2,816.0
Property Tax	953.0	1,138.0	1,229.6	1,304.2	1,510.8	1,482.0	1,638.0
Salaries Tax	10,450.0	13,107.0	17,417.4	20,199.9	22,505.0	23,624.0	26,258.0
Entertainment Tax	128.7	135.7	140.8	14.4	0.7	-	-
Estate Duty	489.0	655.7	683.0	1,025.0	1,186.0	1,459.0	1,277.0
Hotel Accommo. Tax	270.7	269.0	265.9	314.0	375.0	445.0	500.7
Stamp Duty	5,463.9	5,938.0	9,569.0	13,409.0	17,975.8	12,713.0	11,215.0
Departure Tax	668.9	717.4	1,120.0	1,255.0	1,382.6	487.0	521.0
Cross Harbour	195.6	197.0	200.0	201.0	203.0	203.0	202.0
Total	45,596.0	50,139.0	63,958.8	79,098.0	96,645.0	98,956.0	102,187.4

Source: *Hong Kong Government Annual Statistics 1990-1996*

Historical origins

The system of rating property in Hong Kong started with the passing of Ordinance No. 2 in 1845. Originally the system was to be used to 'raise an assessed Rate on lands, houses and premises within the colony of Hong Kong for the up holding of the requisite Police Force therein'. It is interesting that even today the transliteration of the Chinese term for rates is 'chai heung', meaning police pay, retaining the link between the tax and its original purpose.

As the colony developed, rates were used to pay for other services. In 1856 the 'Lighting Rate' was added.

> ... together with and in addition to the Police rate or rates for the year, a further rate called the Lighting Rate, and estimated at one and a half percent on the gross amount of the property included in the police rate assessment for the current year. (Ordinance No 11 1856).

In 1860, when additional revenue was needed to supply water for the city of Victoria (now part of Central district), Ordinance No. 12 provided for a water rate to be set at 2 per cent per annum of the valuation used for the Police Rate assessment. The various Ordinances relating to the collection of tax through property rating were consolidated into the Police and Lighting Rate Ordinance 1863. This ordinance introduced the term 'tenement' into Hong Kong legislation. The term, which is analogous with a hereditament in England and Wales and a heritage in Scotland is defined in the ordinance as:

> ... construed to include any house, cottage, shed, apartment, ground or building, or house together with land annexed thereto and ordinarily occupied therewith by one and the same person or his servants as one entire concern or undivided tenancy or holding, or not so belonging contiguous or occupied.

By 1875, a number of changes had been made. Rates had been extended to include the fire brigade service, and were levied on all property in the city of Victoria. Also in 1875, the definition of tenement was shortened to 'any land, with or without buildings, which is held or occupied as a distinct holding or tenancy, and includes piers and wharves erected in the harbour' (Ordinance No. 12). This definition remained basically unchanged until the 1973 Rating Ordinance. The 1888 Rating Ordinance provided the framework for today's rating system, introducing the terms 'rateable value' and 'interim valuations', the latter being required to deal with the rapid pace of development. Allowances were made for piers in the harbour to be charged at a lower rate, the first of a number of changes in policy towards the harbour piers. Over the years, they have been both rated at various levels and exempted presumably as a reflection of the prosperity of trade at different times.

The next major piece of legislation was the Rating Ordinance 1901. This included provisions to introduce a minimum rateable value and the inclusion of machinery in the rateable value. The 1901 Ordinance was altered by various resolutions during its 70 year life, for example, an additional sum was levied for war funds during the First World War. The 1931 resolution called for a different rate to be set if the water supply was unfiltered and further reduced where there was no water supply. The principle of rate reduction where a tenement has an unfiltered water supply is still found in the current rating ordinance. In 1935 a modified form of rating was introduced in the New Territories. The rates were to pay for services such as street lighting, drainage and water supply and were based on the capital value of the properties in the developing new towns. New Territories villages were not included in this resolution and were not rated.

The Rating (Amendment) Ordinance 1954 repealed the modified capital value rating system. The intention was to gradually extend the general system of rating throughout the rural districts, but in reality little happened until 1974 when the first extensions to the system were implemented. It was not until 1988 that the general rating system was completed for the whole Territory. The current Rating Ordinance was enacted in 1973, 'to consolidate and amend the laws relating to rating'. By 1973 responsibility for municipal services had been divided into the urban areas of Hong Kong and Kowloon, which were administered by the Urban Council and the New Territories, administered by central government. The Rating Ordinance set out that rates in the urban areas were to be paid in two parts, 'General Rates' which would go to the government's general revenue account and 'Urban Council Rates' which would fund the work of the Urban Council. Rates from the New Territories went directly to the general revenue account. In 1986, with the formation of the Regional Council and the introduction of a Regional Council Rate, the New Territories were brought into line with the urban area.

The rate percentage to be levied has varied over the years. It has been as high as 18 per cent but is currently at an historic low of 5.5 per cent, (unchanged since 1991). The allocation between the General Rates and the different council rates also varies from time to time; Table 3.4 refers to the rate percentages.

Table 3.4
Breakdown of rate percentages

1996	General rates %	Urban council rates %	Regional council rates %	Total %
Urban Council Area	2.7	2.8	-	5.5
Regional Council Area	1.1	-	4.4	5.5

Source: *Rating and Valuation Department, Annual Report 1996*

Revenue

In 1996 a total of 1,474,484 properties were subject to assessment. This generated a total rateable value of HK$ 272,303,813 million (Table 3.5). A breakdown of the different property classes indicates that both the highest number of assessments and assessed values were derived from private domestic premises (see Table 3.6). The median rateable value in Hong Kong is approximately HK$ 60,000, with five properties having a rateable value in excess of HK$ 1,000,000,000.

Table 3.5
Rateable value assessments.

	Assessments		Rateable Value	
	No.	%	$000	%
Hong Kong	434,777	29.5	100,557,528	36.9
Kowloon	220,805	15.0	43,355,750	15.9
New Kowloon	242,086	16.4	45,030,261	16.5
Urban Council Area	897,668	60.9	188,943,539	69.5
New Territories	576,816	39.1	83,360,274	30.6
Regional Council Area	576,816	39.1	83,360,274	30.6
Overall	1,474,484	100.0	272,303,813	100.0

Source: *Rating and Valuation Department, Annual Report 1995-96*

Table 3.6
Breakdown of different property class assessments and rateable values -
(1 April 1996)

Property Type	No. of Assessments	Rateable Values
Domestic		
Residential (private)	1,044,715	102,210,479
Non-Domestic		
Retail	96,777	55,785,653
Offices	58,896	28,029,417
Other Commercial	13,074	11,803,914
Factories/Storage	87,829	26,669,961
Hotels	84	2,598,454
Cinemas/Theatres	126	450,927
Petrol Filling Station	186	797,810
Car Parking	28,256	2,557,667

Source: Rating and Valuation Department, Annual Report 1995-96 (modified)

The revenue collected from the property rates is divided between the General Revenue account of the central government and the two local councils, the Urban and the Regional Councils. The total revenue raised by the tax is set out in Table 3.7, which also shows the proportional allocation between the General rates and the Urban and Regional Council rates over the last six years.

Table 3.7
Total revenue raised (in HK$ 000,000)

	90/91	91/92	92/93	93/94	94/95	95/96
General Rates	3,039	3,494	4,424	4,461	5,156	5,805
Urban Council Rates	2,339	3,291	4,174	4,141	4,567	5,135
Regional Council Rates	1,465	1,609	2,026	2,165	3,011	3,408
Total Revenue Raised	6,843	8,394	10,623	10,767	12,734	14,374

Source: Rating and Valuation Department, Annual Reports

Rates account for 85 per cent of revenue for the Urban and the Regional Councils. Other revenue sources for these councils are shown in Tables 3.8 and 3.9.

Table 3.8
Regional Council revenue (in HK$ 000,000)

	89/90	90/91	91/92	92/93	93/94	94/95	95/96
Rates	1,373.90	1,476.00	1,578.80	2,056.00	2,165.80	2,930.00	3,552.00
Rental	75.50	85.50	109.90	119.70	141.40	157.00	n/a
Licences	29.50	35.70	42.30	49.30	55.50	62.00	419.00
Investment Income	159.10	208.20	153.90	103.10	85.80	136.70	n/a
Fees Charges	70.60	90.20	106.00	117.10	133.50	153.20	189.00
Government Grant	273.60	273.60	-	-	-	-	-
Total Revenue	1,983.90	2,169.20	1,990.90	2,445.70	2,582.00	3,439.00	4,160.00

Source: *Regional Council Annual Reports 1990-1996*

Table 3.9
Urban Council revenue (in HK$ 000,000)

	89/90	90/91	91/92	92/93	93/94	94/95	95/96
Rates	2,325.10	2,366.70	3,272.20	4,124.10	4,225.00	4,500.20	5,211.20
Donation & Sponsorship	6.70	8.60	3.90	1.50	15.70	7.30	n/a
Bank Interest	111.60	93.90	51.90	58.70	84.10	143.80	n/a
Licence & Permits	80.20	87.60	95.30	112.30	122.70	132.40	n/a
Fees and Charges	135.10	126.40	110.00	116.50	126.50	121.30	n/a
Admission & Hire Charges	177.80	191.30	232.60	289.80	280.80	283.70	n/a
Sales	20.20	18.90	19.50	18.70	20.60	21.20	n/a
Rental	150.30	172.70	210.10	245.10	267.50	288.50	n/a
Sundry Forfeiture	1.60	2.10	2.40	1.06	1.80	4.60	n/a
Refunds & Reimbursement	31.80	33.70	49.20	43.90	46.20	44.30	n/a
HK Stadium Rev	-	-	-	-	-	90.20	n/a
Total	3,040.40	3,101.91	4,047.10	5,012.20	5,190.90	5,637.50	6,467.10

Source: *Urban Council Annual Report 1990-1996*

The Urban and Regional Councils are responsible for providing similar types of services in different parts of the Territory. However the focus and size of expenditure on each service differs between the rural areas and new towns of the Regional Council and the older, more developed areas of the Urban Council (see Tables 3.10 and 3.11). The two councils have slightly different accounting systems but in both cases the main areas of expenditure are public health and environmental hygiene, markets and street traders. The biggest expense under this category is the provision and management of wet (fresh food) and cooked food markets. All new public and many private housing developments are still built with provision for a market, as the majority of the population of Hong Kong use markets on a daily basis for the purchase of food. The Urban Council manages 62 markets, the Regional Council manages 45. Another feature of Hong Kong life is the hawker or street trader, selling everything from cooked food through to fake cashmere and compact discs. Both councils deal with the licensing of hawkers and the control of illegal hawkers (i.e. street traders without a licence). There are approximately 11,000 licensed hawkers in the Urban Council area, with around 4,000 in the Regional Council area. The estimated number of unlicensed hawkers in the same areas are 6,000 and 2,000 respectively.

Table 3.10
Regional Council expenditure

	89/90	90/91	91/92	92/93	93/94	94/95	95/96
Environmental Hygiene	552.00	736.00	877.30	963.40	1,085.80	1,210.60	1,410.00
Recreation & Sport	257.10	373.50	435.50	543.00	659.40	748.80	908.00
Culture / Entertainment	135.70	180.10	211.30	257.10	293.40	327.00	418.00
Festival Activities	6.30	17.50	10.90	21.40	16.70	31.10	19.00
Project & Capital Works	53.10	234.80	440.10	325.20	478.70	604.90	789.00
General Support	201.00	217.50	262.00	240.80	330.80	289.10	341.00
Total	1,205.20	1,759.40	2,237.10	2,350.90	2,864.80	3,211.50	3,884.60

Source: Urban Council Annual Report 1990-1996

Other expenses in this category include the management and promotion of crematoria as well as the management of public cemeteries and regulatory control over private ones. In land-short Hong Kong, both councils actively promote cremation, providing niches in columbaria for the storage of ashes. Ancestor worship is important in Hong Kong and during special festivals families will visit graves.

The provision and management of recreation and sports facilities is a large area of expenditure. Although categorized under different headings this will cover indoor and outdoor sports grounds, swimming pools, parks and playgrounds. Both councils are also responsible for the management of a number of beaches along the extensive coast line and outlying islands. Two other major areas of expenditure are capital projects and culture and entertainment. Capital projects, which includes the provision of the facilities already outlined, account for some 10-20 per cent of expenditure for each council. Frequently councils build multi-purpose complexes incorporating a wet market, a cooked food market, waste collection point, public toilets and possibly an indoor sports hall or a library. Culture and entertainment covers the funding of libraries, museums, and supports the Hong Kong Chinese and Philharmonic Orchestras and Dance Company. The councils also spend money on the various festivals which take place throughout the year, the most spectacular being the Lunar New Year celebrations with huge fireworks displays in the harbour.

Table 3.11
Urban Council expenditure

	89/90	90/91	91/92	92/93	93/94	94/95	95/96
Admin.	342.10	378.00	455.20	525.10	568.10	671.40	n/a
Capital Works	641.40	589.30	496.80	416.80	532.50	679.00	n/a
Culture	216.60	229.10	258.70	297.90	317.40	375.20	n/a
Entertainment	55.60	58.40	66.60	77.10	90.90	92.20	n/a
Finance	39.50	45.90	56.00	61.90	68.00	76.40	n/a
Libraries	80.30	93.40	108.20	116.40	147.90	168.70	n/a
Liquor Licensing	2.00	2.10	2.60	3.20	3.70	4.10	n/a
Stadium Board	-	-	-	-	187.40	96.30	n/a
Total	3,029.10	3,499.70	3,888.20	4,032.70	4,765.20	5,299.90	6,012.40

Source: *Urban Council Annual Report 1990-1996*

Responsibility for making assessments

The government department responsible for making the assessments throughout the territory is the Rating and Valuation Department, headed by the Commissioner for Rating and Valuation. Under the Rating Ordinance (s4) the Governor appoints the Commissioner and 'such Assistant Commissioners and surveyors as he considers fit'. The professional grade is staffed by valuation surveyors who hold appropriate academic qualifications and corporate membership of both the Hong Kong Institute of Chartered Surveyors and The Royal Institution of Chartered Surveyors. Technical support staff hold certificates or diplomas in the areas of valuation and property studies from local academic institutions. The staff of the Department are highly regarded professionals and the Department has a long history of supporting continuous professional development through such means as the appointment of special training officers, holding in-house training courses and allowing study leave for career development purposes.

Under s12 of the Rating Ordinance the Commissioner is responsible for compiling a list of rateable values of tenements for both the Urban and Regional Council areas. The lists, which are referred to as the valuation list for the area to which it relates, will contain the address and where necessary, a description of the tenement, together with the rateable value. New valuation lists are prepared in legible form and are available for public inspection in the months of April and May of the year in which the list first comes into force. Notice of the place and times at which the lists may be inspected are published in the government gazette and in at least one Chinese and one English language newspaper. Subsequently the lists are retained in a non-legible form although legible extracts can be provided on request.

The Commissioner is also responsible for maintaining the valuation lists. This requires the inclusion of any tenements which have become liable for rates and the deletion of tenements which have ceased to be liable. The process of maintaining the lists is effected by 'interim valuations' and 'deletions'. Under s 24 and 25 of the Rating Ordinance the Commissioner:

> ... may at any time either make an interim valuation of a tenement which is not included in the valuation list and is liable for assessment to rates or delete from the valuation list any tenement -
>
> (a)   if there has been a structural alteration thereto;
>
> (b)   if the tenement comprises 2 or more tenements that were previously valued together as a single tenement; and ... should be valued as separate tenements;
>
> (c)   if the tenement was previously valued as a separate tenement; and ... should be valued together with another tenement as a single tenement ... ; or
>
> (d)   if the tenement or part thereof ceases to be liable for assessment to rates.

The number of interim valuation and deletions in 1995-96 is given in Table 3.12.

Basis of assessment

The statutory provisions relating to rating are governed by the Rating Ordinance (Cap 116) but Hong Kong is also a common law jurisdiction and as noted in Hsu

(1996) the Application of English Law Ordinance (s3) provides that:

Table 3.12
Interim valuations and deletions 1995-96

	Interim Valuations		Deletions	
	No.	Rateable Value $000	No.	Rateable Value $000
Hong Kong	23,598	7,322,762	4,406	3,462,355
Kowloon	7,065	2,371,870	1,855	1,602,837
New Kowloon	8,569	2,602,611	1,461	1,779,536
New Territories	54,686	7,136,644	1,664	1,675,684
Overall	**93,918**	**19,433,889**	**9,386**	**8,520,411**

Source: *Rating and Valuation Department, Annual Report 1995-1996*

... common law and the rules of equity shall be in force in Hong Kong, so far as they may be applicable to the circumstances of Hong Kong or its inhabitants and subject to such modifications thereto as such circumstances may require...

Hence a number of cases from English and Scottish courts have been used in the determination of rating cases in Hong Kong. In *Yiu Lian Machinery Repairing Works Ltd & Ors v Commissioner for Rating and Valuation* [1982] HKTLR32 it was noted that:

... the general principles of rating law in England and Scotland are sufficiently similar to make decisions of a court in either country of potential persuasive value in Hong Kong ...

In Hong Kong the unit of assessment is a 'tenement', defined in the Rating Ordinance (s2) as:

... any land (including land covered with water) or any building, structure, or part thereof which is held or occupied as a distinct or separate tenancy or holding or under any licence.

This definition has been specifically drafted to fit the system of land tenure in Hong Kong where, with the minor exception of the Anglican Cathedral, the Government holds the freehold interest in all land. Under the Ordinance freehold land does not constitute a tenement and is therefore not liable to rates. The

73

question of occupation as a criterion for liability to rating was also covered in *Yiu Lian Machinery etc. v Commissioner of Rating and Valuation* [1982] HKDCLR 32. In this case it was held that the statutory definition of a tenement creates a major difference between Hong Kong and English law. At issue was whether five floating docks and various ancillary facilities could be construed to be tenements under the provisions of the Ordinance and hence rateable. The Hong Kong Lands Tribunal noted that:

> ... in England occupation per se gives rise to liability for rates ... . In Hong Kong under our section 2 actual occupation by itself is not enough. Before any land or building or structure can become rateable it must in addition be held or occupied as a distinct or separate tenancy or holding under licence. So there must be either ownership or occupation under one of these three kinds of limited title...

In Hong Kong the rateable value of a property is assessed in relation to its annual rental value. The definition of rateable value is contained in Part III of the Ordinance (s7(2)) which states:

> The rateable value of a tenement shall be the amount equal to the rent at which a tenement might reasonably be expected to let from year to year if;
>
> (a)   the tenant undertook to pay all usual tenant's rates and taxes; and
>
> (b)   the landlord undertook to pay the Government rent, the costs of repairs and insurance and any other expenses necessary to maintain the tenement in a state to command that rent.'

Therefore, regardless of type, the basis of calculating the annual rental value for all property in Hong Kong will be the equivalent of gross annual value, i.e. where the landlord is responsible for repairs, insurance and maintenance.

Rateable value is also ascertained in relation to market value. (Subject to the statutory assumptions contained in s7(2)). Cruden (1986) notes that in *Warren Chow v Commissioner of Rating and Valuation* [1977] HKLTLR 177 the Lands Tribunal affirmed the principle of open market value declaring:

> What the Commissioner of Rating and Valuation must do, when assessing rateable value, is to look at the tenement at the date of valuation and to determine what rent it would bring on the open market as at that date ...

On the question of the tenancy being from 'year to year' Hong Kong case law has tended to followed English case law and the definition is now construed to imply a tenancy for an indefinite period in excess of one year. The valuations of the tenements are always carried out separately (s10) unless tenements are used in connection with one another and the value of one affects the value of the other, in which case the tenements may be valued together as a single tenement.

Since property in Hong Kong is only rateable if it falls within the statutory definition of a tenement 'chattels enjoyed with land' are not rateable, but tenements which contain plant and machinery are covered under s8 of the Ordinance. In essence s8 states that the rateable value of the tenement will, with the exception of any value ascribable to machinery used for the purpose of manufacturing operations or trade processes, include the value of all machinery which is adjunct to the tenement. The reasonable expenses incurred in working the machinery are allowed in arriving at the rateable value.

In *The Cross-Harbour Tunnel Co Ltd v Commissioner of Rating and Valuation* [1978] HKLTLR 144 whilst it was accepted that the major part of the ventilation system required in the tunnel was machinery the Land Tribunal rejected the submission that the ventilation system was part of a trade process. The Tribunal also held that in this case the water mains in the tunnel were so embedded that they formed part of the tunnel structure and were not therefore machinery. In cases where 'plant' is involved and 'the plant is by means of which a person is occupying the tenement then it will be regarded as part of the tenement for the purposes of assessing rateable value'. Plant is defined as including such items as pipelines, railway lines, tram lines, oil tanks and cables, power stations and electricity transmission systems (s8A).

Since in Hong Kong general revaluations are carried out at approximately 3 yearly intervals the 'tone' of the valuation list is maintained by using a single valuation date known as the 'relevant date'. The last four valuation list effective dates and the adopted relevant dates are shown in Table 3.13.

Table 3.13
Effective and relevant dates

Effective Date	Relevant Date
1 April 1984	1 July 1983
1 April 1988	1 October 1986
1 April 1991	1 July 1990
1 April 1994	1 July 1993

Source: *Williams, 1996*

The last revaluation was undertaken during 1993-94 and took effect on 1 April 1994. The rateable values, which are based on rental levels as at 1 July 1993, remain in force until the next general revaluation. This will be conducted during 1996-97 and is scheduled to take effect on 1 April 1997. However the new Rating (Effective Date of Interim Valuation) Regulation, made under the 1995 Amendment Ordinance, affects the 'relevant date' for new premises. From the 1 August 1995 new domestic premises are assessed to rates 90 days from the issue of the occupation permit or certificate of compliance and for non-domestic premises the effective date is 180 days from either the issue of the relevant occupation document or the date of first occupation, whichever is earlier. In those cases where an interim valuation is required s7A(3) states that:

> For the purpose of an interim valuation, the rateable value of any tenement in respect of which a notice of interim valuation has been served ... shall be the value which would have been ascribed thereto on the relevant date on the assumption that at that date:
>
> (a) the tenement was in the same state at the time of the service of the notice; and
>
> (b) any relevant factors affecting the mode or character of occupation were those subsisting at the time of service of the notice; and
>
> (c) the locality ... was in the same state, with regard to other premises situated in the locality, the occupation and use of those premises, the transport services and other facilities available in the locality and other matters affecting the amenities of the locality, at the time of service of the notice.

Appeals procedure

Proposals to alter, object or appeal against the valuation list are covered in Part IX of the Rating Ordinance. Anyone objecting to any aspect of an existing entry in the valuation list can serve a proposal to alter the entry. There are four bases for objection, either that the tenement in question has been valued at above or below its proper rateable value or that a tenement has been wrongly included or omitted from the list. Under s37(1) the person aggrieved may, within the months of April and May, apply to the Rating and Valuation Department for an alteration to the valuation list. The Rating (Amendment) Ordinance 1995 added a provision that in a general revaluation year a proposal to alter the new list can be made immediately after the list has been declared, which is usually in March, instead of having to wait until the effective date of 1 April. A proposal to alter the list made under s37 must specify the grounds for the proposed alteration (s37(2)).

In the case of interim valuation, deletion or correction to the list a ratepayer can lodge an objection with the Commissioner within 28 days of the issue of the notice. The objector may then serve a notice of objection, specifying the grounds for the objection. Following the service of a proposal or objection the Commissioner will review the valuation and an alteration may be agreed with the ratepayer. A proposal or objection may also be withdrawn, by serving a notice of withdrawal, at any time before a notice of decision is served. In the absence of either withdrawal or agreement a Notice of Decision will be issued.

If a recipient is not satisfied with the decision contained in the Notice of Decision then within 28 days they may lodge an appeal with the Hong Kong Lands Tribunal. The notice of appeal must be served on all the appropriate parties and must be confined to the grounds of the proposal or the objection (s42(2)). In most cases the membership of the Tribunal will comprise of a District Court Judge as the President or Presiding Officer and a Member with expert valuation qualifications. The Lands Tribunal can hear and determine the appeal and may make such order as it thinks proper; award costs to any party; direct the Collector of Rates (the Commissioner) to amend the valuation list and make direction as to the payment of rates as may be necessary (s44(1)).

The Lands Tribunal may also reserve any question of law for the consideration of the Court of Appeal, which has the power to hear and determine the question and send its opinion to the Tribunal. An appeal against a Lands Tribunal decision can be made to the Court of Appeal but only on the grounds that the decision is 'erroneous in point of law' Williams (1995). In principle, a further appeal can be made to the Privy Council in the United Kingdom, but in practice no rating appeals have yet been pursued beyond the Court of Appeal (Williams, 1995).

Following the change of Sovereignty on the 30 June 1997, this option will be abolished and the highest court will be the Hong Kong Court of Final Appeal. But even after the return of Hong Kong to China the common law in force in Hong Kong at that date will be maintained under Article 8 of the Basic Law. Article 84 of the Basic Law will also permit Judges to continue to refer to precedents from any common law jurisdiction in determining cases.

Methods of assessment

When making an assessment the Commissioner of Rating and Valuation has extensive powers to obtain information required for a rating assessment. According to Rating Ordnance (s5), the Commissioner, or any person authorized by him, may:

serve ... a requisition in a specified form, requiring ... particulars ...; require the owner or occupier ... to produce ... for inspection all receipts ... rent books, accounts or other documents whatsoever connected with rent or value ... ; take away for the purpose of making copies any receipts for rent, rent books, accounts or other documents whatsoever connected with rent or value.

The preferred method of valuation for rating purposes is by direct comparison with rents passing for similar properties. The Rating Department holds a substantial data bank, which will usually provide a reasonable body of rental evidence and for the great majority of premises such as domestic, retail, commercial, industrial and storage this approach is normally practicable.

The preference for using a direct comparison approach was indicated in the case of *Mobil Oil v Commissioner of Rating and Valuation* [1991] RA244 when it was held the use of a comparable method is preferable but the adoption of the contractor's approach will be more satisfactory in those cases where only a single comparable is available. In the absence of rental evidence, or where it is considered inappropriate to value by reference to the profits approach, Hong Kong has traditionally adopted the contractor's approach to the valuation of properties such as oil storage depots, golf courses, non-profit making clubs and similar institutions.

There are a number of examples of the contractor's method being applied to the rating of private clubs in Hong Kong. In *Royal Hong Kong Golf Club v Commissioner of Rating and Valuation* (1977) HKLTLR 236 the Lands Tribunal accepted a five stage process to be followed in using this method. This approach required the estimation of effective capital value of the improvements, an estimation of the value of the land, in its existing use, the ascertainment of a market rate and its application to the effective capital value plus the land value. The final sum being subject to adjustments for the basis of the tenancy and what a hypothetical tenant would be willing to pay. This approach was reiterated in later cases relating to the Hong Kong Country Club and the Royal Hong Kong Yacht Club. However, there are a number of problems associated with the use of the contractor's approach in Hong Kong. In particular the high land values disproportionately distort the appearance of the valuation, to the extent that the adjustments become increasingly more problematic. In some cases it is also difficult to adopt values or yields derived from the property market and in a recent revaluation of an oil depot the parties have agreed a decapitalization yield based on adjusted prime lending rate rather than a property based yield.

As a result of some of these difficulties rating valuers are increasingly accepting the use of the profits method as an acceptable alternative to the contractor's approach. The rating assessment of the Hong Kong Jockey Club, (a private members club which organizes all the horse racing in the Territory and is possibly one of the largest single ratepayers) used to be valued on an adjusted contractor's basis but is now valued by reference to profits. In the case of those properties where the likely profit will affect the rent, then the property will normally be valued by reference to receipts and expenditure. Examples of the type of properties falling into this category in Hong Kong include the toll tunnels, the gas, electricity and telephone utility company premises, the tramway, the mass transit rail system and the railway. The leading Hong Kong decision on the use of the profits method for this type of rating valuation is *The Cross Harbour Tunnel Company Co Ltd v Commissioner of Rating and Valuation* [1978] HKLTR 144.

Properties such as multi-storey car parks, petrol filling stations, hotels and cinemas will also normally be assessed by reference to the estimated trading potential of the property in question. However, the use of a profits approach for the valuation of a number of specialized properties does present problems, chiefly related to the extent to which the profitability of the core business is attributable to the use of the property assets. If, for example, a utility company becomes more efficient and generates more profits from the same asset base they will be penalized. One possible solution, which currently does not exist in Hong Kong, might be a system of valuing by reference to statutory formula.

The use of the residual method has, as elsewhere, been the subject of discussion and although there has been a growing acceptance of it applicability the Hong Kong Lands Tribunal still considers that unless comparable evidence is inadequate or unavailable the use of the direct comparison approach is more appropriate. In *Redhill Properties Ltd v Director of Engineering Development* [1984] HKDCLR1 (as discussed in Cruden (1986)) the Lands Tribunal accepted the use residual method and observed:

Because of the relatively few numbers of residential properties remaining in Hong Kong of the age and character of the subject property together with the unusual nature of the hypothetical redevelopment by refurbishing the project, if not unique, would have been a rarity ... in these circumstances both parties were agreed that the preferable method of valuation by comparison was, on the facts, not possible. There simply were no true comparable properties to enable any direct comparison to be made. The valuer was therefore obliged to fall back on the residual method ...

Again in *Hofei Estate Ltd v Secretary for City and New Territories Administration* CLR1/82 (as discussed in Cruden (1986)) the Lands Tribunal observed that because of the substantial number of adjustments required as a result of the nature of the available comparables then a better approach to the valuation would have been to use the residual method. The Hong Kong Rating and Valuation Department has also implemented a system of computer assisted mass appraisal. A detailed explanation of the nature and use of which can be found in Stevenson (1996). Hong Kong has an advantage in that the pattern of relatively dense, high rise urban development naturally lends itself to the use of an assisted appraisal approach, without which the current policy of all properties being revalued every three years, at a common reference date and with all valuations being issued at the same time, would be totally impracticable. Even on an annual basis there are a substantial number of adjustments to the valuation list. In 1995-96 there were 93,918 new entries (with a total rateable value of HK$19,433,889) and 9,386 deletions (Table 3.12).

Hong Kong has been using a system of computer assisted valuations since 1984, when a pilot system was put into place to assist in the revaluation taking place that year. By 1986 a comprehensive system for assessing rental (rateable) values was completed for the majority of residential, commercial and industrial premises. The system is based on a reference assessment approach, which requires the identification and assessment of a representative unit within each building. Multiple regression models, which identify and quantify all the attributes and relationships which affect value, are then used to estimate values for all the other relevant properties and control any intra-building value variations.

Adjustments fall into three categories and are expressed in percentage terms. Specific size and quality allowance are identified separately (QA%), whilst general factors such as age, view, accessibility, nuisance factors, etc. are combined into a composite adjustment (CA%) and ancillary (non main-floor) value items such as balcony or roof areas are also expressed as a percentage adjustments (AV%). The formula for the assessment becomes:

$$RV_i = \$m^2 \times \text{main floor area} \times (1 \pm QA\% \pm AC\% = AV\%)$$

The Department also uses regression based indexing as both a predictive tool and a means of analysing assessment equity. Existing data on price or rateable values can be used to predict prices or rent levels and the regression indexation procedure can be used to update assessed values. Stevenson (1996) notes that the advantages of using computerized assistance and regression based indexing for entry and analysis of all rental evidence and the setting and adjustment of all new values can be clearly demonstrated as the system allowed the values for some 1.105 million assessments to be generated from some 21,000 reference assessments (March, 1995).

In 1993 the Rating and Valuation Department started to develop a comprehensive Information Systems Strategy. By 1998 it is intended that this will provide a fully integrated computerized property data base, valuation and rates billing system with 12 strategic applications. The comprehensive system will not only serve the Rating and Valuation Department but will also provide property related information for other government departments and will include the revaluations, assessment and entry of new premises, property market analysis (price and rental indices) supply forecasts and analysis of rents and capital values.

Exemptions, reliefs and concessions

Exemptions, reliefs and concessions are covered by Parts VII and VIII of the Ordinance. The Governor may exempt any tenement from the payment of rates but tenements which are currently exempt include:

- Government, Urban and Regional Council premises.

- Agricultural land and buildings, (to include fish ponds, market or nursery gardens and orchards).

- Properties occupied for public religious worship.

- Military land.

- Consular premises.

- Traditional village houses (owned by indigenous New Territories villagers).

- Cottage or temporary housing areas managed by the Hong Kong Housing Authority.

- Cemeteries or Crematoria.

Certain other occupiers, such as voluntary welfare organizations, are obliged to pay rates but are subvented by the Government.

The Rating (Amendment) Ordinance 1995 removed the 50 per cent refund for rates on vacant non-domestic property (vacancy refunds do not apply to domestic premises) but 100 per cent refunds are still applicable to vacant undeveloped land and vacancies resulting from a court order. The Rating Ordinance also allows a rates relief scheme to be introduced following a general revaluation. This was first introduced in 1977 and allowed for increases to be phased to cushion the impact of the general revaluation of that year. This form of relief has been removed and reinstated several times over the years. The latest scheme, which followed the 1994-95 revaluation, limited the rates payable in 1994-95 to 120 per cent of the rates payable in 1993-94 . The relief scheme continued in 1995-96 but ended on the 1 April 1996.

Under s18(2) of the Rating Ordinance tenements without filtered fresh water from a government water main are entitled to a concession of 15 per cent in the rates payable. Where the water is available but unfiltered the concession is reduced to 7.5 per cent.

Collection procedures

The computation, liability for and payment of rates is covered under Part V of the Rating Ordinance. Rates are payable quarterly in advance from 1 April each year. Demand notices are sent at the beginning of each quarter and are payable before the end of the first month of the quarter. A surcharge of 5 per cent may be made if rates are not paid by the due date and if the sum is still outstanding after six months then a further surcharge of 10 per cent may be added. Under the provisions of the Ordinance all assessed rates must be paid on demand and before settlement of any proposal or objection. If the rateable value is later amended the alteration will be effective only from the effective date of the list and the appropriate adjustments will be made in subsequent demands.

Although in Hong Kong rates are deemed to be the responsibility of the occupier the Rating Ordinance makes both the owner and occupier of the tenement liable for payment of rates (s21(1)). In the absence of any agreement any amount paid by an owner may be recovered from an occupier (s21(2)). In those cases where two or more tenements are valued together as a single tenement then the assessed rates on the single tenement must be paid either by the sole occupier or by any one of the owners or occupiers (s21(4)). The affected parties may then either apply for an apportionment of the rateable value between the separate tenements, or agree the respective shares between themselves.

Under the Rating (Amendment) Ordinance 1995 the Rating and Valuation Department became the single authority for all matters relating to the administration of rating property. The amendment to the ordinance transferred responsibility for issuing rates demands, processing notification of changes, maintaining rates accounts and instituting an action for recovery of arrears, from the Treasury to the Rating and Valuation Department. The only exception is the collection of rates payments, which remains the responsibility of the Director of Accounting Services as Collector of Rates. The Collector of Rates is also responsible for paying the Urban and Regional Councils the appropriate proportion of the rates collected on the tenements within their respective areas.

Critical analysis

Raising revenue by taxing or rating the occupation of real property has a number of advantages for all governments. The Hong Kong government is no exception and the system of rating property in the territory has a history almost as long as that of the colonial administration. One advantage of such a long existence is that rating, as an approach to taxation, is well understood and accepted. In addition the system, as it is administered in Hong Kong, is relatively comprehensive and straight-forward. All matters relating to rating are governed by a detailed Ordinance, which has been easily amended as required and as Hong Kong is also a common law jurisdiction a substantial body of case law has been built up.

Hong Kong has a further advantage in that it basically covers a very small area and although densely developed, there is a relatively high degree of homogeneity between much of the property within a use class. This has not only allowed the Department of Rating and Valuation to amass a substantial property data base but has also assisted in the use and development of a comprehensive computer assisted mass appraisal system. The use of a computer assisted mass appraisal approach works well in this situation and its implementation has both time and cost saving implications. However, as with any system of taxation, a number of issues arise. The first of which has to do with the nature of the Hong Kong economy and the difficulties of assessing property values in a volatile market. Although Hong Kong is one of the Asian economic success stories, with relatively high rates of GDP growth (+5.5 per cent in 1995) which has been reflected in the demand for real estate, the market has also been subject to the downside element of socio-political risk and is extremely volatile. Hence, although the time frame for rating revaluations is currently three years, which in terms of some jurisdictions may seem relatively short, it is argued that in Hong Kong, where the majority of commercial leases are for two years, a three year time lag between revaluations is a relatively long time period.

The booming economy coupled with a shortage of available land has created high land prices, to the extent that the proportion of the value of a property which is attributable to the land element is higher in Hong Kong. This can distort valuation assessments for rating purposes and has resulted in a general acceptance of the use of the profits, rather than the contractor's approach for the valuation of certain types of special properties.

Any discussion in relation to using rating as a means of raising government revenue must also revolve around the amount of revenue raised in proportion to the time-cost expenses of collection. Although figures are not available as to the relative cost-benefit of different sources of revenue, rating would appear to be one of the more expensive options available to the Government. The amount of revenue raised by the Hong Kong Government is shown in Tables 3.2, 3.3 and 3.7. Currently rates account for some 9 per cent of central government revenue and approximately 85 per cent of the revenue of the Urban and the Regional Councils. But when compared with other sources of government income rates generate substantially less revenue, e.g. the income from rates is currently equivalent to some 30 per cent of the total revenue raised from profits tax on corporations and 55 per cent of revenue from salaries tax. Stamp duty and tax on betting and sweeps both generate some 75 per cent of the revenue raised from rates.

It would be possible for the government to raise more revenue by increasing the rate percentage, which at 5.5 per cent is relatively low. However this decision is influenced by socio-political as well as economic considerations and is presently controlled by the newly elected members of the Legislative Council. It can be argued that the choice of a relatively low rate percentage may act as an attraction or incentive for business, since it reduces the costs of occupation. However in Hong Kong rates form a very small proportion of total occupation costs for commercial interests and therefore the costs per se are likely to have little effect on business location decisions.

Whilst the burden of rates may have little effect on the cost of business occupation this is not necessarily true for all occupiers in the residential sector. The cost of rates may have little or no affect on certain sectors of the housing market, such as public housing tenants or where the costs of residential occupation are met by employers, but rates will affect the middle class housing market where an average 800 sq. ft. (80sq. m.) home would cost some HK$6 million to buy (approximately 500,000 pounds sterling) and in excess of HK$20,000 (£650 pounds) a month to rent. In this case rates, even at 5.5 per cent of rental value, add to the expenses of home ownership. A possible solution to this dilemma might be to have either different rating bands or a differential rate percentage between domestic and non-domestic use.

It has also been suggested that in Hong Kong the use of the Lands Tribunal has developed into a very formalized and expensive system with the majority of appellants feeling obliged to use lawyers. It is felt that the adoption of a lower level and more informal appeal procedure, such as alternative dispute resolution mechanism, might be beneficial. However, the major issue for the continuation of rating property as a system of raising government revenue is the change of sovereignty in June 1997, when Hong Kong will become a Special Administrative Region of China. Although the agreements between China and Great Britain determined that all existing systems would continue unchanged for 50 years, a certain degree of political and economic uncertainty is to be expected and the effects of reunification on the Hong Kong economy and the property market are, as yet, unknown. From the point of view of rating as a property tax the revaluation of 1997 will have been completed before the hand-over, but the implications for the next revaluation in the year 2000 are the subject of much discussion.

References

Cruden, G.N. (1986), *Land Compensation and Valuation Law in Hong Kong*, Butterworths, Singapore.

Ernst & Young, (1995-96), *Taxation in Hong Kong*, Longmans (Far East), Hong Kong.

Hong Kong Government, Rating Ordinance: Chapter 116, Government Printer, Hong Kong.

Hong Kong Government, Annual Report 1996, Information Services, Government Printer, Hong Kong.

Hong Kong Rating and Valuation Department, (1987), *The History of Rates in Hong Kong*, Government Printer, Hong Kong.

Hong Kong Rating and Valuation Department, (1990-1996), Annual Report, Government Printer, Hong Kong.

Hong Kong Regional Council, (1990-1996), Annual Report, Government Printer, Hong Kong.

Hong Kong Treasury, (1990-1996), Accounts of Hong Kong and Annual Report of the Director of Accounting Services, Government Printer, Hong Kong.

Hong Kong Urban Council, (1990-1996), Annual Report, Government Printer, Hong Kong.

Hsu, B. (1996), *A Guide To Hong Kong Taxation*, Open Learning Institute Press & The Chinese University Press, Hong Kong.

Stevenson, R. (1996), Regression Based Indexing, *Journal of Property Tax Assessment & Administration*, Vol. 2, No. 2, pp. 25-39.

Walker, A.W. et al., (1995), *Hong Kong in China: Real Estate in the Economy*, Brooke Hillier Parker, Hong Kong.

Williams, M.J. (1995), Rating In Hong Kong, *Journal of Property Tax Assessment & Administration*, Vol. 1, No. 2, pp. 122-132.

4 Rating in Malaysia

Raja Hizam, Frances Plimmer, Abdul Nawawi and Stuart Gronow

Introduction

The property tax which funds local authority expenditure in Malaysia is called rates. In Malaysia, the basis for the collection of local authority property-based rates is the rateable value, which is the annual value of the ownership of property. This applies in all the ten States of Peninsular Malaysia, except in Johore, where the 'improved value' (capital value) is used. This is because the Malaysian Local Government Act allows a state authority to opt for annual rental or capital value as a basis for rates, at their discretion.

Although based, historically, on the British rating system in Malaysia, rates is a tax payable only by those owners whose property is located within local authority boundaries and that, since a substantial part of the country is not covered by local authority areas and for that reason no services are provided, many landowners are not liable to any rates. There are three distinct historical periods which partly explain the present administrative arrangements in Malaysia. These are the pre-British period, the period of British administration and the post-independence period.

Pre-British period (pre-1786)

The concept of a single political unit covering the whole of the Malay peninsular dates back to the time of the Malacca Empire in the 14th century. Of the 13 states which comprise modern Malaysia, 9 of them are ruled by the Malay Sultans or by other Malay Royal rulers drawn from long established dynasties. Before the British administration, there were generally three levels of government units, where the largest political unit was the 'Negeri' (state), the head of which was the Sultan. He symbolized the unity and welfare of his people and was responsible for foreign relations and providing leadership. The next political unit was the district, known as the 'Jajahan' or 'Daerah'. Each district had a chief, whose duties were associated with local administration, revenue collection, defence and justice.

The third and lowest level was the 'Kampung' (village) which was usually a cluster of between 5 and 40 houses and which was more of a social and economic unit than a political or administrative one. The head of a village was known as the 'Penghulu' (headman) who acted as a link between his villagers and the district chief. Although important within his village, he did not belong to the ruling class and was generally of the subject class. An exception to the above was the social and political structure of the Negri Sembilan, then known as the 'Nine States of Rembau'. This was derived from Sumatra (Indonesia) and had no sultanate or constitutionalized central government until 1870. Instead, it had four major district chiefs known as the 'law givers' and, until 1870, the chiefs had a loose form of confederacy for defence purposes. There were no other structures or political units.

The Malay rulers normally enjoyed almost absolute power, being afforded 'blind loyalty' by their subjects. Government was influenced by the Islamic system of 'mesyuarah', where various decisions are made through agreement, preceded by discussion. There were two traditional Malay concepts which have a strong influence over the people: one is called 'Daulat' (sovereignty) and the other 'Derhaka' (disobedience). The sovereignty of a Malay ruler is not merely a legal concept, it is cultural and religious as well. The 'daulat' endows the ruler with rights and privileges and places him above his subjects and therefore beyond reproach and criticism. The 'daulat' also entails unquestioning loyalty from his subjects. 'Derhaka' has a wider meaning and would encompass both disobedience to the ruler, rebellion, open criticism of the ruler and the attempt to prevent a blatant wrong if it was ordered by the Sultan.

These principles are important for the understanding of the attitude of Malays towards their rulers and helps to explain current attitudes to the present local government and rating systems, particularly in the rural areas. To be disloyal, in the Malay scale of values, was the worst of crimes. Despite the conversion of Malay society to Islam in the 15th century and the presence of the Portuguese from 1511 and the Dutch from 1642, Malay socio-economic institutions were little changed until the traditional indigenous system broke down, mainly because of its inability to accommodate the rapidly rising numbers of aristocrats and members of royal families who vied with each other for the few positions of power and dignity.

The British period (1786 - 1957)

The British influence in Malaysia began in 1786 when the East India Company obtained a grant of control over Penang Island. Malacca, previously in British hands, was handed back to the Dutch in 1814 and was returned to the British by the Anglo-Dutch treaty of 1824. The present system of local government in Malaysia was initially introduced in 1801, when a committee of assessors was set up at Penang. This committee functioned as the local government, having as its roles those of planning, implementing urban development on the island, preserving law and order and raising revenue through rates. It was purely a voluntary body but in 1827, the government recognized its existence by regulation.

The first pieces of legislation were regulations made under the company's charter which were followed by the Municipal Rates Act and the Indian Legislation Act, which applied to Penang, Malacca and Singapore in 1848. British influence was extended further between 1874 and 1914 and Townboards were set up in the urban districts of the areas controlled by the British. A Municipal Ordinance of 1913, based on the British Public Health Act 1875, was introduced and in 1950, the Local Authority Elections Ordinance provided for the municipalities to be administered by a town council with an elected membership.

The British introduced a bureaucratic system which turned the State into the source of authority for the control of the population but not, as before, for the benefit of the ruler himself. British influence provided laws and administrative departments to manage land, collect taxes, develop trade, etc., with the revenue collected belonging to the state and with the state being responsible for the provision of services to the people.

The Chinese and Indian labourers, imported to work in the tin mining and rubber plantations, remained in Malaysia to be a settled part of the colonial population, but distinct from the undisturbed indigenous peasant-based agricultural economy. Economic development was encouraged by improvements in transport and communications systems but these also resulted in a shift in the administrative and economic centre from its traditional location on the coast to the interior. Nevertheless, structurally, the Malay society remained basically the same. The aim of the British policy was to help restore, if not reinforce, the rural character of Malay society, while giving a semblance of political administrative authority to the traditional ruling elite. A separate education system was established which, together with the above, contributed to the emergence of a society divided on racial, geographic and economic lines.

Post-independence (post-1957)

At independence, when the Malaysian Federal government took over national administration from the British, there were five main types of local government authority operating under the control of the state government: the city council of George Town of Penang (fully elected); the two financially-autonomous municipalities of Kuala Lumpur and Malacca; the large towns with town councils (elected and nominated representatives), most of which were financially autonomous; the smaller towns which had town boards or rural boards (nominated members); and autonomous local councils (elected).

Most of the local government units existed in a precarious state, being in many cases bankrupt and suffering chronic shortages of money and manpower. The local councils operated a simple system of rating but received considerable state aid. There was also a lot of confusion in Peninsular Malaysia, caused by the duplication of local government legislation and the creation by the states of a multiplicity of the various types and levels of local authorities. In 1964, the Federal government appointed a Royal Commission of Inquiry to investigate the working of local authorities in Peninsular Malaysia. The Commission's report (the Anthi Nahapan Report) was submitted to the government in 1968, but, as a result of racial rioting, the government did not implement all of the recommendations of the report. However, in 1973, the Local Government (Temporary Provisions) Act introduced new economically viable administrative units which would be capable of providing property services to a modern standard, implementing development projects, town planning measures, etc.

There followed a period of restructuring (1974-89), during which municipal councils and district councils were the only two types of local authorities in the Peninsular, although there was provision to create city councils. The right to elect local government councillors was abolished and local councillors were appointed by the state authorities. The original recommendation of the Anthi Nahapan Report to cover the entire country with local authority administrative control, was not implemented with most states turning local authority areas into an 'octopus' or 'ribbon' shape, based on existing physical development. As a result, 61.5 per cent of the population (excluding Kuala Lumpur) were located in local authorities areas (previously the figure had been 55.8 per cent). In terms of area, local authorities covered 12.7 per cent of the total land area in Peninsular Malaysia (previously the figure had been 3 per cent) and the previous 373 local authorities became 95 in number.

Revenue

Local authority revenue comes from rates; licences, rents, interest and fees for services; and grants from the Federal and/or state government. Rates are the largest source of revenue for most local authorities. Local authority revenue was estimated (1987) to be MYR $1 billions (or 27 per cent of State and 6 per cent of Federal revenues). Operating expenditures were MYR $1.2 billion (or 37 per cent of State and 6 per cent of the Federal operating expenditures) and local authority development expenditure was MYR $462 million (or 18 per cent of the State and 7 per cent of the Federal government).

However, despite the relatively low level of expenditure on local authority services, because their activities impact on the daily lives of their population, the local authorities are the 'front-line' of government and are perceived by the local residents to be more important than the level of revenue and expenditure might indicate. They are, therefore, subject to intervention by Federal, State and other political forces and this, together with the relatively limited level and range of services provided, results in an ineffective and ineffectual provision of local authority services.

Following restructuring, local authorities' responsibilities were extended beyond their traditional role of garbage collection and sanitary inspection or general maintenance functions, to those involving urban development, management, environmental, and social services. Under the relevant local government laws, local authorities may carry out a whole range of functions, limited only by their own ambition and resources. However, in practice, local authorities undertake only a few of the activities laid down in the Local Government Act 1976, partly because of the lack of proper bye-laws and enforcement units to enable the effective delivery of services.

Rates in Malaysia is one of the sources of funding for local government which evolved after the limited reorganization during the period of restructuring 1974-89 following, in part, the recommendations in the Anthi Nahapan Report. Each local authority is a legal entity in itself, with perpetual succession and a common seal. The organization of the restructured local authorities basically remains as before, except for the fact that the Mayor or President and the Secretary (chief administrative officer) are appointed by the state authority. Other officials are employed by the authority concerned and their recruitment and appointment follow a rigid pattern. There is hardly, if ever, any mobility either vertically or horizontally, for such employees.

City and municipal councils are located in the urban centres or state capitals, while district councils are located predominantly in rural areas, with a small urban core as their base. Determination of the status of either municipal or district councils is based on criteria which were formulated by the National Council for Local Government. Thus, municipal councils should have an annual revenue of not less than MYR $5 million (£1 million Sterling) and serve populations of more than 100,000 people. They must have a well organized administrative centre within the core area and the local demand on the administration should be for local government or municipal services rather than for infrastructural development.

District councils are basically rural units, with populations of less than 100,000 living in a dispersed and uncongested rural environment. Revenue is less than MYR $5 million (£1 million Sterling) and they have a more limited capacity to undertake their functions because of their lack of communication facilities and organizational structure. Under the Local Government Act, 1976, inter-governmental communication and coordination is provided for by the National Council for Local Government and the State Local Government Committee and these bodies deal with any complex or policy issues affecting local government and which emerge from state legislation. Under the Malaysia Federal Constitution, the state has absolute authority in local government matters and the implementation (including its manner and timing) of the Local Government Act 1976 is entirely at the discretion of the state. In fact, Federal control is rather weak. For example, there has been a failure of local authorities to communicate information to state authorities which have no power to force compliance.

Importance of the tax

Rates are the largest source of revenue for most local authorities. They account for 64.1 per cent of the total revenue of local authorities in Peninsular Malaysia. But despite this fact, rates are not fully exploited by many local authorities. This has resulted from problems of collection and a lack of commitment to collect new rates and implementing revaluations.

Basis of assessment

Rates are levied on the annual value (or improved value in Johore) of landed property located within the boundaries of local authority areas of Peninsular Malaysia. Since not all of the country is covered by local authority boundaries (refer above), not all owners of landed property pay rates. The unit of assessment is the holding, which is defined in section 2 of the Local Government Act 1976, as follows:

> ... any land with or without buildings thereon which is held under a separate document of title and in the case of a subdivided building, the common property and any parcel thereof and, in the case of Penang and Malacca, 'holdings' includes messuages, buildings easements and hereditaments of any tenure, whether open or enclosed whether built on or not, whether public or private and whether maintained or not under statutory authority.

The only criterion is that there must be an identifiable title which would establish ownership or identifiable occupiers in cases where buildings on State lands are rented.

Vacant land

All holdings are taxable based on the annual value of their occupation. However as vacant land is seldom let and there is therefore no rental evidence, the Local Government Act 1976, section (2)(c) provides a separate basis for the determination of the annual value of land in the case of any land:

• which is partially occupied or partially built upon;

• which is vacant, unoccupied or not built upon;

• with an incomplete building; or

• with a building which has been certified by the local authority to be abandoned or dilapidated or unfit for human habitation.

The basis of the valuation is as follows:

• in the case of (1) the Valuation Officer can choose to value the holding on the annual value or take 10 per cent of the open market value as annual value;

• in the case of (2), (3) and (4) the Valuation Officer must take 10 per cent of the open market value of the land as the annual value and this can be reduced to 5 per cent with the approval of the State authority.

It is pertinent to note that the term 'open market value' has not been defined anywhere in the Act. Therefore, it is necessary to refer to the definition that has often been quoted by the Malaysian Courts in land acquisition cases. The definition, which was stated by *Buhagior J. in Nanyang Manufacturing Co. v The Collector of Land Revenue, Johore* [1954], is as follows:

> The market value of land may roughly be described as the price that an owner willing, and not obliged to sell might reasonably expect to obtain from a willing purchaser with whom he was bargaining for sale and purchase of the land.

The capital value of land is used as a basis to arrive at the annual value at a statutory rate of return. This percentage may or may not have any bearing on the present rate of return for the actual property types.

Another issue is the provision of the rate refund under section 162 of the Local Government Act 1976. If a building is unoccupied and no rent is payable in respect of it for a period of not less than a month in any half-year for which a rate has been paid, the local authority may order the refund or remission of the amount paid proportionate to the period during which the building was occupied. The refund is made once all the following conditions are satisfied:

1   the building is in good repair and fit for occupation;

2   every reasonable effort to obtain a tenant has been made;

3   the rent demanded is reasonable; and

4   the building has been vacant during the whole of the period when the refund is made.

However, land which is vacant is still rateable and the owner is liable for any rates.

Statutory definitions

Annual value

'Annual value' is defined in section 2 of the Local Government Act 1976 as:

> ... the estimated gross annual rent at which the holding might reasonably be expected to let from year to year, the landlord paying the expenses of repair, insurance, maintenance or upkeep and all public rates and taxes provided that:
>
> (a)   no account shall be taken of any restriction or control on rent; and that
>
> (b)   any enhanced value from the presence of any machinery used for the following purposes shall not be taken into consideration:
>
> > (i)   the making of any article or part of article;
> >
> > (ii)   the altering, repairing, ornamenting or finishing of any article;
> >
> > (iii)   the adapting for sale of any article.

However, in practice, very little attention is given to plant and machinery valuation.

Improved value

Section 2 of the Local Government Act 1976 provides for 'improved value' as an alternative basis of assessment and this has been adopted in the state of Johore only. Improved value is defined (section 2 Local Government Act 1976) as:

> ... the price an owner willing and not obliged to sell might reasonably expect to obtain from a willing purchaser with whom he was bargaining for sale and purchase of the holding.

The definition of improved value is identical to the definition of market value used for the purposes of assessing compensation under the Land Acquisition Act 1960, which was quoted in the *Nanyang Manufacturing Co. v Collector of Land Revenue Johore* [1954]. Over a period of years, the courts have clearly identified the methods and principles which should be used in the determination of improved value. According to Mani Usillapan (1988), in the case of *Ng Tiou Hong v Collector of Land Revenue, Gombak* [1984], Syed Agil Barakbah F.J. summarized the following principles, established for the purpose of fixing market value for compulsory acquisition, distilled from various older authorities, but which apply equally to the fixing of improved value:

1   improved value is the price which a willing vendor might reasonably expect to obtain from a willing purchaser. The elements of unwillingness or sentimental value on the part of the vendor to part with the land and the urgent necessity of the purchaser to buy have to be disregarded and cannot be made as the basis for increasing the market value. It must be treated on the willingness of both the vendor to sell and the purchaser to buy at the market price without any element of compulsion;

2   the improved value can be measured by a consideration of the price of sales of similar lands in the neighbourhood or locality and having similar quality and positions;

3   its potentialities must be taken into account. The nature of the land and the use to which it is being put at the time of acquisition have to be taken into account together with the likelihood to which it is reasonably capable of being put to use in the future, for example, the possibility of it being used for building or other developments;

4   in considering the nature of land, regard must be given to whether its locality is within or near a developed area, its distance to or from town, availability of access roads to and within it or the presence of a road reserve

indicating a likelihood of access to be constructed in the near future, expenses that would likely be incurred in levelling the surface and the like;

5   estimates of value by experts are undoubtedly some evidence but too much weight should not be given to these unless they are supported by, or coincide with, other evidence.

Responsibility for making assessments

Assessors are employed by the local authorities which raise the tax. There is a lack of qualified assessors in Malaysia, especially in the smaller district councils, and this has prevented the valuation lists from being updated. In the State of Kelantan, only two out of the nine local authorities have a Valuation Officer. The Local Government Act 1976 (as amended) empowers the local authorities to contract out the service to the private sector (Section 36). However, financial constraints and the lack of qualified assessors led many of the local authorities (especially the smaller ones) to seek the assistance of the Federal Valuation and Property Services Department to update the valuation lists. Up to May 1992, 70 out of a total of 99 local authorities have benefited from this assistance.

Valuation list

Under the Local Government Act, 1976, local authorities are required to maintain a valuation list containing the address of the property, the owner, the occupier, and the annual or improved value. A new valuation list is to be prepared 'once every five years or within such extended period as the State Authority may determine' (Local Government Act, 1976, section 137). Between regular valuations, the list should be kept up-to-date by including new properties which were not in the original list and reassessing values for any upgrading of properties. In both cases, the assessment of the new property is made using the values as at the date of the original list.

Even when the list is prepared, it may not be put into effect because of the political pressures, either in the local councils or in the state government which is required to approve the new list.

Qualifications of the assessors

In 1991, Hizam (1991) reported that, with the exception of a few large local authorities, such as the City Council of Kuala Lumpur and Klang Municipality in the state of Selangor, local authorities have no qualified valuers and valuations are carried out by an assessment clerk. However, Nawawi et al (1996) states that for large local authorities, such as the City of Kuala Lumpur, City of Impon, Seremban Municipal Authority, Pealing Jaya Municipal Authority, Klang Municipal Authority and Seberang Perai Municipal Authority the valuation works are carried out by qualified valuers i.e. valuers with a recognized degree in valuation and property management with some of the valuers registered with the Board of Valuers and Appraisers, Malaysia. In small local authorities, valuations continue to be carried out by an assessment clerk.

Some of the assessors from the Federal Valuation and Property Services Department involved in the rating valuation of the local authority were basically qualified valuers although, in most cases, the local authorities have to work with an assistant valuation officer who may have to carry out the work after only a 'crash' training programme (Hizam, 1991). Assessors from the private sector are mostly qualified valuers.

Frequency of valuations

A further difficulty results from the date of valuation. It should be noted that the valuation is made in the year preceding the one in which the list is to become effective and is to be in force for five years or such extended period as the State Authority determines. But the Local Government Act does not state whether the valuer is required to assess the rent in relation to the year in which the valuation is made or the year in which the list is to be used.

Notification of assessed value

Under section 141 of the Local Government Act 1976 (as amended), the local authority is required to give notice to the public when a new valuation list has been prepared. The notice is published in the Government Gazette and also in the form of an advertisement in two local newspapers, of which one must be in the national language.

Apart from stating that the valuation list is ready, the notices will also state the place where the list or a copy thereof can be inspected. This notice will also specify the date (not less than 42 days from the date of publication in the Gazette) when the local authority will proceed to revise the list. Owners and occupiers of any holding which has been valued for the first time or whose valuation has been revised upwards, will also receive notice to that effect (section 141(3) of the Local Government Act 1976, as amended).

Owners or occupiers whose holdings are included in the list can inspect the list and make extracts without charge. In practice, the notices to the owners and occupiers also state the rate percentage which will be charged and the rates payable.

Appeals procedures

The grounds for objection to entries in the valuation list are contained in section 142, as follows:

1   that any holding for which an owner is rateable is valued beyond its rateable value;

2   that any holding valued is not rateable;

3   that any person who, or any holding which ought to be included in the valuation list is omitted therefrom;

4   that any holding is valued below its rateable value; or

5   that any holding or holdings which have been jointly or separately valued ought to be valued otherwise.

All objections must be made in writing to the local authority, not less than 14 days before the date fixed for the revision of the list. The normal procedure is for the local authority to appoint a Review Committee headed by a President or Chairman to conduct an inquiry into such objections. The law provides for all objections to be investigated and the person making them allowed an opportunity to be heard at such an inquiry either in person or by an authorized representative. The Valuation Officer will normally sit on the Committee as if part of the Committee.

Confirmation of a new valuation list

On or before 31 December of the year preceding the year in which the valuation list is to come into force, the local authority, with the approval of the State Authority, will confirm such valuation list with or without amendments or revision and that list will then become the valuation list until such time as it is superseded by another valuation list. The approval of the State Authority is a prerequisite for the list to be confirmed. All objections need not be heard and determined before the list can be confirmed and inquiries can be carried out after the confirmation of the list. However, holdings that have not been heard and determined prior to the confirmation will continue to be rated at their old levels. If, as a result of the inquiry, the new value is upheld, then it will be treated retrospectively to the date on which the new list came into effect.

The list which has been confirmed is then deposited in the office of the local authority and is available for inspection during office hours by all owners and occupiers. Unlike the post-confirmation list, this list does not expressly include owners or occupiers for the purpose of inspecting the list.

Alteration of assessments

The Valuation Office is empowered (section 144 Local Government Act 1976, as amended) to amend the valuation list at any time for the following reasons:

1   mistake, oversight or fraud in the name of any person or particulars of any rateable holding which ought to have been omitted or inserted in the valuation list, as the case may be, or any rateable holding has been insufficiently or excessively valued, or for any other reason whatsoever any rateable holding has been included in the valuation list;

2   any building erected, modified, altered, demolished or rebuilt, or other improvements made upon a rateable holding, the value thereof has been increased;

3   any building or part of a building being demolished or any other works being carried out on the rateable holding, the value thereof has been decreased;

4   any rateable holding which has been included in a joint valuation and which, in the opinion of the Valuation Officer, ought to have been valued separately or otherwise;

5   the issue of any new titles in respect of any holdings; or

6   any change in the rateable holding effected by any law relating to planning as a result of which the value of the holding has been increased or decreased.

All persons affected by the amendment will be notified not less than 30 days from the date the amendment is to be made. Any person aggrieved on any of the grounds specified above is entitled to object in writing to the local authority not less than 10 days before the date fixed in that notice. Such objection can be heard in person or by an authorized representative. In carrying out this amendment, the law provides the local authority with the discretion to peg the value at the current level or at the level appropriate when the valuation list was prepared. In other words, it accords the local authority the choice of adopting the tone of the list or the existing level of value. All amendments made in the valuation list will, however, need to be confirmed by the local authority.

Any person who had made objections under sections 141 or 144 and is dissatisfied with the outcome can appeal to the High Court (section 145 Local Government Act 1976, as amended). Such a person is, however, required to pay the rate appealed to the local authority on filing the appeal, which is done by an originating motion. This appeal must be filed within 14 days of receipt of the decision of the local authority.

The High Court's decision on questions of valuation is final and conclusive. Either party may, however, on the decision of the High Court, appeal on questions of law to the Federal Court the decision of which is final and conclusive.

Methods of assessment

The principal methods of valuation used in arriving at annual values in Malaysia are:

1   the rental comparative method;

2   the contractor's method;

3   the profits method; and

4   the statutory formula, in accordance with section 2(c) of the Local Government Act 1976, as amended.

In practice, the rental comparative method is most widely used. The contractor's method is used for property which is never let. This method comprises an estimation of the 'effective capital value' of the property and applying to it a rate of return to estimate the annual value. The profits method is used in those instances where there is no bona fide market rental evidence and when the contractor's method is inappropriate. The profits method involves inquiry into gross receipts and profits in an endeavour to determine what an operator would pay as rent for an opportunity to generate profits. The statutory formula, mentioned in section 2(c) of the Local Government Act, 1976, as amended, is generally used for the valuation of land whereby 10 per cent (5 per cent if reduced) of the open market value is deemed to be the annual value.

Use of mass appraisal techniques

Currently, no mass appraisal techniques are used in the valuation of property for rates in Malaysia. Nevertheless, research at the University of Glamorgan (Nawawi, 1996) indicates that the efficiency of the rating system would be dramatically improved by the introduction of an expert system for the valuation of land and buildings. An expert system can be defined as:

> ... a computer system which contains knowledge pertaining to an area of human specialisation. The system can also implement that knowledge in such a fashion as to be able to act as a consultant expert in that field of

specialisation. Such a system typically requires the user to provide answers to relevant questions in order to supply advice based on those responses. In addition, the system is able to justify or explain the reasoning behind a course of action it recommends, in order to defend its deduced solution (Scott, 1988)

The development of an expert system is thus centred on the elicitation of the knowledge from an expert or experts, and representation and validation of the knowledge in a computer program. Based on the feasibility of developing expert systems in property valuation (Scott, 1988; Jenkins, 1992), current research (Nawawi, 1996) is investigating the possibility and practicability of developing an expert system for rating valuation of commercial and industrial properties in Malaysia. Knowledge has been elicited from several experts using various techniques: separate interviews, group interviews and observation. The main source of knowledge has come from several core valuers (from the City Hall of Kuala Lumpur) who acted as the panel providing core domain knowledge. This knowledge was augmented by knowledge from complementary valuers: seven local authority valuers (from Seremban Municipal Authority; Petaling Jaya Municipal Authority; Klang Municipal Authority; Shah Alam Municipal Authority; City Hall and Seberang Perai Municipal Authority), a valuer in private practice and an academic, all of whom contributed local contextual knowledge, market knowledge and legal knowledge, respectively.

Supporting specialists have provided building technology, spatial and macro-economic knowledge. Production rules expert systems (i.e. rules in the format of IF - THEN statements) can be used in the comparison method of valuation. One of the rules represented is that:

IF the comparable is from the same location, AND the comparable is within a suitable date of letting AND the comparable is of the same quality THEN adopt the analysed rent per square foot in the valuation.

Such a concept would be applied to a whole range of aspects of the comparison process within the valuation.

Exemptions, reliefs and concessions

Each state authority has the power to exempt, at its own discretion, any holding from payment of rates if it is used exclusively as a public place for religious worship, licensed public burial ground or crematorium, public school and public place for charitable purposes as well as for science, literature and fine arts.

When any holding is used exclusively for non-profit-making activities, the State Authority may, at its discretion, exempt such holding from the payment of all or part of the rates or otherwise. Because the Constitution provides for the organization of local government and for most municipal services to be a state responsibility, the state government, and to a certain degree the Federal government, have considerable legislative power to control Malaysian local authorities. The Local Government Act 1976, section 136, states that rates shall not be payable for any holding when the assessment imposed is less than 5 ringgit (£1 Sterling) in one year.

Properties entitled to relief

The following are exempt rates at the discretion of the state:

- places used exclusively for public religious worship;

- licensed public burial grounds or crematoria;

- public schools and public places used for charitable purposes, including science, literature and fine arts;

- non-profit-making organizations (either full or partial relief).

The Federal government requires local authorities to exempt from rates:

- holdings where the annual assessment is less than 5 ringgit (£1 Sterling);

- lands, buildings and hereditaments which are occupied for public purposes by or on behalf of the Federal, State or public authorities and in respect of which a contribution in lieu of rate is made by the occupier.

Rates are levied by local authorities on all landed properties located within the local authority areas. However, the whole of Malaysia is not under local authority jurisdiction. For example, a study area, comprising nine districts in the state of Kelantan, has a total area of 12,308 square kilometres, whilst the total area under the local authorities' control is 1,842 square kilometres or only 15 per cent. The area outside the local authorities' jurisdiction is 10,466 square kilometres or 85 per cent and falls within the direct control of the State government. However, the total population living in the selected local authorities area is 688,000 or 73 per cent of the total population in Kelantan.

People living outside local authority areas by and large do not have the benefits of local authority services; nor is the State government in a position to provide any of these services, because of its remoteness and because of the administrative difficulties involved. Therefore, these people do not pay rates to the local authorities. Even though the total population of the local authority area is 688,000 only 53,535 pay rates. About 634,462 people living in the local authority area do not pay rates because the area is not gazetted as an operational area where garbage collection services are provided. Therefore 885,621 out of 939,156 or 94 per cent do not pay rates. This is a main reason why only one local authority out of nine in the State of Kelantan has surplus income.

Collection procedures

Property taxes are collected where the local authority provides services which in most cases is limited to refuse collection only. In some areas, the local authority provides other services, such as local traders markets and local health services. However the residents in these areas are not required to pay rates, because local authorities regard these areas as 'non-operational' areas i.e. without regular refuse collection. It is estimated (Reidenbach, 1988) that less than 50 per cent of the total area of four states was operational and therefore liable to rates.

Many local authorities are not collecting all the property taxes due, based on their existing valuation list and tax rates. The arrears are due to several factors. First, the collapse of land prices in the early 1980s resulted in many developers going bankrupt and housing developments being abandoned or left unsold. Property taxes on these housing developments went unpaid. Second, manual filing and data management made it difficult to track down late payments by individual owners. Third, the local authorities were reluctant to prosecute late payers and seize their property, as allowed under the Local Government Act 1976. The lack of legal staff in councils was often given as a reason for not pursuing late payers.

Some problems in collection are caused by the fact that the title to holdings is not always registered properly, since owner occupiers often fail to inform the local authority of their acquisition. The cooperation from other officers in public departments to improve these records is also unsatisfactory. In some cases, information given by the Land Office is incomplete or there is multiple ownership in one title grant. Problems also arise from residents who live outside a town area within the local authority's boundaries. Because of the lack of infrastructure, such as metalled roads, municipal services are not extended to these areas and as a result people are understandably reluctant to pay their rates. Based on the interviews of 65 ratepayers in four different local authorities (Hizam, 1991), 61.54 per cent complained of the inefficiency of the local authorities in providing local services and this non-provision of services has resulted in the non payment of rates.

The extent of the problem can be seen, for example, in the arrears of revenue as published in the New Straits Times, (8 January 1988). Nearly MYR $80 million was owed to 19 municipal councils in Malaysia. Penang Municipal Council had arrears of MYR $10 million, Ipoh City Council MYR $20 million in arrears and the City Hall of Kuala Lumpur was estimated to have MYR $20 million in rates due. Evidence was also given by the various local authorities in Peninsular Malaysia of the huge amount of arrears of rates that have been allowed to accumulate over the years and which have increased each year with no serious attempt being made to recover them. Some local authorities had large amounts of accumulated revenue outstanding, ranging from 25 per cent to 500 per cent of their accumulated revenue in one year. The power of recovery of arrears is clearly defined in the Local Government Act, 1976. However, the strict enforcement of the law is considered to be a harsh act against friends, relatives or members of the same political party, which gives rise to the fear of losing favour with the people and consequently losing future elections.

Liability for the tax

Although the basic law of rating originated from England via India, one fundamental distinction exists and this was expounded by Good J. in *Tangamah Cumarasamy v Chairman, Town Council Taiping* [1957]:

> A fundamental distinction exists between the English rating law on the one hand and the rating laws of Trinidad and the Federation [Malayan] on the other in that, in England, the liability falls upon the occupier whereas in Trinidad and the Federation it falls on the owner.

Section 146 of the Local Government Act provides that the rates shall be paid by the owner. There is no doubt that the owner who holds the title to a piece of land is a more permanent ratepayer and is therefore more easily traceable for rate collection purposes. This has been recognized in the UK where, for example, the British principle of rating the occupier has been altered in specific cases to make an owner liable for rates, in order to secure ease of rate collection. This was achieved, for example, in section 24 General Rate Act 1967 which made owners rateable for dwellings adapted for occupation in parts (Plimmer, 1987). Although owners pay the tax, they actually collect the rates from their tenants and therefore it is ultimately an occupiers' liability. However, in Malaysia, the absence of beneficial occupation, or for that matter, the lack of occupation at all, is not relevant for the rating of a property. As long as the property can be identified as a holding and it falls within the local authority area, it is rateable.

Computation of the tax

After the annual value has been assessed and there are no objections raised from the owner, the rates payable are based on fixed percentages of the annual value of the landed properties and these percentages can be varied from year to year by the local authorities. The percentages are fixed according to the areas in which the properties are located and/or according to the actual usage of the properties. For example, in Klang Municipality there were six different percentage rates, ranging from 4 per cent to 13 per cent depending on the type of use for the land (Hizam, 1991).

The local authorities cannot exceed 35 per cent of the annual value when imposing such differential rates. For the improved value the maximum rate adopted is 5 per cent of the improved value. Usually, the new rate per cent is applied for a number of years until the expenditure has increased to such a level that the local authority is forced to make another increase. A significant feature of the rate percent is that the present practice among the selected local authorities in Malaysia shows a considerable variation on the amount of rate per cent imposed.

The local government taxation system in Malaysia is difficult to administer because the rate structure is graduated and more than one schedule may apply to a given tax base. In the case of Kuala Muda District Council in the State of Kedah, the rate schedule for vacant land varies from 0.5 per cent to 4 per cent. The tax rate of the property lies below the annual or improved value and is always reduced after a revaluation. For example, in the District of Alor Gajah, Malacca, the rates were reduced from 12 per cent to 5 per cent after the revaluation in 1984 for areas outside town and development areas.

The local authority normally determines the percentage to be applied for rating in the following manner. It first budgets for the year in question, in order to determine the amount of money it will need to carry out the various projects and for the annual recurrent expenditures. From that it deducts the amount of revenue it can obtain from other sources. The balance is then expressed as a percentage of the total of all the annual or improved values on its valuation lists for the year under consideration. The result is the percentage to be levied from that year.

In order to minimize the sudden increase in the property taxes resulting from a new valuation list, some local councils reduce the property tax rate when implementing the new list. In one district in Johore, the new rate was set (1985) at 0.15 per cent (compared to the legal maximum of 5 per cent allowed under the Local Government Act). While the Local Government Act established the maximum tax rates at 35 per cent for properties assessed on annual rental values and 5 per cent on improved values, none of the 14 local authorities visited as part of the research were charging the maximum rate.

Enforcement procedures

Rates are payable half-yearly in advance without demand in February and August (section 147 of the Local Government Act, 1976, as amended). In practice, rates bills are sent out in January and July. Owners who fail to make payment after the specified dates are required to make an additional payment fee fixed by the local authority. If the rate is not paid by the end of the prescribed months, the local authority serves a notice of demand (Form E), calling on the owner to pay within 15 days of receipt of the notice.

Penalties

Where the rate is still not paid after the expiry of the notice of demand, the local authority issues a warrant of attachment, which empowers the local authority to seize any moveable property to whomsoever belonging which is found on the holding concerned. Section 151(5) of the Local Government Act, 1976, as amended, however, gives the local authority the discretion of refraining from seizing and selling or releasing from attachment any property lawfully seizable, where such property belongs to the occupier. The local authority can also refrain from seizing or release from attachment property belonging to a tenant occupier if the tenant occupier pays to the local authority the rent of such holding as it falls due, until the arrears are satisfied, or until the termination of the tenancy.

If the rate is still unpaid within seven days of the issue of the warrant of attachment, the property attached will be sold by public auction (section 149 Local Government Act, 1976, as amended). The proceeds of the sale are then used to pay off the arrears, together with interest at the rate of 6 per cent per annum, plus costs (section 150 Local Government Act 1976, as amended). Any surplus will be paid to the person in possession of the property at the time of the attachment. In cases where the proceeds from the sale of moveable property are not expected to meet the arrears, interest and costs, the registrar of the High Court, upon application by the local authority, can order the attachment and sale of the property concerned. Section 156 Local Government Act 1976, as amended, provides an alternative method of recovery of arrears. Under this provision, arrears may be sued for or recovered as a debt in a court of law.

Critical analysis

The functions of the local authority are legally defined in the Local Government Act, 1976, but their implementation depends on State decisions. The present Malaysian rating system is (or should be) the major source of revenue to the councils but is inefficient as a means of local taxation. The main reasons for this can be summarized as follows:

- inconsistencies in applying the definition of annual value between councils;

- the problems resulting from the differing bases of valuation of annual value and improved value;

- the liability of rates falling on the owner and the consequent difficulties due to incomplete registration of title;

- inconsistencies resulting from the treatment of vacant land;

- the incorrect interpretation of the date of valuation;

- the treatment of exemptions and contributions in lieu of rates varying from council to council particularly with regard to obtaining the necessary certificate;

- unfairness in contributions between those within local authority areas and those outside;

- the methods used to determine rates payable i.e. differential percentages;

- failure to undertake and implement frequent and regular revaluations; and

- the failure in certain local authority areas to collect the rates due and to eliminate the arrears.

The main constraints to improving the system are insufficient qualified staff, allied with the intervention of politicians at all levels which prevent citizens paying appropriate levels of taxes and other contributions. This undermines the adequacy of the supply of services from local authorities which, in turn, is perceived as a justification for citizens to avoid payments. A vicious circle has thereby developed. Although the evaluation can conclude that the rating system in Malaysia has a sound legal, structural and legislative basis, there are constraints which impede the efficient and effective functioning of the system. Allied to this, there is the psychological impact of rates, and the varying ways they are calculated in different councils.

Weakness of local authorities

The effect of the historical pattern of development has resulted in an unequal distribution of income, amenity and opportunity among the ethnic groups. This has resulted in the indigenous population being concentrated in the non-rewarding primary agricultural sector and therefore within the rural areas which have little or no local services. The Chinese immigrants live in urban areas where rewarding employment is located together with superior facilities and services. Local authorities have the task of providing a dynamic role in the economic development of the country, but the structure of local government prevents it from performing such a function adequately. In addition, local authorities in Malaysia face a major constraint in performing their roles effectively as a result of several inherent factors. Their weak financial position affects their capacity to deliver an appropriate level and range of services to the population and to a large extent, this results from the inadequacy of local government finance which relies heavily on rates as a source of income.

Staffing

The ability to employ competent staff is related to the financial ability of the local authorities. Each council is organized according to its own requirements, the subdivision into departments, or units varying accordingly. Based on the analysis of the questionnaire sent out as part of the research, it is evident that most authorities suffer from staffing constraints and certain functions can hardly be carried out. As a result, there is a severe shortage of valuers, records are inadequately maintained and morale tends to be low because of the lack of promotion prospects or established conditions of service.

A comparison between the number of staff employed for valuation and the revenue collection of the property tax shows a distinct correlation between the low number of staff and the level of revenue collected. For example, in the Seremban Municipality in Negri Sembilan State, the number of staff employed in the valuation department was 20 and the revenue from rates comprised 68 per cent of the total source of income. Seremban Municipal Council suffered arrears of 40 to 60 per cent for domestic properties and 20 to 40 per cent for non residential properties. The actual number of staff required according to the Council is 31 (Hizam, 1991).

The poor chances of promotion and less than attractive remunerations that exist as compared to those in the Federal or State governments, or in private enterprise, are the main reasons of inefficient management. In addition, the termination of staff employment (except for technical staff) has its effects, as well as interference from politicians who recruit their own members with insufficient qualification. Staff efficiency suffers accordingly (Lenz, 1986).

Basis of assessment

As improved value and annual value are alternative tax bases, it is pertinent to compare the principles relating to the determination of annual value with the principles (outlined below) for market value. The principles of determining annual value have been well described, for example, Plimmer (1987) and Gill J. - *Overseas Chinese Banking Corporation Ltd. v Commissioner of the Federal Capital of Kuala Lumpur* [1963]. A number of distinct rules have been evolved to distinguish the annual value for rating purpose from improved value, such as the following assumptions which apply to annual value:

1   vacant and to let;

2   premises to be valued *rebus sic stantibus*;

3   the creation of a hypothetical tenancy with a hypothetical tenant and a hypothetical landlord;

4   not subject to any rent control;

5   tone of the list.

A more glaring picture would emerge if a comparison was made with the annual value basis as used in the other states in Malaysia. There is a conflict in rating properties using both the annual value and the improved value basis. Under the annual value system, a separate method of assessment has been prescribed for a holding which is vacant, unoccupied, partially built upon, or unfit for human habitation. The improved value of vacant land must be the value of the land for the use that will be permitted on the land whether by way of a gazette zoning plan or by way of its potential use as ascertained by developments in the neighbourhood.

The application of existing use where land is partially occupied becomes more complicated as no provisions are found in the improved value definition for such lands nor is there any discretion given to the Valuation Officer to adopt a different basis, as is the case for annual value. Apart from the obvious inequity of having both an annual value and an improved capital value as the bases of assessment within the country, there is an inherent problem with the definition and application of improved value, which is used in the state of Johore.

The identical definition of market value and improved value and the use of methods and principles common to both have given rise to a number of problems. In the determination of market value the following are important considerations:

1   the nature and extent of the interest. Usually this is the interest that is affected, e.g. encumbered or short leasehold, etc.;

2   potential. There is an abundance of case law which requires potentialities to be taken into consideration. For example, in the case of *Bukit Rajah*

Rubber Co. Ltd. v Collector of Land Revenue, Klang, Selangor [1968], it was held that the potential development value would be a fair market value of the land acquired.

These considerations when applied to the improved value basis create problems, for example:

1   properties adjoining each other can bear different values in view of the interest therein. It is possible to have two identical properties having different values due to the different lease terms and therefore paying differing amounts of rates;

2   land that is under-utilized by reason of its present use would be valued on its potential use and thus show no relationship to the present income or use;

3   in view of this restriction, interests in, for example, Malay Reservation Land, would have very low improved values or even negative values.

This has led to unfairness in the tax liability between rateable owners. Another incongruity occurs when developed land or improved land is valued on its existing use because of the rule of *rebus sic stantibus*, whilst adjacent vacant land next door is valued at 10 per cent or 5 per cent of its open market value. The result of this is that the latter has a much higher annual value then the former. For example, in an appeal case (file no: PP/1/3/79 - No 102) in the Taiping District Council in Perak, the annual value of land, i.e. the assessment, was increased from MYR $1,080 to MYR $6,000 on the demolition of the building which had stood on the land. The annual value of MYR $1,080 was based on the principle of *rebus sic stantibus*, that is, land with a building on it. When the building was demolished, the annual value was based on 10 per cent of the market value of the vacant site, which was MYR $6,000.

Contributions in lieu of rates

The Federal Constitution exempts the lands, buildings and hereditaments which are occupied for public purposes by or on behalf of the Federal, State or public authorities. Instead the Federal, State or public authorities make contributions in lieu of rates, the amount of contribution being agreed between the parties concerned. There are many problems faced by the local authorities on the administration of such properties. The most critical has been in obtaining the necessary certification from the local heads of the Federal departments.

Under the guidelines set out by the Ministry of Housing and Local Government, there are three forms to be submitted by local authorities before any payment on the contribution can be made. The contents of these three have to be agreed upon and certified by the respective parties before payment can be made by the Ministry of Housing and Local Government. Should there be any delay in the annual certification on the part of the occupier, the contribution in that particular year is forfeited through no fault of the local authority.

Thus, the procedure requires the keeping of proper records of buildings by the occupiers and is open to abuse because occupiers can refuse to complete the forms submitted to them by the local authorities and thereby deny the local authority a share of its revenue. The Federal Constitution provides for the formation of a tribunal to determine any disputes between the councils and the departments. The absence of such a tribunal makes agreement on value almost impossible, causing rating authorities to lose out severely in rate income.

Valuation procedure

The methods and criteria of valuation form the core of the actual valuation process. The valuation procedure allows the Valuation Officer a certain degree of freedom. The opinion of the Valuation Officer, however, is based on a mixture of objective factors and on experience. For a final determination, the valuer can choose from a number of methods which can be applied either individually or in combination. This results in different values for similar properties or the same value for different properties, and consequently complaints are lodged (Lenz, 1986). For example, the Central Valuation Division sent a series of different assessors to the same district councils and the valuations which resulted showed discrepancies in the values assigned to similar property. The owners were accordingly discontent with the results.

In an objection lodged by Hong Peng Koon (PP/1/3/79/1 - 32), a holding, which is situated in Ringan Tupai Industrial Areas in Perak, had been valued at MYR $2,300 (annual value). However the ratepayer's other holding, which was located across the road, was valued at MYR $2,000 (annual value). Even though the size of the land was the same, there was a difference of MYR $300 in the annual values. In valuing land within a 'Malay Reservation', where there is no other material difference in the properties, the annual value is lower than the open market rental, as the land is assumed, to be within a restricted market.

The rates of tax are also low when compare with those applied to other areas. For example, the Kampung Kuantan rate schedule is 4-5 per cent for residential properties but other residential rates are 8-12 per cent. Thus, the payments of rates diverges from area to area.

Valuation lists

Not all local authorities have current valuation lists. A district council in the State of Trengganu has reported that they have yet to prepare a new valuation list for the restructured councils and are still using lists dating back to the 1950s prepared for the old councils. The lack of qualified assessors, especially in the smaller district councils, is an issue which prevents the valuation lists from being updated. In the State of Kelantan, out of nine local authorities only two local authorities have a Valuation Officer. The rating exercise essentially comprises two major processes, i.e. the compilation of the valuation list, and the imposition of the rate for the assessment.

Before 1980, many local authorities had not revalued their properties for many years, although the Local Government Act of 1976 provided for revaluations every five years. Because of this, the Minister of Finance decided in 1981 to assist the local authorities which required the valuation of properties. This free valuation was carried out in stages. Through the assistance of the Valuation and Property Services Division of the Federal Treasury, of the 95 local authorities in Peninsular Malaysia, 32 local authorities managed to update their valuation lists; while another 21 local authorities were in the process of updating their valuation lists (1988). Some 22 further local authorities have completed their valuation lists either with the help of other local authorities or through the services of private firms. Around 19 local authorities have not attempted to update their valuation list and 1 has no rating unit and did not carry out a revaluation at all (Kelantan Valuation Officer, 1988).

Revaluations

All properties have to be revalued and this is a tremendous undertaking, not the least because of the enormous amount of paperwork involved controlling the revaluation itself within the local authorities and the subsequent appeals made by people who are aggrieved by their new assessments. With the exception of a few large local authorities, such as the City Council of Kuala Lumpur and Klang Municipality in the State of Selangor, local authorities have no qualified valuers and valuations are carried out by an assessment clerk. For example, in the Tanah Merah District Council in Kelantan, there is only one staff member and his job description is 'secretary of the council'. He is responsible for the assessment and collection of rates for 4,809 rateable holdings.

Most local authorities merely carry forward the assessment list annually, with no steps being taken to bring them up to the prevailing rental values. This results in an uneven burden of liability for both locality and property types and there is a lack of uniformity in the assessment lists. Most of the revaluations in the local authorities have been carried out by the Central Valuation Division of the Ministry of Finance, and also by private firms (Ariffin, 1986).

The Central Valuations Division itself suffers from insufficient qualified personnel. In most cases, the local authorities have to work with only an assistant valuation officer who may have to carry out the work after only a crash training programme (Hizam, 1991). There are also problems in obtaining the data because of the reluctance of property owners to return completed forms or to complete them fully and correctly. This is because they fear that the returns may be used for other purposes, but the immediate result is that it impedes the process of revaluation. As a result, the revaluation exercise undertaken is restricted to a few councils at a time, and this has created outdated tax bases. For instance, the Kuala Muda District Council in Kedah was established in 1957 and a revaluation has only been carried out once. This was produced in three stages, in 1984, 1985 and 1987. In some cases, in spite of very old valuations lists, the revaluation was postponed by the State or Federal government because of an impending election (Norris, 1977; Lenz, 1986).

Such an occurrence happened in 1985 before the general election when the Federal Valuation and Property Services Department was frustrated by some local authorities which did not implement the new valuation list which it had prepared free of charge for the local authorities. Irregularities among the local authorities in a state include the rate imposed, rateable areas and implementation of the valuation lists.

The failure to undertake and implement frequent and regular revaluations results in an out-of-date and, therefore, inequitable basis on which to levy rates, since different local authorities use lists compiled at different times. Not only are the values out-of-date, so are the relativities between values. The result is that ratepayers do not pay according to the current rental or even the recent value of their properties. This is recognized as unfair, particularly by the ratepayers themselves, who may consider the abolition of the rating system as the best solution. Based on interviews carried out in four local authorities, the research shows that 62 per cent would like a change from the present rating system.

Proposed changes

A study (Hizam, 1991) investigated (amongst other things) the practicability of introducing a community charge-style poll tax into the rural areas of Malaysia. This would involve, initially, ensuring that the whole of Malaysia is included within the administration of local authorities and that all citizens benefit (at least in some measure) from local authority services. In order to avoid the cost

112

and administrative difficulties of revaluing rural holdings (these are mostly wooden houses of low value with little or no rental evidence), Hizam concludes that a community charge-style poll tax:

> ... should be effective and efficient in such areas because people can be easily identified (all Malaysian citizens over the age of 12 have identity cards), there would be a low provision of services and, consequently, a low level of charge.

Recommendations from the study also include a reform of the existing rating system. In addition, a study undertaken by Lim (1991) has also indicated that reform could take place within the framework of the rating system. Lim (1991) is of the opinion that attempts should be made to improve the existing system and to correct whatever shortcomings exist, as follows:

- Establish a central valuation authority - this proposal will enable more frequent revaluations. With all valuation functions of the local authority coming under the central valuation authority, the current problem of the inability to maintain the currency of the existing valuation lists could be overcome.

- Capital value basis of assessment - in those local authority areas, where rental values are lacking, there could be a change to capital value as a basis for the assessment. The provision to adopt capital values is already contained in the Local Government Act, 1976 (at section 130(1)).

- Computerization - there should be a concentrated effort to computerize valuation work, to improve the efficiency of the rating valuation process.

- Local Valuation Court - the replacement of the present Review/Appeals Committee with an independent Local Valuation Court would strengthen the appeal system.

- Lands Tribunal - the establishment of a Lands Tribunal (based on the UK model) would ensure a more uniform and consistent approach to the settlement of disputes involving the valuation of land.

- Publicity and education - by educating the public on rating matters, a more cooperative attitude could be expected.

- Facilitating the payment of rates - ratepayers will find rates less of a financial burden with the opportunity to pay by a reasonable number of instalments.

- Date of valuation - the date of valuation should be made specific.

- Differential rating - the local authorities should resort to differential rating only when necessary. It should be used as the exception rather than the norm.

References

Ariffin, M.A, (1986), The Privatising of the Rating Exercise, *INSPEN*, Bangi, July.

Arshad, M.N. (1986), Rating Revaluation; After This, What's Next?, Second National Seminar on Rating and Local Government Finance, *INSPEN*, Bangi.

Bukit Rajah Rubber Co. Ltd v Collector of Land Revenue, Klang, [1968], MLJ.

Hizam, R.B. (1991), *The Rateable Hereditament and Community Charge Systems: A Comparative Study of Britain and Malaysia*, unpublished MPhil dissertation, University of Glamorgan, United Kingdom.

Jenkins, D. (1992), *The Use of Expert Systems in the Land Strategy of Cardiff City Council*, unpublished MPhil dissertation, University of Glamorgan, United Kingdom.

Kelantan Valuation Officers, (1988), Kadaran Haruskah di hapuskan, First Symposium for Valuation Officers, *INSPEN*, Bangi, June.

Lenz, D. (1986), *Local Government Finance and Taxation - An Initial Study*, Ministry Of Housing and Local Government.

Lim, K.H. (1992), *Rating in Malaysia (Peninsular Malaysia) - A Review*, unpublished MSc dissertation, University of Reading, United Kingdom.

Local Government Act, (1976) (Act 171).

Mani Usillapan, (1986), Improved Value Basis, *INSPEN*, Bulletin, Vol. 4.

Marbeck, A.B. (1986), After This, What's Next?, Second National Seminar on Rating and Local Government Finance, *INSPEN*, Bangi.

Nanyang Manufacturing Co. Ltd. v Collector of Land Revenue Johore, [1954], MLJ.

Nawawi, H.A., Jenkins, D. and Gronow, S. (1996), *Computer Assisted Rating Valuation of Commercial and Industrial Properties in Malaysia*, paper presented at the Cutting Edge Conference, University of the West of England, The Royal Institution of Chartered Surveyors, Bristol, United Kingdom.

Nawawi, H.A. (1998), *Knowledge Elicitation Methodology from Multiple Experts for Rating Valuation by the Comparison Method for Commercial and Industrial Properties in Malaysia*, unpublished PhD thesis, University of Glamorgan, United Kingdom.

New Straits Times, 8 January 1988, Ratepayers $80 million debt.

Norris, M.W. (1977), Modernisation of Local Government, Business Times.

Ng Tiou Hong v Collector of Land Revenue Gombak, [1984].

Overseas Chinese Banking Corporation v Commissioner of the Federal Capital of Kuala Lumpur, [1963].

Plimmer, F. (1987), *Rating Valuation: A Practical Guide*, Longman Group U.K. Limited.

Plimmer, F. (1998), *Rating Law and Valuation*, Longman, United Kingdom.

Reidenbach, M. (1988), Proposal for a new system of grants to local authorities in Malaysia, Ministry of Housing and Local Government.

Scott, D. (1988), *A Knowledge Based Approach to the Computer Assisted Mortgage Valuation of Residential Property*, unpublished PhD thesis, University of Glamorgan, United Kingdom.

Taiping, 1979, File No: PP/1/3/79/1 - No 32.

Tangammah Cumurasamy v Chairman Town Council Taiping, Perak, [1957].

5 The present and future role of property taxation in local government funding in Ireland

Brendan Williams

Introduction

The role of local property taxation in financing local government in Ireland has contracted significantly in recent decades. The option of restoring the central role which local property taxes previously held, or indeed the updating of the legislation dealing with those sectors liable for the payment of such taxes is currently a matter of ongoing policy debate. A general overview of the development of the local property tax system indicates an ongoing important role for local taxation in financing local government activities with an increasing relevance in recent years on direct fees and charges for services provided. This chapter is intended to give an overview of the evolution and contraction of the local property taxation base in Ireland and review current developments and reform of the system.

Since the foundation of the state in 1922 government in Ireland has been administered at two levels, central and local. Central government taxation has evolved a complex system of income, corporation, capital and value added taxes. Property taxes involving central government include capital acquisitions, capital gains, stamp duty or transfer tax and a national residential property tax. By comparison, local authorities' only direct revenue taxation income is from the commercial property rating system, which enables them to carry out the variety of functions for which they are responsible.

A recent government study examining the financing of local government in Ireland outlined the responsibilities of local authorities, their spending requirements and sources of finance as detailed in Table 5.1.

The diminished role of local property tax has caused difficulties for local authorities in recent years with funding perceived as inadequate and with little buoyancy within their revenue systems. Since the discontinuation of domestic

Table 5.1
Current expenditure and financing of local authorities 1995

Activities	Expenditure £m
Housing and Building	232.73
Road Transportation and Safety	332.32
Water Supply and Sewerage	142.03
Development Incentives and Control	36.88
Environmental Protection	168.74
Recreation and Amenity	136.07
Agriculture Education, Health and Welfare	108.13
Miscellaneous Services	67.64
Total	1,224.54

rates in 1978 and land rates in 1984 the dependence of local authorities on direct subvention from central government for substitute funds increased. In the 1980s control of public spending became the paramount concern of national government policy leading to cuts in levels of direct subvention, shortfalls in budgets and cuts in services. An analysis of the shift in funding of the current expenditure needs of local authorities over the period of 1970-1995 illustrates the trends involved (see Table 5.2).

Table 5.2
Funding current expenditures of local authorities 1970-1995

	1970	1983	1995
Government Grants	50%	65%	41%
Fees/Charges	18%	23%	33%
Rates	32%	12%	26%

Source: Department of the Environment, 1996

The high dependence on government grants following discontinuation of rates on the domestic and agricultural property sectors involved major financing problems during the reduction of grant support evident in the 1980s. In the short term, reductions in levels of employment and expenditure in maintenance of housing, along with sales of local authority housing and other property assets, provided means of overcoming such shortfalls. This has been followed by an increased dependence on direct fees and charges for services provided. Since

1983 the scope of areas affected by fees and charges increased with powers widened for local authorities to introduce service charges. A wide range of services now attract fees or charges in many local authority areas such as water charges, refuse charges, sewerage charges, planning application fees, water connection fees and ambulance and fire service fees. The argument in favour of such charges and fees is that a clear link can be developed between service provided and amounts charged.

However attempts to further widen the scope of areas covered by charges and to introduce such charges into areas where they did not previously operate meet with sustained local resistance by affected consumers. In particular taxpayers' sentiment, already politically hostile to what are regarded as excessive general tax levels, resist any imposition of new charges and seek abolition of those is existence. The distrust of the concept of further or double taxation outweighs any argument that general taxation levels could only be reduced by a widening of the available taxation base or improvement in financing mechanisms of local authorities.

For local authorities, dependence on fluctuating levels of central government grants lessens their ability to be responsible and accountable for future provision and management of services. Without guaranteed independent means of raising finance and budgeting for future expenditure, linkage in the decision making process between demand for services, supply of services and payment for same is reduced. The Commission on Taxation (1985) concluded that the most effective taxation measure which could be utilized in financing local government was property taxation. The difficulty in effecting reform in this area is evident in the slow pace at which new legislation to update and protect the existing rates system on commercial and industrial property has proceeded. The greater political problem of introducing an expanded property tax or rating system has resulted in successive governments of different political complexions investigating and evaluating the options (NESC, 1985) but not reaching a political conclusion for action. A negative consensus has emerged in that proposals for introduction of any form of a property tax are regarded as politically unpopular. The updating and legislative security of the existing commercial property rating system is thus regarded as a more limited but necessary priority by recent administrations.

Origins and development of local property taxes

A property tax known as rates has historically been the only form of local taxation in Ireland. The earliest form of this type of taxation is found in the Church Tithe Charges of the fifteenth century and evolved over subsequent centuries with money for public purposes being levied on the basis of the area of land. As the pattern of ownership of land and rights to tenancies in land expanded, the system developed parallel with the English system of expanding the taxation base to the new owners and occupiers. The costs of administration expanded greatly as the state took a greater role in administration of services and all aspects of life throughout the nineteenth century and the need to secure the finances for this involvement necessitated legislative measures. The first measure to introduce a general revaluation for rating purposes was in 1826 based on overall valuations of townlands or localities and it was with the Poor Relief (Ireland) Act 1838 that is found the first general valuation of all property hereditaments as opposed to townlands or estates for the purpose of a Poor Relief Rate.

It was with the Valuation (Ireland) Act 1852 that the first complete set of valuations of all individual tenements was made for public and local assessments. The objective of this act was to provide one uniform basis for valuation upon which taxes and levies could be charged. The basis of valuation of all hereditaments was defined as Net Annual Value, which was to be calculated as the annual letting value over and above the rates, costs of repairs and insurance. This act along with various amending acts in the middle of the nineteenth century remains the core legislation dealing with the valuation system along with two modern statutes updating this legislation passed in 1986 and 1988. As a general principle it can be taken that Irish legislation and case law prior to independence in 1922 mirrored developments in the United Kingdom and that the valuation systems in the period since 1922 have diverged to a large extent with an absence of general revaluations and the consequent lack of relativity within the Irish valuation systems leading to pressure for the abolition of rates. Lack of reform ensured the decline of the system and the consequent reduction in the valuation base to its existing position of encompassing industrial and commercial property only.

The rating system

Organizational control

The Valuation Office was established under the Valuation (Ireland) Act 1852 with responsibility under the direction of the first Commissioner to carry out all valuations for rating purposes for the entire country. This primary valuation was completed during the period 1852 to 1865. Changes to the valuation lists on an annual basis and also general revisions of valuations along with the processing of all appeals are the responsibilities of the Valuation Office; this office, based in Dublin, processes all rating valuation work in Ireland. With additional responsibilities for providing government departments and agencies

119

with advice on a broad range of property valuation matters, including property taxation matters, resources for the updating and reform of the rating valuation system present a serious problem at present.

Responsibility for the preparation and updating of the valuation lists lies with the various local authorities, who are vested with the powers of rating authorities. Requests for revisions of valuations or insertions of valuations on newly constructed properties are forwarded by the local authorities on a regular basis to the Valuation Office. The present local government system in Ireland evolved in the main from the local government, housing and health legislation of the nineteenth century giving a system with over 100 local authorities all with varying degrees of power and responsibilities. In terms of rating valuations the more important of these organizations would be the county councils (29), county borough corporations (5), borough corporations (5) and urban district councils (49), all of whom are statutory rating authorities. The assessment of the amount of rates due is based on the 'rate in the pound' for each year which is a function of the elected councillors of each rating authority. This 'striking the rate' provides the multiplier, which coupled with the rateable valuation, determines the amount of rates levied on occupiers in the following year.

Payment of rates

Liability for rates has, since the Poor Relief (Ireland) Act 1838, been the responsibility of every occupier of rateable hereditaments, with occupier being defined as every person in the immediate use of enjoyment of any hereditaments.

Vacancy in buildings gives rise to the question of liability for and payment of rates. Since 1862, vacant buildings have been deemed rateable with provision for relief being introduced in 1946 whereby the owner, if he is unable to find an occupier or suitable tenant at a reasonable rent, is entitled to a refund in respect of the amount of rates as appropriate for every complete month during which the premises is unoccupied. In applying for relief an owner will be required by the rating authority to whom he is applying for a refund to furnish proof of attempts to let the building during the period for which relief is being claimed. The premises must also be vacant on the date on which the rate is struck.

Categories of rateable hereditaments

A broad definition of all classes of real property is included in s.12 of the 1852 act as being 'all lands, buildings, rights, profits to be taken out of land ... rights of easements and all other tolls...'. The amending act of 1860 made industrial buildings and machinery used therein for the production of motive power rateable but excluded all other machinery from rating. As modern industrial processes

120

became more complex the issue of differentiation between non-rateable machinery and rateable industrial storage tanks and plant became increasingly difficult. The Valuation Act of 1986 was introduced to clarify these categories of industrial plant deemed rateable through the insertion of a schedule listing categories to be rateable. This act also provided for the rating of other property not specifically referred to in the existing legislation.

Whilst the legislation encompasses virtually every category of fixed property and land as being within the scope of valuation for rating purposes, rates are not now payable on agricultural land, farm buildings or domestic buildings. Following a Supreme Court Decision in *Brennan & others v The Attorney General and the County Council of Wexford*[1] in 1984, the collection of agricultural rates on the basis of the existing outdated valuation system without the right of individual appeals was deemed to be a violation of the individuals constitutional property rights as enshrined in Article 40.3.2 of the Constitution and consequently invalid. Attempts to reintroduce a system of property taxes on agricultural land through the 1986 Land Valuations Act were dropped with an electoral defeat of the government who had sponsored the introduction of the system. Agricultural buildings had been derated by legislation since March 1959.

In 1978 payment of domestic rates by owners and occupiers was abolished and replaced by the payment of an annual block grant by the Minister of the Environment to local authorities not exceeding the rates bill for such properties. A national residential property tax was introduced by central government in 1984, which involves both an income threshold and a property valuation threshold. The tax is currently payable on the surplus of domestic property capital value over the value of £101,000 for owners whose overall household income exceeds the limit set of £30,100, the annual payment is based on a taxation level of 1.5 per cent of surplus value. The threshold amounts are index linked to the Consumer Price Indices and are altered within each year's budget. Due to the relatively high threshold figures and other allowances the yield from this tax to date has not been high. This tax is paid to central government and has no linkage with local taxation and finance.

The importance of the rating system to both local authorities and the overall exchequer situation is demonstrated by the estimate of the value of property taxes collected in Ireland in 1994 (see Table 5.3).

Strong negative reaction to a planned extension of residential property tax (RPT) in the 1994 budget and to the continuation of this tax in the rising property market of 1996 which brought increased numbers of taxpayers into a position of liability, demonstrate the political difficulty in Ireland of any taxation proposal affecting family homes. Decisions to abolish RPT and domestic water charges resulted from political pressures prior to the 1997 election. A diversion of some part of exchequer taxation income to finance local government has been debated as a more politically feasible option.

Table 5.3

Estimate of property taxes collected in Ireland for 1994

	£m
Commercial Rates	323
Stamp Duty/Property Transfer Tax	106
Capital Gains	12
Residential Property Tax	12
Total	453

Source: *Department of the Environment, 1996*

Exemptions from rating

The statutory authority upon which the issue of exemptions is based is contained in s.63 of the 1838 act. The main areas involve buildings used exclusively for the purpose of public religious worship, the education of the poor, charitable purposes and buildings used for state or public purposes, (note: buildings occupied by government departments are exempt but the state pays a grant in lieu of rates on such buildings to local authorities). Great problems exist in operating this legislation given that exemption is only available on a strict interpretation of the legislation, if the use to which the building is put benefits 'the poor' exclusively. This narrow definition coupled with the extension of services offered in the twentieth century for charitable or public purposes which could not have been envisaged when the legislation was drafted make the introduction of amending legislation in this area long overdue.

Reform and development of the basis of valuations

The preamble to the 1852 act stated that the intention was to make 'one uniform valuation of land and tenements in Ireland' and laid down in s.11 of the act the basis upon which Net Annual Value (NAV) was to be calculated and reads:

> ... and such valuation in regard to houses and buildings shall be made upon an estimate of the Net Annual Value thereof, that is to say the rent for which, one year with another the same might in its actual state be reasonably expected to let from year to year, the probable average annual cost of repairs, insurance and other expenses (if any) necessary to maintain the hereditament in its actual state and all rates, taxes and public charges, if any, (except tithe rent charge) being paid by the tenant.

This definition is similar to what in today's terminology is known as full rental value on a full repairing and insuring basis being the net annual income to the landlord from a hypothetical tenant. The actual rent may equate to the NAV but frequently adjustments to the rent passing are required based on analysis of the rent payable and those on comparable premises to take account of entire tenancy terms including such items as premiums, rent free periods, rent review patterns, covenants, liability for rates and repairs, etc.

Before 1914 valuations for rateable purposes were made on an exact estimate of NAV as defined in the 1852 act. With inflation non existent, general revaluations although allowed for at intervals of 14 years were not availed of; the city of Dublin was revalued in the seven year period from 1908 to 1915 at 1914 rental values which came into effect in 1915 and Waterford city was revalued between 1924 to 1926 at 1914 rental values which came into effect in 1929.

Absence of general revaluations coupled with specific areas being revalued at different base dates led to a loss of uniformity in the valuation system. Various Commissioners of Valuation through to 1938 sought general revaluations and, in the absence of definite government policy on this issue, a system was introduced in 1946 to fix the rateable valuations at a fraction of the NAV in order to keep valuations relative. The fraction decided on at that time was one-third of NAV and using this fraction, comprehensive annual revisions of all valuations were tested in Galway and Buncrana over 1946-1950 on the basis again of 1914 letting values. These revisions exposed the lack of relativity in the various categories of the rating system which had developed in the absence of a general revaluation. This process of continually adjusting net annual value to ensure relativity came under continual pressure due to inflation of property values, particularly in the period from 1960, and was replaced by a direct comparison system of comparing new rating valuations to be assessed with the existing pattern of valuations on a unitary basis or rate per metre squared. This practice of a valuation base evolving from recent settlements produced gross inequalities both in sections of property use within a rating area and between various locations within a rating authority area. This absence of relativity was noted in several reports most prominent of which was the White Paper on Local Government Finance and Taxation (1971) which called for extensive reform of the system.

Absence of reform to the valuation basis brought forward judicial and political decisions to abolish payment of rates on various sectors of property. Eventually a modern statute, the 1986 Valuation Act specifically dealt with the issue of giving statutory basis to the practice of reducing NAV to give a rateable valuation and also restated the prime importance of NAV in arriving at a rateable valuation.

Following the passing of this act an extensive research project was carried out by the Valuation Office to establish a consistent relativity factor or fraction which could be used in rateable valuations. A factor of 0.63 per cent of 1988 NAV was established as being the ratio in deciding rating valuations for the prime retails areas of Dublin. In the pursuit of uniformity a programme of comprehensive commercial revisions is being carried out using the standard 0.63 per cent factor in the five main urban areas of Dublin, Cork, Limerick, Galway and Waterford with a factor of 0.5 being applied throughout the rest of the country. In the long run some type of uniformity could evolve from such practices but, with a limited areas approach and also limited public acceptance, it provides a poor substitute for a complete revaluation. Court and Valuation Tribunal decisions, most notably the 1990 IMI High Court judgement of Justice Barron[2] stated that these or any other standard relativity factors cannot be applied across all sectors of property based on the statutory basis for assessing comparisons as stated in the act. Variations in the Dublin area previously ranged from suburban shopping centres which were valued at less than 0.5 per cent of NAV to offices in central Dublin which were valued at over 1 per cent of NAV. Obviously the appeal system is used by owners or occupiers of properties which are valued at higher levels than the average to achieve reductions. Difficulties are encountered with owners or occupiers of properties which have been traditionally valued at lower levels when moves to bring these valuations into line are undertaken. A reading of the relevant sections of the Valuation Act 1986 confirms the difficulties involved.

S.5.1 Notwithstanding section 11 of the act of 1852, in making or revising a valuation of a tenement or rateable hereditament, the amount of the valuation which apart from this section, would be made, may be reduced by such amount as is necessary to ensure, insofar as is reasonably practicable that the amount of the valuation bears the same relationship to the valuations of other tenements and rateable hereditaments as the net annual value of the tenement or hereditament bears to the net annual value of the other tenements and rateable hereditaments.

S.5.2 Without prejudice to the foregoing, for the purpose of ensuring such a relationship regard shall be had, insofar as is reasonably practicable, to the valuation of tenements and rateable hereditaments which are comparable and of similar function and whose valuations have been made or revised within a recent period.

Interpretation of the statute to date, would appear to allow a different relationship to be used between different categories of properties and different locations within a rating area. This would appear to give rise to conflict with the original stated intention of the valuation system as stated in the 1852 act to provide 'one uniform basis of valuation'. Based on current legislation the essential elements to be analysed in order to establish a rateable valuation on a subject property would be as follows:

1   recent settlements of similar properties should be used, say settlements at first appeal or Valuation Tribunal stage over the last three to five years;

2   the comparisons should be analysed with particular importance attached to the following: area of property, rent passing, rent adjusted to NAV, rateable valuations agreed, relationship of NAVs to RVs in comparisons, rate per m² as devalued;

3   based on the above analysis the NAV of the subject property should be reduced by the relativity factor as indicated by the comparisons.

This approach now applies to the valuation of all commercial and industrial property with the exception of global valuations of public utilities which are valued on a fixed method prescribed in s.4 of the 1988 Valuation Act. Arriving at NAV in such a manner is somewhat similar to negotiating a new rent at review stage with the following additional important principles:

1   property for rating purposes is valued in its actual state; *'rebus sic stantibus'* as currently used ignoring development potential or higher value uses;

2   the hereditament to be valued is always presumed to be vacant and available for a bid rental from a hypothetical tenant.

Administration of the system

Revision and appeal procedures

The administration of the rating system (Valuation Office, 1989) in regard to procedures to be used has largely been provided for by the 1988 Valuation Act. Responsibility for the upkeep of the valuation lists remains with the rating authority. Information included on the valuation lists is as follows: map reference, local number, occupier, immediate lessor, description of tenement area, rateable annual valuation and observations. A system of continuous revision was introduced to keep the valuation lists up-to-date. Procedures are as follows under s.3:

1   applications for revision are addressed to the local rating authority and can be made by owners or occupiers of properties, rating authorities or the Commissioner of Valuation;

2   a list of all applications is then forwarded to the Commissioner of Valuation each month. If the application for revision is made by a person other than the owner or occupier the local authority must notify the owner and occupier if known;

3   the Commissioner of Valuation is obliged to cause every application made to him to be processed within six months of receipt of the application or as soon as possible thereafter;

4   the Commissioner shall then issue a list of the determinations made in each quarter within 10 days of the end of the quarter;

5   following the receipt of the revised lists each rating authority must publish a notice indicating their receipt of the lists and the time and place at which they can be inspected over a statutory period of 21 days. The rating authority is also obliged to notify the owner where known of the result of his application for revision and his right of appeal.

Appeal to Commissioner of Valuation

If dissatisfied with a valuation or any other aspect of a revision carried out, an owner or occupier of the property concerned or the relevant rating authority may appeal the decision of the Commissioner of Valuation subject to the following conditions being complied with:

1   Notice of Appeal in writing must be lodged within a period of 28 days from date of publication;

2   the notice must be sent to the Secretary of the relevant local authority accompanied by the relevant fee;

3   grounds of appeal must be specified;

4   the Notice of Appeal must be signed by the appellant or his agent.

All valid notices of appeal plus the fee are the forwarded to the Commissioner of Valuation for examination of the grounds of appeal. The Commissioner may then appoint a member of his/her professional valuer staff to investigate the grounds of appeal. Having received the report of the appeal valuer and considered the recommendation attached, the Commissioner then decides on the case in question by confirming the standing valuation or by reducing or increasing the valuation or by making any other changes such as to description deemed necessary. The Commissioner also has the authority to make alterations to the valuations of similar properties which were revised during the same period but not appealed, where such alterations could be considered fair and reasonable.

Appeal decisions are subsequently issued to the local authorities concerned who are obliged to give public notice of the decisions and of inspection facilities as is required in the case of the initial revision lists. Notification of the owners and occupier(s) of the decision is also required where the identity and addresses are known.

Appeal to Valuation Tribunal

Further appeals from the decision of the Commissioner of Valuation are directed to the Valuation Tribunal. The right to appeal the decision from the 'first appeal' applies again to an owner or occupier of property or to the rating authority. The members of the Valuation Tribunal are the appointees of the Minister of Finance, normally including members of a legal and property valuation background. Established in 1988 with a senior counsel as its first chairman, the Valuation Tribunal operates with three of its members hearing each case with either the parties involved or their counsels. Judgements are in writing with reasoned decisions.

A full register is kept of all appeals and any party to an appeal can appeal to the High Court against a decision by way of a case stated on a point of law only. A party so affected by a decision must declare his dissatisfaction to a Tribunal, and within 21 days request the Tribunal to have a case stated for opinion of the High Court, such appeals must be accompanied by the appropriate fee. From the decision of the High Court, there is a right of appeal to the Supreme Court, again based only on a point of law. A full summary of Tribunal cases from 1988 to 1994 was published in 1996 (Killen and Williams, 1996).

Conclusions

The difficulties in operating a valuation system based on nineteenth century legislation are self evident. The absence of revaluations has led to an inequitable system of valuations, resulting in the gradual diminution of the valuation base through political and judicial decisions. Progress in recent years has come through the Valuation Act 1986 which gave a statutory basis to the system of reducing net annual values to arrive at rateable valuations. The existence of different percentages of NAVs for rateable valuations in various sectors will over time be lessened by the results of the appeal system. The same act provided a clearer understanding of those categories of industrial plant deemed rateable. The 1988 act put the administration of the existing system on a modern footing, introduced continuous revision, the Valuation Tribunal and the concept of global valuations. However, the need to introduce a single modern statute which would ideally facilitate a general revaluation remains. Work on this consolidating valuation act is at a very advanced stage and this reform measure would secure the future of the existing commercial rating system.

The serious broad issue of reforming the financing of local government is once again being considered at governmental level (DOE, 1996). Reform in the area of the responsibilities of local government and optimum structures for delivery of local administration are long overdue. Again, consideration of the potential sources of finance is addressed with possible alternatives such as a local income tax, local sales tax, local property tax, charges and poll taxes among the many options considered.

Expansion in the services provided and new regulatory requirements and/or responsibilities are putting further strains on the financing requirements of local authorities. An increasing role in environmental control, new building regulations, dealing with derelict sites and promoting urban renewal provide further pressures on local administration. The obvious difficult combination of increasing demands and funding requirements necessitates reform if the quality of services provided is to be maintained or improved.

Achieving consensus as to what option any reform of such financing will involve remains difficult. The single declared preference of the Commission on Taxations (1985) for a local property tax is not fully endorsed in the government's recent report (DOE, 1996). The Commission had concluded that only a local property tax combined the main characteristics of an effective tax as follows:

•   Easy to operate and administer through existing structures.

•   Capable of producing a large and predictable yield.

•   Low cost assessment, difficult to evade.

•   Flexible that it can be varied from area to area.

•   Clear accountability through elected representatives.

The government's recent report added further criteria against which the options should be judged such as: equity, acceptability, promotes efficiency and transparency. On the basis of this expanded criteria and analysis of the options none was considered a perfect form of funding and choices were therefore made on the basis that those which failed fewer criteria than other options were preferred. Charges, local property tax, local income tax and the existing rates system were thereby preferred with the conclusion that in order to give an element of buoyancy to local authority funding a local property tax or local income tax should be added to the existing system. This conclusion points only to the long term continuation of the present rateable valuation system affecting commercial and industrial property with necessary legislative reform to secure its future. The difficult choices as to the means of supplementing current sources of finance are not yet resolved.

Notes

1   *Brennan and Others v The Attorney General and Wexford County Council* [1984], ILRM 355 Supreme Court.
2   *Irish Management Institute v The Commissioner of Valuation* (unreported judgement) High Court [1990].

References

Commission on Taxation, (1985), *Fourth Report of the Commission on Taxation: Special Taxation*, Government Publications Office, Dublin.
Department of the Environment, (1972), White Paper, *Local Finance and Taxation*, Stationary Office, Dublin.
Department of the Environment, (1996), *The Financing of Local Government in Ireland*, Government Publications, Dublin.
Killen, D. and Williams, B. (1996), *Journal of Valuation Tribunal Judgements*, Institute of Public Administration, Dublin.
National Economic and Social Council, (1985), *The Financing of Local Authorities*, Stationary Office, Dublin.
Valuation Office, (1989), *Valuation of Property for Rating Purposes*, Valuation Office, Dublin.

6 Real property taxation in Pakistan

Simon Keith

Introduction

In Pakistan real property is in principle subject to assessment and possible taxation under three separate systems. Within the rural areas land revenue is administered by the Board of Revenue although very little tax has been assessed or collected in these areas in recent years. Land revenue is in many ways more like a rent charge than a pure tax. In urban areas there are two systems of property taxation. In the federal enclaves within all the major cities, which are known as Cantonments, a property tax is paid to the Cantonment Boards who have most of the functions of a local authority. The law is contained in the Cantonments Act 1924.

In all the major urban areas, excluding the Cantonments, tax is assessed and paid where applicable under provincial laws known as the Urban Immovable Property Tax Acts. The original 1958 Act was common to all four provinces of West Pakistan. Each Province has subsequently made significant changes to the original laws. This chapter describes the situation, particularly in the Province of Sindh, as governed by the Sindh Urban Immovable Property Tax Act 1958 and the many amendments and statutory orders made thereunder. Particular attention is given to the City of Karachi, the main economic centre in Pakistan with a population of about 11 million. It is not a story of success. The situation in Lahore however, is very much better because of the more stable political situation and where they carry out quinquennial revaluations. In Karachi no revaluation has been carried out since 1968! There are 530,000 properties in the valuation list of which less than 300,000 are taxable. The assessments are low and bear little relationship to present day values. In 1991 half the taxable properties paid less than Rs 450 per annum, which was in 1993 about US$ 16. One-quarter paid less than Rs 250. The property tax amounts to only about 7 per cent of the Karachi Municipal Corporation revenue.

Background

In general the amount of tax collected from all sources in Pakistan is not high. It amounts to only about 16 per cent of GDP. There are surprisingly few income taxpayers in the whole of Pakistan. In general Pakistanis have neither the habit of paying taxes willingly nor any expectation that the tax assessment and collection will be administered in a fair and uncorrupt manner. The Federal tax authorities recognize that a considerable amount of income tax is avoided or evaded.

Pakistan is, at least nominally, a Federal State. There are four provinces the largest being the Punjab, the second largest being Sindh with the other two, the North West Frontier Province and Baluchistan being much smaller. About 90 per cent of all taxes collected are by the Federal authorities and of the remainder, 7 per cent is collected at Provincial level and 3 per cent at local level. The yield from property tax is small and has steadily decreased in real terms during recent years and now accounts for only about 0.3 per cent of all taxes collected at all levels of government. For example in Sindh in the years 1988 to 1992 out of total revenues of Rs 63.6 billion only Rs 11.2 came from GOS taxes and receipts. The balance of Rs 52.3 billion came from Federal transfers. Property tax accounted for about Rs 200 million.

The ability of the Provinces to act in an independent manner as would be expected from a truly federal system is, therefore, restricted by the lack of powers to raise their own revenue. Most of the money comes from subventions from the Federal government. Their main sources of locally generated revenues are Stamp Duty and Motor Tax. Stamp Duty is levied *inter alia* on transfers of real property at a rate of 8.5 per cent in the Punjab plus a registration fee of 1 per cent and a Local Government Tax of 2.5 per cent. Although the nature of such a tax is not unusual, the combined level of 12 per cent on the nominal value is exceptional, and seriously distorts the property market. There is little room for increasing levels of Stamp Duty and indeed there are strong reasons for reducing it. However, this would leave the Provinces with even fewer tax raising powers than they have at present.

The third level of government, local governments such as Karachi Municipal Authority, Hydrabad and others, are often in a stronger financial position. They have at their disposal not only 85 per cent of the property tax yield, but also a tax called Octroi which is a form of internal customs duties or tariffs on a wide variety of goods being moved in or out of a city or province. Karachi is the major port for the country and the economic and financial capital. It is not surprising that Octroi yields Rs 2 billion per annum in Karachi. Octroi is a tax that would have been familiar to Parisians in pre-Revolutionary 18th Century France, but is now little used outside the Indian Sub-Continent. It is a tax that appears to be distrusted by economists although there are no signs that Octroi levied at its present levels does distort the Karachi economy. However, it would do so if the rates were raised significantly. The presence of Octroi and its ability to provide a strong source of locally generated revenue has allowed politicians to avoid the dangerous task of bringing property tax up-to-date. The electorate is unaware of the impact of Octroi while the reactions to any change in the impact of property tax will have direct and uncomfortable political consequences.

However, Octroi has reached the limit of its capacity and additional revenue is required from other sources. Property tax is recognized as the only major source of such increased revenue. In Karachi there are good reasons for nervousness about what might be the effect of increasing revenue from property tax. There has been considerable civil unrest in the last few years. In Sindh there are political and ethnic divisions which go back to the partition in 1947. The incoming Muslims from areas that are now part of India generally settled in the major towns, where they form the majority of the population. They are known as Mohajirs or Incomers and now include a strong and better educated middle class. They have not generally assimilated with the indigenous Sindhi population who form the majority in the Province as a whole. They have their own political party, the Mohajir Quami Movement (MQM), which generally controls the towns in Sindh but still remains a Provincial party. Karachi Municipal Corporation (KMC) before it was suspended was controlled by the MQM. The Provincial government of Sindh is controlled by one of the two major national parties. Added to this, there are continuing violent conflicts between Sunnis and Shias and further conflicts between divisions within the MQM itself. With so many inbuilt sources of instability it is not surprising that the politicians have not rushed to embark on a revaluation.

Property market

Property tax can only be understood in relation to the factors that effect the property market generally. There are factors favourable to the successful administration of the property tax. Pakistanis have a high regard for real property as an investment. Almost every owner or occupier of land knows, or at least thinks that he knows, the area of his land, the built area, the rental value and the capital value of it. There is also an excellent numbering system that allows virtually every property to be uniquely identified. There is clearly a thriving property market in both the rental and the sale sectors with an abundance of estate agents and columns of properties for sale and to rent in the newspapers.

There are also factors that are unhelpful to the proper administration of property tax. The first of these is the lack of transparency. In order to avoid Stamp Duty, property is frequently transferred without registration or any other trace in official records. When property is transferred and goes through the official channels the consideration is rarely correctly stated. However such lack of transparency is not an impossible impediment to the experienced valuer seeking to produce a valuation list. It is of course impossible for a property market to operate without exposing properties for sale and the true consideration at which the property changed hands is usually widely known and easily ascertained. The reason that often triggers the declaring of the transaction can be the need for finance.

A much more serious drawback is the existence of laws relating to the restriction of rents and security of tenure. The Sindh Rented Properties Ordinance 1979 applies to all let land and buildings other than hotels, hostels and boarding houses. Rent control has been in existence for many decades. The rent is restricted to the 'fair rent' as determined by the 'Controller', who is in practice, a judge in the Appellate Court. There is no definition of fair rent but Section 4 of the Act defines the factors that have to be taken in to account and these include the rent of similar accommodation in similar circumstances, the rise in the cost of construction and the repairing charges. There is therefore nothing to indicate that the rent in the first instance is meant to be less than the open market rent. However, in practice the law restricts the increases in rent allowable to levels well below inflation and over the years rents have therefore fallen further and further behind the true open market rental value. There has in effect been a transfer of the value to the lessee. It is not uncommon for leases subject of a rent restriction to be transferred on payment of 'pugree', which is a form of premium or key money. Parallel to the restrictions relating to rent are those concerning the rights of a landlord to obtain possession. The circumstances in which he may do so are very restricted.

Another important impediment to the production of a sound valuation list is the lack of any opportunity for training in valuation or estate management in Pakistan. There are very few persons in the whole country with any qualification relevant to valuation and estate management. The lack of such professionals shows up not only in the lack of expertise but also in the lack of ethical standards in much of the property dealings in the country.

Tax base and yield

More than 90 per cent of the property tax collected in the Province of Sindh is from the City of Karachi. This is partly because only in the larger towns and cities in Sindh does the property tax operate. However, it mainly reflects the size of the Karachi economy, its thriving and busy port and its 11 million population. It has become a serious concern that the yield in real terms from property tax in Karachi has been declining over the last decade notwithstanding the increasing size of the city and the growth in its economy. The yield was about Rs 250 million for the financial year 1992/93. The target for 1993/94 was Rs 350 million; this was not achieved. It should be compared with the relatively buoyant yield from Octroi of about Rs 2 billion per annum. The number of properties assessed in Karachi is shown in Table 6.1.

Table 6.1
Statistics on taxable units

	1993	1994
Taxable units	260,830	299,101
Non taxable units	217,317	231,088
Residential	178,196	198,455
Commercial	35,375	52,972
Mixed residential and commercial	41,066	41,253
Industrial	6,203	6,411
Totals	478,155	530,189

The number of properties is lower that might be expected from a city of 11 million. There are a number of reasons for this which are discussed more fully below. A comparison with other bases illustrates the low number of assessments. For instance the number of water customers is 929,655 of whom 743,996 are residential. The Sui Southern Gas Company has 727,245 customers of whom 715,650 are residential. A positive aspect is the recent increase in numbers which probably indicates increased activity in picking up new properties, possibly as a result of increased interest by the World Bank in the subject.

The next largest city in Sindh is Hydrabad with 49,635 assessed properties of which half are taxable. The yield in 1993 was Rs 11.09 million. Lahore is a city of about half the size of Karachi. However in 1994 there were 511,298 properties in the valuation lists of which 214,347 were taxable. In the year ended 30 June 1994 they collected about Rs 220 million. The figures for number of assessments and yield were therefore comparable with Karachi notwithstanding the difference in size. The difference should be even greater than a comparison of population suggests because values in Karachi tend to be higher than Lahore.

There are many reasons for the poor performance of property tax in Pakistan. However, in Sindh it is particularly poor. The causes are not hard to find. There has been no full revaluation since 1968 since then values have risen well over ten fold, whereas in Lahore they have carried out regular revaluations.

Description of property tax

At first sight the general form of the tax is apparently simple and familiar. Tax is levied as a percentage of 'the annual value of buildings and land in a rating area' with the landlord being liable for the tax. The general format is the same in all four Provinces and stems from the Urban Immovable Property Tax Act 1958 and the rules of the same date made under powers contained in that Act. Each Province has over the years made its own amendments and.there are important variations from one province to another. First impressions are deceptive. In practice the assessment, collection and other operations are by no means as simple as might be supposed from the above description. The complications arise from a combination of factors. These include:

1   a system of exemptions and reliefs that is complex, difficult to interpret and which affect a large number of properties;

2   a large number of possible combinations of rates of tax; and

3   a lack of clarity in the assessment process.

The outcome is a muddled and obscure system that fails to collect much revenue and at the same time is mistrusted by taxpayers and politicians alike.

The taxpayer

The taxpayer is the 'owner' and that term is defined in Section 2(e) as follows:

> Owner includes a mortgagee with possession, a lessee in perpetuity, a trustee having possession of trust property and a person to whom evacuee property has been transferred provisionally or permanently ... .

The definition does not cover the occupiers of land and buildings in the unplanned squatter settlements (the Katchi Abadis) although in many of these areas the buildings are permanent structures, sometimes of good quality, and the communities are long established. There are large numbers of buildings outside the tax net as a direct result of the inadequacies of this definition and consequently the tax base is significantly reduced.

Unit of assessment

The unit of assessment is not defined but is taken to be the contiguous area owned by a person within one boundary. However, the taxpayer's liability is calculated by aggregating the values of all the assessments he owns in that rating area.

Basis of assessment

In Sindh under Section 5 of the Urban Immovable Property Tax Act 1958 and subsequent amendments there are two bases of assessment. One for the present list and another that will be used when a revaluation is next completed. For future revaluations the definition of annual value reads as follows:

Annual Value:

1   The annual value of any land or building shall be the gross annual rent at which such land or building together with any fixtures such as lifts, or electric or other fittings, may be let out.

2   The gross annual rent shall be the prescribed amount not exceeding 10 per cent of the total value of the land or building.

3   The total value of any land or building shall, in the prescribed manner, be determined by the prescribed Officer or Authority on the basis of the market value for fixtures, if any, therein.

4   For the purpose of determining the market value, a rating area may be divided into such sub-rating areas, and each rating or sub-rating area may comprise one or more such categories of land or buildings and there may be such different rates for determination of the market value for the lands or buildings in each rating area, sub area or category, as the case may be, as may be prescribed:

> ... provided that the annual value of a building which is subject to any law for the time being in force relating to restriction of rent shall not be greater than the annual value of such building immediately before the coming into force of this section.

In some ways this is the most straightforward of the two definitions of annual value that will be discussed, but it has yet to be tested in practice. Section 1 is relatively straightforward, although there is no definition of what is a fixture in the remainder of the Act nor a large volume of case law upon which to rely. Generally the rule in Pakistan is similar to the common law in the United Kingdom. Attachment to the property implies that it is part of the hereditament. Subsection 2 provides a ceiling. The gross value cannot exceed 10 per cent of the capital value. Subsection 4 would seem to many to be superfluous and the reason behind it will be discussed when the administration of the tax is examined.

The last few lines after subsection 4 will have a very serious effect on the tax yield. Unless amended it will cause property tax to continue to be of only marginal importance. Rent restriction laws do exist in Pakistan. The prescribed rent does not keep pace with inflation. This part of the section has the effect of restricting the gross value to no greater than the restricted rent. Its effect could be as serious as that in India where property tax has been much damaged by the same cause. It is evident why it was considered equitable to insert this restriction. If a landlord who is liable for property tax is only receiving a small percentage of the gross rack rent, he has no resources to pay the full property tax. By its nature it is a tax on ownership. The value of many landlords' interests have been reduced by the effects of rent restriction. It would be inequitable to be taxed on the value as if there were no rent restriction law. Of course, a large element of the value has passed to the statutory tenants as evidenced by the often substantial payments of pugree. As the law stands at present there will be a large element of value on which property tax will not be paid. It would be possible to devise a means of including this value in the tax net. The basis of assessment under Section 5 for the present list is as follows:

> The annual value of any land or building shall be ascertained by estimating the gross annual rent at which such land or building together with its appurtenances and any furniture that may be let for use or enjoyment with such building might reasonably be expected to be let from year to year, less:
>
> (a)   Any allowance not exceeding 20 per cent of the gross annual rent as the assessing Authority in each particular case may consider reasonable rent for furniture let with such building;
>
> (b)   An allowance of 10 per cent for the cost of repairs and for all other expenses necessary to maintain such building in a state to command with the gross annual rent. Such deduction shall be calculated on the balance of the gross annual rent after the deduction, if any, under Clause A; and
>
> (c)   Any land revenue paid in respect of such building or land: provided that in calculating the annual value of any building or land under this section the value of any machinery in such building or on such land shall be excluded.

The first disadvantage is the cumbersome means of reaching the net rental value through the level of furnished lettings. It takes several steps that are unnecessary. There is room for discussion and compromise with the taxpayer at each of these valuation stages. It leaves more to the discretion of the assessing authorities which is not necessarily exercised with probity. The second problem with this definition is that it has been interpreted as not being the annual value notwithstanding the side heading in the Act which is headed '*Ascertainment of Annual Value*' but the actual rent, if any, that is passing. Lastly, for reasons not apparent to the author, all owner occupied properties are assessed at half the amount of that of the equivalent rented property.

Exemptions

The list of exemptions is one of the weaknesses of the system. Not all of them cause problems. There are a number of exemptions that would not be considered unusual and are similar to those found in most countries. These include such as charitable and religious institutions, orphanages, hospitals, almshouses and places of public worship. There are also a number of less usual reliefs the cumulative effect of which severely weakens the effectiveness of the tax. The first of these excludes small properties and applies to any building or land, the annual value of which does not exceed Rs 250, any residential building with a covered area not exceeding 600 square feet, or one flat with a covered area not exceeding 350 square feet on any floor of a building used for residential purposes. However, the effects of these provisions can be negated by the aggregation of the taxpayers ownerships in the rating area.

There is also exemption for any buildings and land the annual value of which does not exceed Rs 3,500 if owned by widows, minor orphans or permanently disabled persons. This apparently charitable provision has a much greater effect than might be expected. Pakistanis typically live in family groups of three generations in one building. As the life expectation of women is greater than men the family group may well include the widowed mother. If the ownership is, or said to be, in her name exemption results. This is one of the causes of the high number of nontaxable properties as shown in Table 6.1.

Rates of tax

In accordance with the Sindh law under Section 3 (2) the tax rates are designed to be progressive and set as follows:

(i) Where the annual value exceeds six hundred rupees but does not exceed twelve thousand rupees - 20 per cent of the annual value.

(ii) Where the annual value exceeds twelve thousand rupees but does not exceed twenty thousand rupees - 22.5 per cent of the annual value.

(iii) Where the annual value exceeds twenty thousand rupees - 26 per cent of the annual value.

The tax rate is determined by the total value of the taxpayer's property in the rating area. There are however a number of complications and exceptions to this general rule for calculating the rate of tax. First, where a building is occupied and used for residential purposes the rates are 15 per cent for owner occupiers and 20 per cent in all other cases. Next, there is an addition to the general rates of tax of 5 per cent for properties 'if used for commercial purposes' and '2.5 per cent if used for industrial purposes'. This additional rate is rather misleadingly known as 'Betterment Tax' and is usually separately listed in the budget and accounts.

In recent years it has been recognized that the yield of the tax is bound to be eroded in real terms if the rates of tax are fixed and no revaluation carried out. Therefore in 1995 under pressure form the World Bank a variable surcharge was introduced. It is usually 30 per cent in addition to the general rates quoted above but only 15 per cent for properties assessed since the 1 July 1979 onwards for properties used for residential purposes. Thus industrial properties all incur a 30 per cent surcharge whenever they are assessed. The variation in respect of the date of assessment recognizes that there is no tone of the list provision in the law and none is recognized in administrative practice. It makes no recognition of the fact that a certain industrial area was revalued in 1973.

The aim of the differential rates is no doubt to provide a progressive tax system. This aim is completely negated by the system of assessing properties and by the exemptions. Many valuable properties are under assessed and a significant number do not pay any tax. The differential rates also cause a complete lack of accountability in that the total amount that should be collected in any rating district is not readily ascertainable. Nor can the taxpayer immediately know what tax he should pay. Differential rates add to the lack of transparency.

Appeals

There is no independent judicial appeals system and many of the weaknesses of the operation and administration of the tax stem from this defect. The provisions relating to appeals in the law and rules are relatively brief and make reference to no-one other than the assessing officer. Appeals are only allowed within a 30 day period after the publication of the draft list or from the date when a taxpayer is informed when the list is altered. In practice the Excise and Taxation Officer deals with the objections and appeals or disagreements with his decisions go to his superior officer, the Director of Valuation. As all appeals are dealt with informally, the system and method of determining them is not transparent. However the outcome is recorded in the valuation list or PT1, which is a public document. In the Karachi area, a large number of valuation list entries have been successfully challenged, in some rating districts more than 70 per cent, and have had their assessments reduced. The system does not encourage probity.

There are other repercussions of the defective system which leaves so much power in the hands of the tax administrators. The public and politicians believe that the assessment process is not being carried out in a fair and incorrupt manner. To correct this defect the intention of the politicians is to try and remove as much discretion from the Excise and Taxation Officers as possible. They attempt to specify the levels of assessment that will apply to different types of property in different areas. The result is that properties are not valued or assessed in a manner that would be familiar to most practitioners in most countries but classified in accordance with a set of rules handed down from politicians.

It is clearly not impossible for an appeal system based on a judicial tribunal to exist in Pakistan. The Cantonments Boards operate such a system in relation to their property tax assessments. There were until recent years independent income tax tribunals. There appears to be no reason why an independent tribunal could not be introduced. It might even be possible to do so without legislation.

Revaluation

The law provides in Section 7 that there should be revaluations every five years. This can, by order, be reduced to three or extended to eight. It is clearly not impossible to do revaluations every five years even in Karachi. The Cantonments Boards, or at least some of them, carry out revaluations every three years. In Lahore they adhere to the quinquennial timetable. In Karachi or the other cities of Sindh no revaluation has been carried out since 1967. Every year of delay in commencing a revaluation makes the task more difficult. There is now little institutional memory of how to commence the revaluation task and no appreciation of the technical difficulties involved.

Enforcement

There are adequate powers of enforcement in the Act. These include attachment of rent, distraint, making the outstanding tax the first charge against a building or land, and the sale of the property. There are also powers to charge interest on arrears.

Administration

The administration of property tax is the responsibility of the Department of Excise and Taxation in the Provincial government. They assess and collect the tax and remit 85 per cent to the local government. There is no separation of the two functions of assessment and collection at any level. The beneficiary of the tax (until very recently the Karachi Municipal Corporation) have no control over it.

The legal responsibility is that of the 'assessing authority' who is more specifically defined in Rule 3 as 'a District Excise and Taxation Officer' (ETO). In theory he has exemplary delegated powers under this and the subsequent rule. It is clear that he has all the powers necessary to assess and collect tax. He in turn can delegate these powers (in writing) to his subordinate officials.

The Excise and Taxation Department also has responsibility for the collection of Motor Tax. It is not responsible for taxation of land in rural areas or Stamp Duty or the fixing of levels of rents for the land leased out by the Development Authorities. Responsibilities for the valuation and management of land in the public sector are widely spread.

Organization

In Karachi the responsibility for property tax lies with the Director of Property Tax who reports to the Secretary of Excise and Taxation. There are 18 area offices each under the command of an Excise and Taxation Officer. Each office deals with both the collection and the assessment but not with Motor Tax. The average office therefore deals with about 30,000 assessments. The staff at all levels including cleaners and constables, amount to about one thousand persons.

In the other towns of Sindh where property tax operates the local offices deal with both Property Tax and Motor Taxes. In Lahore, a city about half the size of Karachi but with a population of about 5 million and almost as many assessments there is one centralized Property Tax office with only about one-third of the staff. They are therefore considered to be more effective and more efficient.

141

Facilities

A visit to a local Excise and Taxation Property Tax Office in Sindh reveals that the staff work under difficult conditions. The offices are of poor standard, shabby, sparsely furnished and crowded. The facilities would be quite insufficient if the all the staff were in the office at any one time. The environment does not promote efficiency.

Records

The records consist of a series of lists. The key document is the valuation list always known as the 'PT1' in accordance with the reference number in the Sindh Urban Immovable Property Tax Rules 1958. The physical state of these records is very poor as might be expected after more than 25 years. Some copies of the PT1s have disintegrated completely and the work is done from the PT8 which are registers with a similar function to a rate book. Notwithstanding the difficulties, the staff do keep track of virtually all the assessments. The clerical work is quite satisfactorily performed with old fashioned equipment and in primitive conditions. In Sindh in 1994 there were no computers in the Department. At that time Lahore was in the process of computerizing its entire property tax operation.

Collection

The aim of the system of collection is that the Excise and Taxation offices should not handle money and that the tax is paid by taxpayers to the banks that are authorized to accept payments. The Property Tax offices issue a demand ('challan') in three parts. These are delivered by the constables to each property. The taxpayer takes the 'challan' to the bank, pays the amount due and retains a receipted 'challan'. One of the copies of the 'challan' is returned by the bank to the Excise and Taxation office. It is a soundly designed system and in theory, it works well but irregularities do creep in. There is little effort made to use the powers available to enforce collection.

Methods of assessment

The PT1s record the information on which the valuation is based. Generally there is no supporting file. The information includes the plot area, the 'plinth' area, the number of storeys and the number of rooms and some rudimentary information on the construction. It also records the declared rent if any. As can be seen this information is not sufficient for any sophisticated methods of valuation even if the information was correct; and it frequently is not. In theory all properties should be inspected internally which causes problems in an Islamic country. If the men of the house are absent it is not thought correct for a male inspector to enter. It is therefore quite common to use a system of self-declaration of the essential facts. There is little opportunity to check them.

Notwithstanding the discretion given in the law to individual ETOs in matters of assessment the methods of assessment are generally prescribed by politicians. The principal method is that of an amount per room variable with location and other factors. It has been shown that the end results bear little correlation to rental values and this relationship is worst in the more expensive properties. The lack of correlation with rental values can be illustrated with a hypothetical example of a good house in a good suburb in, say Cosmopolitan Colony, New Town, on a plot of 500 square yards and with a floor area of 6,000 square feet with some 12 rooms, kitchen and 3 bathrooms. If the house is owner occupied the 'assessed rental value', (ARV) will be about Rs 6,500 and the property tax payable Rs 970 per annum. If let to a private individual the ARV will be Rs 13,000 and the annual payment Rs 2,600 per annum. If the house was let to a government department at the full rack rent it is conceivable that the ARV would be based on the actual rent, less 10 per cent. As the rental value of such a house was in 1992 about Rs 29,000 per month the tax payable could amount to Rs 60,000.

Cantonments

It is worth comparing the system operating in the Cantonments areas of Karachi. It should be noted that these areas form a large part of the city and include a large proportion of the valuable properties. The Cantonments are therefore large and an important part of the city. It is remarkable that a system that operates well should exist next to one that does not. Nor is this a new situation. The legal basis is contained in the Cantonments Act 1924 (CA24) sections 60 to 106 in which is contained a complete code of assessing the annual value and collecting tax from land and buildings. (Referred to as assessment tax in this description to distinguish it from property tax). In many ways the provisions are better than for property tax. The powers of the Cantonment Boards to tax also includes Octroi, terminal tax and tolls. However, it is the assessment tax that is the main and often only source of revenue. Their powers are generally subject to Federal government sanction. The features of the system are in brief as follows:

1   The incidence of taxation (CA24, S.65) is on the owner but there is a right of attachment of the rent if the tax is not recoverable from the owner.

2   The definition of 'annual value' (CA24, S64) is a follows:

> ... (a) in the case of railway stations, hotels, colleges, schools, hospitals, factories and any other which a Board decides to assess under this clause, one-twentieth of the sum obtained by adding the estimated present cost of erecting the building to the estimated value of the land appertaining thereto, ...

For other buildings and land the actual rent is taken into account but if in the opinion of the Board the rent is less than the 'fair letting value' or if unlet it is the amount that it might reasonably be expected to let from year to year.

3   New assessment lists should be prepared 'at least once every three years'.

4   There are rights of objection when a new list is published or when alterations are made to an existing list and these are heard by the assessment committee. A right of appeal lies with the District Magistrate or such other officer as may be empowered by the Federal government on his behalf. It is therefore possible to have an assessment reviewed by independent persons.

5   All transfers and erections of new buildings must be notified to the Boards.

6   The exempt properties include places of public worship, buildings used for educational purposes, hospitals maintained wholly by charitable contribution, burning and burial grounds and lands belonging to the Boards or Federal or Provincial governments.

7   There are adequate powers of enforcing payment including powers of distraint.

It is a relatively short, simple and sensible code with none of the complications that beset the property tax. It cannot be said that they have available valuation expertise that allows them to make assessments in the manner that might be expected in many other countries however, the major inconsistencies of property tax are avoided. Furthermore in most Cantonment areas the system as a whole works well enough. The reasons for this are probably that the inhabitants want it to work because they relate to the particular Board in which they live, they know how the money is spent and want the services it provides. They see outside their boundaries examples of local government not providing the essential services.

Valuation profession

There are no opportunities in Pakistan to obtain training as a valuer or estate manager. Pakistan is in much the same situation as India and Bangladesh. It is otherwise unusual for a major Commonwealth country to be in this position. It is in strong contrast to Singapore, Malaysia and Sri Lanka all of which have facilities to train in valuation, estate management or land economy. Not only are there no such training facilities but there are now few people with any relevant foreign qualification. There is no doubt a need for such persons not only in relation to property tax assessment but also elsewhere in the public sector for Wealth Tax assessments, assessments for Land Revenue, acquisition of land by various bodies and the management of land by many government departments and para-statals to name only the most obvious instances. Persons unqualified in valuation or land management perform these functions without training.

In the private sector there are all the needs for valuation and estate management that would be expected in a country where land and property are highly regarded as an investment. However, it cannot be said that this deficiency is thought important or even recognized to exist. The absence of such persons is significant not only at the working level but also in relation to policy. It is possible to see in the property tax law the results of legislation without access to advice on valuation matters. It is not clear what can bring about any change. A change in attitude could happen through foreign valuers being brought in to carry out the Karachi revaluation.

Critical analysis

Lack of transparency

There are certainly many in Pakistan who hold that the lack of transparency and complexity are not there by chance. They would say that they form a pattern which is designed to keep all the power in the hands of the officials administering the tax. It is not so much that the law is difficult to understand but its application is not straightforward. The PT1s are open to public inspection but no pattern is apparent on first inspection due principally to the lack of any tone of the list and the unusual owner occupier concession. There are many exemptions that can affect properties but these will not necessarily be obvious to the taxpayer. If the taxpayer does succeed in understanding the law and practice and wishes to dispute the assessing authorities findings there is no independent arbitrator to whom he can turn. On the other hand the officials do have a grasp of the law and can if the circumstances are right assist a taxpayer in finding his way through the maze.

145

Legal defects

There are a number of important defects in the law which if not rectified will certainly greatly reduce the yield. The definition of who is liable for tax will continue to prevent a large number of properties, probably more than 100,000 being assessed and appearing in the list at all. The list of exemptions will require modification.

The future

The World Bank have taken an interest in the performance of the property tax since at least 1990. Improvements in property tax and a revaluation of all the properties in Karachi form part of the IDB loan under the Sindh Special Development Project and at the time of writing this chapter bids from the private sector to carry out extensive revaluation work are being evaluated. At present no attempt has been made to rectify the structural and legal weaknesses identified above. No part of that project yet addresses the need for the establishment of a valuation profession. Even if the attempt at a revaluation succeeds the new list will be flawed unless the legal defects are addressed. There can be no useful institutional building without appropriate valuation training.

The revaluation task is of great complexity and magnitude. When considering the problems that will be encountered and the chances of success it is instructive to compare other successful revaluations in the developing world in recent years. Karachi is for instance about twice the size of Lagos in Nigeria where the private sector was successfully used to revalue the 240,000 properties in 1990 after a similarly long interval since the last revaluation at a cost of rather more than US$ 2 million. There are many similarities between the circumstances of the two cities. In both cases they are port cities with all urban problems of the developing world. They also represent the economic capitals of their respective countries. However, in Nigeria the Chief Valuation Officer for Lagos State had the advantage of a valuation profession that is quite numerous, well trained and educated, and with an overcapacity in the private sector. There was also previous experience of using the private sector in revaluation work elsewhere in the country. The law was fundamentally sound. By contrast none of these advantages exist in Karachi.

Revaluations have also been completed in Accra, Ghana in the mid-1980s, Harare in Zimbabwe in 1991 and Kampala in Uganda in the early 1990s. In all cases there were persons trained in valuation available and the law was fundamentally sound. It may be that lessons can be learned from Jakarta, Indonesia where the magnitude of the revaluation task was similar. There, the need for technical training was recognized. Training courses were run by the

Malaysian Valuation Division. The technical task of a revaluation was successfully completed in the early 1990s but at a cost reported to be in the region of US$20 million. The resulting tax revenue has reportedly been disappointing.

There is no doubt that a satisfactory system of property tax could be operated in Karachi. Although there are many technical problems, none of these are insurmountable. It has been calculated that the new tax base would be in region of Rs 30 billion. If the tax rate was then reduced to 10 per cent and allowing for about a 66 per cent success rate, which are both quite modest assumptions, the yield would be in the region of Rs 2 billion or roughly the same as Octroi. Research indicates that such a tax rate would be affordable. However, whether the political will exists to carry through this major undertaking remains to be seen.

References

The majority of the information for this work was gathered by the author as a consultant to the World Bank in connection with the preparation work for the Staff Appraisal Report for the Sindh Special Development Project of October 1993. He was also part of the PE Inbucon Ltd team that prepared the Resource Generation Study of Metropolitan Karachi in 1992. In Lahore in the Punjab he was a member of the ODA funded research project by the Polytechnic of East London which produced reports on 'Urban Land Management and Land Information Management' in 1991.

The data relating to property tax, assessment numbers and yields was provided by the Excise and Taxation Departments of Sindh and Punjab.

7   Property tax in Thailand

Sakon Varanyuwatana

Introduction

In Thailand there are currently two taxes which can be considered as property taxes, namely, the House and Buildings Tax, and the Land Development Tax. The House and Buildings Tax was introduced as part of the reforms implemented following the change in government from an absolute monarchy to a constitutional one, whilst the Land Development Tax evolved from the return to a land tax which had been used some 100 years before. It can be seen from Table 7.1 that these two taxes are important revenue sources for local self-government units. The House and Buildings Tax represents 82.9 per cent of total local tax revenues, whilst the Land Development Tax accounts for only 4.95 per cent of the total. However, their actual significance is greatly diminished when compared to the total local tax and total government tax revenues as illustrated in Table 7.1.

This chapter attempts to explain the general characteristics of these two tax revenue structures, including the basis of assessments, reductions, reliefs, exemptions, appeals and penalty procedures. Defects in the taxes have led to several disadvantages in terms of buoyancy and economic growth.

A brief structure of local government administration

Local government in Thailand represents two distinct forms. Firstly, there are territorial administrative systems of which local jurisdictions are extensions of the central government. Secondly, there are local self-governments, each with an elected assembly. In principle, the two systems are separate, but in practice the identifying features of the two are somewhat blurred. The primary unit of local administration under the territorial system is the province (Changwat). Currently there are 76 provinces across the country. Every province is under the administrative power of a governor who is appointed (except the Bangkok Metropolitan Area where the governor is elected) by the Ministry of Interior. The governor is the head of the provincial administrative body on which almost every central government agency is represented. They (the governor and central officers) have to follow instructions and policies from their own central agency. The purpose of their assignment in each province is to render specific services to the residents of that particular geographical area, with their expenditures being financed directly from the central budget. This arrangement creates some administrative problems for the governor, as he has the difficult task of co-ordinating the activities of each central officer, without having direct control over their line of command and their budget within the province.

Table 7.1
Share of House and Buildings Tax and Land Development Tax to total tax revenue, 1995

Tax revenue	Amount (million baht)	% to locally levied taxes	% to total local taxes	% to total net* government tax revenue
House and Buildings	4,941.48	82.90	13.30	0.65
Land Development	294.85	4.95	0.79	0.04

* *Excluded tax return from value added tax and other taxes*

Source: *Department of Local Administration, Ministry of Interior and Fiscal Policy Office, Ministry of Finance*

Local self-government, the second form of local government in Thailand, is based on a series of statues enacted between 1933-1995 by the national assembly. They are composed of:

1   provincial administrative organizations (PAOs);

2   municipalities (Taseban): there are three classes of municipalities namely, the city (Nakorn), the town (Muang) and the village (Tambon). They are classified under the basis of population size, revenue capacity and political importance. For example, all locations of provincial governments are established as city municipalities regardless of other criteria;

3   sanitary districts (Sukapibans);

4   Bangkok Metropolitan Area (BMA);

5   City of Pattaya;

6   the latest form of local self-government, i.e. village councils and village administrative organizations (VAOs).

There are no clear distinctions between the two basic forms of provincial administrative organizations and local self-government. The overlap is most apparent in the case of the PAOs and the provincial administration headed by the governor. In general the PAO provides governmental services to all inhabitants outside the geographical jurisdiction of municipalities and sanitary districts. The PAO itself is composed of two major elements firstly, the provincial governor who acts as executive body of provincial administration, and the province council which act as the legislative body. As head of the provincial executive body and as the representative of central government, the governor serves in a dual legal capacity which tends to create some confusion in local administration.

The municipality is a corporate entity intended to provide large urban areas with limited self-government. All municipalities are deemed by law to be comprised of an elected municipal assembly and a municipal council. The former is the legislative body of the municipality with the remit to review and act on the annual budget and to pass ordinances dealing with subjects compatible with the central government laws and within the legal boundaries of municipal government. The municipal council functions as an executive committee and has two major responsibilities: to determine policy and present appropriate ordinances and recommendations to the assembly, and to supervise the operations of the municipality and its employees.

The sanitary district is a quasi-urban local self-government jurisdiction established with the consent of the Ministry of Interior. As the name implies, to be a sanitary district the area must meet certain demographic characteristics required by the Ministry of Interior. Unlike the municipalities, sanitary districts do not have a separate legislative body but are administered by a committee. The governing body is composed of both elected members and members appointed by the provincial governor. The committee is administered under the direct control of the provincial governor.

The village administrative organization, established under the Village Council and Administrative Organization Act, 1995 replaced regional administration which was previously under the supervision of the provincial governor. The village council and village administrative organization both have a similar management structure. Membership of the village council is composed of chiefs of every hamlet and village, the village doctor, and local elected members from each hamlet. The composition of the village administrative organization is similar to the village council. The remits of the village council and village administrative organization are to act as both legislative and executive bodies for respective villages.

To summarize, in Thailand central government, through the Ministry of Interior, has historically exercised a great deal of central control over all forms of local self-government. This control is manifested in two ways firstly, in the broad supervisory powers delegated to provincial governors and secondly, in the issuing of rules and regulations governing financial practices, budgeting, and services by the Ministry of Interior. Though there are attempts to decentralize power from the central authorities, much remains to be done.

House and Buildings Tax

The House and Buildings Tax was first introduced in 1932 to replace taxes levied on shop stalls in the market place, buildings, boats and rafts. Initially, this tax was designed to be levied only within the Bangkok area, but was later extended throughout the whole country. The Ministry of Finance was initially assigned the control and implementation of this tax. The Director General of the Revenue Department could determine objections against assessments under the act, with taxpayers having the right of appeal to court. However, over time many changes have been made to the legislation and it is the Ministry of Finance and the Ministry of Interior who are currently jointly responsible for the tax. Both the Minister of Finance and the Minister of Interior have the power to issue rates and regulations relating to the implementation of this tax. However, the actual administration of the tax is in the hands of local self-government units.

Taxable property

Taxable property under the House and Buildings Tax is defined as houses not owneroccupied, industrial and commercial buildings and the land appurtenant to these buildings. Structural additions to taxable property are also subject to taxation.

Taxpayers

Owners of buildings, structures and land appurtenant thereto are liable to pay the House and Buildings Tax. Where the land and the buildings belong to different owners, the owner of the buildings is liable for the whole amount of the tax.

Tax base

In respect of each taxable property the tax is calculated on the basis of the annual rental value, actual or imputed. Thus actual or imputed rental income from buildings and land utilized for all purposes, is taxable with the exception of owner occupied residences. From a local authority point of view, it may not be possible to say with any degree of certainty that evidence of the annual rental value of a house or building is totally reliable, since rental values are normally under-declared to mislead the officials responsible for making the tax assessment. In addition, some classes of property are not rented, and in these cases it is usual for the Ministry of Interior to direct that the annual value shall be a prescribed percentage of the capital value of the property. That provision is designed primarily to assist the authorities in tax collection. The tax prescribes the 'annual rate' which is defined as the sum for which the property might be expected to lease from year to year. The statute provides that where there is a lease, the rent is to be adopted as the basis for determining the annual value, unless there are reasons to indicate that the rent does not correspond to the sum for which the property might reasonably be expected to let from year to year. If it is difficult to specify accurately the actual rental value, the Committee Officers under the Act may rectify or calculate otherwise, the annual value by taking into consideration the characteristics of the property, its size, location, and benefits received from the property. To make a proper assessment of the tax (nationwide) each year, the Ministry of Interior issues general guidelines for annual value assessments for local self-government units to follow in tax assessments and collection.

Exemptions and reliefs

The following building structures and adjacent land are not subject to the House and Buildings Tax:

1   royal palaces owned by the Crown;

2   buildings owned by the government which are utilized for public purposes, and property utilized by the State Railway of Thailand;

3   public hospitals and educational institutions not run for personal profit;

4   religious buildings;

5   buildings unoccupied for 12 months or longer; and

6   buildings occupied by owners and not being used for profit.

Tax rates and reductions

The House and Buildings Tax is a proportional tax, specified at the rate of 12.5 per cent of the annual value. In addition, to encourage manufacturing investment, the Act also provides for a reduction for factories and dwellings in which machinery has been installed to a value of one-third of the annual value of the property. Damaged buildings are subject to a reduced valuation in proportion to the extent of the damage. This applies only to damage which requires major repair and subject to the fact that the buildings have not been restored for normal use. Similar reductions apply to buildings which become unoccupied during the year. It is one of the main weakness of this tax that exemption is granted to owner-occupied residential houses and other buildings.

Collection

Municipalities, sanitary districts and the provincial administrative organizations have the responsibility to collect the House and Buildings Tax in their respective areas of jurisdiction. The date of tax filing and payment is announced within the first four months of each calendar year. Taxpayers must file tax returns within 30 days of the announced date at the municipal office or the sanitary district office or, if the buildings are located outside a municipal or sanitary district area, at the district office of the provincial administrative organization.

Appeals

A taxpayer who is dissatisfied with his tax assessment may appeal and request a revised assessment, however, if the tax return has been filed after the due date the taxpayer forfeits his appeal rights.

Surcharges and penalties

If the taxpayer does not pay by the due date but pays within one month thereafter, he must pay an additional amount equal to 2.5 per cent of his tax liability. The penalty for late payment is 5 per cent in respect of payments made between the first and the second month after the due date, rising to 7.5 per cent after the end of the second month and to 10 per cent after the third month. If delinquency extends beyond four months, the tax authority may apply to the court to seize and sell the taxable property to recover the tax arrears.

In the case of transferred property both the previous and the new owner are jointly responsible for payment of tax arrears at the date of the transfer. Failure to file tax returns results in a fine not exceeding 200 baht. Perjury and other attempts to evade or avoid payment of the correct amount of tax is punishable by imprisonment for a period not exceeding six months or a fine not exceeding 500 baht or both. A taxpayer who is uncooperative in supplying requested information or who fails to produce documents or answer questions is liable to a fine not exceeding 500 baht.

Criticisms of the House and Buildings Tax

As illustrated in Table 7.1 the House and Buildings Tax is the most important of locally levied taxes to local self-governments. Its share of total tax revenue is normally around 80 per cent. Despite its large revenue contribution, the House and Buildings Tax has a very low tax yield when compared to its potential. This poor yield is primarily a result of the defective structure of the tax and the inefficiency of the tax administration. The major cause of the problems relates to the exemption of owner occupied houses and buildings. It narrows the tax base and encourages the building of large houses by wealthy people. Moreover, the tax exemption for dwelling houses and buildings also creates administrative problems in determining whether or not the houses and buildings are really used for residential purposes. Since house ownership is indicative of a relatively high income for house owners, it is recommended that, in terms of equity and for preventing tax revenue loss through exemption, as well as reducing tax evasion, the exemption for residential houses and buildings be terminated as soon as possible. However, it is still remains desirable from the equity point of view to exempt those houses having a low rental value. This would adjust the incidence of the House and Buildings Tax which at present tends to fall mainly on those tenants who generally fall into the low income group.

Similarly, the exemption of tax for houses and buildings which have been left vacant also creates loopholes in the tax because it is difficult to verify the claim made by the owners that the houses or buildings really are vacant. The low yield is also due to the fact that the tax assessors have in most cases to accept the rent which has been declared by the taxpayers in the tax returns, as the annual rental for tax purposes. Such a rent does not always reflect the true value which is likely to be earned by the land and buildings. Even though the rent declared by the taxpayers can be compared favourably with the rent paid in respect of similar buildings and land in the vicinity, the rent may still be low as there is a prevalent practice of making advance lump sum cash payments by tenants to landlords whenever the lease agreements expire and new agreements have to be negotiated. The size of these cash payments can in some cases be substantial resulting in the actual rent paid being subsequently far below the rent which ought to be paid. If the annual rental for tax purposes could be increased to reflect the true rent earned, i.e. by incorporating the lump sum payments in the rent, it would substantially raise the revenue potential from this tax.

Apart from the practice of accepting actual rents, etc., the low yield of the House and Buildings Tax is also attributable to the poor system of tax administration. This is particularly evident in the lack of enforcement and measures to track the potential taxpayers. Despite the fines and penalties imposed on tax avoidance, rates of compliance are considered low.

Land Development Tax

This tax can be considered as representing a real property tax. It is assessed on the value of land excluding structures and crops. The basis for this tax is the land value and is collected in accordance with the Land Development Act of 1954 (as amended). It is of some relevance that local development should be financed, in part, from a tax secured on this particular basis because it is development which has resulted from earlier national and community expenditures which is reflected in current land values i.e. the so called unearned increment. Local development can take many forms, with local taxation on a land value basis making a worthwhile contribution to meeting public costs.

The origin of the Land Development Tax can be traced to the early Ayudhya period, when contributions in kind (usually rice) were made to the King by the tenants of the land, which in theory was owned by the King. A major reform was introduced during the reign of King Rama V in 1874 which authorized the assessment of land taxes based on its soil condition and productivity. When the Revenue Department was established, it was made responsible for administration of the land tax, which became an important source of revenue for the country. In 1960, however, the government transferred the Land Development Tax to local self-governments, under the supervision of the Revenue Department. Since then the large municipalities and the Bangkok Metropolitan Area have collected the tax. Finally, in 1965, the responsibility for its assessment and collection was assigned to the provincial administrative organizations, municipalities, and sanitary districts for those lands situated within their jurisdiction. The Ministry of Interior through the Department of Local Administration still exercises general supervision of the tax. Taxable property comprises all land, including mountains and water basins.

All persons or groups of persons, individual or corporate, who own land or are in possession of land not owned by other individuals are liable to pay the Land Development Tax.

Exemptions and reliefs

The following classes of land are excluded from the Land Development Tax:

- land owned by all levels of the government;

- land on which royal palaces are located;

- land on which public hospitals, public educational institutions or other structures of public use are found;

- land owned by religious bodies or used for religious purposes;

- non-profit cemeteries;

- land which is a part of, or attached to a building structure that has to pay the House and Buildings Tax;

- land used for the government rail service, water works, electricity, sea ports or airports;

- land owned by a private individual(s) but used by the government in the public interest; and

- land on which embassies, consulate or offices of international agencies are located.

Exemption is also granted to a taxpayer of land which is used for his personal residence, for husbandry, or cultivation, according to the following rules:

- land located outside a municipal or sanitary district, the exemption is not more than 5 rais but not less than 3 rais (1 rai = approximately 0.4 acres);

- land located in a tambon municipality or in a sanitary district, the exemption ranges from 200 square wah (or 800 square meters) to 1 rai;

- for land located in Pattaya city and municipalities other than a tambon, the exemption is not more than 100 square wah but not less than 50 square wah;

- land located in the Bangkok Metropolitan Area, the exemption is as follows:

  i   50-100 square wah for a densely populated area.

  ii   100 square wah to 1 rai for a populated area.

  iii 3-5 rai for a rural area.

The basis for determining the type of district is in accordance with prescribed ministerial regulations. Whether a taxpayer owns one parcel or several parcels of land in a province, he can only claim one exemption. Moreover, this exemption is granted for land in one province only. Even though several individuals jointly own one parcel of land, only one exemption applies to that land. No exemption is granted for land with buildings used for business or rental purposes. In addition, cultivated land in excess of the exempt area, is subject to only one-half of the statutory rate. If cultivation is carried out by the landowner the maximum tax liability is fixed at five baht per rai. In adverse circumstances, taxes on cultivated land are waived. However, idle land is subject to twice the statutory rate.

These exemptions are of concern and represent one of the major reasons for the low revenue base of this tax, especially the exemption for land used by its owners. These exemptions also exacerbate local wealth and income inequality as residential houses and lands are excluded from tax liability at both the local and national level.

Tax base

The tax is assessed on the land value of the property with no account being taken of any improvements to the land or of any crops. The land value is the product of the area of the property and the medium value of land within the tax district or part of the tax district in which the particular property is situated. The medium value is computed by the local committee from at least three recent sale prices of land located in the district with no account being taken of improvements, value of structures or crops which may be included in such sale prices. Once determined, the medium price of land for a given district is used for a period of four years. This medium price is made known to the general public and if dissatisfied, a landowner can appeal for its revision.

If there are no land transactions in the area, the medium value is calculated by reference to the closest neighbouring areas which have similar land conditions and usage. The provincial governor has the authority to appoint appraisal committees for each jurisdiction. Membership of the committees vary with the different types local self-government:

1   in municipalities, the membership is composed of the provincial permanent secretary, provincial land officer, local sheriff, mayor and two appointed experts;

2   in sanitary districts the committee comprises the provincial permanent secretary, province land officers and two experts appointed by the board of the sanitary district;

3   for areas outside municipalities and sanitary districts where there is no village chief, the committee is composed of the provincial permanent secretary, provincial land officer, and an expert appointed by the provincial governor.

The committee must meet to appraise the medium land value every four years. After the medium land value has been determined and there is reason to believe the value has changed significantly, the governor has the authority to order the committee to reappraise the medium value. In October of the forth year, the committee must submit the medium value to enable the governor to announce the value to each provincial and local office.

Tax rates

The tax rate schedule for the Land Development Tax is shown in Table 7.2. The rate of this tax is progressive with the size of land holding, however, the rate itself is low when compared to the medium value of land on which the tax rate is based. The assessed value once determined will be used for a period of four years. However, when an average tax rate is calculated for each tax bracket, it is obvious that the overall rate structure is regressive with respect to the value of land.

Collecting organization

As with the House and Buildings Tax, municipalities, sanitary districts and the provincial administrative organizations are responsible for the collection of the tax. Under the Act of Village Administrative Organization 1995, village administration organizations are taking over tax collection from the provincial administration organizations.

Tax payment and return

The land owner, or his representative, must file a tax return for each parcel of land on a form provided by Ministry of Interior. Filing is made at the district office, if the land is located outside a municipality, and is made at the municipal office if the land is located in a municipality. In both cases filing must be made during the month of January in each year. If there are several owners of a parcel of land, all owners have a collective responsibility for ensuring that the filing has been completed. A new land owner must report his purchase to the survey official within 30 days of the acquisition. A similar requirement applies to an owner whose land area has changed or who has altered the use of the land which

Table 7.2
Tax rates and brackets of Land Development Tax

Bracket	Tax rate medium price of taxable land (baht per rai)	Taxes per rai (baht)	Estimated tax rate per rai %
1	<200	0.5	0.50
2	200-400	1	0.33
3	400-600	2	0.40
4	600-800	3	0.43
5	800-1,000	4	0.44
6	1,000-1,200	5.5	0.50
7	1,200-1,400	7	0.64
8	1,400-1,600	8	0.53
9	1,600-1,800	9	0.53
10	1,800-2,000	10	0.53
11	2,000-2,200	11	0.52
12	2,200-2,400	12	0.52
13	2,400-2,600	13	0.52
14	2,600-2,800	14	0.52
15	2,800-3,000	15	0.52
16	3,000-3,500	17.5	0.54
17	3,500-4,000	20	0.53
18	4,000-4,500	22.5	0.53
19	4,500-5,000	25	0.53
20	5,000-5,500	27.5	0.52
21	5,500-6,000	30	0.52
22	6,000-6,500	32.5	0.52
23	6,500-7,000	35	0.52
24	7,000-7,500	37.5	0.52
25	7,500-8,000	40	0.52
26	8,000-8,500	42.5	0.52
27	8,500-9,000	45	0.51
28	9,000-9,500	47.5	0.51
29	9,500-10,000	50	0.54
30	10,000-15,000	55	0.44
31	15,000-20,000	60	0.34
32	20,000-25,000	65	0.29
33	25,000-30,000	70	0.31
34	For land with a value over 30,000 baht tax paid is:		
	1. first 30,000 baht	70	
	2. each additional 10,000 baht	25	

Source: *Royal decree on Land Development Tax*

could lead to a change in the tax liability. The survey official must in turn report the change to the assessment official within 30 days.

Tax assessment must be finalized and land owners notified in March of the first year in which the new medium value is in effect. This tax assessment remains constant for the next three years. Tax payment must be made in April of each year or 30 days after the date of assessment. If the tax liability is less than one baht, payment is waived. A new owner is jointly liable together with the previous owner, for tax arrears over the past five years, including the year in which ownership changes. Tax arrears of over five years remains the responsibility of the previous owner. Joint liability of tax arrears does not apply if the change of ownership is as a result of forced sale by court order or through bankruptcy proceedings. Seizure and auction of taxable properties can be carried out by the tax authority to enforce payment of tax arrears.

Tax refunds

Taxpayers may claim refunds for any overpayment. These claims must be made to the district officer for land located outside the municipality or sanitary district or in other cases with the mayor for land located in a municipality. Such a claim must be made within one year after payment or after the day on which an appeal has been decided. An appeal to the provincial governor can be made within 30 days of assessment notification. Appeals to the courts regarding a decision rendered by the governor can also be made within 30 days of the decision.

Surcharges and penalties

A taxpayer who fails to file a tax return within the specified period is liable to pay an additional 10 per cent of the assessed taxes. This surcharge is reduced to 5 per cent if the taxpayer later files a tax return on his own volition. In reporting information which reduces his tax liability, the taxpayer is liable for the deficient taxes and an additional 10 per cent on the deficient amount. A taxpayer who misinforms a survey official regarding the area of his property for the purposes of tax reduction is liable to pay double the increase of the additional taxes. Late payments are subject to a surcharge of 20 per cent per annum on the tax arrears.

Perjury for whatever reason can lead to imprisonment for a period not exceeding 6 months or a fine not exceeding 2,000 baht or both. A taxpayer who fails to show land location and size and to observe a tax official's instructions may be imprisoned for a period of one month and fined a sum of 1,000 baht or both. A similar penalty may be imposed for obstructing a tax official in the discharge of his duty.

Issues

The major problem of the Land Development Tax relates to the level of tax rates which are not only regressive because they fall less heavily on highly priced land, but also because they are extremely low by international standards. In addition, the medium value used as the tax base should be reviewed every four years, however, at present 1978 medium values are still being applied, as a result of unsettled criteria in land appraisal and unfinished tax amendment legislation.

Recent developments and conclusions

It is obvious that there are many problems and loop-holes in both the House and Buildings Tax and the Land Development Tax. There have been several attempts to amend the laws which have resulted in relatively minor changes. This may be due to the broad effects of both taxes on taxpayers, thus any attempt to change the taxes would tend to attract opposition from both taxpayers and politicians who scrutinize the bill in the House of Representatives. So far, the structure of the taxes has remained largely intact and changes which have occurred relate to how taxes are paid, changing membership of local assessment committees, etc.

In 1995 the government designed a draft act to replace both taxes which proposed to abolish both taxes and introduce a new property tax, retaining the name Land Development Tax. Unlike the current tax structure where there are many loopholes from tax assessments and exemptions, the structure of new property tax has as its assessment base property value, including both land and buildings. More importantly under the new tax the exemption for owner occupied properties is removed. Under the new proposal the collection organizations, penalties, reliefs and concessions remain as per the present system. However, the new tax proposal is still under review by the government, since if it is passed, there is likely to a redistributive impact on taxpayers.

References

The Land Development Tax Act of 1954.
The House and Buildings Tax Act of 1932.
Royal Decree for Medium Land Value Assessment for 1986, 1988, 1989, 1990-1993.
Royal Decree for Exempting Royal Property of 1943.
Royal Decree for Using House and Buildings Act of 1932 inside and outside Municipal Jurisdiction of 1973.

Lewchalermwong, A. (1972), *Taxation and Tax Reform in Thailand*, Kurusapha Press, Bangkok, Thailand.

Ingram, J.C. (1971), *Economic change in Thailand 1850-1970*, Oxford University Press, Singapore, 1971.

Lent, G.E. and Hirao, T. (1970), *A Survey of Thailand's Tax Structure*, Fiscal Affair Department, International Monetary Fund.

Dhiratayakinant, K. (1990), *Urban Finance: Existing Situation and Future Alternatives*, Thailand Development Research Institution Foundation, Bangkok.

8   Immovable property taxation in Cyprus

Panayiotis Panayiotou, Frances Plimmer,
Antonakis Panayi and David Jenkins

Introduction

There are several taxes in Cyprus which are levied on the basis of the value of landed properties. Some of these are paid to the local authority and some are paid to central government. The taxes and rates levied by the Government of Cyprus on immovable property are: Immovable Property Tax of 1980, Town Rate, Improvement Rate, Towns Tax, Estate Duty Taxation, Capital Gains Tax, Betterment Charge and Sewerage Charges.

Property taxes levied by local authorities afford some financial independence from central government, thus reducing central government's burden of providing local services. The central government is a recipient of the revenues from the Immovable Property Tax of 1980, Towns Tax, Estate Duty, Capital Gains Tax and Betterment Charge. Municipalities and Improvement Boards are the recipients of the Town Rate and Improvement Rate respectively. The Sewerage Charges are received by the local Sewerage Councils. Betterment Charge law has not been applied, mainly because of difficulties in defining the area in which betterment has occurred and also in providing the quantum of the betterment.

Overview

The Republic of Cyprus is the third largest island in the Mediterranean with an area of 3,572 square miles (9,251 square kilometres) and a population of approximately 700,000 (see Figure 8.1 for a map of Cyprus). Its open-based economy is relatively poor in natural resources and is thus highly dependent on the import and export of goods and services. The Cypriot Employers and Industrialists Federation (1996) explain that since its independence in 1960, Cyprus's development has been internationally acknowledged as a success story

163

in both the economic and social fields. Despite the acute political problems which emerged in 1974 when Turkey invaded the island, occupying about 38 per cent of its territory, the economy quickly recovered as a result of the concerted efforts of both the public and the private sector.

Kotsonis (1990) explained that after the establishment of the Republic in 1960, agriculture continued to be a backbone of the economy of the island. However, with the post-independence days came the boom of an expanding tourist industry, coupled with an unprecedented residential, commercial and industrial expansion. All this exerted a tremendous pressure on the limited available land resources and the competition of uses became more acute.

Administration

The Republic of Cyprus, for administration purposes, is divided into six districts (Lefkosia (or Nicosia), Ammochostos (or Famagusta), Larnaka, Lemesos (or Limassol), Keryneia (or Kyrenia) and Pafos). The island's capital and seat of Government is Lefkosia. Each district is headed by the District Officer who is essentially the local representative of central government. The District Officer acts as the chief co-ordinator and liaison for the activities of all ministries. The administrative power in Cyprus is a two tier system, but the structure is rather centralized, delegating limited power to the local authorities from central government. There are three types of local authorities: Municipalities, Improvement Board Areas, and the Villages. Municipalities have more power and a larger population than the other local authorities. According to the 111/1985 law, one of the limits of an area to be a municipality is its population, which must not be less than 5,000.

The Lands and Surveys Department for administration purposes is divided into six District Offices and a Headquarters. Because Turkish troops occupy Keryneia and part of Ammochostos, their District Offices are situated in Lefkosia and in Larnaka respectively. According to the Immovable Property (Tenure, Registration and Valuation) Law, Capital 224, 1946, Cyprus's Lands and Surveys Department is entrusted to produce valuations of all taxable landed property for taxation purposes. This is called a general valuation and occurs whenever required by the Council of Ministers, and so far this has occurred only in 1909 and 1980. The basis of tax assessments used in Cyprus today have been the 'market value' and the 'assessed value'. Market values were used to produce the capital value as at 1 January 1980 of immovable property, based on sales evidence of open market transactions: this was the last general valuation. 'Assessed' value is the 1909 value, based on the experience of Lands and Surveys Department's employees who at the time had no sales records on which to base open market valuations. It can be argued that the assessed value was only an approximation of the 1909 open market value because it was performed by non-qualified valuers based on their professional experience alone and that the evidence of open market sales at that time was very limited. Both values are used as a base for various taxes on landed properties.

Overview of taxes

The Immovable Property Tax of 1980 (Law 24/1980 amended by the Laws 60/ 80, 68/80, 25/81 and 10/84)

This is levied by the state on the open market capital value as at 1 January 1980, on all of an owner's property. The owner may be either a legal body or private individual who is registered in the Lands and Surveys Department records or who is entitled to be registered, according to sections 9 and 10 of the Immovable Property Law, Capital 224. According to section 9, no title to immovable property shall be acquired by any person by adverse possession against the Republic or a registered owner. According to section 10, subject to the provisions of section 9, if a person can provide proof of undisputed and uninterrupted adverse possession for a period of 30 years, that person shall be entitled to be registered as the owner. Properties belonging to the state, the municipalities and the communities (i.e. villages) are exempt, so are churches, places of worship, non-profit making organizations, properties owned by farmers in rural areas and properties owned by foreign states for diplomatic purposes. Markides (1991) explained that the current law replaced the old laws 30/77, 38/78 and 93/79 under which the tax was levied on 1909 (assessed) values of properties. The tax is payable to the state on 30 September each year. The rates at 1980 market value based on the value of an owner's properties are as follows:

up to £100,000	-	0.2% for legal bodies and 0% for individuals
from £100,001 to 250,000	-	0.2%
from £250,001 to 500,000	-	0.3%
from £500,001	-	0.35%

Delays on tax payment are penalized with 9 per cent interest on the outstanding amount.

The Town Rate (Capital 240 and Laws 64/1964, 15/1966)

This is paid to the municipalities on all immovable property of legal bodies or individuals, according to the municipality Law 111/85 (as amended), within the administrative limits of any municipal corporation. Properties belonging to the state and the municipalities are exempt, as are churches, places of worship, charitable institutions and properties owned by foreign states for diplomatic purposes. The 1995 rate was 0.05 per cent on the market value of such property as at 1 January 1980 as is registered or recorded in the books of the District Lands Office. The tax is payable to the municipality on 30 June. A penalty of 5 per cent is levied on payments made after the 30 September.

The Improvement Rate Law (Capital 243 and the amendment Laws 46/61, 58/ 62, 4/66, 31/69, 7/79, 49/79, 65/79, 7/80, 27/82, 42/83, 72/83, 38/84, 72/87 and 66/89)

This tax is levied on all immovable properties within the geographical limits of any improvement area. According to the Villages (Administration and Improvement) Law, Capital 243, an improvement area is any area declared by the Council of Ministers as an 'improvement area', for improvement purposes (i.e. construction of roads, national parks). Properties belonging to the state and the Improvement Boards are exempt, as are churches, charitable institutions and properties owned by foreign states for diplomatic purposes. The tax rate, decided by the Improvement Board is subject to the approval of the government. This is up to 1.5 per cent on the 1909 assessed value of such property as registered or recorded in the books of the District Lands Offices. This tax is payable to the Improvement Boards by the owner on the 30 June each year and is used to support improvements and local services. A penalty of 5 per cent is levied on payments made after the 30 September.

The Immovable Property (Towns) Tax (Laws 89/1962 and 73/1965)

This is levied on immovable property in towns or other areas defined by the Council of Ministers as 'Towns', according to section 3. The tax rate is 1.5 per cent on the 1909 assessed value of property as registered or recorded in the books of the District Lands Offices. Properties belonging to the state, municipalities, communities are exempt, as are churches, charitable institutions and properties owned by foreign states for diplomatic purposes. It is payable on 30 June of each year. Payments after the 30 September are fined by 5 per cent on the amount payable. This tax is collected by the state and is allocated to the Ministry of Education (note: it has replaced the Education Tax).

The Estate Duty Taxation (Law 67/62 and the amendment Laws 71/68, 3/76, 13/ 85, 93/86, 138/86, 323/87, 66(1)/94, 6(1)/96, 78(1)/96, 17(1)/97)

This is levied on immovable properties left by a deceased and is collected by the state. The properties are valued at their open market capital value as at the date of death. For deaths before 1 December 1942, Estate Duty is not levied. According to the amendment Law 138/86, inheritances due on deaths after 17 October 1986 incur the following level of relief:

£50,000	-	for husband or wife surviving;
£75,000	-	for every child under 21 years old at the date of death;
£75,000	-	for every disabled child surviving;
£50,000	-	for a 21 years old child;
£50,000	-	for all the children surviving.

Furthermore, there are rebates in some cases where the heir is a non-profit making organization or religious organization. These cases are examined by the state individually. Additionally, according to the 17(1)/97 amendment law, if the property left by the deceased is a residence used by the deceased or his/her family and the open market capital value at the date of death is less than £150,000 tax is not levied on heirs. The rates of tax on evaluated immovable property are as follows:

up to £20,000	-	0%
from £20,001 to £25,000	-	10%
from £25,001 to £35,000	-	13%
from £35,001 to £55,000	-	15%
from £55,001 to £80,000	-	17%
from £80,001 to £105,000	-	20%
from £105,001 to £150,000	-	23%
from £150,000	-	30%

These rates are valid from March 1997.

The Capital Gains Tax (law 52/1980 and 135/1990)

Capital Gains Tax applies to both individuals and companies. Owners are charged at 20 per cent on gains arising from the disposal of immovable property and shares in a company which owns immovable property. Gains are based on the open market capital values as at 1 January 1980 (or actual cost if acquired later) adjusted for the increase in the Consumer Price Index (CPI) up to the date of sale. Tax is paid to the state, and the main exemptions include:

1   immovable properties left by a deceased (which is liable to Estate Duty);

2   immovable properties given as a gift:

- from parents to children;

- from husband to wife and vice versa;

- from relatives up to second generation relatives (e.g. grandfather to grandchild).

Betterment Charge (Law 90/1972 Section 80)

The enforcement of the provisions of the Town and Country Planning Law, 1972 may cause an increase in value of immovable property. Such an increase may result either from a change to a more profitable use, or a higher density, or it may come about after the carrying out of development by a public authority in an area. Nicolaides et al (1983a) commented that in the same way as it is 'fair' to pay compensation to owners whose property rights are being materially adversely affected, it could be argued that it would also be fair to ask from those owners whose properties are being benefited by public activities to pay back at least some part of their gain. One way for the state to collect betterment is the levying of a Betterment Charge. Betterment Charge is levied on the increase in value which is attributable to the scheme. The betterment is ascertained by the carrying out of two open market capital valuations, one at the date prior to the scheme and a second one at a date falling within the period starting two years after the date of the decision and finishing two years after the date of completion of the scheme. The difference between the two valuations, after deducting any increase which is not attributable to the scheme, is the 'betterment' which is subject to the charge. Betterment Charge has been fixed up to a maximum of 30 per cent on the betterment, and is payable to the state in 20 annual instalments. Betterment Charge has not yet been levied because of:

1   the difficulties in defining the area in which betterment has occurred and also in proving the quantum of the betterment;

2   limited number of staff of the Lands and Surveys Department;

3   the use of manual procedures by the Department; and

4   the political cost.

Sewerage Charges (Law 1/1971)

The aim of this law is the establishment, construction, control and administration of sewerage systems, including the processing and the disposal of waste. The Sewerage Council, according to section 30 of the law, has the right to levy tax and fees. The tax is levied on the open market capital value as at 1 January 1980 and is payable on 30 September each year. Sewerage charges are levied on landed properties in areas where sewerage systems were constructed and are in use. The rates vary depending on the property type e.g. in Larnaka, in 1995, the rates on hotels, hotel apartments and industries was 0.932 per cent and for all other property types was 0.285 per cent. Sewerage charges are also levied on properties in areas where sewerage systems are under construction, e.g. in Larnaka, in 1995, for all property types, the rate was 0.07 per cent. However, charges on landed properties in areas where systems are under-used are likely to be replaced by charges levied on water consumption. The argument for this is that it is a fairer method for those areas, since the greater the water consumption, the greater the use of sewerage systems.

Origins and evolution

Kotsonis (1990) commented that evidence uncovered in a 5th century BC excavation at Dali village revealed that the King of Idalion and the town itself rewarded a physician who had cured those wounded during a siege with the grant of royal lands, to the value of one silver talent in full ownership. Kotsonis explained that this indicated there was then not only royal lands but also land in private ownership, describing the properties donated as neighbouring lands of certain named individuals. The inscription also indicates the existence of land taxation and rights of inheritance even in those early days.

Ioannou (1990) and Markides (1991) explained that the property tax system in Cyprus dates back to the Ottoman Empire. The Turks were the first to introduce a system of property tax during the period 1850-1878, which has been altered through the years to accommodate the subsequent administrators and social changes. The first general valuation began in 1909 under the Law 12/907 by which a cadastral survey, registration and valuation to cover the whole island was authorized. The general valuation was completed some 20 years after it was first started. The values adopted (1909) were known as assessed values and were based on the experience of Lands and Surveys Department's employees after visiting the areas, e.g. villages, and not always after an inspection of individual properties. The valuers were unable to use sale records because they did not exist. Today, the assessment is a desk-based exercise and it can be argued that these assessed values are suspect because of the extremely low values of properties in 1909 compared with today's values and the fact that it is not worth applying appropriate valuation methods for such little return. The general valuation was used for property taxation as soon as it was completed and currently the 1909 assessment is still used as the basis for the Towns Tax (previously the Education Tax) and the Improvement Rate.

The second general valuation was carried out for a specific purpose and only covered the sewerage areas of Lefkosia and Ammochostos at 1971 values in order to levy tax for the establishment of a sewerage system. This is a general valuation for specific purposes and could not be used as a tax base for other taxation purposes. This tax was in fact levied only in Lefkosia because in 1974 Ammochostos was invaded by Turkish troops.

The third general valuation was carried out for the whole of Cyprus (except the occupied area) at 1980 values and is known as the market (capital) values of 1 January 1980. It was completed in 1991 and its main purpose was to create a record of uniform values all over the country for all purposes e.g. central government taxation, municipalities rating. It is already in use for the Immovable Property Tax, Town Rate (previously the Municipal Tax), Sewerage Charges and Capital Gains Tax, but not for the Towns Tax and Improvement Rate.

The place of the tax within the general tax system

Taxation of landed property has always been a significant financial resource for the socio-economic development of the island because such resources have been extensively used for local authority services, education, sewerage, construction of roads and generally for the improvement of areas.

Statistics on the size of the tax base

Table 8.1
Government ordinary revenue raised by Immovable Property Tax (1980), Towns Tax, Estate Duty and Capital Gains Tax

Year	Im. Pr. Tax 1980 £	Towns Tax £	Estate Duty £	Capital Gains Tax £	Betterment Charge
1991	4,754,000	449,000	1,433,000	5,001,000	-
1992	3,461,000	348,000	2,373,000	4,719,000	-
1993	2,997,000	410,000	2,203,000	5,181,000	-
1994	3,126,000	408,000	2,022,000	5,974,000	-
1995	5,949,000	488,000	2,318,000	9,336,000	-
Total	20,287,000	2,103,000	10,349,000	30,211,000	-

Table 8.2
Calculated Town Rate and Improvement Rate by the Lands and Surveys Department and sewerage revenue from tax levied on landed properties

Year	Town Rate	Improvement Rate	Sewerage Charges
1991	502,796	101,438	2,465,714
1992	761,319	104,502	4,050,446
1993	1,204,970	130,823	5,462,187
1994	1,835,115	114,889	6,520,881
1995	2,013,885	101,260	8,472,102
Total	6,318,085	552,912	26,971,330

Total revenue raised

Table 8.3
Total government ordinary revenue raised by Immovable Property Tax (1980), Towns Tax, Estate Duty and Capital Gains Tax

Year	Total £
1991	11,637,000
1992	10,901,000
1993	10,791,000
1994	11,530,000
1995	18,091,000
Total	62,950,000

Comparison with other taxes

According to the Statistical Abstract (1994) and the Financial Report (1995) the most important sources of government revenue is Income Tax, as a direct tax, and Import Duties, as an indirect tax (see Table 8.4).

Table 8.4
Government ordinary revenue raised by Income Tax, Import Duties and Excise

Year	Income Tax (Direct Tax) £	Import Duties (Indirect Tax) £	Excise (Indirect Tax) £
1991	131,075,000	100,170,000	80,600,000
1992	154,390,000	108,402,000	96,670,000
1993	169,513,000	88,446,000	67,794,000
1994	217,075,000	88,167,000	98,900,000
1995	237,239,000	91,830,000	118,535,000
Total	909,292,000	477,015,000	462,499,000

Table 8.5
Government ordinary revenue raised by Lands and Surveys Fees

Year	Lands & Surveys fees (Direct Tax) £	Lands & Surveys fees (Indirect Tax) £	Lands & Surveys fees (Sale of Goods & Services) £	Total £
1991	3,341,000	6,809,000	3,341,000	13,491,000
1992	4,083,000	8,276,000	4,084,000	16,443,000
1993	4,130,000	8,241,000	4,130,000	16,501,000
1994	5,277,000	10,504,000	5,277,000	21,058,000
1995	6,136,000	12,248,000	6,136,000	24,520,000
Total	22,967,000	46,078,000	22,968,000	92,013,000

The total revenue raised by Immovable Property Tax (1980), Towns Tax, Estate Duty and Capital Gains Tax from 1991 to 1995 is £62,950,000 (see Tables 8.1, 8.2 and 8.3). This means that this revenue is 1.7 per cent of the total government income, (total revenue raised by taxes levied on landed properties divided by total government revenue). Furthermore, this revenue is 10.9 per cent of the total government development expenditure, (total revenue raised by taxes levied on landed properties divided by total government development expenditure).

172

Both taxes in Table 8.1 and Lands and Surveys Fees in Table 8.5 are government revenue. The total amount raised by those categories is 4.2 per cent of the total government income and 26.8 per cent of the total development expenditures. Income tax provides the greatest contribution to the government revenue. Immovable Property Tax is 2.2 per cent of Income Tax (Immovable Property Tax divided by Income Tax).

Table 8.6
Government total revenue raised, development and ordinary expenditures

Year	Government Total Revenue £	Government Dev Expenditure £	Gorvernment Ord Expenditure £
1991	563,142,000	90,082,000	794,232,000
1992	635,219,000	104,807,000	803,603,000
1993	731,500,000	114,977,000	915,985,000
1994	847,530,000	120,948,000	1,011,108,000
1995	940,475,000	146,325,000	1,112,400,000
Total	3,717,866,000	577,139,000	4,637,268,000

Purpose of the tax

The Immovable Property Tax of 1980, Estate Duty, and Betterment Charge are spent by central government under normal development expenditures. Town Rates and Improvement Rates are collected by municipalities and Improvement Boards respectively. These are incorporated into their budgets for administration and development projects e.g. public works, roads. The Towns Tax is spent by the Ministry of Education for educational purposes and Sewerage Charges are spent by Sewerage Councils for the construction and maintenance of sewerage systems.

Basis of assessment

The unit of assessment for taxation purposes is immovable property, as defined by the Immovable Property Law, 1946, at its highest and best use with all improvements. According to the Immovable Property (Tenure, Registration and Valuation) Law, section 2, 1946, immovable property includes land, buildings, trees, wells, water rights and easements.

According to the Immovable Property Law, Cap. 224, 2 of 8/53: 'value in connection with immovable property, means the amount which the immovable property, if sold in the open market by a willing seller to a willing purchaser, might be expected to realize', i.e. its capital value, based on open market transactions. The basis of general valuations in Cyprus has been capital value since the second general valuation in 1971 in Lefkosia and Ammochostos; it was also used in the third general valuation in 1980 for the whole of the country (except for the occupied area). Capital value was used after the establishment of the Immovable Property (Tenure, Registration and Valuation) Law in 1946 for other purposes such as compensation for compulsory acquisition. A capital value basis satisfies general valuation criteria and has fewer practical problems in Cyprus than annual value because of the Rent Control Law (23/83 and the amendment laws) which limits free market rental information required as market evidence for valuing residential and retail properties.

Landed properties are sold on the open market by a willing seller to a willing purchaser and this represents a useful volume of open market sales as evidence of comparable transactions. In Cyprus, whilst sale evidence exists, there is not a large volume of sales. However, it can be argued that these limited sales transactions provide strong and sufficient evidence for a capital value tax base, with the condition that sales are reliable, genuine and not understated. The capital value basis is an approach based on the full open market capital value of immovable property in its existing condition, with all developments, improvements, and potentialities (considering the best use of property).

Responsibility for making assessments

According to the Immovable Property (Tenure, Registration and Valuation) Law, Capital 224, Section 69, the Lands and Surveys Department in Cyprus is required to produce a valuation of landed property for taxation purposes, called a general valuation, whenever and wherever required by the Council of Ministers for the purposes of securing the up-to-date and uniform valuation of immovable property in any municipality, village or quarter.

According to section 67, any immovable property can be revalued at the instance of the Director or on the application of the registered owner at any time after five years from the date of the last valuation, provided that the property has materially changed, causing a substantial increase or decrease in value or if a general valuation has been ordered.

General valuation criteria

According to legal advice given by the General Attorney of the Republic of Cyprus (35/69, dated 20 September 1969), the following legal principles must be applied in a general valuation:

1   equal treatment of the taxpayers by the state and the fixing of the taxpaying ability on the basis of objective criteria;

2   for general purposes, a revaluation must cover the whole state;

3   for specific purposes, the valuation must cover the whole area which is specifically affected; and

4   a valuation for specific purposes cannot be used for general purposes.

Under the first principle, the Attorney-General requires not only equal treatment of taxpayers but also requires that the tax levied be an amount reasonably payable. Under the third principle, when the Council of Ministers in Cyprus decides to levy a new tax in order to develop a project in a specific area and for specific purpose e.g. construction and maintenance of a sewerage system such as in Lefkosia, the municipality requires a revaluation, known as a 'general valuation for specific purposes'. The last principle means that if a revaluation is made for a specific area for a specific purpose e.g. a sewerage system, it can not be used to levy the Town Rate which is for general purposes. If it is applied in this way, then it will be in conflict with the first criteria of equal treatment of taxpayers because each valuation is carried out using different criteria e.g. date of valuation.

The Lands and Surveys Department has developed both manual and computerized systems for maintaining sales records. The manual system will be abandoned as soon as the Cyprus Land Information System is developed and the integration between the legal and fiscal data of properties and plans is provided for the whole of Cyprus. This will enable valuers to read sales information simultaneously with plan information. The present manual system offers only limited access to this facility. As soon as a contract of sale is deposited or a sale is accepted, land clerks write a file number, date and price on the back of plans used by the valuation section. So whenever a valuer works on a specific area, sales information is available on the back of the plan. Property sales information (excluding the specific set of plans) are sold to the private sector, to valuers and to real estate agents in hardcopy and in digital formats.

The majority of assessors in the Lands and Surveys Department were trained in courses organized by the Department. Some of the staff are university graduates in real estate management and valuation, law and economics.

Furthermore, some land officers of the Headquarters in Nicosia are members of the Royal Institution of Chartered Surveyors and members of the Scientific and Technical Chamber of Cyprus which is the local professional organization recognized by the Government. Locally trained staff are supervised by the qualified staff at the Headquarters.

Use of private sector assessors

General valuation assessment is the sole responsibility of the Lands and Surveys Department. The private sector may be used by the owners in order to question or appeal the Lands and Surveys' assessments and decisions.

Frequency of valuations

According to the section 70 of the Immovable Property Law, Capital 224, when a general valuation has been ordered under section 69, the following provisions take effect:

1   the Director of the Lands and Surveys Department publishes a general valuation notice to inform the public that a general valuation will take place;

2   when the valuation is completed, the Director prepares a valuation list which is deposited by the Director and the Chairman of the town, village or quarter and is also published in the official Gazette of the Republic. The valuation list is used to inform people about property values.

Within 60 days from the date of the notice, any person whose property is affected may object in writing to the Director. Nicolaides et al (1983b) explained that an owner must deposit a fee equal to 1 per cent of the difference between his own valuation and the valuation appearing in the valuation list. The purpose of this limitation is to discourage owners from supplying the Director with inadequate or false information. The Director examines any objections submitted to him with the required fee and notifies the person objecting of his decision. If the owner is not satisfied with the Director's decision, he has the right to appeal to the Court.

Revaluation of individual properties

According to Section 71 of the Immovable Property Law, Capital 224, a revaluation of any individual property can be made at the instance of the Director. The Director may give notice of the proposed valuation or revaluation to the person or persons affected, requiring the owner to supply the valuer with information about the immovable property and, if it is necessary, to give the valuer the opportunity to inspect the property. When a valuation or a revaluation has been made, the Director gives notice of the value to the owner of the affected property. The owner may object in writing to the Director within 30 days from the date of receipt of such notice. The Director may consider any objection made to him and notify the person objecting of his decision. If the owner is not satisfied with the Director's decision, there is a right of appeal to the court.

Notification of assessed value

Once a year the municipalities or the district officers supply the Lands and Surveys Department with a list of building permits issued in their respective areas. The Director of Lands and Surveys Department orders the revaluation of the properties with the effective date being that of the last general valuation, that is, 1 January 1980. Valuers visit the properties, complete a standard revaluation form and estimate values manually. Because of the great number of revaluation cases, the use of manual methods and the limited number of staff of the Department, valuation lists are not posted, as required by the section 71 of the Law. However, owners are informed of the date of tax payments.

Appeals procedure

For the dates of tax payments, owners are reminded by the mass media. In the case of sewerage charges, notices of property values are sent to taxpayers by mail. Owners may not pay their tax and object in writing to the Director. The Director considers any objection made to him and notifies the person objecting of his decision.

Appeals system

If an owner is not satisfied with the decision of the Director of the Lands and Surveys Department regarding the valuation of a certain property, he has the right to resort to the District Court. The District Court after hearing both parties (the owner and the Department) will give its decision on the market value to be adopted. If either party feels that the decision of the District Court is not correct, an appeal may be made to the High Court. Individuals and legal bodies are represented by attorneys at all appeal cases and may hire expert property valuers and surveyors. An appeal does not postpone the deadline for payment and tax payments are fined with the pre-defined rate of interest on the payment amount.

The number of appeals is generally quite small because owners are normally satisfied with the assessed property values. As values are estimated as at 1 January 1980, owners have the illusion that the taxes are based on underestimated values. The constitution of Cyprus does not allow the use of valuation tribunals.

Methods of assessment

Capital values are achieved using comparisons made by Lands and Surveys Department based on open market transactions of similar properties for the last two general valuations because:

1   of the availability of appropriate sales records of immovable properties;

2   sales of immovable properties in the open market are the same as 'capital value' with the provision that they are reliable and genuine and not understated. Furthermore, if a property sale is much higher than similar property sales in the same area, these may not be included as sales evidence in a general valuation because the sale price may include other assets, e.g. goodwill; and

3   it is the simplest and most direct method of valuation.

The profits and contractor's valuation methods are not widely used because they are not as reliable as the comparative method which, moreover, is accepted by the Cyprus courts.

Use of mass appraisal techniques

Manual appraisal techniques were used for the 1909 and 1980 general valuations. The Lands and Surveys Department is in the process of computerizing and developing the Cyprus Integrated Land Information System (CILIS), with mass appraisal techniques being designed and developed by the CSC Datacentralen A/S, Denmark. Datacentralen is the software and hardware supplier to the Department since it succeeded in an international 'request for tenders' competition in 1995. According to the contract between the government and Datacentralen, CILIS will be delivered by the end of 1998. As soon as the Council of Ministers decide to perform the next general valuation, this will be implemented using the developed mass appraisal techniques.

When it was decided to introduce a fully computerized Land Information and Management System, the Department of Lands and Surveys invited Sagric

International to carry out research and prepare the request for tender documents (RFT) in 1991. The main proposal in the area of computer assisted mass appraisal systems (CAMAS) was to utilize simple multiple regression analysis. The Danish valuation system known as the 'Total Value System' or the 'base home approach' is based on multiple regression analysis.

Exemptions, reliefs and concessions

Properties belonging to the state, the municipalities and the communities (i.e. villages) are exempt. Additionally churches, places of worship, non-profit making organizations and properties owned by foreign states for diplomatic purposes are also exempt. It should also be noted that in Cyprus, central government taxes and local authorities rates are mainly payable by those owners whose property is located within municipal, town and improvement board areas. Thus, properties in rural areas are not affected directly by taxation laws. The Immovable Property Tax of the 1980 affects rural areas, provided that the owner is not a farmer and the total value of the owner's property exceeds £100,000. There are three main reasons for this:

1   to motivate people to develop agriculture and farming without the burden of taxes on the landed properties;

2   to discourage people from leaving rural areas and moving to towns, by reducing the cost of living in the rural areas; and

3   the reduction of administrative costs. Generally, land values in rural areas are much lower than values in towns, so an economic tax system in rural areas would have relatively high rates of tax, unless some form of complex equalization of funds was introduced by the state.

Properties entitled to relief

The following properties are exempt from Towns Tax (S.9, Law 89 of 1962), Town Rate (S.92, Cap. 240) and Improvement Rate (S35 D, Cap. 243):

1   any public burial ground;

2   any church, chapel, mosque, meeting house or premises or such part thereof as shall be exclusively appropriated to public religious worship;

3   any premises used as public hospitals;

4   any immovable property:

- held and registered in the books of the District Lands Office in trust for any school operating under any Law in force for the time being relating to Elementary or Secondary or Higher Education (this last for Towns Tax and Improvement Rate only);

- belonging to the Republic;

- owned or used exclusively for the purposes of any charitable institution of a public character supported mainly by endowments or voluntary contributions in so far as such immovable property is held for such purposes. (Such properties will not be exempt from taxation unless and until local enquiry is held on the application by the institution concerned and on payment of fees for the purpose, and the Director to whom the report of the DLO, is referred signifies his approval for such exemption);

5   'Supply Lines' belonging to the Electricity Authority of Cyprus. 'Supply Line' (S.2 Cap. 171) includes any building or apparatus connected with a conductor, etc., for the purpose of transforming, etc., electricity (S.25, Cap. 171);

6   property owned by any foreign state and used by such state as an embassy or consulate or as an official residence of the diplomatic representative of that state, provided that such state has signed the 1961 Vienna Agreement on Diplomatic Privileges (Art. 23 of the Agreement, Law 40/68).

The following properties are exempt from Towns Tax (S. 9, Law 89 of 1962) and Improvement Rate (S. 35D Cap. 243):

1   property owned by the offices or any other body or authority of any Communal Chamber of the Republic;

2   property registered or recorded in the books of the District Lands Office as common pasture ground;

3   property recorded or assigned *abantiquo* for the common use of the community. (This includes all village domestic water supplies, whether issuing from wells or otherwise (D.L.S. 314/48 of 24.1.1951).

The following properties are exempt from Town Tax (S.9, Law 89/62 as amended by S. 2 of Law 73/65):

Property owned by a municipality or a public utility body. The Council of Ministers must decide on this after recommendations by the Minister of Finance and the Council of Ministers may impose on this such conditions as they may think fit.

Property belonging to the Improvement Board of the area are exempt from Improvement Rate (S.35D, Cap 243)

Reference should be made to the provisions of the Persons who sustained Losses (Exemption from Taxation) Temporary Provisions Law, 62/1975. This is a temporary Law and it affects all immovable property which is situated in the area or is adjacent to the area occupied by Turkish troops. Such properties are temporarily exempt from taxation. On the approval of the Director of Lands and Surveys Department, any tax paid for the year 1974, is refunded to the owners of such property. (S. 2-3, Law 62/75).

Collection procedures

The central government tax collectors are located in each district and are responsible for the collection of Immovable Property Tax of 1980, Towns Tax and Capital Gains Tax. Municipalities and Improvement Boards collect Town Rate and Improvement Rate respectively. Sewerage Boards collect the sewerage charges. Taxes are payable, in one payment, within a specified period of time applicable throughout the country.

Liability for the tax

Generally the payment of taxes in Cyprus is the responsibility of the owner. Where legal ownership records are not updated, usually taxes are paid by those beneficiaries who are entitled to be registered as owners. Frequently leaseholders of government land have not been asked to pay taxes.

Computation of the tax

The rates of the Immovable Property Tax of 1980, Towns Tax, Estate Duty and Capital Gains Tax are determined by the Ministry of Finance and are approved by the House of Representatives. Town Rates and Sewerage Charges are imposed by municipalities and the Sewerage Boards respectively subject to the approval by the government. Improvement Rate is imposed by the government and collected by the respective Improvement Boards. There is no differential taxation on land and buildings since all taxes are levied on property as it stands.

Enforcement procedures

Enforcement procedures for the collection of taxes are provided by law. Late payments generally carry interest and in some cases, penalties. Delays on Immovable Property Tax payment are liable to 9 per cent interest on the payment amount and delays on Town Rate, Improvement Rate and Towns Tax are each fined with 5 per cent interest. It is worth noting that in order for a property to be transferred to another person, the owner must present proof that he has paid all the taxes related to the property. As a consequence the government and the local authorities can be sure that all taxes and interest will have been paid.

Penalties

When the total amount of tax owed by an owner represents a substantial sum, the authority may decide to sue the owner. In that case, the owner may be liable to a fine or imprisonment.

Critical analysis

The 1909 and 1980 general valuations are used as the base for a number of taxes. The basis of assessment should ideally be a single valuation base, since uniformity of property values is one of the general valuation purposes and conforms to the legal principle of the Attorney-General, i.e. equal treatment of taxpayers. Furthermore, property taxes, e.g. the Immovable Property Tax, the Town Rate, the Improvement Rate and the Towns Tax should be a single tax paid to a single authority because it would be easier for owners to pay one tax to one authority instead of paying several taxes to many authorities. Additionally, central government and local authorities' administration expenses would be reduced significantly.

If capital values for a general valuation are kept updated at regular intervals, for example every two or three years or whenever an assessment ratio study indicates that reassessment is needed (IAAO, 1990), the assessment of tax will be based on what actually exists on the land, including buildings, at the date of taxation. It can be argued that this is an equitable system since the capital value reflects all the valuable characteristics of the property. It increases the social equity of the tax because it reflects current values and up-to-date relativities of 'wealth' (assuming 'wealth' equates to capital value and not exclusively to taxpaying income). Examples of an out-of-date assessment tax system are the Town Tax and the Improvement Rate, simply because the 1909 assessed values are used as a basis of taxation even though these values have no relation to the actual values of the properties taxed.

If an owner's properties are located in Strovolos Municipality only, in that part of the area affected by Towns Tax, and the following values apply:

	evaluated at 1980 Capital Values	evaluated at 1909 General Valuation
building site	£15,000	£50
house	£30,000	£250
apartment	£20,000	£200
Total	£65,000	£500

Each year the owner would pay the following taxes:

1 Immovable Property Tax of 1980. As the total value of the owner's property is less than £100,000, and providing the owner is not a legal body then he is exempt from paying this tax.

2 Town Rate. The rate is 0.05 per cent on the total value of the property in the Municipality, so at 1980 values, the owner will pay £32.50 (£65,000 multiplied by 0.05 per cent).

3 Towns Tax. The rate is 1.5 per cent on the total value of the property in the Municipality, so at 1909 values, the owner will pays £7.50 (£500 multiplied by 1.5 per cent).

The Town Rate is £32.50 because the basis of assessment is 1980 values. An up-to-date valuation base would ensure that taxpayers pay according to an updated liability in proportion with their current relative liabilities, i.e. if someone's property is now worth £30,000, he should pay half the tax of his neighbour, whose property is worth £60,000, even if both properties were worth £15,000 in 1980.

Land records are not updated immediately with landed property changes because manual systems are used at present for the interchange of information between the Lands and Surveys Department and the local authorities.

Recommendations

It is considered (Panayiotou et al., 1997) that all property-based taxes in Cyprus could be improved both from the taxpayers' and the tax collectors' point of view so that an equitable, convenient, certain, up-to-date system would result and the operational and administrative costs decrease. The following recommendations would provide the means for practical improvement, thereby giving local authorities a strong and stable financial foundation on which to build the provision of quality services.

1 The central government of Cyprus should adopt an up-to-date capital value basis of assessment, so as to provide consistency throughout the country.

2 Current capital values will not only assist equity and uniformity but also can be a useful tool to discourage purchasers and vendors from declaring a lower price. Lands and Surveys Department could present capital values of similar properties in the area, as evidence to support estimated sale prices for transfer fee purposes. This would result in greater levels of Capital Gains Tax and transfer fees.

3 Once a revaluation has been carried out and implemented, the new values should be adopted for all taxes.

4 In order to make revaluations more frequent, say every two or three years, it is recommended that the benefits of new technology be utilized. The introduction of Computer Assisted Mass Appraisal (CAMA) systems would assist in estimating property values at a certain date, based on limited sales data, using different techniques for the prediction of a property value, e.g. multiple regression analysis and knowledge-based systems. The best technique will predict values at a certain date, with minimum acceptable mean error, minimum data, minimum cost, fast response, minimum human skill and effort.

5 The Lands and Surveys Department is able to provide digital information on ownership for a number of municipal areas and within five years, for most of the country. Tax collectors, including central government, should use computer technology to send separate bills to each owner, where it is possible, as well as reminders, if necessary.

6 Even if all ownership records in Cyprus are computerized, it will not be possible to estimate an owner's total property market value because Lands and Surveys Department has only started to record personal identity numbers and company registration numbers systematically since 1986. It will lead to erroneous results if Lands and Surveys digital records are used for the calculation of Immovable Property Tax 1980. The Department has to adopt methods to find the ID numbers of the owners where that is possible.

7   Rebates for the poor will make collection more acceptable i.e. recognition that a high property value does not mean a high income.

8   The state should examine the likely effect of merging existing property taxes into a single one, including the resulting procedures of collecting revenues and appeal procedures against those who refuse to pay taxes. Revenue could be distributed to local authorities in those cases where collection is by central government. Since the administration of income is by local authorities, they will not lose financial control. The procedural cost of property taxation will be minimized and as a result the system will be more efficient, cost-effective, time-effective and flexible.

9   The state should examine the inclusion of rural areas which are currently not affected directly by taxation laws, because of the continued rise of land values, the computerization of Lands and Surveys Department, the need for local services and the improvement of those areas. Rates can be regulated by local authorities, and specific rebates or cash-back schemes introduced where and when appropriate.

10   Government should clarify its position as to whether leaseholders should pay taxes as they enjoy services provided by local authorities and central government.

11   Because of the dated records held by the Lands and Surveys Department, the application of computer assisted mass appraisal techniques will not operate efficiently and will result in inaccurate assessments. The Lands and Surveys Department should re-examine the procedures of updating the land records with local authorities and the District Officers. Furthermore, since the last general valuation was in 1980, a further revaluation should be implemented.

Acknowledgements

We would like to thank the Lands and Surveys Department and the Ministry of Finance for the supply of valuable statistical information. We would also like to thank Mr Christoforos Christofi (retired, ex-Senior Land Valuation Officer) for his consistently helpful and valuable comments.

References and Bibliography

Beardshaw, J. (1986), *Direction of the Economy and Public Finance, Economics*, A Student's Guide.

Britton, W., Davies, K. and Johnson, T. (1989), *Modern Methods of Valuation*, 8th edition, Estates Gazette, London.

Cypriot Employers and Industrialists Federation (1996), 'Cyprus', *CBI European Business Handbook*.

Cyprus Betterment Charge Law (90/1972 Section 80).

Cyprus Capital Gains Tax Law (52/1980 and 135/1990).

Cyprus Estate Duty Taxation Law (67/1962 and the amendment Laws 71/68, 3/76, 13/85, 93/86, 138/86).

Cyprus Immovable Property Registration and Valuation Law (12/1907).

Cyprus Immovable Property Tax Law (24/1980 and the amendment Laws 60/1980, 68/1980, 25/1981 and 10/1984).

Cyprus Immovable Property (Tenure, Registration and Valuation) Law (1946), Capital 224.

Cyprus Immovable Property (Towns) Tax Laws (89/1962 and 73/1965).

Cyprus Improvement Rate Law (Capital 243 and the amendment Laws 46/61, 58/62, 4/66, 31/69, 7/79, 49/79, 65/79, 7/80, 27/82, 42/83, 72/83, 38/84, 72/87 and 66/89).

Cyprus Municipalities Law (111/1985).

Cyprus Sewerage Charges Law (1/1971).

Cyprus Town Rate Law (Capital 240 and Laws 64/1964, 15/1966).

Diplomatic Privileges (Law 40/68).

Eckert, J. (1995), *Building A Property Taxation System in Poland using CAV Technology*, paper presented at IRRV 3rd International Conference on Local Government Taxation, Copenhagen.

General Attorney of the Republic of Cyprus (35/69).

Harvey, J. (1989a), The Incidence of Taxation on Land Resources, Urban Land Economics, *The Economics of Real Property*.

Harvey, J. (1989b), Theory of Urban Public Finance, Urban Land Economics, *The Economics of Real Property*.

International Association of Assessing Officers, (1978), *Assessment-Ratio Studies and the Measurement of Assessment Performance*, Chicago, United States.

Ioannou, C. (1990), Immovable Property Taxes and Rates, Cadastre, Functions, Main Laws and Proceedings.

Kotsonis, A. (1990), *Multi-Purpose Cadastre in the Context of Cyprus*, Seminar on Land Information Management in the Developing World, Adelaide, South Australia.

Lipsey, R.G. (1987), Aims and objectives of Government policy, *An Introduction to Positive Economics*.

Markides, C. (1991), *Immovable Property Taxes, Historical Review and Cadastre Proceedings 1857-1990*, Lands and Surveys Department, Cyprus.

Maunder, P., Myers, D., Wall, N. and Miller, R.L. (1987a), Income and Employment Determination: Government and Trade, *Economics Explained, A Coursebook in A level Economics.*

Maunder, P., Myers, D., Wall, N. and Miller, R.L. (1987b), The Role and Size of Government, *Economics Explained, A Coursebook in A level Economics.*

Nicolaides, R., Mouzouris, Chr. and Aristidou, A. (1983a), The Town and Country Planning Legislation, *A Handbook on Land Valuation*, Phase B, Department of Lands and Surveys, Cyprus.

Nicolaides, R., Mouzouris, Chr. and Aristidou, A. (1983b), General Valuations, *A Handbook on Land Valuation*, Phase B, Department of Lands and Surveys, Cyprus.

Panayiotou, P.A., Plimmer, F., Panayi, A. and Jenkins, D. (1997), Immovable Property Taxation and Rating in Cyprus: Facts and Problems, *Journal of Property Tax Assessment & Administration* Vol. 2, No. 2.

Persons who sustained losses (Exemption from Taxation) Temporary Provisions Law 62/1975.

Rent Control Law 23/83.

Statistical Abstract, 1994 and the Financial Report, 1995.

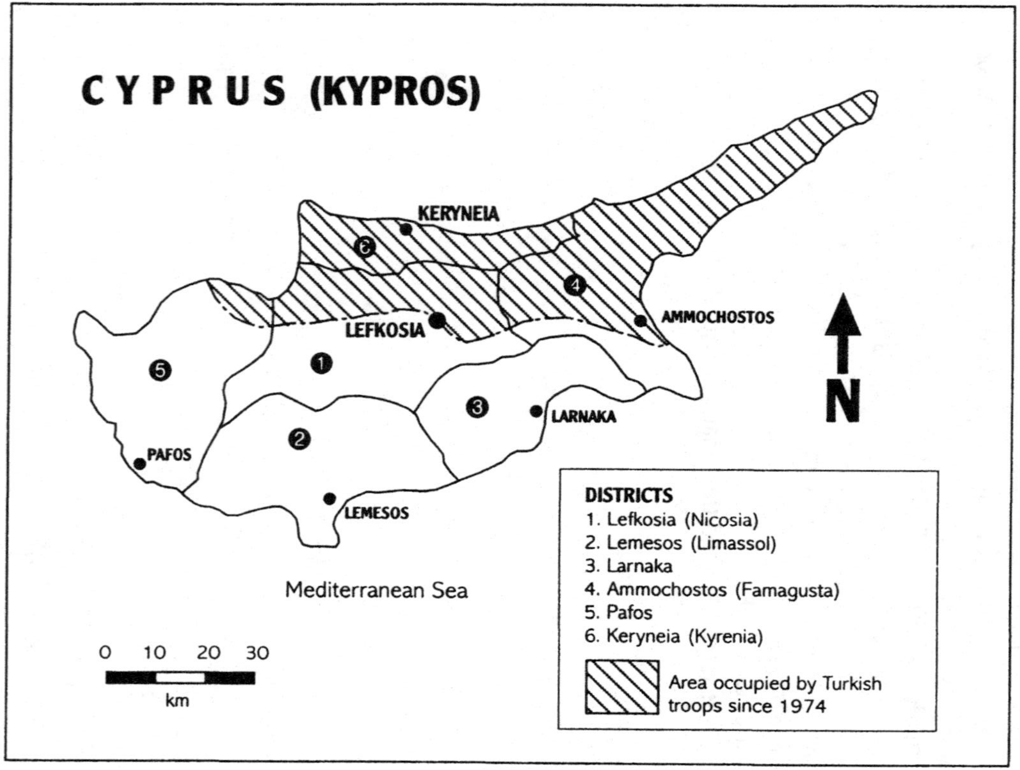

CYPRUS (KYPROS)

DISTRICTS
1. Lefkosia (Nicosia)
2. Lemesos (Limassol)
3. Larnaka
4. Ammochostos (Famagusta)
5. Pafos
6. Keryneia (Kyrenia)

Area occupied by Turkish
troops since 1974

Mediterranean Sea

0 10 20 30
km

KERYNEIA
LEFKOSIA
AMMOCHOSTOS
LARNAKA
LEMESOS
PAFOS

Figure 8.1   Map of Cyprus

9 An analysis of local government finance in Botswana

Ngaka Monagen

Introduction

After 80 years as a British Protectorate, Botswana gained independence in 1965. It is a landlocked country in of approximately 582,000 square kilometres. It shares its borders with Zimbabwe, South Africa, Namibia and Zambia. The population is 1,326,796 (de facto) as per the 1991 national census statistics. The country is often referred to as the fastest growing mixed economy in the region. The changing structure of the economy is dominated by the mineral sector and greatly affected by movements in the international markets. The Gross Domestic Product (GDP) grew by 3.1 per cent in 1995 compared to 4.1 per cent in 1994. However, the non-mining GDP increased by 5.5 per cent in 1995 compared to 2.3 per cent in 1993 which underpins the government's effort of diversifying the economy.

Since 1987, property investment has been experiencing a minor development cycle . The Accelerated Land Servicing Programme (ALSP), also perceived as a deliberate government intervention, made an impact in the free operation of the property market. Immediately following the first delivery of development land there was a downturn in the property performance which remains to date. Some observers believe a false market existed and values are now dropping to natural levels. Not so for developers, who are finding it difficult to service mortgage loans through rental income resulting in numerous repossessions by financiers.

The property tax system was first introduced under the Townships Act 1955 and its management is guided by Part VI of the Town Council Regulations 1966 under the Act. In this law, all towns declared as town/city councils, unless excluded by the Minister, are empowered to fix and levy rates. A council is immediately required to prepare a general valuation and produce a valuation roll for the purpose of levying rates. Over the years, these institutions did not have the resources to prepare valuation rolls which were prepared by the private sector until 1988. Central government has, since this date, been preparing these rolls on behalf of councils with substantial cost savings. The councils continue to experience serious resource constraints and the government plays a prominent role in facilitating the management of property rates.

The government is committed to a rationalization policy with the view to reducing capital spending and, in particular, to reduce the size of its funding to councils. It is, therefore, considered unwise to allow councils to raise property rates in order to finance unworthy projects and for the government to sponsor such projects by way of increased revenue support grants. This is a government's perception when a council is administered by an opposition party. Gaborone, Francistown, Selebi Phikwe, Lobatse and Jwaneng are all under such an administration. To this end, the Minister may not approve a budget that is not in balance and there is no economic justification for new undertakings.

Rates are a form of local property tax levied on rateable land in urban centres declared as Rating Authorities. The authority to levy rates is contained in the law which also sets out the powers and duties of councils. The government attaches great importance to property rates and this is evidenced in the manner in which a rating bye-law is processed. The Minister fixes the tax rates (rate in the Pula) for the financial year which are thoroughly discussed with other ministries at cabinet level before they become a bye-law. A policy was adopted that allowed for the increase of tax rates only if it is apparent that a budget will not balance. It is more common, however, to adjust these rates after a revaluation where property values have also changed. The midterm increases, so far, were for Gaborone and Francistown in the financial year 1994/95 due to increased recurrent expenditure.

This chapter analyses the framework of the property tax system with the view to facilitate a meaningful comparison with other regions. It traces the origin of councils' funding, the relative size of local authority finance and, more importantly, the operational model for better comparison. It reviews the assessment procedure, the objection process and concludes with a more general analysis of broad policy and legal issues.

Tax revenue

The source of revenue for the recurrent budget of councils includes user charges, property rates and revenue support grants as shown in Table 9.1. The duties of councils are specified in the law and include the provision of township services such as education, health care, refuse disposal, roads, building control, town planning. Property rates are an important source of revenue needed to provide and maintain such services.

Expenditure

In the 1992/93 financial year, the contribution of property rates towards the councils' budgets was, on average, 11 per cent compared to 26 per cent in 1995/96. The total expenditure increased from P82 million (local currency) to P137.4 million in the same period representing an increase of approximately 68 per cent. Gaborone alone has a share of about 75 per cent of the total. Its budget progressed from P32 million (1992), P41 million (1993), P56 million (1995) and continues to rise to P62 million (unaudited figures) in 1996. This is attributable to four distinct factors; firstly, the local economic growth with corresponding rising incomes generated demand for improved services. Secondly, population growth as revealed in the 1991 population census placed a considerable burden on existing services and expansion was necessary. Thirdly, single lane roads are being converted to dual lanes in order to ease traffic congestion. Lastly, maintenance costs on infrastructure increased due to more land from the ALSP. It is also clear that in the past five years Gaborone has experienced a tough economic cycle. The Bank of Botswana annual report suggests that the primary objective in national development planning would be to strive for a growth rate that is increasingly higher than the rate of population growth. A parallel message contained in the NDP7 is that the growth of recurrent expenditure must be reduced to more sustainable rates that are consistent with the projected growth of recurrent revenue.

Table 9.1
Expenditure and revenue 1995/96 (Pula million)

Council	Budget	Charges	Rates	Grants
Gaborone	55.880	3.915	22.610	29.354
Francistown	29.671	3.322	6.126	20.223
Jwaneng	12.301	1.227	2.199	8.875
Lobatse	17.218	2.059	2.127	13.032
Selebi Phikwe	17.757	2.808	2.250	12.699
Sowa	4.549	0.393	0.201	3.955
Total	137.376	13.723	35.514	88.139

(1 Pound Sterling = Pula 5.4755 as at September 1996)

Source: MLGLH 1995

191

There is no anticipated increase in tax rates for 1996/97 despite the rising expenditure; user charges remain lower than the highest in 1993/94 and councils would require increased revenue support grants to balance the budgets. Due to the new system of a formula based revenue grant, this would not be possible and there is a shortfall in councils' budgets in the current year (1996-97) except for Sowa. The solution for this shortfall by the Ministry is that additional rates income arising from new developments will bridge the gap. There is an assumption that interim assessment for all towns is possible. Sowa Township Authority (STA) was established in 1991 with fewer properties being predominantly residential and relies heavily on the grant for the upkeep of the town. The grants are financing an increasing share of the councils' budgets which led government to adopt a formula based recurrent grant. The formula is based on the remoteness of the district, assumptions about the prevailing economic performance and the population growth in each council. This effectively means that with the persistent economic decline as one factor of the formula, smaller towns in terms of population are likely to be disadvantaged. A pattern could develop where small towns having a low revenue base, with high demand for quality services, would resort to a high taxation regime out of necessity.

Revenue

The total revenue of P137.4 million in 1995 was nearly 0.01 per cent of the GDP comprising 10 per cent user charges, 26 per cent property rates and 64 per cent revenue support grants. In contrast, the predominant source of revenue for central government is general taxes. Over this period, income tax and corporate tax generated P300 million, transfer duty P6 million, customs duty P832.9 million and sales tax P185.7 million. Overall recorded total non-mineral revenue was P5,144.6 million and with spending being P5,414.1 million, yielded a deficit of P269.5 million. The Bank of Botswana has said that additional revenue over the original projection is possible from its contribution to government and the potential increase in the taxes above. The size of the deficit has pushed government to slow down on overspending by pursuing a policy of budget rationalization and councils are expected to follow the same principle.

The mineral's revenue has played a significant role on local government finance and there was little focus on user charges and tax rates. The probable increase of a contribution of property rates to the budget over the five year period in Table 9.2 is largely a result of an increase of rateable properties in the list. The tax rates, in particular, were not even adjusted for inflation except in the case of Gaborone and Francistown. As a result, Botswana enjoy services that are seemingly under priced compared to the region as a whole. The recurrent expenditure must be restrained and charges for services must be adjusted to economic levels. For this to be effective, councils must have a significant degree of fiscal autonomy in trying to balance expenditure with revenue. The quality of services being provided and the willingness of people to finance that quality of services would be difficult to measure for as long as government remains in charge.

It is often argued that property rates income is a major source of revenue to councils, determined on the basis of the total rateable values and the budget. In reality, contribution by property rates to the budget is not substantial if compared, for instance, with the revenue support grants to the same. Where the recipient council is comparatively small like Sowa, it can be adduced that this contribution is negligible. This argument is fairly subjective because, taken on its own, the 41 per cent for Gaborone in 1995/96 equates to approximately P23 million. However, if these figures were intended to gauge central government's share in councils' budgets, then both the charges and property rates revenue would need to increase to lessen dependency on government. This is now acknowledged by government and according to the Budget Speech, 'The thrust of the changes will be to transfer to the local authorities, whenever possible, the full authority to set the level of the user charges and fees which they collect and to streamline the procedures by which they do so.' (Mogae, 1996).

The eminent control over councils is in the form of setting the tax rates for property tax, deciding on the level of user charges applicable in the financial year and offsetting council savings by reduced grants. The government requires councils to submit their proposals relating to charges and fees for vetting and approval. If the proposal is considered unreasonable it is referred for revision. This supervision shifts the blame from councils for failing to provide satisfactory services. Ideally, councils should know in advance the level of income they will generate to facilitate proper planning. This entails removal of unnecessary constraints on the level of charges they can impose for the provision of services. By affording councils the opportunity to decide on the appropriate fee structure for their services, in effect, promotes accountability as well as enhances efficiency.

Table 9.2
Property rates income as a percentage of the budget

Council	1992/93	1993/94	1994/95	1995/96
Gaborone	9	39	38	41
Francistown	19	16	20	21
Jwaneng	9	18	18	17
Lobatse	12	11	11	12
Selebi Phikwe	8	12	11	13
Sowa	8	6	6	4

Source: MLGLH, 1995

There have been discussions to expand the revenue base for councils and a study was commissioned to identify new sources of revenue. This was conducted by the Task Force on Local Government Finance (LGF) captioned 'Increasing the own-source revenue of Councils' and the report was submitted on the 22 November 1993. The transference of existing revenue sources from central government to councils is considered not feasible as it would weaken the financial standing of the former whilst improving the latter. The move to explore new sources of revenue, however, connotes more taxes on services that are currently exempt and may not be welcomed by the public. The proposal includes local government tax, hotel tax, petroleum fuel tax, retail turnover tax, etc. which are currently being seriously considered by government.

It should be explained and will further be discussed that the figures contained in Table 9.2 are only indicative largely due to tax evasion. Rates income is not always collected in full in any given year. Table 9.3 illustrates the extent of such tax evasion over a three year period. There is continuing reluctance by rateable owners to pay property tax, the main reason being, that the services rendered by councils are not satisfactory. The money being owed to councils causes some delays to the development programmes.

Table 9.3
Rates arrears (Pula million)

Council	1993/94	1994/95	1995/96
Gaborone	9.28	11.23	11.17
Francistown	3.92	1.19	1.68
Jwaneng	1.03	1.36	1.50
Lobatse	0.78	0.89	1.20
Selebi Phikwe	1.52	0.84	1.29
Sowa *	0.00	0.00	0.00

* All rateable properties are currently owned by the Government and BHC

Source: Council Reports as at 31st March 1996

The councils should reassess the methods of rates collection, foster closer cooperation with ratepayers and improve efficiency in order to make the tax more acceptable and effective. Rates arrears are substantial and indeed a serious concern to the authorities. If councils cannot collect the annual rising arrears, they experience cash flow difficulties leading to delays in providing services. It was observed that when rates defaulters were threatened with court action, the arrears were greatly reduced implying that ratepayers are unwilling rather than unable to pay. The point raised by Department of Local Government Audit (DLGA) is that rates arrears are consistently increasing and councils need a strong policy on rates collection to redress the situation. This will be discussed further under legal and policy issues later in the chapter.

Basis of assessment

It is a legal requirement that the property tax is based on the assessed value, which is an estimation of the open market value realizable if the property is offered for sale in the market. Regulation 65 provides that the basis of assessment:

> ... shall be the capital sum which the land might be expected to realise if offered for sale ... at the time of the valuation on such reasonable terms and conditions as a bona fide seller would require.

Further, to have regard to comparable rateable land and to disregard any 'exceptional circumstances of a temporary nature'. Therefore, the tax is based either on the improved or unimproved value which is determined by way of comparable market evidence. There are some problems with this approach because of lack of sufficient market evidence to support assessments. In the early 1980s, the investment market for residential properties performed well mainly as a result of a reducing supply. Good returns on property investment were notable and banks were, generally, willing to finance the construction or purchase of houses by up to 100 per cent of the price. Even where a contribution was required, the income levels were sufficient to afford a deposit.

In the late 1980s, government introduced the ALSP and, as the name implies, more land was allocated to citizens for owner occupation and consequently there was a housing boom. As more people built their own houses, the user market took a down turn and sales became sluggish. The trend continued to date and virtually all sales are auctions on repossessions where banks only wants to recover the outstanding loans. Commercial and industrial properties are rarely sold in the market however, there is ample rental evidence. The institutional properties market is usually not active.

It is against this background that the 'capital sum' basis of assessment is sometimes criticized as inappropriate. The Rating Review Committee recommended to cabinet in November 1995 to change the basis of assessment for commercial and industrial properties to rental value in view of the abundant rental evidence of such properties. The proposed amendment provides that 'the rateable value of any rateable land not used for residential purposes and not described as residential in any approved plan ... shall be the gross annual rent which might reasonably be expected to be obtained for the land ... on the open market at the date of valuation ...'. There is the usual assumption that a landlord pays all the outgoings. The main constraint on the current approach is demonstrated under methods of assessment where an assessor is forced to break a building into components and relating that to value. In some cases, the cost approach is used. The argument put forward by Botswana Housing Corporation (BHC) in the Sowa Local Valuation Court (LVC) rejecting this method was that an assessor should reflect the fact that it is difficult to sell its properties in the market. The proposal to change the basis of assessment received a broad support of councils during the consultation stage, stating that it will produce better supported assessments when finally approved by cabinet. The methods used to derive the rateable values are discussed later in the chapter.

Tax base

Rateable properties as defined in the law include land and buildings which represent about 40 per cent of urban land in each council area. A fairly large amount of the land is not rateable, i.e. low cost housing. Land comprises residential, commercial, industrial, civic and agricultural unless exempt under the law and is further categorized as developed or undeveloped. The tax rate for residential land is lower than the other land uses and the undeveloped rate is four times higher than the developed rate. The rationale to impose such a high tax is the presumption that business can afford to pay more tax and to encourage land owners to develop quickly to avoid pockets of vacant land in built-up areas.

There are approximately 54,000 properties in the list with a total rateable value of P2.71 billion, as detailed in Table 9.4. After applying the appropriate tax rates, the figure translates to roughly P35.5 million being the actual rates income for councils in the 1995/96 financial year. By far, residential land represents the largest share of rateable properties within each council area. The number of rateable properties in the country could be larger than recorded. The low cost housing, about 60 per cent of the total land, locally referred to as the Self Help Housing Agency (SHHA) continues to pay service levy which is a disguised form of property tax operated in an inefficient manner. Currently, these properties are exempt from property rates because title is held by councils and the occupier is issued with a certificate of right for beneficial occupation.

When the land is developed and satisfies all other conditions of a certificate of rights, the occupier would excise the right to purchase a fixed term grant (being simply a conversion of title). It is at this point that councils lose revenue due to the manner in which a transfer is processed. The position starts with an application by an occupier to purchase the land, issuance of the Service Levy

Clearance Certificate (SLCC) and final registration of title. The time between SLCC and the registration of title creates a void period in the collection of rates. Perhaps a decision should now be made to bring this land within the rating system in its existing status.

Table 9.4
Size of tax components 1995/96

Council	No. of Properties	Rateable Values (Pula Million)	% of Total Rateable Values
Gaborone	29,800	1,414[1]	52.2
Francistown	6,706	499	18.4
Jwaneng	5,172	189	7.0
Lobatse	4,705	241	8.9
Selebi Phikwe	6,948	304	11.2
Sowa[2]	1,018	62	2.3
Total	54,349	2,709	100.0

1   *1987 Tone of the List*
2   *New Town since 1991*

Source: Department of Lands 1996

Tax rates

The earlier discussion on revenue indicates that the property rates income is a product of the rateable value and the tax rate (see Table 9.5). The latter is a ratio of the rateable value estimates and the rates income component of the budget. The rateable value estimates are based on values contained in the normal valuation roll and figures derived from additional properties that would otherwise be included in a supplementary assessment for the next financial year.

The law provides that councils must 'fix and levy rates upon land'. The councils are further required to pass bye-laws that are approved by the Minister and published in the Government Gazette if they wish to raise own-source revenue. The determination of the tax rate is a tripartite affair involving councils' budgets, Department of Lands (DoL) rateable value estimates and the Ministry of Local Government, Lands and Housing (MLGLH) fixing the tax rates. This arrangement is often criticized as the real source of delay in rates collection as well as cumulative rates arrears. In 1993, The Task Force which was appointed to investigate additional sources of revenue for councils observed that the routine work involved every time a council wishes to revise its charges needs to be streamlined.

Table 9.5
Tax rates 1995/96: thebe in the Pula *

Council	Residential Developed	Residential Undeveloped	Non-residential Developed	Non-residential Undeveloped
Gaborone	1.07	4.28	1.30	5.20
Francistown	0.80	3.00	1.00	4.00
Jwaneng	0.78	3.12	0.95	3.80
Lobatse	0.60	2.40	0.75	3.00
Selebi Phikwe	0.65	2.60	0.75	3.00
Sowa	0.30	1.20	0.40	1.60

*   *100 thebe equals P1*

Source: *MLGLH 1995*

Ideally, tax rates should be fixed and gazetted before the beginning of a financial year to ease collection within the first four months as required by law. In 1995, tax rates were gazetted in September allowing councils little time to collect rates before the end of the financial year mainly due to the concern raised above. The Task Force noted that councils would shift the blame for failing to provide more and better services on central government's control over their financial affairs. The Rating Review Committee advised that a bye-law procedure can be replaced by a council resolution in order to speed up the process. The central intervention is also not consistent with the government's commitment to allow councils fiscal autonomy.

There is a confusion about the operation of this tax system amongst the general public particularly as regards the source of property tax increases. Quite often the public query the increase in assessed values as the source of higher tax bills. In practice, if assessed values increase and the tax rates remain the same or vice versa, property tax revenue will increase. In other words, a rise in property values allows councils to generate more revenue without increasing tax rates. A house which has been assessed at P50,000 and a tax rate of 0.65 per cent will produce an income of P325. After a revaluation, the value of the property increases to P120,000 and with the same tax rate, the income rises to P780. Assuming a council still requires the P325 income, the tax rate will be dropped to 0.27 per cent. Given this situation, a council would adjust the amount of required revenue by simply varying the tax rates. A resolution to retain the previous levels of tax rates after a revaluation is a decision to increase property tax income. However, tax rates have remained the same for the past five years and, with no increases in either charges or grants, this is seen as a grip on overspending.

Property assessment

Property rates are, primarily, a local government affair even though central government is inadvertently playing a leading role. The key issues to be considered are (i) appointment of assessors, (ii) listing of rateable properties and (iii) preparation of valuation rolls. In all these cases, councils are specified as the responsible authorities. This is an onerous task because, as discussed earlier, councils do not have the capacity to carry out these duties. The DoL remains largely responsible in providing the service free of charge. It assists in identifying rateable properties and preparing all assessments.

Assessors

The regulations provide that councils appoint assessors and no qualifications are specified. It is, however, common practice to nominate personnel who hold professional qualifications and have attained the relevant experience to carry out the assigned duties. Assessors have, in the past eight years, been appointed on a yearly basis from the staff of the DoL as councils can still not afford the services of the private sector. It should further be reiterated that assessments were previously prepared by the private sector, which continues to be involved as the need arises. Government does not charge councils for the services provided. The only costs to government is subsistence allowance and salaried officers which is negligible compared to what the private sector would otherwise charge for the valuation service. Notwithstanding this good gesture, there is a great shortage of assessors in the public sector which hampers progress. If the trend continues, the only logical solution would be for government to play a coordinating role and allow the private sector to do most of the work. The revaluation of Gaborone has been pending for the last four years is now going to tender after approval of the project memorandum.

Identification of rateable land has been done by assessors with councils playing a diminishing role. The management of land is fragmented and often information on available land is difficult to collect. The process of land delivery is lengthy involving planning, cadastral survey, land allocation and finally title registration.

In the absence of a full fledged land information system, an assessor moves from place to place in search of new properties for listing in the roll. It is a requirement that valuation rolls should contain names and addresses of rateable owners. In the past, these rolls contained few details in this regard and needed to be updated. As this information is not easily available, the inspection teams work long hours to gather the relevant details. In some cases, property owners are away on different engagements which then means collecting information over weekends.

The problem should not exist at all; allocation of land is based on completed application forms containing all the necessary personal details. The subsequent transfer of land requires Rates Clearance Certificate (RCC) and a deed of transfer is issued, both containing individual particulars. The conversion of low cost housing to fixed term grant (leasehold title) is based on SLCC issued by councils and is similar to the other two. All this information is currently not easily accessible to assessors and the collection of names and addresses continues to be a problem. The denial of this valuable information to the assessor is indicative of lack of cooperation and proper coordination between authorities handling land related matters. The problem is that the information is confidential or records are not organized in a systematic manner.

Appointment of assessors is a light weight issue but with some connotations for future operations. The debate ensued during the rating review exercise regarding the appointment of assessors. The Committee argued that councils have a vested interest in the collection of rates and, therefore, their involvement in appointing assessors might be seen as a conflict of interest. The facts are that councils should not be seen to be involved in property assessments which ratepayers should feel are being handled by a party independent of the amount of rates to be collected. Further, that all matters relating to assessment of properties like the power of inspection and the right to property information should be shifted to assessors once appointed. Currently, DoL identifies candidates from the staff for appointment, councils appoint assessors on the basis of the recommendation and MLGLH approves the appointees. The councils also provide written authority conferring the power of entry on assessors to inspect rateable properties having given 24 hours notice of the intention to do so. In the long term, councils are expected to internalize this process. If the regulations are changed to cater for a temporary arrangement, they will need the same changes when councils are finally in control.

Valuation roll

Immediately following declaration of a township status, a council is required to carry out a general valuation and produce a valuation roll for the purpose of levying rates. It is a further requirement that revaluations are done once in every five years. It is unfortunate that the assessments remain fixed for the duration of this period regardless of any changes in the property market. In the interim period, all new properties are brought into the system by way of a supplementary valuation roll based on what the value would have been at the last general valuation. It effectively means that the rateable values, once the roll is signed, cannot be updated in any form until the tone of the list is changed by a revaluation.

Property values change from time to time largely influenced by both the business and development cycles. The experience came to light in Selebi Phikwe immediately after the revaluation in 1992; the boom period came to an abrupt stop and there was clear evidence that property values were dropping. The town was quickly becoming a ghost town also due to the collapse of copper and nickel prices in the international markets. Later, other towns followed because of the general downturn in the economy as a whole. This would logically necessitate an adjustment in the rateable values to reflect the changed conditions.

Rating work is held in database files in the network at DoL. The benefits of the system cannot be fully realized because there is still no connection between the Department, councils and other authorities dealing with land matters. The Botswana Land Information System (BLIS) exists on Oracle at the Government Computer Bureau (GCB) and, at the moment, is only accessible to the Deeds Registry and the State Land Allocation Policy (SLAP). This system was put in place following the introduction of ALSP mainly to speed up allocation of state land. It is an assembly of land database files capable of multi-purpose use, i.e. property assessments, rates invoicing by councils and property transfers. There is a pending conversion of rating database files to Oracle which will then ease the flow of information between the Deeds Registry and other authorities. The computerization of council offices is also reported to be nearing completion. When the whole project is finally completed between these authorities, the need for names and addresses as specified in the law will diminish. The volume of work currently operated manually will be automated allowing for more accurate assessments and better return on investment.

Once a valuation roll is completed, it is published for public knowledge in the Government Gazette, local newspapers and in such other places as a council may determine. Such a notice calls upon all ratepayers to lodge in writing any objections they may have against the assessment of their properties and to do so within 21 days from the date of the first publication. If no objections are received, the valuation roll is certified and then binding on all. Where objections are received, the matter is referred for consideration by the Local Valuation Court (LVC) after giving six weeks notice to other parties. If such roll is a supplementary it is immediately merged with the normal roll.

Appeals procedures

The objections arising from a new valuation roll, when lodged within the statutory period, lead to the sitting of a local valuation court. The process can be long and frustrating; the revaluation of Francistown was completed in June 1995, the objection period expired in July 1995 and the court finally sat in June 1996 to consider the objections that were received. This caused a general confusion amongst ratepayers some of whom refused to pay the rate bills pending the decision of the court. On the other hand, the regulations provide that the levying of rates should be treated as if no appeal were pending and that due adjustments be made after the decision is finalized. In situations where ratepayers persistently refuse to pay and the court later confirms the assessments, all outstanding bills attract interest payments which increases the rates burden.

From time to time, errors are discovered after valuation rolls have been gazetted and certified. Such errors mostly consist of wrong identification and description of assessed properties. In some instances, assessed properties have changed ownership and needed to be corrected in a roll. The regulations specify that, in the circumstances, councils may cause any errors to be corrected after giving seven days notice to the owner of the subject land. It is not necessary to refer the matter to court unless the owner, having been served with a notice and complied with all the requirements, objects to the suggested corrections. These corrections are not considered serious and almost all such corrections are made out of court.

The LVC is established under the Town Council Regulations to the Townships Act to settle valuation disputes. It consists of a chairperson appointed by the Minister as being a person qualified to hold a judicial office in terms of the Magistrates' Court Act. The other two members are nominated by individual councils and approved by the Minister. The three members constitute the LVC and serve at the 'Minister's pleasure'. The Clerk of the Court is appointed by a council from its members of staff or a member of the public deemed capable to hold that office. All members are paid allowances provided that they are not employed by either council or government.

The importance of this court lies in resolving conflicting issues being submitted for arbitration and its strength is in the ability to make use of the evidence being presented before it. The speed at which decisions are finalized is obviously desirable and, therefore, a reasonable justification for a professional court structure. The law regulating the tax system is not simple, the assessment process is an art and there can never be simple decisions arising from a complex system. The current structure, where none of the LVC members has any knowledge of valuation, complicates the appeals procedure, particularly, in view of a lack of local understanding of the system. Perhaps what is needed in the case of this tax is for councils to embark on a mass public education programme in appreciation of the contribution they receive from ratepayers.

The authority of the court is mainly in its power to summon witnesses; to hear, receive and examine witnesses under oath. It may demand that any document be presented in court as evidence. After all objections have been considered, the Chairperson is required to certify the valuation roll which then supersedes any previous rolls. In the event that any party is not satisfied with the decision taken, that party may appeal to the High Court within one month whose decision is final.

Methods of assessment

The practice, which is also a legal requirement, is to assess land and improvements separately and the sum of the two is the rateable value of the subject property. The difficulty in acquiring comparable market evidence was discussed earlier in the chapter and the situation is worse with regard to land value. The government has been the main supplier of development land with the sale price being either cost recovery or affordable price. Recently, the private sector was encouraged to participate in the delivery of land. Improved land transactions are analysed to derive a value attributable to vacant land. The rate per square metre determined for each is a 'tone' for all similar properties in a location.

The most common methods are a comparison based on direct open market sales evidence and the cost approach being the equivalent of the actual construction costs adjusted for time. The comparison method analyses the sales data and property characteristics to estimate rateable values of properties in the same locality that are otherwise not for sale. To date, the method is predominantly used in assessing residential, commercial and industrial properties being capable of sale whilst the cost approach is used to assess other properties. In using the comparison method, beacon properties with reliable sales evidence are identified and the sale prices separated according to different components of the property, i.e. land, improvements, services, etc. A building is further divided into different features and the improvement value is then apportioned to estimate implicit value for property characteristics. This is necessary since properties being assessed are not always identical and it would be inappropriate to apply the same rates without any adjustments. The following parts form the main features for value purposes:

Land: size
                                     location

Improvements:		floor area
		finishes and condition
		accommodation
Outbuildings:		garage
		maid quarters
		swimming pool
		boundary walls
Services:		full/partial/none

A common practice for determining land value is to analyse the open market sales of properties and derive patterns of value for various localities according to different land uses. Currently, the exercise involves the collection of sales data from the Deeds Registry and land value maps and schedules of improvement rates are produced. The sales data is verified to determine if the values are true open market sales. The analysis is then translated into a value expressed as a rate per square metre which is applied to the land size to arrive at land value.

The assessment of the improvements requires the collation of physical features listed above and their value related directly to the main building. The next step is to apply a rate per square metre (derived by analysis in the same way as for land) to the gross floor area of a building. The actual floor areas of other parts of a building are transformed into equivalent area of the main building floor space. In this way the floor areas of all elements are expressed in terms of the main building according to their value relationship so that a rate per square metre for the main building can be applied once to the transformed area. The breakdown below loosely illustrates the relationship of the parts to the main building;

Main building	-	100%
Maid quarters	-	50%
Garage	-	40%
Patio/Veranda	-	25%

Example:

What is the rateable value of a house with a gross floor area of 150 square metres with a front veranda of 12 square metres? The size of land is 1,200 square metres, garage 20 square metres and maids' quarters 30 square metres. Also in the grounds is a swimming pool, car port and boundary wall. The analysis shows a rate of P800 per square metre for improvements and P20 per square metre for land.

	Gross Floor Area (square metres)	Factor %	Effective Floor Area (square metres)
Main building	150	100	150
Maid quarters	30	50	15
Garage	20	40	8
Veranda	12	25	3
Total area			176
Rate for improvements			800
Value of improvements			140,800

Some features cannot be directly related to the value of the main building whilst, in effect, contributing to the value of the property. However, they often carry a standard value throughout the locality being assessed once the value is fixed and, therefore, repeated to all similar cases. From the previous example, the following adjustments are made:

Improvement value		140,800
Car port say	750	
Swimming pool	12,000	
Boundary wall	6,000	18,750
Total improvement value		159,550
Land value: 1,200 square metres @ P20		24,000
Rateable value		183,550
		Say P184,000

The cost approach is based on the assumption that the market value of property is not higher than its total costs. An assessor uses age bands to determine a depreciation rate which is then applied to the assessment to estimate the equivalent replacement cost; the age bands are 0-5 years = 0 per cent, 5-10 years = 5 per cent, 10-15 years = 10 per cent, etc. The approach was adopted for the valuation and explained in the Sowa LVC during an objection raised by the BHC. The Corporation had built houses for Soda Ash Botswana (mining company) and an agreement was signed to the effect that rent levels are based on cost recovery for the duration of the agreement. In the general valuation, the assessor relied on costs with no depreciation because all the houses were new. The Corporation argued that values were high as there was a thin market due to the town being recently established. The decision of the court was that the values were consistent with the costs which are recovered through rent.

The property market took a down turn in 1993 and continues to do so to date. The rateable value in the example represents the state of the market during that period and has declined drastically since then. Even when revaluations were possible on an annual basis, the assessing authority still faced serious resource constraints to fulfil this role. The issue is not helped by the lack of mass appraisal techniques and value banding. In 1995, DoL proposed to introduce a computer assisted valuation system incorporating both the geographic information and land information systems but with little success. The terms of reference were prepared and presented to government in December 1995 and there has been no progress since then. This system is seen as the only viable option to aid frequent assessments and improve the revenue base for councils.

Exemptions and reliefs

All land in a council area is rateable unless it is exempt under the regulations. There is also a requirement that the owner of any land makes application to the council for the determination of rateable status of the property owned. Land is exempt on the basis of one of two factors firstly, ownership and secondly, use. In the case where payment of rates includes the cost of defrayal for services, the land being exempt by reason of use is liable to proportionate rates for such services. The rates chargeable in this regard are cost recovery except that the limit is half the rates that would otherwise be payable if the land was rateable. Another exception to use is that such land will not be exempt if the owner derives income from the use of the land.

The exemption from rates by virtue of ownership comprises of land that is:

1   vested in government;

2   vested in the council;

3   owned by Tati Concession Limited; or

4   owned by Botswana Railways but excluding staff housing.

It should be explained that the exemption from rates in the first three cases is irrespective of the purpose to which the land is used. Further, land vested in the council refers to land owned by itself. Any land owned by another council in the council area is rateable unless exempt from rates by virtue of use. Whilst government land is exempt from rates, there is a discretionary payment of a contribution in lieu of rates which is equivalent to the rates that would otherwise be payable on the land. The exemption from rates by reason of use comprises of:

1   public library or museum;

2   public religious worship;

3   residence for the clergy;

4   school and hostel but not staff houses;

5   public hospital or institution for mental patients;

6   orphanage or charitable institution;

7   public cemetery or crematorium;

8   recreation but excluding horse racing or where there is an admission fee;

9   agricultural shows;

10   hostels for the destitute, handicapped or for the old people;

11   land used for a public service but with Minister's special consent.

If any of the exempt land is used for some other purpose at the same time or at different times during the year, such land may be regarded as rateable in part, or rateable during a portion of the year and rates are apportioned accordingly. The owner of non-rateable land is required to notify the council of any change in the use of such land and expected to respond to any subsequent enquiries that will enable the council to determine whether such land is properly listed. If the land remains non-rateable because of the owner's failure to notify the material changes in the use of the land, then the owner shall remain liable for rates from the date on which the change took place. The regulations do not cover foreign missions and embassies but such properties are protected under Article 23 of the Articles of the Vienna Convention on Diplomatic Relations of 1961. The exemption appears in the First Schedule of the Diplomatic Immunities and Privileges Act and excludes the general staff housing.

What is not clearly explained and, therefore, causing confusion to the general public is the exemption of land on the basis of 'a public service'. A public service is usually provided by government and would be exempt under ownership and not by land use as discussed earlier. The Rates Manual contests that the land is exempt in this category if it is leased by government from a private owner either at a sub-economic rent or rent free which sounds unrealistic. Other observations separate 'service' from the organization providing that service, that is in the light of either ownership or use. The confusion arises if a public service is provided by an organization other than government. This would lead to numerous applications being lodged by organizations who are convinced that their product is a public service within the meaning of the law. Moreover, the actual land use involved would invariably be either office or residential, both of which are difficult to exempt as a category of land use.

The only relief specified is rates abatement. First, the council should fix a date upon which rates are due and payable. Then a notice of abatement is published together with a rating bye-law to afford ratepayers the opportunity to take advantage of a discount. The notice should also specify that the abatement is only allowed if payment of the bill is made on or before the fixed date and does not apply in the case of rates arrears. However, when all arrears including interest payment and the current bill are paid on the specified date, then such discount is allowed. The amount of discount is derived from a formula which should be applied by all councils.

Collection of rates

Regulation 77 of the Town Council Regulations provides that:

> ... a council may not more than once every financial year, assess, raise and levy by bye-law, a rate upon all rateable land within the council area and ... collected in such amounts ... as the council may determine.

Rates become due and payable on a date fixed by councils and published at least 30 days before collection starts. A rating bye-law which, in practice, sets the tax rates should give the details of the effective date. Irrespective of this date, the period for which rates are payable covers 12 months (financial year) and is usually from the 1 April to 31 March the following year.

A ratepayer is allowed three months from the fixed date within which to settle the bill for the current year. If the bill is paid on or before that date there is a discount whereas if there is no remittance after the three months grace period, interest is charged. There is also a provision in the regulations for councils to accept payment of rates in instalments and to specify the conditions under which such payment by instalments is made. The conditions include:

1   interest payment;

2   all rates are paid before the end of the financial year; and

3   monthly payment of a fixed amount.

As soon as a valuation roll is certified and the tax rates are known, a council will dispatch rates invoices to all ratepayers. In the case of an interim valuation, such notices are sometimes based on the roll which is not yet gazetted. The interim valuation for Gaborone was completed in May 1995 and was not gazetted until March 1996 because names and addresses of some individuals (being a legal requirement) were missing in the roll. Within this period the City Council was invoicing individuals on the basis of the roll and claiming authority of the law. Regulation 62(4) provides that any interim valuation shall be merged immediately with the current roll and the interpretation by councils is that rates collection based on the roll which has been merged is also due immediately. Ratepayers are allowed the opportunity to raise any objections that they may have against the assessments and payment of rates, nevertheless payment cannot be withheld on the basis of a pending objection. Indeed, this is further clarified in Regulation 64 where it states that if the rateable value is subsequently reduced by court, a ratepayer is entitled to a refund of 'any rate in excess of that which would have been paid if the rate had been levied on the value as fixed by the said valuation court'.

As explained previously, the owner of any assessed land is liable to pay rates unless the land is exempt. If the rates remain unpaid for more than three months from the date of the invoice, the council may demand payment from the occupier of the land. The assumption is that the occupier is a tenant and will withhold the equivalent of the rates paid from the rent. The production of a receipt by the occupier for such payment is considered good and sufficient discharge of the amount paid out of the rent. It is acknowledged that a lump sum payment of rates at the beginning of the council year is necessary to allow councils the opportunity to meet their statutory obligations. In retrospect, it is difficult for an average person to pay the amount at the same time; the inclusion of interest payment thereafter makes it even more difficult. The government pays a contribution in lieu of rates in two instalments. An advance is paid at the beginning of the year and the balance at the end. Even though the advance is a substantial amount (about 90 per cent) the arrangement could go a long way in reducing the burden on ratepayers. The councils would then schedule their development programmes in line with the pattern of the cash flow.

Enforcement

The importance of rates income to councils is such that if arrears are allowed to accumulate, councils will experience serious financial difficulties in the implementation of their plans. It is against this background that councils are empowered to take all reasonable steps to recover the money and guided to make efficient and timely collections. The councils are required to issue a written notice of demand immediately rates are overdue and request payment within 14 days from the date of the notice. If there is still no payment after the notice, the name of the defaulter is published in the Government Gazette as well as local newspapers. The council is then expected to apply to a magistrate court for a summary warrant for the recovery of the money overdue and any interest that may have accrued. This warrant is executed as if it were a writ of execution to recover the arrears.

Before action is taken by a service of a demand notice, all details on the matter must be confirmed and a certified statement prepared to serve as evidence in a court action. The notice is served either on a duly authorized agent or at the last known physical address. Where the recovery is dependent upon determining the whereabouts of a defaulter and all reasonable efforts have failed, the services of an investigator may be considered provided the expenses are justifiable. In extremely exceptional cases, i.e. before write-offs, a council may engage a debt collector on a commission basis, usually 10 per cent of the amount collected. Attorneys are commonly used in case it leads to litigation. To date, no case has been through the courts in spite of the seriousness of the rates arrears as shown in Table 9.3 A somewhat interesting provision is contained in Regulation 91:

> Where any rateable land in any council area is unoccupied, and the rates thereon ... have been unpaid for five years, the council may take possession of such land and grant leases.

and Regulation 92 that:

> Every such lease shall be for such term not exceeding three years ...

If the definition of land includes vacant land then the action is not worth the effort. Of course it would be easy to take possession of a building and lease it for a period of three years even though there will still be some problems. If the subject property has a registered mortgage bond with the Botswana Building Society (BBS) and occupied by a tenant, the rent is collected directly by the Society towards the loan in terms of the loan agreement. Logically, all charges attached to the property should be serviced out of that income but instead the property owner is still expected to settle the charges. The councils' nonchalance on this rule is a clear testimony of its insignificance.

The measures prescribed in the regulations for the recovery of rates arrears are confrontational, hardly ever used and imply that councils would prefer a friendlier approach. An application for a 'summary warrant' to the magistrate court is cumbersome; 12 per cent interest charge on unpaid money increases the rates burden; taking possession of a vacant site for a term of three years is unrealistic. There is a much easier way which surely starts with public awareness campaigns. The message should be to persuade the public to want to pay this tax as in most other countries.

The use of rates clearance certificates should be investigated; the transferor of property has an obligation to notify the council in writing of any change of ownership and remains liable until such a process is completed. The new owner becomes liable from the date of the transfer. Section 87(1) of the Deeds Registry Act provides that 'No deed of grant or transfer of land shall be registered unless accompanied by a receipt or certificate of a competent public revenue office that the taxes, duties, fees and quit-rent (if any) ... have been made.' Consequently, the Registrar of Deeds would request a clearance certificate from the council before any transfer can be effected. The council needs to satisfy itself that all rates including arrears and interest are paid before the certificate is issued. The certificate may be issued annually and extended to other forms of property transactions. If banks and utilities would demand evidence of rates payment as a condition of providing the required service or an exemption certificate, then the public will be persuaded to settle the rates bills in time.

Legal and policy issues

The Townships Act 1955 authorizes the Minister, by statutory instrument, to declare any area a township. Section 6 of the Act empowers the councils to make bye-laws for the 'health, order and good government of the township' and such bye-laws will have no force or effect until approved by the Minister and published in the Government Gazette. Section 7 also empowers the councils to 'fix and levy' by bye-laws rates, charges, fees and tariffs for the services they provide. It follows that councils' attempts to raise revenue by way of a bye-law should first be acceptable to the Minister. The processing of these bye-laws is long, involving councils, MLGLH, AGC, DoL and consultation with other government ministries. This is a serious constraint in raising revenue by councils.

There is continuing discussion within government that councils require fiscal autonomy in order to function effectively and efficiently. In particular, the recommendation by the Task Force to 'remove requirement for Minister's approval where there is no national interest threatened by a council's use of the authority'. There is, nevertheless, a worrying reservation for complete transference of authority to councils. A model bye-law is proposed which incorporates two types of schedules; Schedule A comprising of items where the Minister's approval is required and Schedule B where no such approval is required. The general belief is that once councils gain fiscal autonomy, they will overcharge for the services they provide. The primary objective for devolving authority is to speed up the process by which councils would raise revenue and reduce uncertainty to guide planning. The real source of concern should be rates arrears which, in one part, are a result of the current procedure.

211

The formula which determines support grants are based on economic and population growth projections. It is observed that without any additional fiscal effort, the recurrent revenue of councils will expand with the growth of these two factors. In the unlikely event that recurrent revenue should fall if there is a decline in the two factors leading to unmatched recurrent expenditure. Further, if expenditure is allowed to increase at faster rates, councils will be tempted towards a corresponding increase in revenue which will have to come from higher taxes on existing services as well as new options of own-source revenue. The baseline is that as councils grow, their revenue base improves and an increasing share from the revenue support grants should be redirected to encourage other growth areas. The government should ultimately move away from automatic grants towards loans where councils are expected to repay through cost recovery efforts.

The government study on a formula based support grant is suggesting otherwise; a projection is made over a five year period up to the year 2001. Based on the two factors, the total grant is increasing from P88,130,000 in 1995 to P137,666,500 in 2001 showing a growth rate of 6.4 per cent in 1995/96 prices. This, summarily, confirms that the grant will continue to rise for as long as the population grows thus bringing into question the basis of the formula. If the basis is shifted from population growth and economic performance to the need assessment, the annual grant will fluctuate based on prioritization of development projects and become consistent with the central policy of balancing recurrent expenditure with the projected growth of the recurrent revenues. The size of the grant will be competitive, determined on project basis rather than on rising intra-migration and birth rates.

The public is extremely silent about the property tax system; it will be interesting to determine the real reasons for this silence. There is general consensus that the 21 day statutory requirement for the advertisement of the valuation roll is not sufficient taking into account the level of local understanding of the system. The presumption is that once an advertisement comes out, everybody should see it and respond accordingly. Because the rates income is crucial to the councils' budgets, there is a need for a rates collection strategy that encompasses both persuasion and enforcement techniques. The collection of rates is fraught with problems basically due to two critical factors, viz lack of public awareness and method of rates payment.

After 30 years of the tax system, the public still does not know why it has to pay the tax; some people argue that it is a direct payment for township services and others believe it is simply a land tax. The people holding land in urban centres pending the registration and issuance of title deed default on payment with a genuine belief that they are not rateable. These people are convinced that for as long as they are not registered owners, they are necessarily not rateable owners. This is often the case because immediately following land allocation, an allottee signs a purchase agreement and pays 10 per cent of the purchase price as deposit which concludes a binding contract. It then takes many more years before the balance is paid and, like in the conversion of SHHA properties, the arrears start to build up. The definition of rateable owner does not make any reference to registered owner and possession of title deed is irrelevant in this instance. Regulation 2 of the Town Council Regulations provides that the rateable owner is 'any person who lawfully occupies or holds land in accordance with an agreement whereunder he is entitled to obtain transfer of such land on the fulfilment by him of the conditions prescribed by such agreement'.

The gazetting of the valuation roll for 21 days is necessary to afford ratepayers an opportunity to lodge objections if not satisfied with the assessment of their properties. Quite often no such objections are received and the roll is then certified and binding. The concern should be why there are no objections to the gazetted roll; is it because ratepayers are satisfied with the assessments? The public neither knows the purpose of the tax nor how to go about making an objection to the assessments. The 21 days gazette notice is probably too short a period. All these issues need to be explained to the public and it is the duty of councils to do so in order to foster closer cooperation with the public.

The level of rates arrears (see Table 9.3) confirms a lack of enthusiasm amongst potential ratepayers. The annual council budgets are always in balance without due regard for arrears from the previous years and, therefore, provides no incentive for councils to apply themselves more rigorously to recover the outstanding money. The law assumes that rates are paid annually in advance and any unpaid balance after four months grace period attracts an interest payment. In comparison, income tax is collected monthly from the source and according to Section 67 of the Income Tax Act, 'Every person shall furnish a tax return ... in respect of any tax year ... within two months after the end of that year ...'. The purpose of a tax return at the end of the year is to determine the precise level of a liability within the given tax bands. Transfer duty is paid at the time of a transaction and generally regarded as part of the transfer costs. In one instance, tax is deducted from salary and in another, there will be no transfer without payment. The approach tends to eliminate any possibility of build-up arrears over a target period but it is not appropriate for rates collection because councils demand lump sum payment at the start of the financial year. Paying utility bills every month is affordable and failure to pay leads to immediate disconnection of service which could be assimilated, with adjustments, to the rates model. Rate payment should be collected from source where possible and in the event of defaulting, proper measures like RCC, discussed earlier, are used before any court action.

Conclusion

There is a clear recognition of the desire by councils to manage their own affairs without undue intervention from central government. This is a welcome move but will be introduced in stages until the fundamental structure is in place. The public expects these institutions to mobilize resources to accomplish their aim and objectives, to produce long term strategic plans with mid-term reviews and to be transparent in their dealings. This is not achievable at the same time as government continues to influence the plans on a large scale. Such control was possible in the past because the Minister would minimize the blame by increasing the support grants as well as maintaining the lower tax rates which had a compensating effect.

Government grants to councils are not guaranteed, being largely dependent on the performance of the mining sector which is not a renewable natural resource. Spending can get out of control to the extent that it exceeds the target revenues. The solution is not in increasing revenue to finance that expenditure but may require an appraisal of planned projects with the view to rationalization. The economy creates winners and losers and without proper planning and management, economic opportunities are lost to other districts or competing regions. The success of councils in providing services is dependent on an effective rates collection strategy which needs to be put in place. Public knowledge of the tax system is crucial to collection; payment of rates from the source is the ultimate goal and enforcement procedure should be simplified and made more realistic. There is no economic sense in taking possession of vacant land for a term of three years as no developer is prepared to lease the land for that period of time. The councils need to reshape the finance structure and until that is completed the burden of collection transcends all possible efforts.

References

Bank of Botswana, (1995), Annual Report.
Deeds Registry Act (CAP 33:02).
Diplomatic Immunity and Privileges Act (CAP 39:01).
Income Tax Act (CAP 52:01).
Local Government Audit, (1993), Audit report and accounts of the Gaborone City Council.
MFDP, (1996), Annual Economic Report.
Statutory Instrument Nos. 67-71 of 1995.
Townships Act (CAP 40:02).
Transfer Duty Act (CAP 53:01).

MFDP, (1996), Financial statements, tables and estimates of consolidated and development fund revenues 1996/97, Government Printer, Gaborone.

MFDP, (1991), National Development Plan 7 (1991-1997), Government Printer, Gaborone.

MLGLH, (1996), Model Bye-Law: phase two report.

MLGLH, (1996), Costing manual: phase two report.

MLGLH, (1995), Formula determined revenue support grant model.

MLGLH, (1995), Town and City Councils recurrent budgets for 1995/96.

MLGLH, (1994), Town and City Councils recurrent budgets for 1994/95.

MLGLH, (1993), Increasing the own-source revenues of councils: a report.

MLGLH, (1993), Town and City Councils recurrent budgets for 1993/94.

MLGLH, (1992), Town and City Councils recurrent budgets for 1992/93.

MLGLH, (1988), Draft rates manual.

Mogae, F.G. (1996), Budget Speech, Government Printer, Gaborone.

Rating Review Committee, (1995), A Report.

10 Property taxation in Zimbabwe

Geoff Brakspear

Historical background

In order to begin to understand the levying of taxes for local government administration it is necessary to understand the historical background to the ownership and occupation of land in Zimbabwe. Prior to 1890, most land in the country, now known as Zimbabwe, was occupied by small numbers of black Africans. Land was plentiful and with a subsistence economy there was no need for the indigenous population to lay private ownership to land; when the resources of the occupied land were depleted then the people merely moved on to any unoccupied land. Apart from stone cities that were abandoned well before the 1800s and the 'city' of the Paramount Chief of the Ndebele people, no major urban centres were developed and, due to the construction of most dwellings (pole, mud and thatch), villages could be abandoned with ease and reconstructed elsewhere.

Traditionally, the indigenous people considered that the land was held in trust for their forebears and descendants. Thus no living person had any absolute rights of occupation or ownership that could be sold or transferred. Without entering into the history of the land occupation of the Rhodesian settlers, it is suffice to say that under the Land Apportionment Act, 1930 and the Land Tenure Act, 1969, the entire country was split into three broad occupation groupings, being:

1   Land allocated for white settlement, where no black African was permitted to own land.

2   Land allocated for black settlement, known as the 'Tribal Trust Lands', could continue to be used in the traditional African way. In addition there

216

was a small amount of land set aside for black African ownership, known as the 'African Purchase Areas'.

3   Land allocated for the conservation of wildlife and flora, which was controlled by the government.

Needless to say, the apportionment of land was by no means fair on the indigenous population. Generally speaking, about 47 per cent of the country was allocated for white settlement, 6 per cent for national parks and woodlands and the last 47 per cent to the indigenous black Africans. In 1979 there were approximately 250,000 whites and 7 million blacks. This system of land ownership continued to 1979 when the Land Tenure Act was repealed thus allowing all races to occupy or own land in any part of the country, except of course, the national parks.

With the arrival of white settlers came central and local government, both of which inevitably required to finance its activities by the raising of taxes in one form or another. The system of property taxation was largely based on the rating systems in South Africa, particularly of the Cape colony, which had the following fundamental aspects:

1   All ownership of land by the private sector was in terms of title deeds registered in deeds offices.

2   All original title deeds for a particular piece of land would have a land survey document attached to it.

3   Property taxes or rates would be charged on the basis of ownership of all registered land in deeds offices, with certain exceptions.

4   The registered owner of land would be responsible for the payment of property taxes or rates.

But with some 47 per cent of the country in communal ownership, it was necessary to change the system of property taxation in respect of these areas. In this case, property taxation is payable on the basis of land occupation and by people living in the communal areas. These are the basic principles of the land taxation system in Zimbabwe.

Local government administration

Due to the historic and political history of the country, three forms of local government administration evolved prior to 1980 based on the previous allocation of land on racial lines. Up to 1988 there were three acts of parliament controlling three forms of local government area, these being:

1 Urban council areas in terms of the Urban Councils Act (Chapter 29:15), which were principally the four cities (Harare, Bulawayo, Mutare and Gweru) plus the larger towns such as Masvingo, Marondera, Chinhoyi and Kadoma. Historically, all urban council areas were within areas designated for white occupation.

2 Rural council areas in terms of the Rural District Councils Act (Chapter 29:13), which covered the remaining land previously designated for white ownership. The areas were largely agricultural and included a few small towns and villages which inevitably became the administrative centres of the districts.

3 District council areas in terms of the District Councils Act (Chapter 231), previously designated as Tribal Trust Land, now known as the Communal Lands.

Together with these different administrative areas, different forms of property taxation evolved as follows:

1 Urban rates: applicable to urban council areas and to designated land within the rural council areas. Rates in these areas were based on a formal valuation of the property.

2 Rural rates: also known as unit tax, were based on land ownership and the size of land owned.

3 Supplementary charges: devised for the incorporated areas (formerly African Township Areas).

4 Communal land rates: applicable to the Communal Lands which were based on a per capita basis, stock or buildings in the possession of an individual or on the value of the land belonging to the inhabitant.

It should be emphasized that the responsibility of assessing and levelling the property taxation payable is in the hands of the local government authority. There is no centralized system of any form for property taxation, except in so far as the Minister is responsible for giving his consent to the charges proposed.

In dealing with property taxation, I have chosen to initially concentrate on the basis of the taxation, under urban rates, rural rates, supplementary charges and communal land rates. Thereafter I shall examine how the particular taxation is levied and applied.

Urban rates

The governing legislation for the valuation of property for rating purposes is contained within Part XVII (section 186 to 215) of the Urban Councils Act (Chapter 29:15). In terms of clause 101 of the Rural District Councils Act, 1988, the provisions of the Urban Councils Act shall apply, to the land within the council area declared to be 'urban land'. 'Urban land' in terms of the Rural District Councils Act is defined as:

(i) areas containing stands used or intended for use for residential, commercial or industrial purposes;

(ii) land set aside in terms of section 10 of the Communal Land Act, 1982 for the establishment of a township, village, business centre or industrial area. Whilst land in the Communal Areas cannot be sold into private ownership certain land in these areas is held by individuals and organisations on a permit. As it is necessary, due to the capital investment in property of this nature to have some form of security of tenure, the permit must, therefore, be of sufficient duration to be attractive; and

(iii) land declared as urban land by the Minister after consultation with the Council.

Each local authority is responsible for the valuation of the relevant areas of its administration. The council is responsible for the appointment of a Valuation Officer who shall undertake and supervise the valuation and preparation of the valuation roll. In practice it is only the larger towns that are able to employ full-time valuation officers on their payroll, other councils usually request the Chief Government Valuation Officer to undertake the valuation or, the valuation officer is appointed, after tendering, through the Estate Agents Council.

The council as soon as it is established shall ensure that a general valuation of all properties within its area is undertaken. For this purpose the council must fix a date falling within the period during which the valuation is to be carried out and 'all property within its area shall be assessed so as to arrive at a fair and equitable valuation of property'. The valuation roll must thereafter be updated by a revaluation of all property not less than three years and not more than ten years after it came into effect. However by notice in the Government Gazette the Minister may extend such interval to not more than 15 years. During the intervening period supplementary or amended valuations shall be undertaken in the following instances:

- where a property did not appear in the general valuation roll;

- the value of the property has been affected by flood or other disaster;

- the value of the property has been affected by alterations, additions or demolitions;

- the property was not previously within the council or urban area;

- the value of the property has been affected by a town planning scheme or the construction of public works;

- properties have been consolidated or the property has been subdivided into lots on any approved diagram or general plan in terms of the Land Survey Act;

- the value of the property has been materially affected by any cause peculiar to that property; and

- any property where errors occurred in the general valuation roll which affected the value of the property.

Any property valued in a supplementary or amended valuation roll shall form part of the general valuation roll and shall be valued at the same valuation date.

Rateable property

All property within a council or urban area shall be rateable, except property which is:

1   vested in the state; or vested in and occupied by the council and is not held by a person who is either a party to an agreement which, on the fulfilment by him of a condition in the agreement, which entitles him to take transfer of the land; or a statutory authority or body to which the ownership of land has been transferred by any Act of Parliament;

2   any of the following types of property: (there are slight variations between the two acts) -

- property used exclusively for public religious worship, or public religious worship and religious educational purposes;

- property used exclusively for public libraries, art galleries or museums of natural history or of fine art;

- property exclusively used as a university or university college, registered school, registered nursery school or a boarding house or hostel used in connection with these facilities;

- property used exclusively as a public institution for aged persons or mentally or physically disabled persons or any other charitable cause, public hospital or orphanage or a nursing home or hostel which is maintained in connection with an institution referred to;

- public cemeteries or crematoria;

- mining locations exclusively used for mining purposes;

- property used exclusively for amateur theatre, active athletic sports, horse racing, motor racing, Boy Scouts, Girl Guides or other similar youth organization, or functions and activities of the church or members of the church;

- property owned by an agricultural society and used exclusively for showground purposes;

- railway property;

- property owned by any other local authority in respect or improvements thereon or which is less than 5 hectares in extent and on which works of a public nature have been erected. (10 hectares under Rural District Councils Act).

Basis of valuation

The basis of valuation for commercial property shall be 'the estimated price which a buyer would be willing to give and the seller would be willing to accept if the property to be valued were brought to voluntary sale in the open market' at the valuation date fixed by the council. The Valuation Officer shall ignore any exceptional circumstances of a temporary nature in undertaking his valuation of the property as a whole or the valuation of the land only.

The council may request the Valuation Officer to apportion the valuation of the property between land and improvements on the basis that the value of the land shall be the value as though it were unimproved and the value of the improvements shall be the difference between the value of the property as a whole, less the value of the land.

A council may if it so wishes elect to have a general valuation roll made on the basis of the value of land only, in which case the valuation is undertaken as though the land is unimproved. This is an important section within the Acts, as within Zimbabwe there is a shortage of suitably qualified valuers and some councils, having extended the period of the current valuation roll to 15 years, may have to opt for the valuation roll to be compiled on this basis.

Within the Act 'property' is defined as land including improvements, while improvements are defined to include:

1   all buildings, moveable or immovable;

2   incomplete buildings which are occupied in whole or in part; and

3   all work actually done or material used upon any land and the expenditure of capital or labour by the owner or occupier, but only in so far as it effects the value of the property.

Improvements does not include the following:

1   the clearing of land of trees, undergrowth or rock or the levelling or draining of the land or works of a similar nature;

2   work done or material used on or for the benefit of any interest in land by the State or by any council, unless such work or material has not become the property of the State or such council; and

3   plant or machinery which is situated on or in any property that is occupied and used wholly or mainly in connection with one or more of the following activities; the making of any article, altering, repairing of any article, generation of electricity for sale, the production or storage of gas, the slaughtering of livestock, the freezing, chilling or storage in cold storage of any article or material.

The basis of valuation is fairly clear and specific, in general the methods of valuation used are those used for open market capital valuation purposes. Basically the five principal methods of property valuation (direct capital comparison, investment, residual, contractor's and profits methods) are utilized in respect of different types of property.

Assessment of residential property

The assessment of residential property for rating purposes consists of calculating the number of 'rating units' to be assigned to the property and determining the rating zone within which the property is situated. The 'rating unit' is an area equal to the minimum size of plots permitted under any town planning scheme applicable within the locality in which the property is located, or in the absence of such a planning scheme, such an area as determined by the council. The number of rating units assigned to any specific property is calculated by dividing the area of the property by the rating unit applicable to the property. Each council shall divide the council area into one or more rating zones having regard to the following:

1   each rating zone should contain residential properties of approximately the same size and value;

2   should contain properties which are adjacent to each other; and

3   no rating zone should consist solely of one property.

The valuation roll

During the course of the valuation the Valuation Officer must prepare the general valuation roll to contain the following:

1   the name of the owner of the property;

2   the description of the property;

3   the area of the land;

4   the valuation of the property. The valuation of the property if required by the council being split between land and improvements, with the total value of the property being included. If the land is valued then this value only should appear; and

5   any other particulars that a council may require.

Once the valuation roll has been completed, the Valuation Officer shall sign it and submit it to the council, which shall then:

1   have a copy made available for inspection in the council offices for any owner, occupier or duly authorised representative to inspect and make copies;

2   by notice in the Government Gazette, and in two issues of the local newspaper, call upon owners and occupiers of property to object to either the valuation of the property concerned or its apportionment between land and improvements or in respect of any error, omission or incorrect description in relation to the property. All objections shall be lodged in the prescribed form within 21 days of the notice appearing in the Government Gazette.

In addition, if the council objects to any valuation appearing in its valuation roll, it shall give notice in writing to the owner or occupier of the property concerned and to the Clerk of the Valuation Board at least 28 days before the day upon which the Valuation Board sits to consider the valuation roll.

Valuation Board

In every council area a Valuation Board shall be established, made up of the President of the Administrative Court (to act as the President of the Board) and two additional members, one of whom shall be selected by the Minister and the other nominated by the council.

Objections to the valuation roll

Once the Clerk of the Valuation Board has received all objections within the allowable time period, he shall give notice in the Government Gazette and a local newspaper stating the place, hour and date at and on which the Valuation Board will sit to consider objections lodged in terms of the Act. In addition, the Clerk shall, at least 28 days before the date of sitting of the Valuation Board, forward a copy of the notice referred in the Gazette to every objector and to the Valuation Officer, who shall also receive copies of all objections which are to be considered by the Valuation Board.

The owner or occupier of the property may appear before the Valuation Board personally or may be represented by a legal practitioner or any other person duly authorized by him in writing. The council may appear before the Valuation Board at any of its sittings for the purpose of making any representations or objections on behalf of the council and shall be represented by any person, except the Valuation Officer, as the council may appoint. Finally, the Valuation Officer shall appear before the Valuation Board. Any representative of the council, the Valuation Officer and any objector or his representative may call evidence and cross examine any witness.

If an objector fails to appear before the Valuation Board, the Valuation Board shall nevertheless consider the objection and the matter shall be determined.

After considering the objections in terms of the Act the Board may either confirm any valuation or make such alterations or amendments to the valuation roll in respect only of separate individual properties as it may deem expedient, whether or not an objection has been made. If no objection has been lodged no alteration or amendment shall be made to the valuation roll unless the owner or occupier of the property concerned and the council have received 28 days notice in writing from the Clerk of the Valuation Board of the time and place of the sitting of the Valuation Board at which an alteration or amendment will be considered and the nature and extent of the proposed alteration or amendment.

However, the Valuation Board shall not be entitled to reduce or increase the valuation of property in the whole or any portion of the council area by a percentage. It would appear that if the valuation officer has valued the whole or part of the area at figures that would appear to be higher or lower than the general market value at the valuation date, the Valuation Board would be required to determine the valuation on each and every property and thereafter shall allow the owner and occupier of the property and the council to object. It is unlikely that the Board will revalue every single property within the town or a particular area unless there are overriding circumstances to justify this action.

All decisions of the Valuation Board shall be final and binding and without further appeal. However, on questions of law arising from the proceedings there are certain defined channels whereby an aggrieved party may appeal to the High Court.

Changes to the valuation roll

Once the valuation roll has been brought into effect, the council may through its Valuation Officer, have supplementary valuations or amendments to the valuation roll made. The procedures for both of the methods of changing, adding to, reducing and the like to the valuation roll follows much the same procedures as with a general valuation roll. Of importance is the 'tone of the list' provisions contained in the act which pertain to the assessment of new property or altered property to be included within supplementary rolls with regard to the level of values to be adopted. The general rise or fall in values since the last general revaluation are disregarded in determining the new assessed values.

Rural rates

Unlike urban council areas, rural land (defined within the Rural Councils Act as land not being urban land) is not subject to valuation. The whole concept of the tax is based on the area of land owned, or the number of employees in a mining venture, or on the output from certain mines, or the number of licenses issued or on the use of rural land.

In order to assess the tax payable it is necessary to have a common basis upon which to levy the tax. The tax in terms of the Act is called the 'Land Development Levy' and the basis of assessing the levy payable on all use-types is a 'unit', which is defined in great detail within the Third Schedule of the Rural District Councils Act.

Rateable property

All the following owners of property are subject to the payment of the Land Development Levy:

1   an owner of rural land;

2   owners of mining locations situated on rural land within the council area mining for base metals, gold, silver, platinum or precious stones;

3   an owner of land which is deemed to be rural land by virtue of a resolution of the council in terms of the Act; and

4   a person who carries on a specified business on rural land within the council area or is the owner of rural land within the council area on which a specified business is carried on.

Within the Rural District Councils Act there is no exemption for similar organizations exempted from paying urban rates. However, a council may reduce by one unit the land development levy in respect of land which exceeds 120 hectares in extent and has on it any church or school maintained by religious or other body, society or association which has as objects the spiritual, physical, intellectual or industrial welfare or vocational guidance of persons.

Units of land

As previously mentioned, the Land Development Levy shall be levied in accordance with the Third Schedule of the Act. Alternatively, if the Minister directs the Land Development Levy shall be assessed in the same manner as the Urban Rate as if the rural land concerned were urban land. This would involve the valuation of rural land, which in itself may not be easy when it comes to permits issued for the use of Communal Land which may have no transferable rights attached.

Supplementary charges

There is no specific Act of Parliament that sets out how supplementary charges shall be calculated in respect of any Incorporated Area. In terms of the Urban Councils Act, the Minister may make regulations for 'fixing and imposing in respect of immovable property in a local government area, except such property as may be exempted in the Regulations, a supplementary charge to cover the expenses incurred by the State for the maintenance and administration of the area'. This however, only relates to where the State is administrating the Incorporated Area.

In terms of the Rural District Councils Act, a council in terms of section 89 may make bye-laws applicable for an Incorporated Area to provide for 'fixing and imposing in respect of immovable property in the area concerned, except such property as may be exempted in Regulations by the Minister, a supplementary charge to cover the expenses incurred by the council in the maintenance and administration of the area concerned'. In terms of this Act the supplementary charge shall be based on a unit of land and additionally, or alternatively, a unit of residential or business accommodation, as determined by the council and the council may vary such charges according to any or all of the following:

1   the type of tenure under which the property is held;

2   value of the property, whether based upon the value of the land or improvements, or both;

3   the area of the property, being either that of the land or the improvements, or for the use to which the property is put.

This provision did not previously exist in the Rural Councils Act or indeed the District Councils Act, and to date no subsidiary legislation has been passed in order to ascertain how these particular provisions will be implemented. It is interesting to note that in this section the value of the property could be used as a basis upon which to assess a supplementary charge, but no basis of valuation is offered. In terms of these bye-laws every user of residential hostels and other nonresidential uses shall pay a monthly supplementary charge for each property he is the user of. This supplementary charge shall be calculated according to the use to which the premises are put and shall be payable on the first day of each month to the appropriate office.

The supplementary charge is calculated by reference to the floor area which is defined as the area of floor space enclosed by the external walls and includes areas above and below ground level. Every unit user of a dwelling unit within

227

the incorporated areas shall pay to the council a supplementary charge for each dwelling unit of which he is the user. For the various incorporated areas different charges are made for different types of accommodation or structures and much depends on the present legal title of the occupier of the unit.

Communal land rates

The rates chargeable in the communal lands and the resettlement areas has recently changed in terms of the Rural District Councils Act. In terms of the Rural District Councils Act a council may impose a 'development levy' (note that the Rural Rates were described in terms of the Act as 'land development levy'). The development levy shall be imposed upon all persons who, on the date any charge becomes due and payable to the council concerned, are 'Heads of Household' within any communal or resettlement ward of the council or who, at any time during the period of 12 months following the date the levy was imposed becomes a Head of Household within any such ward. The Head of Household is defined as a person who occupies or uses:

1   communal land for agricultural or residential purposes other than a spouse, child or dependant of any person who occupies the same land; or

2   any resettlement land for agricultural or residential purposes by virtue of an agreement, whether written, oral or tacit, between himself and the state.

Clearly the development levy is imposed upon the Head of Household of a family unit occupying land within the council area. The land is not leased to him but is granted as a traditional right of occupation and use. The rate that it charged on each Head of Household could be uniform throughout the area concerned no matter how well developed the land is or indeed the quality of that land, or the number of persons in the household. However, the council may, with approval of the Minister, charge different rates for different classes of Heads of Household.

Implementation and charging of local government taxation

With four types of local authority taxation it is possible within the rural district councils for all four types of tax to be imposed at the same time. This is not necessarily true of the urban council areas as it is unlikely that there will be any communal or resettlement land within its boundaries. However, it is possible for the other three types of taxation to be found in the urban council areas.

228

I have not ascertained from the two acts of Parliament how a council should view the imposition of its taxation in respect of the different types of land ownership and occupation. It is however, probable that the council will attempt to show an equitable balance between the different land uses bearing in mind the ability to pay of the individuals concerned. If there was only one type of local government taxation applicable clearly the council would estimate the income it requires and thereafter calculate the tax chargeable based on either the rateable values; or the number of units; or the numbers, types and uses of premises in the Incorporated Areas; or on the total number of heads of household.

Methods of levying rates

In terms of the Urban Councils Act, a council shall have the power to fix and levy in respect of each financial year or part thereof a General Rate upon all rateable property within the council area. The General Rate, may be assessed on the valuation of the land only or that apportioned to the improvements only or of the whole property or on the land and improvements valuation. The council may levy different rates on the land and improvements. In addition, the council may, with the approval of the Minister, determine that a lower rate or rates than that generally applicable shall be levied for a particular class or classes of property, or that a different general rate shall be levied in respect of commercial, industrial and residential properties.

The City of Harare, for example, levies a general rate on all nonresidential properties and a special lower rate on all residential properties. For example, the City of Harare levied rates as shown in Table 10.1 for the period July to December 1988.

Table 10.1
Rates in cents per dollar of value

	Land	Improvements
General Rate	2,323c	1,572c
Residential Rate	1,014c	0,711c

Unlike the urban councils, the rural district councils may only impose the Land Development Levy (Rural rates or unit tax) and the Development Levy (Communal land rates) once during any 12 month period. The levy shall be imposed in order to meet expenditure on matters which are prescribed in regulations and reflected in estimates or supplementary estimates provided and approved in terms of the act. The only variation to the levy imposed is that the council may fix different rates in respect of different classes of heads of household. It would appear from the act that if the council needed to raise a specific figure then in respect of the unit tax, for example, the levy is easily calculated by dividing the total number of units by the amount required.

Methods of payment

Within the Urban Councils Act, rates are usually chargeable twice a year for the periods January to June and July to December. In the City of Harare, the rate is usually charged and becomes payable by 31 May or 30 November in any year. Ratepayers can however, choose to pay the rates on a monthly basis and must make application to their council for paying by this method.

In terms of the Rural District Councils Act, the rate is chargeable once a year and is payable on the date specified by the council. Levy payers may choose to pay the levy on the due date or by monthly instalments. In both cases where a ratepayer chooses to pay by monthly instalments, interest can be charged by the council at the prescribed rates, currently 10.5 per cent per annum. Supplementary charges are usually payable on a monthly basis.

Special rates, levies and charges

In both of the relevant acts the council may impose special rates, with the consent of the Minister, to meet a specific expense or development project that it wishes to carry out. For example, the City of Harare imposes a special rate on all industrial land that is served by a private railway siding. In this instance, the City of Harare provided railway sidings to industrial stands at its expense and owners of these stands have had to pay an annual rate for the maintenance and service of these railway sidings.

A special rate has been levied by one of the smaller towns for the supply of a particular area of that town. With the ability of being able to raise special levies, demands by residents can be met out of expenditure specifically raised for a particular project.

In addition to this special rate, councils may impose specific rates for the entire town or city in respect of a particular service supplied by the council. For example, the City of Harare, imposes a waste management tariff and a sewerage tariff on all owners of land, including owners of non-rateable properties. Both special rates and specific rates or charges vary from town to town and much depends on the services provided by the council concerned.

Non-payment of rates

If a rate or levy remains unpaid for a period of 30 days from the fixed date relating to that charge, a council may charge interest at the prescribed amount. However, if the rate or levy remains unpaid the council may take action against the individual concerned through the courts. In cases of private land, the council would normally request the courts to attach the property concerned and to have that property sold by public auction.

Interestingly, no transfer of land shall be registered for land contained within a council area unless a valid certificate is attached stating that all rates and charges made and levied in respect of the property during the last five years have been paid, or, if not paid are deemed irrecoverable.

Conclusions

The four types of local government taxation presents a colourful and varied picture of the financing of local government. It is unlikely that there will be many major changes, with the exception of supplementary charges. There are insufficient valuers within Zimbabwe at the present time to value for rating purposes all privately held land particularly if the rating is to be based on the value of the improved property. Thus the Urban and Rural District Councils in implementing urban rates, value the properties at their own convenience depending on the availability of sufficient valuers to undertake the necessary work. Property valuers must make enquiries at all council offices prior to undertaking their normal non-rating valuations, in order to ascertain the rateable values, date of valuation and rates imposed.

In view of the nature of land holding within the Communal Lands, it would be difficult to impose a system of rating based on open market values in these areas, as the land in terms of section 8 of the Communal Land Act allows a person to occupy and use communal land without giving that individual any saleable interest.

With the Government policy of 'a single city (or town) concept', it is likely that we will see the end of supplementary charges within the incorporated areas once all land has been placed in private ownership in terms of a registered title deed.

Unless there is a major change to the local government taxation, concepts of Roman Dutch Law and a rapid increase in competent property valuers, any major changes in the way local government taxation is viewed are not foreseen. Whilst the system of local government taxation has its peculiarities and problems the system appears to work and is generally accepted by most taxpayers.

11 Property tax systems in The Netherlands

Jan Paul Kruimel

Origins and evolution

Property taxes were introduced in the Netherlands in 1970. They replaced the old land tax and the personal property tax levied by central government, the public street tax and the fire insurance tax, levied by the municipalities. The abolished land tax was based on an assessment of rental value which dated from 1892; the personal property tax was based on the rental value of the household effects.

The introduction of property taxes throughout the country took some time; the last municipality which reformed its tax system did so in 1980. Since 1970 there have been three major changes made to the laws concerning the property tax. The first considered the basis of valuation of unmarketable property, the second with regard to limitations on revenue from the property taxes and thirdly, in 1995 a general overhaul of the municipal taxes. The most important change to affect the property tax was the abolition of the area based system with effect from 1997.

Local property taxes

In the Netherlands the municipalities have the power to levy four taxes on moveable and immoveable property.

Immovable property taxes ('onroerende-zaakbelastingen'):

- a tax levied on those who have a right *in rem* over immovable property; and

- a tax levied on those who use immovable property.

Movable property taxes ('belastingen op roerende woon-en bedrijfsruimten'):

- a tax levied on those who have a right *in rem* over non-immovable residential accommodation or working accommodation which is of a permanent nature and is to be used permanently; and

- a tax levied on those who use non-immovable residential accommodation or working accommodation which has a permanent nature and is to be used permanently.

Taxes on movable property were introduced in 1995 after legal disputes concerning the taxing of house boats. The High Court decided that a house boat, a so called water-mansion, was not an immovable property. Movable property taxes are levied by only a few municipalities. The rules for the taxation of immovable property are equally applicable to movable property taxes, while the rates applied on the latter must be the same as the rate for the corresponding tax on immovable property. In this chapter only the rules concerning immovable property taxes will be described. Property taxes are known as the owners' tax and the users' tax. Theoretically, the municipalities are permitted to levy either one of the property taxes, both or none, however, in reality all prefer to levy both taxes.

Statutory regulations

The main sections dealing with the rules concerning property taxes can be found in the Municipality Act. The municipalities are empowered to levy the tax through a municipal bye-law.

From the fiscal year 1997 the rules for the assessment are to be found in the Immovable Property Assessment Act. According to this act the assessments for the municipal property tax, the tax on built property levied by the water boards, the net wealth tax and income tax (imputed rent) which are levied by central government are carried out by the municipalities.

Revenue and limitations

The total revenue of the tax is currently in the region of Dfl. 4,000 million which represents almost Dfl. 250 per inhabitant or Dfl. 750 per family. These figures include the taxes levied on nonresidential property. Whilst in 1980 the taxes collected represented only 3.5 per cent of the total income of municipalities, by 1995 this percentage had risen to almost 8 per cent. Municipalities are not constrained as to how the revenue should most appropriately be spent; there are no constraints on the provision of special investments or services rendered.

Until 1990 the revenue from the taxes was limited by statutory rules. Effectively the revenue from the owners' tax was not allowed to exceed 15 per cent of the block grant which the municipality received from the Municipality Fund. As to the users' tax the limitation was 12 per cent. From 1990 these percentage constraints on revenue have been replaced by a relative limit: now the rate of the owners' tax may not exceed 125 per cent of the rate of the users' tax. The rates applied to the owners' tax and users' tax when considered together show large variations between municipalities. The maximum tax burden at present would tend not to exceed approximately 1 per cent of the market value of the property.

The property tax base

Property taxes are levied on all immovable property. This includes everything in the ground, built upon the ground and fixed to the structures. Whether a property is immovable has to be decided according to civil law. It includes the land as well as the buildings and improvements.

Delineation of individual property

Contained within the Immovable Property Assessment Act are the rules concerning the delineation of the individual property upon which the taxes are levied:

1   built property with the land under the property;

2   non-built property (land);

3   if part of a property referred to under 1 or 2 above is of such nature that it is intended to be used as a separate entity; whilst it is understood that if two or more of such parts are being used as one entity, those parts are considered as one property;

4   if two or more of the properties referred to under 1, 2, or 3, are being used by one taxpayer and belong together, according to general understanding such a complex is considered as one property.

Rule 4 is also applicable to all complexes of land and buildings such as a house with a garden.

235

Only property that lies within the boundaries of a municipality can be taxed by that municipality. In principle there is no delineation for the property in a vertical direction. However, in practice municipalities only tax the built structures and everything that is connected to it, such as gas exploration pipelines in the ground.

Consequences of irregular delineation

If the delineation of the property has not been carried out according to the law, the tax court has the power to nullify the assessment notice, with the consequence that the revenue is lost to the municipality. This can occur when too much property has been taken into account. There is no opportunity for a new tax bill to be issued for the same property to the same taxpayer. This represents a different situation to the case where the wrong person has been sent the tax bill, in which case, a new tax bill can be sent to the right person or corporation. In all cases tax bills should be sent within three years of the beginning of the fiscal year.

Date of assessment

With regard to the two property taxes, one is normally levied on the occupier, and the other on the owner. Both property taxes are levied according to circumstances at the beginning of the fiscal year, i.e. 1 January. No relief is granted if the circumstances change during the year, however, it is generally accepted that the public notary settles the owners' tax on any future sale of the property. The fact that a person has a right to use the property does not affect his liability. The fact that he uses the property is sufficient justification for the issuance of the assessment notice and the tax bill.

Assessment for the owners' tax

The owners' tax is levied on those who have a right *in rem* over the property. The major part of this group consists of those who are the owners of the property or those who have a long lease on the property. Within the national cadastre of the Netherlands all properties together with the names of the owner and other persons who have a right *in rem* to the property are registered. There is only one exception to this, the right of possession is not registered. On the other hand, the so called economic ownership, which is often coupled with the right of possession, is registered.

The users' tax is levied only on those who use the property. With reference to residential property this means that the occupier will be taxed. When a property is occupied by a household, the choice of taxpayer, in this case, is at the discretion of the municipality.

If parts of a property, though not separate properties, are being used by different persons or corporations, the person or corporation who has made this use possible is liable for the users' tax even if he does not use the property himself. In this way the landlord of the property is taxed for the use of the property by different persons who do not form one household.

If a property is successively used by different persons or corporations during the year, which is generally the case with holiday homes and sports halls, the person who has made the use possible is liable for the users' tax.

The value basis

From 1997 the rules concerning the basis of the property tax are to be found in the Immovable Property Assessment Act. Prior to 1997 the rules were prescribed in the Municipality Act and before 1983 in the Municipal Property Tax Decree. All properties are required to be valued according to a specific date, which needs to reflect the physical situation, state of repair, as well as to the legal situation, for example the land planning rules.

The tax base for residential property

The statutory basis adopted is the market value of the property. This is defined as follows:

> ... the true economic value determined as that which could be assigned to the property if re and unencumbered right could be transferred for immediate and complete acquisition by a purchaser of the property in its actual condition.

In other words, the market value is calculated on the basis of the price which the property would fetch if it were sold in a free market with full vacant possession and without encumbrance or mortgage. In addition, the following are to be ignored, the fact that the property is let or where there is a current lease. This means that property taxes are not a form of personal taxation, the amount payable relates solely to the property itself and is not effected by the personal circumstances of the user or the owner.

The market value is the tax base for residential property and from 1997 also applies to buildings listed as historic monuments.

The tax base for non-residential property

Since 1983 the Municipality Act has a separate set of rules with regard to the tax base for non-marketable properties. These special rules were introduced following decisions of the tax courts which were generally unfavourable to the municipalities. For example, a water purification plant belonging to a public water board recently built for several million guilders would, according to court decisions, be assessed at nil, owing to the fact that only the present owner can use it for this purpose, and land planning regulations do not provide opportunities for alternative uses. Similar decisions were given concerning industrial properties. In 1983 new rules were introduced.

In 1995 a review was implemented which means that all non-residential property except listed historic buildings are to be assessed at market value unless the corrected replacement value of the property was higher, in which case the corrected replacement value becomes the taxable value.

The corrected replacement value is the replacement cost corrected for functional and technical obsolescence. Technical obsolescence refers to the structure and will generally be expressed as a percentage related to its remaining useful life. Functional obsolescence relates to a fall in value resulting from economic changes: new buildings meeting current criteria will generally offer economic advantages when compared to older structures. Account must be taken in this respect of general developments in the economy and developments within the particular sector.

Methods of valuation

The methods of valuation to be applied, are in principle left to the discretion of the valuer. From 1997 the Immovable Property Assessment Instruction contains criteria concerning which method is to be used for determining the market value.

Residential property is to be valued by one of the following methods:

1   comparison with reference to residential properties;

2   comparison with properties in a homogenous group of residential properties;

3   statistical models; or

4   combinations of the above methods.

Non-residential property is to be valued by one of the following methods:

1   capitalization of the gross rent;

2   comparison to other similar properties; or

3   discounted cashflow calculation.

For the corrected replacement value the value of the land is to be added to the value of the building(s). The value of the land is determined by comparison, reflecting the land use planning rules. The value of the building is calculated by reference to the cost of building an identical replacement building, corrected for technical obsolescence in relation to its remaining useful life and for functional obsolescence based on economic obsolescence, antiquated construction methods and excessive running costs.

In determining the corrected replacement value for church buildings and buildings of historical interest which are not listed, the functional obsolescence is to be applied in such a way that the value is equivalent to the utilization value.

The functional obsolescence is determined in such a way that the value is equal to the operating value of the property reflecting the relationship to economic developments in the particular sector concerned.

From 1997 it is obligatory to use a network of comparables as a reference basis. The references consist of comparables with an assessed value and reference figures. A plan for the revaluation has to be approved by the (national) Valuation Board. Quality control by the municipality on the reference network and on the valuations is compulsory. A report on the results has to be sent to the Valuation Board.

Special valuation rules

Since 1995 special valuation rules prescribed by the Municipality Act and the Immovable Property Assessment Act relate specifically to exemptions. The property tax in the Netherlands has a number of statutory exemptions. In addition, the municipalities have the power to prescribe additional exemptions within their bye-laws. In general all exemptions granted by the municipal authorities must not be in defiance of Article 1 of the Constitution, which states that all persons present in the Netherlands will be treated equally; discrimination owing to religion, political faith, race, sex or any other reason is not permitted. With regard to the property tax this requires that exemptions must be formulated generally and must not be designed for any one particular taxpayer.

Statutory valuation rules (exemptions)

The most important valuation rule/exemption concerns cultivated land which is professionally exploited for agriculture or forestry purposes. It includes all structures built over the land such as greenhouses. Suggestions to abolish this exemption have not been enacted. According to the Immovable Property Assessment Exempted Property Decree, the Municipality Act for valuation purposes no account is taken of:

1   Cultivated land which is professionally exploited for agriculture or forestry purposes. According to the Municipality Act this also includes properties built on such cultivated land.

2   Landed property that is part of an estate protected by the Nature Protection Act (which contains fiscal privileges).

3   Natural sites, including dunes, moorland, sand-drifts, swamps and lakes, administered by nature corporations.

4   Public roads, waterways and lanes for public transportation by rail, including all constructions, but not railway stations.

5   Machinery which can be removed whilst retaining its value as machinery and which is not considered to be built property.

6   Property that is mainly used for public worship, or meetings of spiritual societies. Not included are such parts of buildings which are used a residences.

7   Water-defence works and water-control works that are administered by public authorities. Excluded are such parts of buildings that are used as residences.

8   Water-purification plants administered by public authorities. Excluded are such parts of buildings used as residences.

9   Foreign embassies and consulates except the honorary-consulates.

Valuation rules (exemptions) in the model municipal bye-law

The model bye-law on property tax contains, in addition to the statutory exemptions, the following valuation (exempt) rules:

In the valuation for the municipal property taxes no account is taken of:

1   Properties used for public service by the municipality except those used for teaching (education).

2   Street furniture provided for the general public, such as lampposts, seats, traffic-lights and traffic-signs, monuments, fountains, gates, etc.

3   Public gardens, parks and ponds owned or managed by the municipality.

4   Cemeteries, crematoria and urn-gardens, except for those parts used as residencies.

Date of valuation

Up until the 1997 fiscal year a new reference date could be chosen every year, although very few municipalities took the opportunity to implement an annual revaluation. The majority of the municipalities have taken the alternative approach by adopting a five year revaluation period with only about 20 preferring a shorter period.

The majority of the municipal bye-laws on property tax contain a clause to the effect that a revaluation will take place in the case of alterations. The new valuations will have effect for the year following the completion of the alterations. The reference date will always be the one that is applicable for the next fiscal year. The result is that for each year all the properties are valued according to the same reference date. Generally, municipalities do not take into account improvements that have not been completed, in these cases only the land will be valued.

In 1997 the Immovable Property Assessment Act gave 1 January 1995 as a fixed revaluation date for the entire country. These assessments were applicable from 1997 for a four year period. After that a new assessment date, 1 January 1999, will be valid for the next period of four years and so forth. Thus every four years a revaluation will take place. The Immovable Property Assessment Act also contains rules concerning alterations during the assessment period. A new valuation will be carried out in the following circumstances:

1   the splitting up or merging of delineated properties or of parts of such properties which results in a change in the value of the property, to which property was added of more than 5 per cent or more than Dfl. 250,000 or in a change of the value of the property from which property was removed of more than 5 per cent or more than Dfl. 250,000;

2   changes in value as consequence of building of (additional) property, removal, improvement, demolition or destruction, which results in a change

in value of at least 5 per cent with a minimum of Dfl. 25,000 or Dfl 250,000 or more;

3   a change in value as mentioned under 2 as the result of circumstances that are exceptional for the property such as soil contamination.

The interim valuations are related to the reference (revaluation) date applicable and will have effect for the fiscal year following the completion of the alterations.

Exemptions

In addition to the valuation rules mentioned earlier the municipality has the power to introduce an efficiency exemption. Thus, properties with an assessed value not exceeding Dfl. 25,000 can by municipal bye-law, be exempt. The exemption applies to both the users' tax as well as the owners' tax, and not limited to specific properties.

Responsibility for assessment

Property taxes in the Netherlands are essentially municipal taxes. This means that municipalities can choose to either levy the taxes or not, and are responsible for the procedures necessary to produce the required yield. This procedure begins with the drawing up of the bye-law on property taxes by the municipal council. In the following paragraph the different responsibilities are outlined to illustrate the organization of the property tax. As far as possible the description follows the Immovable Property Assessment Act, effective from 1997.

Valuations

A committee comprising the Mayor and Aldermen are charged with the levying of the taxes, however, the responsibility for the work lies with municipal civil servants. The manner in which the valuations are carried out is at the discretion of the municipality: either municipal appraisers or private appraisers are employed to prepare the valuations. The schedule and basis concerning the valuations is prepared under a master plan which is determined by the committee of Mayor and Aldermen and must be further submitted to the (national) Valuation Board.

Furthermore, the municipality is obliged to carry out the continuous registration of sales transactions for all properties, information on rental contracts, building prices for nonresidential property and land value information. The basis for the valuations must be in accordance with a reference book consisting of equalized valuations of a random sample of properties within the municipality. The majority of the municipalities employ private appraisers. The largest property tax consultancy, 'Kafi', provides around half of the municipalities with appraisal services. The consultancy practices also assist the municipalities in defending the tax bills in court.

Appraisers are not yet required to have professional qualifications, however by 1998 they will be required to have passed the examination of Immovable Property Assessment Valuer, combined with the NFM qualification of the Netherlands Federation of Housing Agents.

Assessment and tax bill

Prior to 1997 in the Netherlands unlike in other countries, there was no difference between the assessment and the tax bill. The notification of the assessed value is given on the tax bill, which includes the address of the property, the assessed value and the name of the taxpayer. The tax bill is sent to the taxpayer by the municipality. Furthermore, it states for which tax the tax bill is being levied. The appeal process in terms of the assessment starts with receipt of the tax bill.

However, from 1997 the taxpayer receives a separate assessment notice from the municipality before 1 March. These assessments are used for the municipal property taxes, the water board tax on built property and for both the income tax (imputed rent) and net wealth tax which are levied by central government. The municipalities send an assessment notice to the user of the property and to the person who has a right *in rem* on the property. As noted previously the appeal process against the municipal property taxes starts with the assessment notice.

The assessment notice is sent on one occasion for the period of four years for which it is applicable. If during this period the valuation changes, then according to the rules of the law, a new assessment notice must be sent.

Under the Immovable Property Tax Assessment Act any person who proves that he is being taxed for the property, and who has not received an assessment notice, can request to be sent a (new) assessment notice.

An assessment notice can contain information on the assessments concerning various properties situated within the municipality for which the person named on the notice will be assessed. Normally, the municipalities will place all properties of a taxpayer disregarding whether he is the user of the property or in possession of a right *in rem* on the property, on one assessment notice.

Powers to call for return

The municipalities have the power to call for returns for the property taxes. They also have such powers under the Immovable Property Assessment Act. These powers are primarily used for nonresidential property and cover such aspects as construction plans and rental information. In valuing residential and several other property types returns are not used as all information concerning sales prices can be found in the public registers of the national cadastre, which is at the disposal of the municipality.

Public information

By law, the distribution of any information collected for tax purposes is illegal, unless this is necessary for the application of the tax laws. The taxpayer can ask the municipality for all the information it possesses concerning his own property. All persons and corporations who are liable for a tax bill, users' tax and owners' tax, are in the same position. No public information is given, though the municipality will generally give information concerning comparable properties in an appeal to the tax court. In addition, information from public sources, such as the national cadastre, will usually be given when requested. If the municipality refuses the taxpayer's request for information concerning the property in question, he can submit an administrative appeal to the Administrative Court.

Under the Immovable Property Assessment Act any person who has received an assessment notice can request the municipality to send him a copy of the valuation report. Furthermore, anyone who has a reasonable interest in knowing the value of a specific property - for example to compare assessed values, can ask for the assessment figure. In cases like this the valuation report is not supplied.

Appeal procedure

Under the Immovable Property Assessment Act there is an appeal procedure against the assessment notice and a separate procedure for the tax bill. The procedure against the tax bill is not normally concerned with the assessment, except on the question, whether the tax bill has been correctly calculated on the figure of the assessment notice. For all practical purposes the appeal procedures for both are identical.

The first stage of the appeal procedure is a written appeal to the Mayor and Aldermen given that they are the body responsible for sending the assessment notice and the tax bill. The written appeal must contain the reasons for the appeal, and must be received by the Mayor and Aldermen within six weeks after the date of mailing of the assessment notice or tax bill. The appeal against the assessment notice will be reviewed by an appraiser who may be the same appraiser who prepared the original valuation, but this is not mandatory. The appraiser will then advise the Mayor and Aldermen regarding the assessment. At the taxpayer's request he can be heard by one of the civil servants. The taxpayer will in due course receive a written decision. In some municipalities, especially the larger ones, the Mayor and Aldermen have delegated the responsibility on deciding appeals to senior civil servants, for example the Director of Taxes.

Against the decision of the Mayor and Aldermen an appeal can be made to the Tax Court. The written appeal must be received by the Tax Court within six weeks after the mailing of the decision of the Mayor and Aldermen and must contain the reasons for the appeal. It is not a requirement that the taxpayer be professionally represented. The Tax Court hears the evidence from both parties in private but the decision is given in public.

It is possible to instigate a further appeal against the decision of the Tax Court to the High Court. This appeal must be sent to the Tax Court and must be received within six weeks after the mailing of the Tax Court's decision. The Tax Court will forward the appeal to the High Court together with all the papers concerning the appeal.

A copy of the appeal is sent to the Mayor and Aldermen with an invitation to submit their case within a maximum period of six weeks. The High Court can only set aside the decision of the Tax Court on the basis of violation of the law with the exception of the law pertaining to foreign countries or neglect of formalities for which the penalty is nullity. Oral pleadings in the High Court are possible but rather infrequent in tax cases, mainly due to the fact that it can only be effected by a barrister. The decision of the High Court is generally the final decision.

Administrative procedures

Tax rates

The rate of tax is determined by the municipal council, with rates of property taxes being found in the municipal bye-law. Since 1990 the rates of the owners' tax and users' tax are related in the following way; the rate of the owner's tax must not exceed 125 per cent of the rate of the users' tax. Though this is not a statutory requirement it actually means that it is not possible to levy only the owners' tax. The tax rates are applied on a 'flat' basis. The following example should demonstrate the appropriate rules. The rates are given in an amount per full Dfl. 5,000 of value. Assume the assessment is Dfl. 32,000, the rate for the owners' tax is Dfl. 8 per full Dfl. 5,000, and the rate of the users' tax is Dfl. 7 per Dfl. 5,000. The owners' tax is therefore 32,000/5,000 = 6.4 x Dfl. 8 = Dfl. 48; and for the users' tax 32,000/5,000 = 6.4 x Dfl. 7 = Dfl. 42.

Since 1997 the municipalities have the power to increase the tax rates for nonresidential property or residential property subject to a maximum of 20 per cent. This is possible for the owner's tax as well as the user's tax and can be separately and differently used for each of these taxes.

Generally the tax can be paid in two instalments, the first ending on the last day of the month after the date of the tax bill and the second instalment expiring two months later. However, the municipality has the right to implement a different regime of instalments than that given in the municipal bye-law.

Collection and enforcement procedures

The tax collector for the municipality has the responsibility for the collection of property taxes. The tax is normally paid into the bank or giro account of the municipality, or in some cases cash payments are accepted at the town hall.

The person or corporation whose name is printed on the tax bill is liable for the payment of the tax. In the case of the owners' tax the co-owners are also liable for the payment of the tax. If the tax is not paid by the due date, the tax collector will furnish a demand notice. If no payment is subsequently made the tax-bailiff can serve a distress warrant. Finally, he can use distraint procedures without the need to call for a court judgement. Thus, all properties belonging to the taxpayer, including immovable property can be sold at public auction. All the costs of enforcement procedures have to be paid by the taxpayer.

A taxpayer can ask for an extension of payment or for payment to be spread across more instalments. This request would normally be granted, however the taxpayer has to pay interest on the amounts which are overdue.

Refunds and remission

If the tax bill is disputed and the taxpayer successfully appeals, any overpayment is refunded including interest. In some cases, especially with regard to the owners' tax, if the person liable for the payment of the tax is not in a position to pay the tax, the tax collector may grant him a remission. Generally, the tax collector will first consider whether payment could be spread over more instalments. Remission is not possible when it is found that the taxpayer has the ability to pay.

Conclusion

The most important development regarding property taxes has been the introduction of the Property Assessment Act which now requires only one assessed value for each property. This value is used as the basis for taxes levied by three different levels of government, i.e. central government, municipalities and water defence boards. In addition the preparation of the assessment is solely the responsibility of the municipality.

12 Decentralizing property taxation: the Philippine perspective

Oscar Baraquero

Introduction

The implementation of Republic Act (RA) No. 7160, known as the 1991 Local Government Code (LGC), gave high hopes, among others, of improved financial resources for local government units (LGUs) in the country. The Code, which integrated all laws related to the administration of the province, city, municipality and barangay (barrio), expanded the powers of the elected officials for each LGU, and revolutionized the operations for all departments delivering the basic and essential services including the administration of real property assessment. RA No. 7160 had been considered as central to the political program under the administration which overthrew martial law in the Philippines. It became the law to 'free the local government units from the total grip of an overly centralized government which left our LGUs with very little room for decision-making'. Powers and resources were devolved to the LGUs from central government, aimed to facilitate development in the countryside.

National leaders declared that the territorial and political subdivisions of the state should enjoy genuine and meaningful local autonomy, to enable them to attain maximum development as self-reliant communities and make them more effective partners in the attainment of national goals. Toward this end, the state shall provide for more responsive and accountable local government structures, instituted through a system of decentralization, whereby local governments shall be given more powers, authority, responsibilities and resources.

> Devolution of powers, no matter how small or vast powers are, becomes meaningless and ineffective without the necessary finances to support and sustain the functions of local governance.
>
> *(Quote from former Finance Secretary).*

Devolved functions to LGUs such as health and social services, housing policies, agriculture and quarrying activities, expanded the responsibilities of the local officials. To sustain the devolved functions, new sources of revenue had to be introduced. Existing local sources of income, like property taxation had to be optimized through effective fiscal administration.

Legal basis of assessment

The appraisal and assessment of real property as well as the levy and collection of the tax are guided by the following fundamental principles:

1   real property shall be appraised at its current and fair market value;

2   real property shall be classified for assessment purposes on the basis of its actual use;

3   real property shall be assessed on the basis of a uniform classification within each local government unit;

4   the appraisal, assessment, levy and collection of real property tax shall not be let to any private person; and

5   the appraisal and assessment of real property shall be equitable (Section 198).

Definition of terms

Appraisal is the act or process of determining the value of real property as of a specific date for a specific purpose.

Assessment is the process of discovery, listing, classifying and appraisal of real property subject to tax.

Fair market value is the price at which a property may be sold by a seller who is not compelled to sell and bought by a buyer who is not compelled to buy.

Assessment level is the percentage applied to the fair market value to determine the taxable value of the property. Simply stated, assessment level is the fraction/portion of the fair market value enacted by Ordinance of the local legislature which should not exceed the rate as prescribed by law.

Assessed value is the taxable value, a product of the fair market value multiplied by the assessment level.

Depreciated value is the value remaining after deducting from the acquisition cost.

Improvement is a valuable addition to a property or an amelioration in its condition, amounting to more than a mere repair or replacement of parts involving capital expenditures and labour which is intended to enhance its value, beauty or utility or to adopt it for new or further purposes. Improvement is often used interchangeably to denote real property other than land.

Reassessment is the assigning of a new assessed value to property, particularly real estate, as the result of a general, partial or individual reappraisal of the property.

Machinery embraces machines, equipment, mechanical contrivances, instruments, appliances or apparatus which may or may not be attached permanently, or temporarily to the real property.

Acquisition cost for newly acquired machinery not yet depreciated within the year of its purchase, refers to the actual cost of the machinery to its present owner, plus the cost of transportation, handling and installation at the site.

Actual use refers to the purpose for which the property is principally or predominantly used by the person in possession thereof.

Remaining economic life is the period of time expressed in years, from the date of appraisal to the date when the machinery becomes valueless.

Remaining value is the value corresponding to the remaining useful life of the machinery.

Changes in the property tax system

The integration of the Real Property Tax Code (PD No. 464) in the Local Government Code of 1991 or RA No. 7160, significantly changed the administration of real property assessment, appointment and supervision of the Municipal Assessor, mass appraisal or general revision of assessments, assessment level and the sharing of property tax revenues.

Section 200 of the LGC provides that the provinces and cities including municipalities within the Metropolitan Manila Area (MMA), shall be primarily responsible for the proper, efficient and effective administration of the real property tax. In compliance with this provision, the majority of LGUs through the Office of the Assessors, prepared the revised schedule of unit values, intended for the first general revision under the Code, as follows:

> The provincial, city or municipal assessor shall undertake a general revision of real property assessment within two years after the introduction of the Code and every three years thereafter.

Before its use, the review and approval of same, earlier exercised by the Department of Finance, has been shifted to the Provincial and City Board (Sangguniang Panlalawigan or Panglungsod).

The schedule of unit values for all types of property, land, buildings and other structures enacted by Ordinance are to be published in a newspaper of general circulation or posted in the provincial capital, city or municipal hall and in two other public places of the LGUs, where the unit values are intended for use. Assessment levels whether in accordance with the percentage established by law or lesser are also covered by Ordinance. An Ordinance may incorporate miscellaneous provisions on appraisal procedures for property used differently than those classified by law or property with combined usage.

Public hearings on the proposed schedule of unit values are conducted by local officials in an attempt to reduce protests on the revised assessments. Although public hearings for the imposition of higher values for taxation of property is not required by law, the local officials, businessmen and non-government organizations engaged in real estate, consider it proper to share views and information on price trends in real property. Public consultation about property values has assisted taxpayers in being able to understand the basis of the revaluation.

Enforcement of the new schedules of unit values assists assessors in estimating the value of real property discovered, declared or listed for the first time, mass appraisal and reclassification or conversion of uses, e.g. agricultural to residential, residential to commercial, etc., and appraising real property upon request of the property owner. An assessment made shall not be increased more frequently than once every three years except in the case of new improvements which substantially enhance the value of the property or where there is a change in use of either the land or the building.

The fixing of previous assessment levels for all classes of property under the Real Property Tax Code (PD 464) and consistently applied in the past, is also now exercised by the Local Board through Ordinance. The maximum percentage permissible under Section 218 of the new Code may be reduced by the Board. Assessment levels lower than those prescribed by law may be recommended by the assessor if resistance to the increase in valuations persists.

Appointment of assessors

Subject to the Civil Service Law, Rules and Regulations, a provincial, city or municipal assessor is now appointed by the respective local executive, the provincial governor in the case of province, the city mayor and municipal mayor in the case of city and municipality, respectively. A college degree holder in engineering, commerce, law or other related courses, first grade civil service eligible with five years experience in assessment practice or any related field may qualify for the position of provincial or city assessor. The same educational qualifications and civil service eligibility plus three years experience in appraisal or assessment field are required for the position of municipal assessor.

Mass appraisal methods

In compliance with Section 201 of the Code, the Department of Finance issues rules and regulations for the appraisal, assessment and classification of real property. Local Assessment Regulations No. 1-92 (series of 1992) embody the periodic mass appraisal procedures in the preparation of unit values, the classification of property based on actual use, sending of Notices of Assessment and Tax Bill to the local treasurers or bill collectors and property owners.

The unit values prepared by the assessors and approved by Ordinance, are generally, reflective of sales prices of land three years prior to the finalization of the schedule of unit values. Sales data including declared values by taxpayers in compliance with Sections 202 and 203, wherein a sworn declaration of property value is enjoined a year before the preparation of the unit values, and within 60 days upon acquisition or renovation of property in case of a building and other structures, are abstracted, analysed and computed as shown in Table 12.1.

New sets of unit values for different classes of property are the result of applying the sales or market data approach, income approach or the cost approach. The unit value may be adjusted depending upon the condition of the property. For example, it is recognized that lot value tapers from street frontage to the rear. If a standard depth is established for a residential lot, with a dimension of 20 by 75 metres, a unit value of P100 per square metre, can be applied as shown in Table 12.2.

Table 12.1
Sale prices and declared values

Sale No.	Sale Price/Declared Value, Etc. P
1	231.00
2	269.50
3	300.00
4	333.33
5	350.00
6	541.66
7	578.03
8	600.00
9	743.49
10	990.00
11	1,000.00
12	1,020.40
13	1,075.27
14	1,261.83
15	1,394.12
Total	10,688.63

Average: 10,688.63 / 15   =   P 712.57

Median: 600.00

Unit Base Market Value :   712.57   +   P 600.00 / 2

                                     =   P   1,312.57 / 2

                                     =   P   656.28

                              Say   =   P   700.00

Table 12.2
Zones and percentage values

Zone	Width	x	Depth	Area	% Value
1	20	x	20	400	100
2	20	x	20	400	80
3	20	x	20	400	60
4	20	x	15	300	40
Total				1,500	

Zoning of the lot area is restricted to four zones. Parcels situated on street corners are also appraised at higher values than those located along the street. The percentage adjustment for a corner location may be determined by reference to the following example;

Example:

		P
Average price per square metre for a corner lot first class residential location		500.00
Average price per square metre of lot along street sides		400.00
Difference		100.00
Corner Influence	100 / 400	25%

Note: *Corner location adjustments do not apply to industrial land.*

Historically, the mass appraisal or the general revision of assessments of real property every three years, as provided in PD No. 464, has not been fully implemented. Notwithstanding the clear provisions of law, the frequency of property revaluations did not comply with PD No. 464. Whilst compliance with PD No. 464 regarding periodic reassessment was ineffective, the subsequent collection of tax as a result of the last mass appraisal in 1983 was deferred in succeeding years, from 1984, 1985 then to 1988 and finally to mid-1987. This deferment had the result of reducing the effectiveness of the tax.

The first mass appraisal exercise under the 1991 Local Government Code, commenced in 1992 with the corresponding tax being collected as from 1994.

Due to the lack of time and other constraints, the conduct of the general revision of assessment under RA No. 7160 differed from those under PD No. 464, as in the latter case, the majority of assessors complied, whilst in the former many assessors were prevented or persuaded to set aside the project.

Assessment levels

Another critical aspect covered by the Local Government Code was the reduced assessment levels, especially for buildings and other structures. Comparatively, lower percentages of assessment are generally beneficial to taxpayers, however, in rural areas the amended assessment levels for dwellings drastically reduced the revenue from the property tax. The assessment levels for different types of property, which may be further reduced by the Local Board, are as follows:

Land

Class	Assessment level (%)
Residential	20
Agricultural	40
Commercial)	
Industrial)	50
Mineral)	
Timberland	20

Buildings and other structures

(a) Residential

Fair Market Value		
Over	**Not over**	**Assessment level (%)**
	175,000	0
175,000	300,000	10
300,000	500,000	20
500,000	750,000	25
750,000	1,000,000	30
1,000,000	2,000,000	35
2,000,000	5,000,000	40
5,000,000	10,000,000	50
10,000,000		60

(b) Agricultural

Fair Market Value

Over	Not Over	Assessment level (%)
	300,000	25
300,000	500,000	30
500,000	750,000	35
750,000	1,000,000	40
1,000,000	2,000,000	45
2,000,000		50

(c) Commercial

Fair Market Value

Over	Not Over	Assessment level (%)
	300,000	30
300,000	500,000	35
500,000	750,000	40
750,000	1,000,000	50
1,000,000	2,000,000	60
2,000,000	5,000,000	70
5,000,000	10,000,000	75
10,000,000		80

(d) Timberland

Fair Market Value

Over	Not Over	Assessment level(%)
	300,000	45
300,000	500,000	50
500,000	750,000	55
750,000	1,000,000	60
1,000,000	2,000,000	65
2,000,000		70

Machinery

Class	Assessment level (%)
Agricultural	40
Residential	50
Commercial	80
Industrial	80

Special classes - the assessment level for land, buildings, machinery and other improvements

Actual use	Assessment level (%)
Cultural	15
Scientific	15
Hospital	15
Local Water District	10
Government owned or controlled corporation engaged in the supply and distribution of water and/or generation and transmission of electric power	10

Although there are assessment levels assigned for properties classified as, cultural, scientific and hospital, these are recorded as exempt from tax. Generally, real property owned by the government or controlled by it are deemed taxable under the provisions of the new Code except for plant and machinery used for water distribution and the generation of electric power. Privately owned property is similarly treated.

Sharing of the property tax

The Basic tax and the Special Education Fund tax which were previously considered as state taxes are now earmarked solely for local government units as specified under Section 223. For each province, city and municipality within the Metropolitan Manila Area (MMA), the basic rate should not exceed 1 per cent and 2 per cent of the assessed value of the property, respectively. The Special Education Fund is set at a constant rate of 1 per cent.

The sharing of the Basic tax, slightly favours the lowest unit of local government - the barangay located outside the MMA from 10 to 25 per cent, the provincial share was reduced by 10 per cent (from 45 to 35 per cent), the municipal share was also reduced to 40 from 45 per cent. A different sharing arrangement is applied to the cities; 70 per cent goes to the city budget which was reduced by 20 per cent or from 90 to 70 per cent, while 30 per cent goes to the barangay which was increased from 10 per cent. In the Metropolitan Manila Area, the Basic tax is apportioned to give 35 per cent to each of the MMA and the municipality and 30 per cent to the barangay.

The Special Education Fund is shared equally (50 per cent) between the province and the municipality in which the property is located. The Special Education Fund is automatically released to the local school boards and allocated for maintenance and the construction of public school buildings, purchase of equipment, books and periodicals, education research and sports development. On the other hand, the distribution of revenue from the SEF in the city is not clearly defined in RA No. 7160, thus the existing apportionment of 60 per cent to the city and 40 per cent to the national treasury under RA No. 5447 may still prevail.

Liability and collection system

Liability for the local property taxes and the additional tax for the Special Education Fund begins on the first day of January and from that date it constitutes a lien, mortgage or encumbrance on the property, only to be extinguished upon payment of the delinquent tax.

The assessment roll containing a list of all property owners with the corresponding assessed value and detailed information about the property are submitted to the local treasurer by the assessor on or before 31 December each year. As prescribed by the Local Board, the treasurer is expected to post notice in conspicuous public places, stating the date and period of payment of tax without penalty. The same notice shall similarly be published in a widely circulated newspaper in the locality once a week for two consecutive weeks.

Payment of tax

The property owner or any person having a legal interest in the property may pay in four quarterly instalments the basic property tax and the additional Special Education Fund without penalty . The Local Board (Sangguniang Panlalawigan or Panglungsod) may, under Section 251 of the Code grant a 10 per cent discount on payments made within the prescribed schedule and not exceeding 20 per cent for advance payments.

A 2 per cent penalty every month or a fraction thereof, not exceeding 36 months is charged on the unpaid amount both for Basic tax and SEF. In the event of erroneous or excessive assessment or if the levy of tax is found illegal, the owner upon written request, can claim a refund or tax credit from the treasurer within two years from the date the taxpayer is entitled to the refund or tax credit. The treasurer is obliged to make a decision within 60 days from receipt of the written taxpayer's claim.

Remedies for the collection of tax

Coercive measures under Section 256 may be relied upon by the treasurer to collect delinquent taxes through administrative remedies such as the issue of a Warrant of Levy on real property and sale at public auction. These remedies are cumulative, simultaneous and unconditional, that is, any or all of the remedies or a combination may be resorted to and the use of one remedy shall not be a bar against the application of the others.

If the property tax and other taxes levied under the Code is uncollected within five years from the date they become due, no action whether administrative or judicial, can be instituted after the expiration of this period. However, the period of prescription to collect can be suspended on a number of grounds including:

1   if the local treasurer is legally prevented from collecting the tax;

2   the owner or person having an interest in the property requests an investigation and executes a waiver before the expiry of the period to collect; and

3   the owner is out of the country or cannot be located.

In case of fraud or intent to evade payment of tax the prescription period to collect may be extended and the appropriate action may be instituted for the collection of the tax within 10 years from the discovery of the fraud or the intent to evade payment of tax.

Additional tax on idle lands

The appraisal and assessment of idle land is based on the same process of valuation and classification as for other property. The local government unit by Ordinance, may levy an additional 5 per cent of the assessed value over and above the regular rates, if such property is established as idle or the owner fails to maximize its use. For land considered as agricultural, suitable for cultivation, dairying, inland fishery or other uses, with a minimum area of one hectare, if one-half of which remains uncultivated it shall be considered as idle. Land, other than agricultural, measuring one thousand square metres located in the city or municipality, if one-half of the area is not improved or used it shall be listed within the same category. A parcel or lot within an approved residential zone, regardless of the area, not developed by the owner or developer will also be classified as idle.

In an area where civil disturbances have occurred, or a natural disaster, the additional levy if already imposed, shall not be collected.

Exemptions

The exemptions from real property taxation under RA No. 7160 are limited to:

1   those owned by the Republic of the Philippines or any of its political subdivisions;

2   properties actually, directly and exclusively used for religious, charitable or educational purposes;

3   machinery and equipment used for the supply and distribution of water, and the generation and transmission of electric power whether privately or government-owned or controlled corporations;

4   property owned by cooperatives registered under RA No. 6938; and

5   machinery and equipment exclusively used for pollution control and environmental protection.

Appeals

Excessive assessments can be appealed against by filing within 60 days from the date of receipt of the written notice of assessment with the Local Board of Assessment Appeals (LBAA). The LBAA is composed of the Registrar of Deeds as Chairman, the Provincial or City Prosecutor and the Provincial or City Engineer as Members. Any decision made by the LBAA which is contested either by the petitioner or the respondent can be appealed to the Central Board of Assessment Appeal (CBAA) whose chairman and two members are appointed by the President.

Mass appraisal in a LGU

The recent mass appraisal and reclassification of property undertaken by the majority of Assessors' Offices in the country, has updated unrealistic assessments which had existed for some 10 years. Generally, the reassessment carried out manually was a long-drawn-out process. Within the constraints of limited funding and human resources, the completion of all assessments for existing real property units within a two year period is unrealistic. Confronted with this situation, the Department of Finance stated in LAR No. 1-92:

> ... if there is not sufficient time or resources to finish simultaneously the general revision work for all real property units (RPUs) within the territorial jurisdiction of a particular local government unit (LGU), a partial revision may be undertaken by kind or class of real property.

In Rizal Province, one of the major local government units in the country comprises 14 municipalities and 206 barangays, saw an average increase of 150 per cent in assessed value after the 1992-1993 mass appraisal project. This was equivalent to P19,286 million of total assessed value, as compared to P7,756 million before the general revaluation. From the total revised assessed value, P15,570m represents taxable land, increasing from P4,284m or approximately 263.43 per cent after the mass appraisal. All other assessed properties had similar increases in values.

Tables 12.4 to 12.7 contain comparative statistics relating to assessments, collection of revenue from all local sources, and state tax allotted to the LGU. National information for the reassessment could not be established due to fragmented sources of data. However, the data for the Province of Rizal, a fast growing community, could be representative of the national trend in terms of reassessment.

Conclusion

Decentralizing the powers of national government per se, is a positive sign towards self-reliance of local government units through improved fiscal administration. Self-governance should guide local officials to be responsive to the goals and objectives of central government. In addition, central government wants LGUs to be self-reliant through effective administration of the property tax.

If all LGUs had conducted the mass appraisal under the new Code, local revenue would have increased considerably. The disinterest of many local

Table 12.3

Comparative class valuation of property in Rizal Province

(in 000's pesos)

	Assessed Value Before Mass Appraisal	Assessed Value After Mass Appraisal (Effective 1994)	Percentage Increase
TAXABLE:			
Residential	P3,286	P8,209	150.00
Agricultural	1,860	3,237	74.06
Commercial	467	1,518	225.82
Industrial	1,971	5,569	182.60
Mineral	20	78	291.61
Special	153	675	339.87
Total Land, Bldg.,etc.	**P7,756**	**P19,286**	**150.00**
EXEMPT:			
Religious	P 35	P 97	174.00
Government	441	248	(43.63)
Others	34	190	456.00
Total Land, Bldg.,etc.	**P 510**	**P 535**	**5.00**

officials to support the general revision of assessment defeats the uniformity principle important to property taxation, for while several LGUs complied, taxpayers owning property in other LGUs did not see an increase in assessed values for that property.

The administrative control over the assessors is now affected by political intervention. Political pressures prevail over the standard operating procedures in appraisal and assessment, making it extremely difficult to establish the fair market value of real property. Although being aware of this the Department of Finance has not tackled the problem.

Out of the P283 million actually collected in 1995 by the Province of Rizal P51 million represents real property tax. For the city in MMA, P420 million represents the collections of property tax from the amount of P1,907 million earned for the same year.

Table 12.4
Comparative data of real property after mass appraisal in Rizal Province for the period ended 31 December 1993

	Percentage of RPU (Quantity of Record)		Percentage of Land (In Hectares)	Percentage of Assessed Value		
	Land	: Bldg.		Land	:	Bldg.
TAXABLE:						
Residential	78.00	: 94.84	15.04	46.72	:	25.15
Agricultural	17.10	: 0.75	82.41	19.49	:	5.43
Commercial	0.75	: 2.84	0.13	7.19	:	10.75
Industrial	0.35	: 1.45	0.25	21.97	:	57.83
Special	3.75	: 0.09	2.06	4.24	:	0.35
Mineral	0.05	: 0.03	0.11	0.39	:	0.49
	100.00	: 100.00	100.00	100.00	:	100.00
EXEMPT:						
Religious	7.60	: 3.15	2.60	17.76	:	19.19
Government	48.60	: 2.55	37.40	47.66	:	41.36
Others	43.80	: 94.30	60.00	34.58	:	39.45
	100.00	: 100.00	100.00	100.00	:	100.00

The zero per cent assessment level for residential buildings and other structures worth less than P175,000 seems peculiar and cast doubts upon its rationality. Proponents of this assessment may have in mind alleviating the poor, but imposing a nil assessed value on houses with an estimated market value of less than P175,000 represents a significant effect on LGUs' revenue. Rural towns suffer markedly from this policy, made more apparent when logistical support for supplies, manpower, etc., are involved in the reassessment and records maintenance of properties grouped into this category. Taxing other properties such as, government owned and controlled corporations would not offset the loss in revenue due to nil assessment, given that there are few LGUs which have this type of property.

Devolving the power of administering property taxation and the supervision over the assessor by the elective officials is, to some extent, untimely. In the Philippines, local officials are the key to the smooth implementation of the Code. The common issues on inadequate revenue will remain resulting in difficulties

Table 12.5
Comparative revenue from real property and internal revenue allotment of State Tax 1995

Regions	Actual Collections (In Million Pesos)			IRA (In Million Pesos)
	BASIC	SEF	TOTAL	
MMA	2,675.30	1,745.10	4,420.40	3,492.20
I	105.80	94.30	200.10	2,268.80
II	49.30	48.30	97.60	2,053.60
III	253.10	244.00	497.10	3,500.20
IV	673.90	621.20	1,295.10	7,127.40
V	103.40	92.80	196.20	3,302.10
VI	299.70	245.80	545.50	4,605.90
VII	289.80	187.90	477.70	3,877.70
VIII	82.20	74.90	157.10	3,477.50
IX	37.40	34.90	72.30	2,640.90
X	142.40	117.90	260.30	3,898.40
XI	193.40	183.10	376.50	3,253.50
XII	130.60	106.60	237.20	1,887.10
CAR	51.70	36.30	88.00	1,576.40
Total	5,088.00	3,833.10	8,921.10	46,961.70

Table 12.6
Comparative percentage collection of revenues from all sources 1995

Sources	Local Government Unit Percentage of Collection	
	Rizal Province	City of Manila
1 Property Tax (Current, Prior Years and Penalties	18.04	20.7090
2 Taxes on Goods and Services	6.59	30.8203
3 Operating and Miscellaneous Revenues	7.17	9.9134
4 Capital Revenue	5.07	0.0002
5 Other Taxes	2.44	3.3420
6 Grants and Aids	0.08	0.0000
Sub-Total	39.39	64.7852
7 Internal Revenue Allotment (Share from State Tax)	60.61	35.2148
Total	100.00	100.0000

in being able to access the maximum revenue source available to the LGUs due to partisan politics. The collection of revenue from all sources demonstrates that LGUs will continue to remain dependant on state tax.

Attempts are being made to amend several provisions within the Code. The Association of Treasurers and Assessors through the Department of Finance have filed resolutions to the Oversight Committee of Congress with regard to the adverse effect of the new Code.

References

Baraquero, O.R. (1996), *An Evaluation of the Periodic Mass Reassessment of Real Property in Rizal Province*, unpublished thesis, PSBA.

Department of Finance, LAR No. 1-92, Series of 1992.

Estrada, A.S. (1996), *The Collection of Real Property Taxes in the Province of Rizal from 1991-1995: An Assessment*, unpublished thesis, PSBA.

Presidential Decree No. 464, The Real Property Tax Code.

Republic Act No. 7160, The Local Government Code of 1991.

The Rules and Regulations Implementing the Local Government Code of 1991.

13 The property tax system in Brazil

Claudia De Cesare and Les Ruddock

Introduction to the property tax system

This chapter outlines the structure of the property tax system in Brazil. As the tax is administered at local government level, the system in the city of Porto Alegre is used as a case study. Porto Alegre is the capital of the state of Rio Grande do Sul, which is the southern-most state of Brazil, and is one of the chief industrial and commercial centres in the country. The city has approximately 1.5 million inhabitants, being the largest city in the South Region. Property tax is defined in Brazil as an annual tax on urban land and buildings *(Imposto sobre a propriedade predial e territorial urbana - IPTU)*. There are other taxes on real property, such as the Tax on Real Estate Transfers (ITBI) and a Tax on Rural Land (ITR), which is administered at central government level. Income raised from letting real estate properties is also taxed. This chapter is limited to examining property tax only.

The National Fiscal Code (CTN) lays down the fundamental principles of the property tax in Brazil. The code defines the components of the tax base, the tax liability, and the general exemptions from the tax base. Other specifications concerning property taxes are defined at local government level. As a consequence, procedures related to establishing the tax base and rates for the property tax may vary considerably around Brazil. Since the reform of the taxation system undertaken in 1967, the property tax has been imposed at local government level. Until 1988, the only sources of raising revenue from taxes administered by municipalities were the property tax and a tax on services (ISSQN).

Large transfers of revenue from central government to municipalities complemented the revenue raised by the collection of the cited taxes. As a result, local authorities did not have much interest in collecting their own taxes.

In summary, both a low level of effort in the collection of their own taxes and an extreme dependence on transfers of revenue were observed in Brazil. Taxpayers used to pay insignificant property tax bills.

Since the 1980s, the progressive and continual reduction in transfers from other levels of government to municipalities has been contributing to the financial impoverishment of local authorities. In contrast, local authorities have been required to undertake large public investments in infrastructure and services due to a population explosion and a rapid spread of the urban area over recent decades in most large Brazilian cities. Therefore, local authorities are facing the challenge of recovering revenue using their own sources of taxation in order to provide their community with, at least, the minimum standards of living.

The Brazilian Constitution, promulgated in 1988, partially favoured local authorities, allowing the imposition of two new sources of taxation at local government level. The new sources of taxation were a tax on real estate transfers (ITBI), and a tax on sales of liquid and gas fuels (IVVC) which was subsequently abolished from the taxation system in 1996. Additionally, according to the constitution, property tax (IPTU) could be used as an instrument of urban policy. In this context, progressive rates over time could be applied to promote a rational use of urban land with social benefits to the community at large. An extensive series of studies identified that the property tax is the most inefficiently explored source of revenue at local government level in Brazil (Alonso, 1991; Smolka and Furtado, 1996). The need to explore the potential of property tax for raising revenue is largely recognized by government authorities, urban economists, scholars and fiscal experts. Due to the high visibility of property tax, the efforts to improve its revenue collection often result in the tax being highly unpopular. As a consequence, government authorities that effectively undertake initiatives in this sense are subject to extensive pressures.

Statistics on the size of the tax base

Table 13.1 illustrates the pattern of real estate property recorded in 1996 in the city of Porto Alegre. There were approximately 472,000 real estate units in total. The residential segment accounted for about 81 per cent of the properties and more than 55 per cent of them were residential apartments. Non-residential properties and undeveloped sites (vacant land) represented approximately 13 per cent and 5 per cent of the real estate units respectively.

Table 13.1
Pattern of real estate property in Porto Alegre 1996

Property use class	1996	%
Vacant land	25,193	5.35
Houses	119,543	25.37
Apartments	263,563	55.94
Stores, stores/shops	22,726	4.83
Offices	37,211	7.90
Industries, factories, warehouses	1,747	0.37
Miscellaneous	1,140	0.24
Total (units)	471,123	100.00

Total revenue raised

At national level, revenue from property taxes represents 3.26 per cent of the total revenue from taxes in Brazil (World Economic Forum, 1994), or 0.8 per cent of gross domestic product (Meneghetti Neto, 1995). Property tax is the second most important source of revenue from taxes at local government level. When all the state capitals of Brazil are considered together, property taxes represent on average 30 per cent of the revenue from taxes raised at local government level (Smolka and Furtado, 1996). For instance, the property tax contributed in 1992 approximately 28 per cent of the revenue from local taxes in Rio de Janeiro, the second largest city in Brazil. However, it represented only 10 per cent of the total revenue for the municipality.

Table 13.2
Revenue sources in the city of Porto Alegre

Revenue	1995	
	US$	%
Group 1 - Current revenue	**432,343,591**	**97.97**
a. Revenue from taxes	165,253,361	37.44
b. Revenue from assets	25,715,856	5.83
c. Transfers from central government	43,225,285	9.80
d. Transfers from state	155,851,302	35.32
e. Others	42,297,787	9.58
Group 2 - Capital revenue	**8,941,620**	**2.03**
Capital revenue	8,941,620	2.03
Total	441,285,211	100.00

Table 13.2 illustrates the revenue sources in the city of Porto Alegre. As with the majority of the cities in Brazil, the transfers from the State still represent an important source of revenue. Table 13.3 illustrates the distribution of revenue raised from taxes in the city of Porto Alegre. The property tax contributed approximately 32 per cent to the total amount collected in 1995. The revenue from taxes increased by almost 61 per cent between 1993 and 1995.

Table 13.3
Distribution of the revenue from taxes in the city of Porto Alegre

Revenue from taxes	1995	
	US$	%
Property tax (ITPU)	52,170,173	31.57
Tax on real estate transfers (ITBI)	22,537,515	13.64
Tax on services (ISSQN)	86,868,734	52.57
Tax on sales of liquid and gas fuels (IVVC)*	2,965,512	1.79
Charge for services	711,427	0.43
Total	165,253,361	100.00

* *IVVC abolished in 1996*

Table 13.4 indicates the distribution of the total revenue from property tax considering the different property use classes in 1996. Residential properties accounted for approximately 39 per cent of the tax revenue. However, they represented more than 81 per cent of properties. In contrast, only 5 per cent were vacant sites (undeveloped sites) but this accounted for almost 29 per cent of the tax revenue.

Table 13.4
Contribution of property use classes to property tax revenue in Porto Alegre 1996

Property use class	Units [%]	Revenue [%]
Vacant land	5.35	28.75
Residential	81.32	39.15
Non-residential	13.33	32.10
Total	100.00	100.00

Comparison with other taxes

Taxation in Brazil represented approximately 25 per cent of the gross domestic product (GDP) in 1992 (World Economic Forum, 1994). Income tax represented only about 1.5 per cent of GDP, while taxes on goods and services represented approximately 12 per cent of GDP. As discussed earlier, revenue from property taxes represented only about 0.8 per cent of GDP (Meneghetti Neto, 1995).

Meneghetti Neto (1995) highlights the regressive structure of the taxation system in Brazil, since consumption is its principal source. Taxes on consumption tend to absorb a larger percentage of income from low-income than high-income earners. The preference for taxes on consumption associated with the huge inequality of income distribution suggests that the taxation burden is unfairly distributed in Brazil.

Purpose of the tax

The property tax revenue is spent in an integrated way with the other sources of revenue administered at local government level. Local authorities are responsible for financing an extensive number of public services in Brazil. They supply and maintain the water, sewerage, sanitation, public illumination, and traffic system. They are responsible for refuse collection and disposal, and city cleaning. Additionally, they control and manage public transport services. Their responsibilities also include the provision and maintenance of public areas, such as parks, recreation areas, and centres for entertainment, sports and culture activities. They are partially responsible for education, health services, environmental control and social services. Moreover, they have the difficult task of providing assistance to low-income families in the area of housing.

Municipal legislation lays down the minimum spending limits for expenditure on education and health services in Porto Alegre - 30 per cent and 13 per cent of the total revenue must be spent in education and health services respectively. The difference between the total revenue and the expenditure on personnel and maintenance of essential urban infrastructure and services is spent on public investment. In 1989, the local authority in Porto Alegre implemented a form of participative budget scheme (*Orcamento Participativo*). The plan for expenditure with the revenue allocated to investment is defined in conjunction with the community. It means the community is organized for discussing, defining priorities and deciding the activities that local government will supply. The city pioneered this scheme in Brazil and the initiative has achieved high popularity at national level. The public budget is approved on an annual basis by a Chamber of Councillors, elected by the local community and responsible for taking decisions on matters concerning strictly local affairs.

270

From 1992 to 1995, the distribution of total revenue according to the three levels of government in Brazil followed the model illustrated in Figure 13.1 (PMPA: SMF – Gaplan, 1995). Local authorities often argue that the division is not fair and the revenue administered at local government level is insufficient to cover their constitutional responsibilities with the community. It is the responsibility of local authorities to collect the property tax in Brazil.

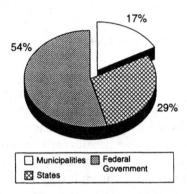

Figure 13.1   Distribution of the total revenue from 1992-1995

Importance of the tax

Property tax in Brazil is important for two main reasons. Firstly, the tax is the second most important source of revenue from taxes imposed at a local government level. When efficiently administered, the property tax can provide local authorities with a large yield, guaranteeing certain independence from other government levels. Secondly, the property tax can be used as an instrument of urban policy for deterring land speculation and for promoting urban development and a rational use of the urban land. Unfortunately, few local authorities in Brazil are making the best use of this powerful instrument.

Basis of assessment

The basis of assessment is the market value of each individual real estate property. The tax covers all property use classes, including vacant land, residential and non-residential property. Classes of properties exempt from the property tax will be discussed later. The National Fiscal Code (CTN) establishes the property tax base, which is defined as that market value considering land and immovable improvements attached to land. Therefore, the tax base does not vary among different local authorities in Brazil.

271

Slight variations can be observed in the usual concepts adopted for defining market value in Brazil. The basic legislation in Porto Alegre defines market value as 'the most probable price in terms of money for which a property would sell in a competitive and open market, assuming that seller and buyer are acting prudently and knowledgeably, without any special stimulus' (*Legislacao Municipal de Porto Alegre* - Basic law of Porto Alegre, 1973).

Responsibility for making the assessments

Local authorities are entirely responsible for valuations for taxation purposes. In other words, there is no central office responsible for assessing properties at national level. In Porto Alegre, the tax is administered integrally by the Municipal Secretary of Finance. There are three departments involved in establishing the tax base for taxation purposes. One department is responsible for assessing properties, where internal staff perform all activities needed for real estate valuation. Another independent department is responsible for keeping the real estate cadastre updated, and finally, there is a department responsible for carrying out inventories on properties. Due to the dynamic growth of the city with the consequent introduction of new dwellings and renovation of existing ones, a team of fiscal agents continually collect information about the physical characteristics of properties. This information is provided to the sector responsible for the real estate cadastre for updating of property records.

There is a public company that provides computational support principally in the management of the real estate cadastre.

Qualification of assessors

In Porto Alegre, the staff responsible for real estate valuation is composed of administrators, architects, civil engineers and economists. Additionally, a group of undergraduate assistants support the technical team in a large number of activities, including collecting, recording and mapping information. Alternatively, local authorities can decide to hire external services provided by private offices to establish the property tax base.

Frequency of valuations

No legal requirement exists concerning intervals between general valuations. However, all properties must be assessed at the same assessment date. Since 1987, general valuations have taken place in 1988, 1990, and 1991 in Porto Alegre, with the next revaluation being planned for 1997.

Notification of assessed value and the valuation roll

In Porto Alegre, tax bills are sent to taxpayers on an annual basis at the beginning of year. Tax bills indicate not only the amount to be paid, but also the basic characteristics of the property, its assessed market value and the tax rate. An information leaflet describing the basic procedures undertaken for establishing the tax is also provided to all taxpayers. Additionally, a brief valuation list is published in an official newspaper containing summarized information about taxpayers and their tax bills.

Intervals between general revaluation

For those years between revaluations, the tax base is indexed generically according to the prevailing rate of inflation in Porto Alegre. Some capping systems have been adopted in order to guarantee that taxes between consecutive periods do not critically affect the ability-to-pay principle.

Appeal procedures

Taxpayers can consult, at any time, the local authority in Porto Alegre in order to have explained the procedures used for assessing the property tax or to check the cadastral information about their properties. In the case of a dispute over tax bills, taxpayers can apply for a revision. Proposals for reassessing any individual property are accepted up to 30 days from the delivery of the tax bill to taxpayers. When appealing against a bill, taxpayers must identify their reasons for non-agreement with the tax bill. The local authority analyses the proposals and informs taxpayers about its decisions.

If an application to alter the tax bill is not supported by the local authority, taxpayers can further object against the decision to a Municipal Councillor who revises the decision undertaken in the first instance. After the two levels of objections, in case of dispute between taxpayers and the local authority, a formal appeal can be made to the Court of State and, finally, to the Supreme Court of the Nation.

Alterations of assessments

Valuations for taxation purposes are altered in the following situations:

1   The local authority realizes that there was an inaccuracy in the procedures undertaken for assessing the property, such as the valuation being based on an incorrect record of the physical characteristics of the property;

2   The local authority agrees with the proposal to alter the tax bill;

3   The judiciary power requires the local authority to alter the tax base.

Methods of assessment

The cost approach is the method employed traditionally for assessing real estate property for taxation purposes in Porto Alegre. According to the cost approach, the following model establishes the property market value:

$$MV = LV + BC \tag{1}$$

where MV is market value, LV is land value and BC is building cost.

$$LV = ULV \times LA \tag{2}$$

$$BC = UBC \times BA \times (1 - D) \tag{3}$$

where ULV is a typical land value per unit land area (US$/square metre), LA is land area (square metre), UBC is a typical building cost per unit building area (US$/square metre), BA is building area (square metre), and D is the depreciation factor [%]. The land value is estimated according to the methodology described as follows:

1   The city is classified into 88 urban zones that represent a type of stratification into geographic areas with similar characteristics.

2   Data related to sales of vacant land (undeveloped sites) that have been sold in a period close to the assessment date are collected for each zone.

3   An average land value per unit land area is calculated for each zone according to the information collected about sales of vacant land.

4   The typical land value per unit of land area established is adjusted for each site, considering basically two groups of information, which are the infrastructure equipment and services, and the physical characteristics of the site.

The infrastructure indicators taken into account and their adjustment factors are summarised in Table 13.5. These factors are applied to the typical land value, when the site is not supplied with these infrastructure facilities. A large group of objective factors defined deterministically are employed in trying to adjust the typical land value to each individual site.

Table 13.5
Adjustment factors for land value

Infrastructure equipment	Adjustment factor
Electric light and power	if not, 0.85
Water supply	if not, 0.85
Sewer System	if not, 0.85
Paved roadway	if not, 0.95
Public School	if not, 0.90

According to the specific physical characteristics of each site, the typical land value per unit land area can be further adjusted. Adjustments in typical land value are applied to an extensive number of situations. The basic adjustments are due to site depth, shape and corner influence. The present section only summarizes the most common adjustment criteria. For nonstandard sites, an adjustment factor is computed according to equation (4). Standard sites are sites with 30.00m or 40.00m of depth according to the zone in which they are situated.

$$AF = \sqrt{SD/RD} \tag{4}$$

where AF is adjustment factor, SD is standard depth for the zone, and RD is the real depth of the site.

Additional reductions are provided for sites without frontage to a public street (60 per cent reduction in the typical land value), for triangular sites (30 per cent reduction in the typical land value), and for sites with irregular shapes. Adjustments due to corner influence are attributed up to a 30 per cent increase in the typical land value. Considering all the adjustment factors, the adjusted land value can not be greater than the typical land value established for each zone. For each individual site, the land value is estimated according to equation (2) considering the typical land value per unit land area, already adjusted, multiplied by the land area of the site.

The building cost is estimated considering a cost per unit area of constructing various types and styles of building. The estimated costs are arranged for classes of building in cost tables and they are used to estimate costs for each individual property. There are about 30 different typical building costs defined, classified according to type of building, walls, roof, storeys, and building quality. For each individual property, the building cost is estimated according to equation (3) considering the typical building cost value per unit building floor area multiplied by the property floor area and its respective depreciation factor. Depreciation factors vary from zero to 45 per cent for brick wall construction and from zero to 50 per cent for other types of wall, taking into account only the year of construction.

The system used for valuation in Porto Alegre is totally developed using computational resources. Basically, the property data management for taxation purposes involves three distinct systems. The structure of the property data management for taxation purposes in Porto Alegre is illustrated in Figure 13.2.

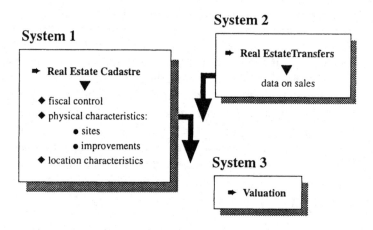

Figure 13.2   Property data management

System 1, the real estate cadastre, is a general registry that manages information about taxpayers and their properties. The information managed allows the tax base to be assessed and the tax bills to be produced at the individual property level. This system includes information about the name of the taxpayer, property address, and previous bills and debts related to the tax. The principal characteristics of sites, buildings and zones are recorded. The basic idea of this system is to gather information to explain variations in the market value in different geographic areas. Assessed values are computed with the information provided by this system.

System 2 and System 3 are related to provide information for valuation purposes. The systems allow the establishment of the market value not only using the cost approach, but also using other mass appraisal techniques, such as multiple regression analysis or artificial neural networks. Because of a tax on real estate transfers, also administered at local government level, all ownership transfers are recorded in System 2. New owners declare sale prices. In order to avoid taxation, part of the price is declared under the real value of the sale. A team of assessors is responsible for judging if declared prices can be considered as evidence of market price. When declared prices are accepted for taxation purposes, this information goes to System 3.

System 3 aims at recording information for valuation purposes. Sale prices come from System 2. The basic attributes of improvements, sites and zones are also inserted, which come from System 1. Major problems concerning the real estate cadastre are observed in large cities like São Paulo and Rio de Janeiro. São Paulo is the major industrial and financial centre in Brazil, accounting for almost 30 per cent of the national gross domestic product. It is the biggest city in South America with almost 18 million inhabitants. Local administrators of the property tax in São Paulo argue that the rapid spread and development of the urban area is the major problem in the administration of the property tax. As a result, a large number of new inventories are not recorded in the real estate cadastre. A large increase in revenue might be achieved simply by recording these inventories.

In the city of Rio de Janeiro, approximately one out of three residential properties is not recorded in the real estate cadastre (Smolka and Furtado, 1996). Less than 40 per cent of these properties are slums. The rest of the properties are located in areas provided with urban equipment and services, and high-income families occupy them.

Exemptions, reliefs and concessions

The general exemptions from property tax are common in all local authorities in Brazil. They include the following:

1   properties used for governmental purposes (administrative purposes);

2   properties used for defence and infrastructure purposes;

3   properties used for political organizations without profit purposes;

4   properties used for public or social interest without profit purposes;

5   public schools and properties used for cultural and scientific purposes;

6   national parks, preservation areas, etc.; and

7   properties used for health services (e.g. hospitals), religious and charitable purposes.

In Porto Alegre, for individual taxpayers, relief is guaranteed for pensioners, retired people, orphans, widows, and others with a unique property used for owner occupation and an income up to three times the minimum salary. Under the same conditions, other taxpayers with property assessed up to approximately US $3,000 are also entitled to relief. Approximately 13 per cent of properties were exempt from the property tax in 1996.

Collection procedures

Bills are sent to taxpayers at the beginning of the year with financial incentives given to encourage full payment in Porto Alegre. Otherwise, payments can be made in 10 monthly instalments. Other local authorities in Brazil have adopted similar payment schemes. The property owner is primarily responsible for paying property tax. An occupier or user, even without legal authorization to use the property, can be requested to pay the tax. The tax results from the market value estimated for each property multiplied by a property tax rate.

Differential taxes between land and buildings

In Porto Alegre, rates for the property tax are progressive according to the assessed market value. The progressive rates aim at inserting an element to identify the ability-to-pay in the property tax. Table 13.6 illustrates rates for properties located in zones supplied with all basic infrastructure services and equipment. Properties situated in other zones are granted further reductions in rates. The tax is calculated by the sum of the market value corresponding to each class of value multiplied by its respective rate (sliding scale of rates).

In Table 13.6, the information about classes of assessed value is expressed in Fiscal Monetary Units (UFM). Due to high-inflation periods, a monetary unit for fiscal purposes, which is adjusted monthly according to the rate of official inflation, is adopted to update values for taxation purposes. The UFM was equivalent to approximately US$ 0.90 in January 1996. Different property use classes attract different rates. Rates for vacant land vary from 5.0 to 6.0 per cent of the assessed property value, while the maximum rate for residential property reaches 1.2 per cent. High rates applied to vacant land aim to stimulate land development and deter land speculation.

Enforcement procedures

In the case of non-payment, interest and fines are the enforcement measures available. The debt is subject to the court and may result in the sale of the property by public auction in order to pay the debt.

Table 13.6

Table 13.6
Rates for property tax

Property use class	Assessed market value [UFM]	Rate [%] sliding rates
Vacant land	up to 6,652	5.0
	over 6,652 to 33,259	5.5
	over 33,359	6.0
Residential property	up to 3,326	0.2
	over 3,326 to 6,652	0.4
	over 6,652 to 13,304	0.6
	over 13,304 to 33,259	0.8
	over 33,259 to 66,518	1.0
	over 66,518	1.2
Non-residential property	up tp 6,652	0.6
	over 6,652 to 13,304	0.8
	over 13,304 to 33,259	1.0
	over 33,259 to 66,518	1.2
	over 66,518	1.4

Note: *UFM is a fiscal monetary unit that varies according to inflation.*

Critical analysis

Property tax is in fact a good option for raising revenue at local government level for a number of reasons including: revenue from the property tax can be allocated easily to a particular local authority, the tax is capable of producing a large and predictable yield, and is relatively difficult to evade. In Brazil, the property tax was implemented at local government level in 1967. Therefore, the tax represents a familiar concept to taxpayers and local authorities. Taxpayers have a reasonable understanding of the property tax system, the tax base, the rates, and how the bills are computed. By the same token, local administrators are familiar with the procedures related to administering the tax.

The general structure of the property tax system in Brazil seems to be adequate. The tax base is market value. A large amount of evidence for open market transactions is recorded in the majority of municipalities in Brazil. Additionally, the real estate market for sales suffers from fewer governmental interventions than the rental market, considering the annual rental value is the second option for the tax base. Moreover, market value represents a familiar concept to local administrators and taxpayers.

As discussed earlier, local authorities provide the entire urban infrastructure. In general, the provision of urban equipment and services results in the market value of properties increasing with benefits to their owners. This argument may be a strong reason in favour of the acceptability of the tax among taxpayers, since the property tax revenue can be associated with these public investments to supply and maintain the urban infrastructure. Alternative taxes to replace the property tax might not be readily accepted and could result in revolts by taxpayers.

In Brazil, the alternative of imposing progressive rates contributes to the use of the tax as an instrument of urban policy. In developing countries, due to unstable economic period cycles, land and real estate are a major way of concentrating wealth. For these countries, the importance of having a tax on real estate is vital for encouraging investment in productive activities and deterring real estate speculation. The progressive rates of property tax can also be used to incorporate an element of ability to pay in the property tax systems. In spite of the extensive series of advantages related to having a tax on real estate, the property tax has been inefficiently and unfairly administered in the majority of local authorities in Brazil. The following weaknesses are frequently identified in current property taxes.

Assessment bias in the tax base estimated

A fundamental requirement of valuation for taxation purposes is to present uniformity. Perfect assessment uniformity would be achieved if the ratio between assessed value and market value were constant for all properties at the assessment date. In the great majority of cases, high-value properties are under-assessed relative to low-value properties in Brazil (Smolka and Furtado, 1996; De Cesare and Ruddock, 1997a, 1997b). Part of the assessment bias can be attributed to the inaccuracy of the current techniques used for valuation for taxation purposes. Inaccuracies of the real estate cadastre and capping systems also contribute to the assessment bias.

Inaccuracies of the real estate cadastre

Real estate cadastres need to reflect the real conditions of properties and taxpayers. Moreover, all properties must be recorded in the cadastral information systems. The vexing problem faced in large cities in Brazil, such as Rio de Janeiro and São Paulo, where no records exist for a large number of properties should not be tolerated. It penalizes taxpayers that are effectively paying the property tax, exposing them to a disproportionately heavy burden. This fact may encourage these taxpayers to lose confidence in the taxation system.

Inefficient exploitation of the property tax as a revenue source

For a long time in Brazil, taxpayers were used to paying relatively low property tax bills due to an out-of-date tax base. Many local authorities have undertaken general revaluations on a regular basis. However, capping systems have been used largely for guaranteeing that tax bills would not override the ability-to-pay. The Chamber of Councillors, a group of politicians elected by the local community, is responsible for promoting and arguing in favour of the capping systems in order to protect the poor and the retired taxpayers. However, the capping systems actually favour high-income taxpayers. Low-income and retired taxpayers can easily be exempted from taxation with relief based on income, as applied in Porto Alegre. Therefore, the great challenge faced by local authorities is still how to best explore the potential of property tax as a source of local revenue.

Proposed changes

The fundamental principles that regulate the property tax in Brazil are not expected to change in the short term. However, the administration of property tax can be improved greatly in order to, simultaneously, explore the potential of the tax as a source of revenue and achieve assessment uniformity. Some local authorities in Brazil are already improving their property taxation systems. Tax bases for the property tax are being re-established at periodical intervals using more accurate valuation techniques and equalization factors. Real estate cadastres are being updated and mechanisms are being adopted to guarantee a continual update of information. However, local authorities still need to face the political risk of radically changing part of the tax bills.

Focusing on the city of Porto Alegre, the process of reform has already been started. After many years, the traditional method used for valuation is finally being discarded and multiple regression analysis is to be used. The valuation process will include tests for assessment uniformity and eventual adjustments on the estimates of market value. Additionally, a geographic information system is being implemented and is expected to be available for use at the end of 1998.

References

Alonso, J.A.F. (1991), O Papel do IPTU face as transformacoes na economia de Porto Alegre, *Indicadores Economicos da Fee: Analise Conjuntural*, Vol. 19, No. 3, pp. 138-145.

Código Tributário Nacional (1990) Lei No 5172 de 25 de Outubro de 1966, 22ed., Ed. Saraiva: São Paulo, Brazil (The Brazilian national fiscal code).

Constituição da Republica Federativa do Brasil - 1988 (1993) 3ed., Ed. Atlas: São Paulo, Brazil (The Brazilian Constitution).

De Cesare, C.M. and Ruddock, L. (1997a), An Empirical Analysis of a Property Tax System: A Case Study from Brazil, *The International Conference on Assessment Administration (63rd Annual Meeting):* Toronto, Canada.

De Cesare, C.M. and Ruddock, L. (1997b), Devising a fairer property tax system: a case study from Brazil, *Journal of Property Tax Assessment & Administration*, Vol. 2, No. 3, pp. 41-68.

Legislação Municipal de Porto Alegre (1973), Lei Complementar No 7 de 7 de Dezembro de 1973 com as alterações introduzidas pelas Leis Complementares Nos 27, 29, 35, 60, 66, 94-97, 112, 138, 166-69, 209, 212, 228, 232, 263 e 285. Porto Alegre: Brazil (Basic law of the municipality of Porto Alegre and its several alterations up to December 1996).

Meneghetti Neto, A. (1995), Tributação: Alguns Pontos para Reflexão, *Indicadores Econômicos da FEE*, Vol. 23, No. 1, pp. 138-149 (Paper on taxation).

Prefeitura Municipal de Porto Alegre – PMPA: Gaplan (1995), Orcamento Publico (Internal publication about the public budget).

Smolka, M.O. and Furtado, F. (1996), Argumentos para a Rehabilitacao do IPTU e do ITBI como Instrumentos de Intervenção Urbana (progressista), Espaco e debates, Vol. 39, Ano XVI, pp. 87–103 (Paper on the need to improve the taxes on real estate property in Brazil).

World Economic Forum (1994), *The World Competitiveness Report.*

14 Rating systems in New Zealand

Garry Dowse and Bob Hargreaves

Introduction

This chapter reviews the history of rating systems in New Zealand over the past 150 years, with attention primarily focused on the major administrative, land policy and valuation principles current to 31 December 1997. New Zealand is one of the few countries in the world adhering to a rating system based on the value of land exclusive of improvements. New Zealand has two levels of government - central government, a Westminster type parliamentary system, and local government. The local government system is largely independent of the central executive government. However, it has a subordinate role with the powers of local authorities being conferred by Parliament. New Zealand local government is divided into three categories: regional, territorial and special purpose authorities. The Local Government Act 1974 is the statute constituting regional councils and territorial authorities. Their boundaries are usually defined by the Local Government Commission.

Taxes levied by central government include - income tax, duties (e.g. sales tax, wholesale taxes, etc.), estate duty, and goods and services tax. The country has no capital gains tax as such. The tax levied by local government is a rate levied on land holdings. Apart from the income from trading activities under the control of territorial authorities, local rates on land holdings are the main source of funds for local authorities. Local authorities have considerable individual control on what property will be rated, how it will be rated and the quantum of rates to be paid. The principle source of control on rating are statutes enacted by central government. The two most important of these are the Rating Powers Act 1988 and the Valuation of Land Act 1951 and amendments. Additional legislation that is also relevant includes the Local Government Act 1974.

Rates are paid on 'rateable property' under one of three rating systems - the annual value system, the capital value system or the land value system (O'Regan, 1985). Local authorities using the capital or land value rating system are required to fix their rates on the capital and land values appearing on the district valuation roll prepared by Valuation New Zealand (a department of central government) directed by the Valuer-General. Local authorities who adopt the annual value rating system are required to appoint valuers for the preparation of annual values for their district. These appointed valuers may be their own valuation staff, the Valuer-General or public valuers. The values which provide the basis of these rating systems are defined in the Valuation of Land Act 1951. This Act allows for formal objections to valuation before courts of the land, and has resulted in a system of determining value that is largely governed by case precedent and legal requirement.

Historical development of the rating base

The native ownership of land in New Zealand lies with the New Zealand Maori whose system of ownership is based on tribal ownership with boundaries between tribes usually being natural geographical features. European colonization of New Zealand during the 1800s was dominated by British settlers. In 1844, the new colony's government introduced a number of laws, including the Municipal Corporation Ordinance, allowing local authorities to raise revenue through taxation of property. A system of provincial government was established in 1853 and continued to 1876. Each province was autonomous and self funding. The principal system of rating became the annual rental value system which was the English system transposed almost without change. However, such a system did not prove successful as the landlord/tenant relationship was not the normal pattern of landholding in the new colony. In a young and developing country where land was often bought outright, capital value rating became increasingly popular.

Ultimately the early settlers, arriving from Europe, favoured the system of taxing unimproved land values because it did not penalize them for making improvements. Both the annual value and capital value systems increased the burden of individual ratepayers as they improved their properties. Underdeveloped land areas attracted almost no rates, thereby encouraging the non-development of potentially productive land. Developing farm land out of bush was back breaking work (in those days the main tools were an axe and cross cut saw) and the idea that farmers could be taxed for their hard work was unpopular.

Advocates of unimproved land value taxation argued that another important advantage was that it raised the cost of holding vacant land thereby discouraging speculation. Also by encouraging improvements to the land, intensive rather than extensive farming systems would be adopted, and this would lead to the closer settlement of farm land. To overcome these apparent defects in the early annual rent and capital value rating systems the concept of unimproved value rating was introduced, with the province of Wellington leading the way in 1849. This early concept of unimproved value envisaged the value of the land without any buildings and improvements whatsoever.

In 1876 New Zealand's early provincial structure was abolished and replaced by the present central and local government structure. This resulted in the first national rating statute - the Rating Act 1876. This act proposed annual value as the only form of rating and was largely based on the English system which used the annual rent as the basis for setting rates. Under this act local authorities appointed one valuer who was responsible for the preparation of a valuation roll which would become the rate roll for the district.

The 1876 Act was repealed and replaced by the Rating Act in 1882. This statute gave local authorities the choice of using either capital value (land plus improvements) or annual value rating system. However, it also applied a universal system of determining values and took the assessment of these values out of the hands of local bodies, creating a new occupational class known as 'Property Tax Assessors'. The effect of this statute was that almost all the counties (rural areas) adopted capital value rating with the boroughs (urban areas) adopting an annual value system. The reasons given for the 1882 change were:

1   Undeveloped land and land held for speculative purposes (of which there were large tracts) had no rental value but a definite market (or capital) value.

2   Farm improvements usually added more to the annual rental value than to the capital value.

3   The introduction of a national property tax based on capital value justified the introduction of a common valuation and tax base.

However, the main criticism of the annual value and capital value systems remained - they both penalized rate payers who improved their properties. This was seen as an inhibitor to growth and development in a young lightly populated country. In 1896 the Rating on the Unimproved Value Act was passed. The Act was limited in its application and required a successful ratepayers poll to adopt the new system.

In 1896 the Valuation of Land Act was also passed and the Valuation Department (later to become Valuation New Zealand), a central valuing authority, was established for the purpose of providing a full and impartial valuation service for use by central and local government, and the general public. Since 1912 central government has legislated, quite deliberately, to leave the choice of rating systems to local government. The Rating on the Unimproved Value Act was consolidated in 1912 and the rating system then remained largely unchanged until the Rating Act 1967. The 1967 act has since been replaced by the Rating Powers Act 1988, essentially a consolidating Act with few major changes.

One notable feature of the period 1896 to 1967 was the increase in popularity, to almost complete dominance, of the unimproved (or land) value rating system (Table 14.1). Unimproved value was replaced by land value for rating purposes with the introduction of the Valuation of Land Amendment (No. 2) Act 1970. The 1970 amendment to the Valuation of Land Act was introduced in response to the numerous difficulties that arose over the years in assessing unimproved land values.

Table 14.1
System of rating used by local authorities (by percentage)

Year	Capital Value	Land Value	Annual Value	Land Value and Capital Value	Total (%)
1942	37	55	8	-	100
1955	27	66	7	-	100
1972	16	80	4	-	100
1985	10	80	5	5	100
1995	30	64	2	4	100

Up until 1976 local authorities could switch from capital values to annual values rating systems without reference to the ratepayers but any change in or out of land value required the majority approval taken from a poll of ratepayers. There was also provision in the legislation for 15 per cent of ratepayers to initiate a change in the rating system by demanding that a poll be taken. Local authorities can now change the rating system without taking a poll of ratepayers. As rating burdens are a very politically sensitive issue local authorities have been careful not to make changes without a broad consensus of support.

Over the last 50 years land value based rating has clearly been the dominant system. Since 1985 there has been a small swing back to the capital value system (Ralston, 1978). This is particularly evident in the main cities. Today, the strong theoretical arguments advanced by Henry George of single tax fame favouring the land value system are probably of much less concern to the typical New Zealand ratepayer than the more pragmatic question of how much has to be paid under each system (Hargreaves, 1991).

Revenue

Since November 1989 New Zealand local authorities have experienced major restructuring as a result of central government initiated research undertaken by the Local Government Commission. These reforms were initiated on the rationale that local government had remained unchanged for 100 years and was long overdue for reform. Previous attempts to reform local government had been largely ineffective. As at 31 December 1987 there were 828 agencies of regional and local government, and special purpose authorities. There are now 12 regional councils; 74 territorial authorities (designated district or city); and 6 special authorities. The dramatic reduction in agency numbers was achieved through large scale amalgamations, as well as absorption of ad hoc authorities (e.g. pest control boards) into district, city and regional councils.

The aim of the amalgamations was to produce public cost saving through significantly improved efficiencies. There has been a separation of activities into regulatory type functions and business units which compete with outside businesses for council contracts.

Both regional councils and territorial authorities have the power to levy rates. The regional councils main functions are: the functions under the Resource Management Act; the functions under the Soil and Conservation and River Controls Act; control of pests and noxious plants; harbour regulations and marine pollution control; regional civil defence; to oversee transport planning; control of passenger transport operators. Some regional councils also have other functions, such as those formally undertaken by land drainage boards. Territorial authorities functions include the administering of land use consents under the Resource Managements Act 1991; noise control; litter control; roading; water supply; sewage reticulation and disposal; rubbish collection and disposal; parks and reserves; libraries; land subdivision; pensioner housing, health inspection; building consent; parking controls; and civil defence.

Total revenue raised by local authorities is shown in Table 14.2 (Statistics New Zealand 1996 Official Year Book.

A breakdown of rating revenue raised by Palmerston North City Council (PNCC) is shown in Table 14.3 (Palmerston North City Council Annual Plan 1996/97). PNCC is the territorial authority used as an example throughout this chapter. It is a city of approximately 75,000 people (the 10th largest in New

Table 14.2
New Zealand local authorities statistics

Rates (including water rates)	1,658.6 Million
Petroleum tax	34.4 Million
Grants, subsidies and levies	300.5 Million
Fees and fines	113.9 Million
Sales and other income	640.2 Million
Investment income	128.2 Million
Total current receipts	**2,875.8 Million**

Zealand). It has approximately 27,000 rateable properties. Rating revenue
the 1996/97 year is budgeted at $30.438 million or approximately 46 per cent
its total funding budget.

Table 14.3
Palmerston North City Council sources of funds 1996/97

Loans	14%
Trading revenue	29%
Special funds and asset sales	11%
Rates	46%
Total	**100%**

It would appear that this level of rating revenue is fairly typical of the level of
rates collected by other local authorities throughout the country. Rating revenue
varies depending on the level of an authority's trading activities. Higher amounts
of rating source funds are common for councils who generally have less trading
activities.

Basis of assessment

The two acts of Parliament in New Zealand that determine the manner in which rates are assessed and determined are the Rating Powers Act 1988 (RPA) and the Valuation of Land Act 1951 and amendments (VLA).

Rating Powers Act 1988

The purpose of this Act was to consolidate and amend some 97 statutes that either wholly or in part affected rating. There are no major changes within this statute, it being essentially a consolidation statute. It sets out the statutory requirements for:

• Rateable property	• Valuation rolls
• Powers of local authorities	• Rate records
• Rates as a charge	• Rates postponement
• Differential rating	• Special rateable values
• Rating liability	• Remission of rates
• Rates recovery	• Maori land rating
• Rating systems	• Valuation equalization

Rating systems

The Rating Powers Act provides for four different rating systems:

1   'Annual value' rating - rates are set and levied on the annual rental value of rateable property.

2   'Capital value' rating - rates are set and levied on the capital value of rateable property.

3   'Land value' rating - rates are set and levied on the land value of rateable property.

4   'Land area' rating - rates are set and levied on the basis of an amount for each hectare of rateable property.

The rating system in use shall be that system that has prevailed historically, however, a rating authority may change the system by:

1   passing a resolution to that effect;

2   disseminating knowledge on the proposed change;

3   giving public notification of the resolution.

There is no right of objection. This is one major change from earlier legislation which, as discussed earlier in this chapter, required a poll of ratepayers to change the system.

'Land area rating' may only be used for assessing a special rate for drainage or water race purposes.

Making of rates

The Rating Powers Act requires the following:

1   the rates be assessed for a period of one year or less;

2   pre-calculated as an amount per dollar of rateable value;

3   give public notification of its intent to make rates.

Valuation of Land Act 1951 and Amendments

The valuation of land for rating purposes is governed by the Valuation of Land Act 1951 and Amendments. Under the Rating Powers Act 1988 (Section 105) a local authority is required to accept valuations prepared by the Valuer-General under the VLA, if rating on either a land value or capital value system, or the authority appointed valuer if on an annual value system.

Definitions of value

These are precisely detailed in Section 2 of the Valuation of Land Act 1951. The exact definitions are provided hereunder as it is the wording of these definitions that are responsible for much of the code of practice that surrounds the assessment of these values.

Annual value is defined as:

> the rent at which the property would let from year to year, deducting therefrom 20 per cent in the case of houses, buildings, and other perishable property, and 10 per cent in the case of land and other hereditaments, but in no case shall it be less than 5 per cent of the capital value of the fee simple of the property.

Assessments for annual value are normally carried out by territorial authorities that have their own valuation division. However, these assessments may be undertaken by Valuation New Zealand, or an appointed practising valuer. When there is a clearly defined rental market, e.g. commercial, retail and industrial space, then annual values are assessed by direct reference to the rental market. Where there is no established market, then the '5 per cent of capital value' provision is used.

Capital value of land means:

> the sum which the owner's estate or interest therein, if unencumbered by any mortgage or other charge thereon, might be expected to realize at the time of valuation if offered for sale on such conditions as a bona fide seller might be expected to require.

Land value in relation to any land means:

> the sum of the owner's estate or interest therein, if unencumbered by any mortgage on other charge thereon, might be expected to realize at the time of valuation if offered for sale on such reasonable terms and conditions as a bona fide seller might be expected to require, and if no improvements (as defined) had been made on the said land.

Value of improvements means:

> the added value which at the date of the valuation the improvements give to the land.

Improvements in relation to any land means:

> all work done or material used at any time or for the benefit of the land by the expenditure of capital or labour by any owner or occupier thereof, in so far as the effect of the work done or material used is to increase the value of the land and the benefit thereof is unexhausted at the time of valuation.

The Act goes on to detail certain improvements that are deemed to be part of the land value. These are:

1   Draining, excavation, filling, reclamation or improvements relating thereto.

2   Grading, levelling, and the removal of rocks and soil.

3   Removal or destruction of vegetation.

4   Alteration of soil fertility.

5   Prevention of erosion or flooding.

It is this definition of improvements that differentiates 'land value' as brought in by the Valuation of Land Amendment (No. 2) Act 1970 from the previous concept of 'unimproved value' wherein land was considered in its raw undeveloped state. In the case of farm land it was assumed the millable timber was removed and the land remained in a cut over state.

The concept of unimproved value required the valuer to assess land in its probable present condition exclusive of improvements. In the case of depreciated land the probable present condition is different from the original condition of the land. Over time wide variations of interpretation became common as to the natural condition of much of the country, and this was further complicated by a lack of unimproved land sales.

Under the current legislation land value includes all improvements or expenditure of capital or labour to the land to make it suitable for development. For example, with farmland the processes of laying underground drainage or clearing bush and converting the land into pasture are incorporated into land value. In an urban situation, an example could be the case of where over and above a $40,000 purchase price for a block of land $10,000 is spent on site filling, drainage and earth retaining works for the provision of a house building site. This has the effect of immediately increasing land value. With this urban example the assessment and recording of values on the district valuation roll before and after the introduction of the Valuation of Land Amendment (No. 2) Act 1970 would be shown as:

Unimproved Value (Pre 1970 Amendment)		Land Value (Post 1970 Amendment)	
UV	$40,000	LV	$50,000
VI	$10,000	VI	$ 0
CV	$50,000	CV	$50,000

In effect, in the current practical situation land value is viewed as the value of the bareland together with its 'invisible' improvements. Actual improvements assessed with a value are generally only those structural improvements erected on or above ground. While this concept of certain improvements being included as part of the vacant land value may appear to be an unusual concept it has become widely accepted, and there have been very few objections that dispute the nature of improvements to be included.

Responsibility for making assessments

The VLA gives statutory power to the Valuation Department (a department of central government which became Valuation New Zealand in 1987). Under the Act the country is to be divided into districts. These districts are determined from time to time by Valuation New Zealand (VNZ). Under sections 9 and 10 of the VLA the Valuer-General is required to prepare valuation rolls for each territorial authority within a valuation district at any time up to five yearly intervals. Section 8 directs that for each property on the district roll the information to be supplied is:

1   Name of the owner.

2   Nature of the estate or the owners interest in it.

3   Name of occupier.

4   Situation, description and land area.

5   Nature and value of the improvements.

6   Land value.

7   Capital value.

8   Where applicable special rateable values or rates postponement value.

9   Such other particulars as are prescribed.

Under Section 8(1A) an annual value valuation roll is also to be compiled where a territorial authority has adopted annual value rating system. The information required to be shown is similar to that on the district valuation roll, with the annual value substituting capital, land and improvement value.

Up until the 1980s rolls were revised at five yearly intervals. During the 1970s the Valuation Department as then known developed multiple regression techniques which, when used in conjunction with newly installed computers, allowed full mass appraisal techniques. The utilization of computer technology led to some experimentation in one year revisions in the early-mid 1980s. This early experimentation was not entirely successful and ultimately VNZ has settled on the implementation of three yearly revision cycles since 1988. The exception in most recent times is in Wellington City (New Zealand's capital city; fifth largest city by population) where territorial authority requirements have seen VNZ adopt one year revision cycles.

Under Section 12 of the VLA there is provision for alterations to be made during the currency of the roll but all values are backdated to the previous revision date. Typical reasons for ongoing roll maintenance and amendment are land subdivision and new improvements.

Valuation rolls

The values for the purposes of assessing rates shall be:

1   For the capital value and land value system the figures shown on a valuation roll as supplied by the Valuer-General (head of Valuation New Zealand).

2   For the annual value system figures shown on a valuation roll prepared by a valuer. The valuer may be the Valuer-General or a Registered Valuer (Valuers Act 1948) employed by or contracted to the territorial authority.

VNZ is the largest valuation organization in New Zealand employing a total of approximately 400 staff in 1996. It has 27 district offices, 3 regional offices and a head office. It maintains a nationwide database on the country's 1.54 million properties. Currently the only local authority using the annual value system is Auckland City, who utilize their own valuation staff to carry out the assessments. The valuation roll is a public record and is open for inspection during normal office business hours.

On the sale or letting of a property there is a requirement for the owner to supply the territorial authority with details of the sale. The information gathered in this way forms the basis for compiling sales databases supplied by the VNZ (VNZ-Link) and Headway Systems Limited (Valpak). These two organizations databases are currently dominant in the provision of property sales information in New Zealand.

Appeal procedures

When a district valuation roll has been revised, it is publicly notified and open for objection. Any alterations to roll values made during the currency of a roll also carry with them a right of objection. Those entitled to object to values are:

1   The Valuer-General.

2   The Valuer (where an annual value rating system is in force).

3   Any local authority.

4   Any owner or occupier whose name appears on the roll.

Objection rights are contained within Sections 18, 18A, 19, 20-25 of the VLA. Objections are required to be made in the prescribed form. VNZ investigates all objections and makes such amendments to values as it sees fit. The onus of proof in pursuing an objection to value lies with the objector. Either the Valuer-General or the objector may require an objection to be heard by the courts. The local Land Valuation Tribunal (chaired by a District Court Judge) is the first level of hearing and their decision is sealed as an order of Court, unless it is appealed. On the appeal of a Tribunal decision, the case will be heard by the Administrative Division of the High Court.

Objections and the resulting Tribunal (Court) decisions have given rise to a large body of case precedent that has been responsible for the development of valuation practice for rating purposes. Such has been the influence of these objections that many of the principles determined in this manner have also become part of general valuation practice in New Zealand.

At the time of writing this chapter VNZ is being restructured using a regulatory/ service delivery model. Legislative changes mean that a fully contestable market for government valuation services for territorial authorities will exist from the year 2000.

On 1 July 1998 VNZ became a Crown-owned company. It operates on a commercial basis, and will be progressively exposed to competition for the provision of government valuations. A separate Office of the Valuer-General (OVG) has been established within Land Information New Zealand. This regulatory body will set and monitor standards for the completion of rating valuations within the contestable environment.

Territorial authorities tendering out their valuation work will be held accountable by the OVG for complying with the standards. Under the new framework current appeal procedures to valuation will remain: an objection to value to the valuation provider, followed by the Land Valuation Tribunal, then the courts.

Methods of assessment - principles

New Zealand valuation practice recognizes the three basic approaches to the determination of value:

1   The cost, summation or contractor's approach; (the last term is not used in New Zealand practice).

2   The market data or sales comparison approach.

3   The capitalization, income or productive approach.

There are two schools of thought: the first and oldest is that the valuer should use all three methods, correlating the estimates into a value conclusion. The second and more recent view is that the valuer should adopt the method(s) of approach that is/are most relevant. District Valuers in charge of VNZ district offices have considerable flexibility as to which method and which philosophy should be adopted. However, the emphasis has always been on the market approach, either by direct comparison or an analytical approach using net rates, gross rates, income capitalization, income multiples or some other appropriate units of comparison (Jefferies, 1990; and 1991).

In recent years VNZ has developed a computerized valuation system based on a series of multiple regression models. This method has been generally adopted in residential areas where there are a large volume of sales recorded. Between government revaluations, in areas where mass appraisal computer generated values have been adopted, ongoing inspections by district office field staff of properties where sales transactions, new improvements and land subdivisions are advised help maintain the accuracy of VNZ's database.

The general principle of valuation for rating purposes is that the property shall be valued in accordance with its underlying zoning under the relevant local District Plan. District Plans are required in accordance with the Resource Management Act 1991. The purpose of the Resource Management Act 1991 (RMA) is to promote the sustainable management of natural and physical resources in New Zealand. It repealed the Town and Country Planning Act 1977 together with many other enactments. The RMA requires all territorial authorities to have a District Plan. This provision was formally provided for under the Town and Country Planning Act 1977 (TCA) in the form of District Schemes. Effectively each parcel of land in the country has a zoning, with the broad classifications being rural, residential, industrial, commercial and recreational. Currently, New Zealand is in a transitional phase, i.e. the preparation of many District Plans under the RMA are still only in their 'infancy' stage while others are in lengthy public submission stages. To date there are a small number that have become operative. On planning application where a District Plan has been prepared, but, is not yet operative, the proposed District Plan is read in conjunction with the existing District Scheme (McVeagh's, 1994).

The basic approach to valuations for rating purposes under the capital value and land value systems may be stated by the equation:

$$LV + VI = CV$$

where the valuer establishes the value of the land as vacant site, the unexhausted value of the improvements and sums them to give capital value; or

$$CV - LV = VI$$

where the valuer establishes the capital value of the property first (by capitalization or direct comparison or by some other appropriate technique), then determines the value of the land as a vacant site and by deduction determines the unexhausted value of the improvements.

The land residual approach ($CV - VI = LV$) is not acceptable for rating purposes as it does not establish the value of the land from market evidence. Land value must be assessed separately and independently of a property's capital value and value of improvements (*Thomas v Valuer-General* [1918] NZLR 164).

The concept of determining the land value as a vacant undeveloped site and adding the unexhausted value of the improvements is fundamental to all valuations for rating purposes. This has given rise to a number of anomalous situations:

1   House on a subdivided site: *Valuer-General v Epps* [1964] NZLR 810

In this case the existing on site house was situated over the common boundary of two separate lots, as such it prevented the sale of the sites individually. Value as a single large house site (say) $60,000. It was held the rating valuer must ignore this and pretend the improvements do not exist, (i.e. value as two vacant lots).

Therefore land value for rating purposes $80,000

2   Specified departures: *McKee and Another v Valuer-General* (1970) NZ Valuer, Vol. 22, No. 7

In this case three attached dwelling units were erected on a site by way of special planning permission. As of right (a permitted activity) only two may be erected. It was held that the valuation principle to be applied is that the land is to be valued as vacant, i.e. suitable for a two-unit development only but any likelihood of permission being granted for a higher use is to be included.

Value for two units @ $40,000 per unit	$80,000
Value for three units @ $30,000 per unit	$90,000

Likelihood of higher use being granted - say 50 per cent (i.e. $90,000 - $80,000 / 2 = $5,000). Therefore land value for rating purposes $85,000 (i.e. $80,000 + $5,000 = $85,000)

3   Non-Conforming Uses: *Valuer-General v General Plastics (NZ) Ltd* [1959] NZLR 857

This case centred around an industrial building, in use and operating, situated on a site zoned for residential purposes. It was held the land must be valued as vacant, therefore, its only potential use is residential. Therefore:

(A)	Value of Improvements (Industrial)	$100,000
	Land Value (Residential zone, industrial use)	$ 50,000
	Market Value	$150,000

(B)	Value of Improvements	$ 50,000
	(Industrial on residential site)	
	Land Value (Residential)	$ 30,000
	Capital Value	$ 80,000

This decision resulted in the VLA being amended in 1965 by the introduction of *special rateable values* (SRV). The valuation under (A) would now become the SRV.

Exemptions, reliefs and concessions

Generally all land is rateable but with several notable exceptions. The First Schedule of the RPA defines land which is not rateable. Non rateable land includes:

Crown lands that meet the following criteria:

• Land occupied by a vice-regal residence.

• Roads owned by the Crown.

• National Parks.

• Crown reserves (e.g. scenic reserves, historic reserve).

• Communal accommodation for education and health purposes.

- Crown land forming part of an aerodrome.

- Land occupied by railway track and railway passenger or goods terminals.

- Land associated with education uses.

Non-Crown lands that meet the following criteria:

- Private schools/universities/kindergartens.

- Hospitals.

- Certain charitable trusts.

- Places of religious worship.

- Cemeteries/crematoria.

- Land owned by the N.Z. Historic Places Trust.

- Marae (Maori meeting place).

- Certain land vested in Regional Councils (e.g. land required for river control).

- Harbour Board Land and Wharf Areas.

- Airports.

This list is by no means extensive and there are further exclusions:

- Private land leased to Crown for the above purposes are exempt.

- Productive areas (e.g. farms) associated with education may be rated.

- In many cases the non-rateable area is limited to 1.62 hectares.

- Crown land leased for more than 12 months is rateable.

- Defence land is subject to land value rating only.

The non-rateable exemption is for general rates only and these properties will remain liable for rates levied in respect of; water supply, refuse collection, sewage disposal, or any separate rate. It has become increasingly difficult to determine what is and what is not rateable property. In recent years government has pursued a policy of corporatization and/or privatizing many government departments and quasi government agencies. The ownership and the status of occupiers of

'Crown' land is no longer certain. Within the next two years this situation is likely to be reviewed as local government conducts major funding and rating reviews.

Rates postponement

Part X of the RPA 1988 contains provision for farmland rates relief where farm land value is influenced by potential for residential, industrial, commercial or other non-farming development. Section 25A of the VLA provides for the assessment of rates postponement values. These rates were introduced to maintain equitable relativity with farmland values which are not influenced by potential for urban development. Where farm land has a higher value for urban development then two sets of values are required; one for the lower use and one for the higher use. The difference between rates assessed on the lower value and the higher value may be postponed. Conditions that apply in respect of rates postponement are:

1   The postponed rates become a charge on the property and are recoverable if the property is sold or if it ceases to be used for farming.

2   If the circumstances surrounding the property remain unchanged the accumulated postponed rates are written off at five yearly intervals.

3   The postponement may be transferred to successive owners if the use remains unchanged.

Under the act the onus is on the occupier to satisfy the territorial authority or VNZ that they are eligible.

Special rateable values (SRVs)

Within the current New Zealand rating system a further category of rating relief exists, known as 'Special Reliable Values'. SRVs are assessed where the use of the land is different from that permitted by its zoning and where a value based on uses would give rise to a higher or lower value than that based on zoning, e.g. commercial/industrial use in residential/rural zone, single or double unit dwelling in a high density (multi unit) residential zone. They attempt to provide for equitable rating between differing intensities of actual land use. SRV assessments reflect a property's actual use rather than the highest and best value as influenced by zoning. They are assessed and entered on the district valuation roll in addition to the values determined under Section 2, VLA. It is the SRV on which the rates assessment is based. The VLA provides for five categories of special rateable value:

SRVs of industrial or commercial land in residential or rural areas (Section 25B, VLA) An example here could be a factory that was an existing land use in area that was subsequently re-zoned residential.

SRVs of residential land in commercial or industrial areas (Section 25C, VLA) Similar to above but excludes existing rural land uses in areas subsequently rezoned. The rural aspect is now provided for in Section 25A rates postponement values.

SRVs of single or double unit dwelling houses where values are influenced by the demand for multi-unit housing (Section 25D, VLA) Developers buying up old houses for multi-unit redevelopment establish the land values. If property sales for redevelopment are used to value all the sites in a street then existing improvements of houses which still have economic life will be depreciated and equate to demolition or removal value only.

SRVs of existing use properties (Section 25E, VLA) This could arise when the building is larger than permitted under current planning controls. For example, an existing 10 storey building might be situated on a site where planning controls would now only permit 8 floors. The larger building may give an existing land or capital which is in excess of that which would be assessed for a smaller building.

SRVs of land subject to special preservation conditions (Section 25F, VLA) An example could be an early 1900s building with a Historic Places Trust National Preservation Order, situated on a prime 500 square metres commercial site. On a highest and best use basis a nil value of improvements arises because when the rental income from the undercapitalized site is assessed the capitalized income is less that the land value. For SRV assessment purposes, the site is well undercapitalized by the presence of the existing building and a lower land value will be attributable. The capital value assessed on the capitalized income basis now exceeds land value and hence a value of improvements is arrived based on the formula CV - LV = VI. The following example illustrates a typical situation where SRV are assessed:

> A residentially zoned site with an industrial building erected thereon would be valued as residential land, say $50,000, and the improvements valued on the basis of their added value to a residential site, say, $20,000. Thus, the capital value would be $70,000. However the value as an industrial property may be $100,000.
>
> The values shown on the district valuation roll would be assessed under Section 25B, VLA:

301

	Roll value	S.R.V.	
LV	$50,000	LV (industrial land value)	$ 70,000
VI	$20,000	VI	$ 30,000
CV	$70,000	CV	$100,000

Rating apportionment

The RPA allows for the provision on request of a separate rating assessment for each tenant in multi-tenanted properties. The following rules relate to the assessment of these apportionments:

1   The rateable value of the parts must equal the rateable value of the entire property.

2   If the lease stipulates a proportionate payment then that figure shall be adopted.

The act is silent as to whether these apportionments should be based on floor area or rents. Consider the following example of a multi-tenanted four storey building where the ground floor is retail and the upper floors are commercial office.

Location	Contract Rent	Market Rent	Floor Area
Ground	$ 80,000	$ 112,000	280 sq.m
1st floor	$ 75,000	$ 75,000	300 sq.m
2nd floor	$ 65,000	$ 75,000	300 sq.m
3rd floor	$ 75,000	$ 80,000	300 sq.m
Total	$ 295,000	$ 342,000	1,180 sq.m

The apportionment for rating purposes under any of these three scenarios, based on a capital value of $3,000,000 would be:

Location	Contract Rent	Market Rent	Floor Area
Ground	$ 813,000	$ 982,000	$ 711,000
1st floor	763,000	658,000	763,000
2nd floor	661,000	658,000	763,000
3rd floor	763,000	702,000	763,000
Total	$3,000,000	$3,000,000	$3,000,000

These three different methods of apportionment give quite different results. In practice all of them could legitimately be adopted as SRV. The need for rates postponement or a SRV is determined on the motion of the Valuer-General or on the application from the territorial authority, owner or occupier concerned. Any valuations assessed under rates postponement, SRV and rating apportionment provisions carry with them the right of objection under the VLA.

Remission and postponement of rates

Rates may be remitted or postponed in the following cases:

1   in cases of extreme hardship (requires an occupier application to the authority);

2   on land that is applied for some recreation or charitable purpose.

Where a development is considered to benefit the whole community an authority may also formulate a rating relief policy for the period of such development.

Rebate of rates

The Rates Rebate Act 1973 provides for the granting of a rebate of rates payable on residential property to the property occupier, provided their income does not exceed certain limits.

Valuation equalization

Under the RPA provisions are made for a rating authority to request the Valuer-General to equalize the roll values of different territorial authorities. This provision is available to overcome inequitable situations which would otherwise arise through an authority, which levies rates over two or more territorial authorities, striking the rate on valuation rolls which were implemented at different times.

Collection procedures

Rate liability and recovery

Under Part VIII of the RPA the occupier, (as opposed to the owner), is primarily responsible for the payment of rates. The territorial authority is required to issue to the occupier a rates assessment providing the following information:

303

- Name and address of local authority.

- Name and address of occupier.

- Valuation roll number.

- Legal description and location of the property.

- A description of the rates being levied.

- Number of instalments by which rates are payable.

- The date the rates are due.

- Special rateable or rates postponement values if applicable.

- Place where rates are payable.

Section 123 requires rates on a separate property to be levied in accordance with the values shown on the district valuation roll. Rates become a charge on the land and non-payment of rates may ultimately be recovered by the sale or lease of the property. There is a contradiction in that, although the occupier is primarily liable, in the instance of occupier default an authority may ultimately sue the owner or any party holding an interest in the property (including a mortgagee) for recovery of rating arrears. Payment of rates can be made by lump sum or by instalments. Discounts may be granted for early rates payment. Likewise penalty charges may be added to unpaid rates.

Rating powers of local authorities

Territorial authorities have the power to levy the following types of rate:

1   A general rate - the income from which is used for the general purpose of the territorial authority. This rate must be at a uniform rate in the dollar but this may vary between wards.

2   A separate rate - is a rate charged for some particular work or service that will benefit the district, e.g. to finance a new library. A separate rate may be levied for part of a district where that part will be the beneficiary of the work. This rate may be either a one off payment or may continue over a number of years.

3   A service rate - property provided with specific services (e.g. reticulated water, sewage disposal, rubbish disposal) may be separately rated for that service.

4   A uniform annual charge - a fixed amount levied against each property, i.e. it is not related to the value of the property. The general rate plus any charge shall not exceed the maximum rate that may be levied. The income from an annual charge shall not exceed 30 percent of the total rates revenue.

5   Consolidated rate - A single rate to replace a rate levied for general, separate or service purposes.

6   Lump sum contribution - A single dollar amount to finance a particular work within all or part of the district.

The general rate shall not exceed 1.25 cents in the dollar on the capital value or land value or 18 cents in the dollar on annual value, however, total rates may exceed this amount.

Differential rating

A local authority may levy a rate on a differential basis so that the rates made and levied in respect of any one or more specified types or groups of property may vary from those rates levied for another specified group or type of property. One of the often heard arguments about rating is the question of how the rating burden is distributed within the community. Differential rating allows the territorial authority to establish a different value in the dollar charge for various parts of the district or for various types of property. It is most frequently used to distinguish between commercial and residential locations, low density and high density residential locations or single and multi-unit dwellings.

The first form of differential rating used in New Zealand was introduced in 1886. Counties were given the power to divide their area into ridings and levy different rates according to the needs of the riding. At this stage the main issue was roading and the argument was those that benefit should pay. Municipalities were given the same power in 1900. This type of differential rating became relatively insignificant as local authorities gradually moved away from separate riding or ward accounts to consolidated accounts.

The Urban Farm Land Rating Act of 1932 recognized that farm land with potential for urban subdivision may face 'excessive or unduly burdensome' rates. In cases where the council judged that the land would not be subdivided for at least five years provision was made to strike a lower rate in the dollar on rateable value. The modern form of differential rating used in New Zealand was introduced into counties in 1970 and municipalities in 1976. The objective of differential rating is to allow each local authority to adopt the system in a way that is best suited to its own needs.

Through to today it appears local authorities have retained differential rating to maintain the status quo of rating share contribution from different property sectors and to minimize the 1970 effects of changing the rating base from unimproved value to land value. The criteria for establishing a group or type of property for differential rating are:

1   The use(s) to which the property is put.

2   Zoning of the land.

3   The land area.

4   The situation within a particular district.

5   Such other distinctions as the territorial authority deems fit.

Such wide discretionary powers are not favoured by all sections of the community. Individual rights are protected by an objection system that prevails when a differential rate is introduced or amended but there is no provision for the community to revoke it once it is in force. Ratepayer objections normally relate to properties being incorrectly classified into a certain differential group. Palmerston North City Council rating levies for the year 1 July 1996 to 30 June 1997 are used as an illustration. It has 16 individual coded differential general rating groups (Table 14.4). In the determination of rates for an individual property the appropriate differential rate (based on property type classification) is applied to that property's land value. A set uniform charge is also added to derive the annual rates levy.

Therefore, a property with a land value (Palmerston North City Council rates on land value) of $40,000 and filling the requirements of Code 1, i.e. a single house property, the rates would be $40,000 x $0.0110315 = $441.26 + $430.00 (uniform charges) = $871.26. Whereas the same property under code 2 would be rated at $1,149.82 including uniform charges.

In New Zealand territorial authority and regional council rates are either billed collectively or individually. In urban areas it is common for territorial authorities to collect rates on behalf of a regional council by incorporating the regional council levy within territorial authority annual rating demands. This situation prevails in urban Palmerston North. With the PNCC illustration above regional council rates would be added to the PNCC levy as a separate entry in the rating notice sent to property owner(s) or occupier(s).

Table 14.4

Palmerston North City - differential groups 1996/97

Code	Brief Description	Rate (Cents in $)
01	Single unit residential	1.10315
02	Two unit residential	1.79956
03	Three unit residential	2.28406
04	Four unit residential	2.42249
05	Five unit residential	2.42249
06	Six unit residential	2.83777
07	Seven unit residential	3.04542
08	Eight or more unit residential	3.18384
10	Miscellaneous	1.38428
20	Central City non-residential	3.04542
30	Other non-residential	3.04542
31	Research institutions	3.04542
40	Hotels, motels etc.	3.18384
50	Rural/semi-serviced (5 hectares or more)	0.19380
51	Rural/semi-serviced (0.2 hectares or less)	0.69214
52	Rural/semi-serviced (between 0.2 & 5 hectares)	0.41528

Critical analysis

Uniformity

Uniformity is the cardinal principle for rating valuations. In New Zealand the land value system remains the most popular system of rating used by local authorities. The land value system is favoured by assessment authorities for reasons of cost and uniformity in value between similar land holdings. However, in heeding to the VLA definition of land value the question of whether the land component is being valued at market level is disputable.

A fundamental difficulty with land value rating is the valuer is specifically instructed to ignore the existing on site improvements and to value the land as if it were vacant. Therefore, identical sites will have the same value for rating purposes even though they may have quite different levels of improvements.

In built up areas it is often difficult to obtain land sales evidence. The few sales that exist may be from buildings purchased for demolition and site redevelopment. The land prices being paid in this situation normally cannot be imputed across a whole range of similar properties because the demand for redevelopment sites is usually quite limited.

Market value versus capital value

There are many definitions of market value, most revolving around the idea of making some sort of predictions about a property's sale price. The Appraisal of Real Estate (1978) defines market value as:

> The highest price in terms of money that a property would bring in a competitive and open market under all conditions requisite to a fair sale, the buyer and seller each acting prudently and knowledgeably and assuming the price is not affected by undue stimulus.

Most valuers would see market value assessments as the art of estimating sale price within prevailing market conditions. Among other things the Valuer may consider:

1   A reasonable time frame in which the property would sell.

2   Any tenancies or leases that the property is subject to.

3   Mortgages that may be transferred with the property.

4   Inhibiting registrations on the title.

The definition of capital value provides for an immediate sale on the valuation date: '... at the time of valuation ...', and allows the valuer to ignore leases, mortgages and title encumbrances; '... if unencumbered by mortgage or other charge thereon'.

This approach to value is of particular relevance to investment property where the rating valuer may ignore existing leases on the property and assess a value based on optimum lease conditions. In recent times this has led to instances where, in trying to maintain relativity between similar properties, over assessments have occurred, see following example.

> There are three identical and neighbouring industrial properties. The only difference is the terms and conditions under which they are occupied.

Property A: - Vacant

Property B: - First class tenant, long term lease, two year rent reviews.

Property C: - Third class tenant, 12 year lease, no rent review. Contract rent $20,000.

The net market rent for each of the properties is $30,000 p.a.

In this situation the practising valuer determining market value (as in predicting sale price) would probably vary the capitalization rate according to the quality of the tenant, and would also make allowance for rent shortfalls, thereby arriving at a different value for each. Valuation New Zealand, when assessing capital value, would use 'optimum or market' lease conditions for each property, thereby arriving at the same capital value for each. Clearly, there is a conflict between achieving uniformity for rating purposes and market values.

For investment property it is interesting to note that in the past five years there have been court decisions which challenge VNZs approach to valuation on an unencumbered basis. *Valuer General v Radford and Co. Ltd* [1993] 3 NZLR 721. This case related to a land holding in inner city Wellington owned by Radford and developed with leased retail shops. The Land Valuation Tribunal found in favour of Radford's objection, that the district roll valuation should be reduced by an amount equivalent to the burden of the leases on the owners estate or interest in land. On appeal by the Valuer-General the High Court upheld the Land Valuation Tribunal's determination.

Differential rating

Rating is ultimately a political process and local authority politicians are very conscious of maintaining the status quo in terms of rating burden. Differential rating has been used as a tool to maintain the status quo. The use of differential rating and uniform charges is a significant departure from a purely ad valorem rating system. One of the problems of trying to maintain the status quo over the years of various sectors rating share is that it may create current inequities. It is interesting to note in some instances that the differentials have been manipulated so far away from a pure land value system that the result is now closer to capital value rating. Is this the explanation for the more recent trend of local authorities adopting capital value rating systems? The effect of differential rating in Palmerston North can be seen in both Tables 14.5 and 14.6. Table 14.5 is taken from information produced in 1990 as part of a Palmerston North City Council proposal to change the rating system from land value to capital value. The proposal failed on the back of ratepayers opposition. However, in viewing Table 14.5 it can be seen how the effects of differential rating for 1988/89 distorted the rating base to such an extent that it became closer to a capital value system

Table 14.5

Palmerston North City rates for 1988/89 - share to be extracted from each major sector

Type of Property	Land Value (%)	Capital Value (%)	Actual Yield (%)
Single unit residential	63.78	58.94	52.54
Multi unit residential	4.72	4.95	7.29
Non-residential			
- Central city	10.25	12.21	15.68
- Multi-storey	1.06	2.92	1.75
- Suburban	12.03	13.71	15.00
- Motels, etc.	1.05	1.94	1.63
Miscellaneous	7.11	5.33	6.11
Total	**100.00**	**100.00**	**100.00**

Table 14.6

Palmerston North City Council - rates incidence 1996/97

Type of Property	No. of Ratepayers (%)	Land Value (%)	Capital Value (%)	Total Rates Levy (%)
Single unit residential	82.9	61.3	62.7	60.4
Multi unit residential	2.9	3.3	3.7	5.5
Non-residential	7.5	17.5	19.3	28.1
Rural/semi serviced	4.4	13.2	7.3	2.1
Miscellaneous	2.3	4.7	7.0	3.9
Total	**100.0**	**100.0**	**100.0**	**100.0**

rather than a land value system.

Table 14.6 shows the current Palmerston North City Council rating incidence as at 1 July 1996. Its layout and contents are slightly different from Table 14.5, to include: an indication of the percentage number of ratepayers per property type, the aggregation of figures for non-residential (i.e. commercial) property types, and separate figures for rural/semi serviced category property - the latter having previously been incorporated in the miscellaneous property figures in Table 14.5. In Table 14.6 the distortions caused by differential rating are still clearly evident, with the current rating base still generally remaining closer to the capital value system rather than the land value system.

Within the next two years some important rationalization of rating systems in New Zealand is likely to occur. The recently introduced Local Government Amendment Act (No. 3) 1996 requires all local authorities to conduct a funding and rating review before the middle of 1998. In late 1996 Kapiti Coast District became one of the first local authorities in New Zealand to initiate such a review. Its review has included the production of a discussion document for public comment on a proposal to change from a land value to a capital value rating system.

Summary

This chapter has reviewed the development and components of local government property taxation in New Zealand. Rating practice in New Zealand is determined by the requirements of the Rating Powers Act 1988 and Valuation of Land Act 1951 and Amendments. The former covers the manner in which rates are levied and the latter the assessment of the values on which the rate is based. Capital values, land values and value of improvements are assessed at regular periodic intervals by the Valuer-General (Valuation New Zealand). Where annual values are required for rating purposes these are assessed by local authority appointed valuers, which can include the Valuer-General.

Under the Valuation of Land Act objection rights are available on all valuations made for general revaluation purposes and all alterations to value made during the currency of a valuation roll. Parties to a valid objection have the right to have the case heard by the Land Valuation Tribunal, with the High Court the ultimate authority on appeals. The decisions of the courts have resulted in a large volume of case precedent most of which now forms the basis for the determination of valuations for rating purposes.

Anomalies arise where the courts have continually emphasised that capital value is market value but have then gone on to determine the correct procedural approach in specific circumstances. These approaches are required by the definitions of 'capital value', 'land value' and 'value of improvements' contained

311

in the act. Many of these situations now require the assessment of rates postponement values, special rateable values, and rating apportionment values.

Historically the New Zealand system has allowed local government a free choice of which rating system it uses. The current statute allows territorial authorities to change the rating system. Although required to consult the ratepayers there is no requirement to heed the collective opinion. In recent times there has been a trend towards greater use of capital value rating. However, the land value system of rating continues to be the most popular basis utilized by local authorities in New Zealand. The arguments in favour of the capital value system appear to be based on ability to pay for the services provided, i.e. those with higher valued properties can best afford to carry a higher rating burden.

References

American Institute of Real Estate Appraisers, (1978), *The Appraisal of Real Estate* (7th Ed.), American Institute of Real Estate Appraisers, Chicago.

Hargreaves, R.V. (1991), Is Site Value Still an Appropriate Basis for Property Tax?, in *Proceedings, International Conference on Taxation and its Interacting with Land Policy*, Lincoln Institute of Land Policy, Cambridge, Massachusetts.

Jefferies, R.L. (1990), *Urban Valuation in New Zealand, Volume II*, New Zealand, Institute of Valuers, Wellington, 1990.

Jefferies, R.L. (1991), *Urban Valuation in New Zealand, Volume I (2nd Ed.)*, New Zealand, Institute of Valuers, Wellington, 1991.

Mc Veagh's, J.P. (1994), *McVeagh's Land Valuation Law (8th Ed.)*, by Mulholland, R.D., Butterworths, Wellington.

O'Regan, R., (1985), *Rating in New Zealand*, Baranduin Ltd, Wellington.

Palmerston North City Council, Annual Plan 1996/97, Palmerston North City Council, New Zealand.

Ralston, S.W.A. (1978), Land Value for Taxation, *New Zealand Valuer*, Vol. 23, No. 9.

Statistics New Zealand, *New Zealand Official Yearbook 1996 (10th Ed.)*, Wellington, New Zealand.

Acknowledgement

This chapter is an extended and revised version of the earlier chapter, Rating Systems in New Zealand, authored by T.H.C. Taylor, and published in Comparative Property Tax Systems (1991).

15 Property taxes in Australia

David Hornby

Introduction

The modern tax on immovable property (the property tax) has old ancestry, being one of earliest forms of taxation. Although its popularity in Australia has waned recently in favour of the income tax it is still the most important tax at the local level of government. This chapter provides an overview of property taxation in Australia, compares taxes on immovable property with other taxes under the criteria of 'good taxation', considers the relative merits of improved property taxes versus land taxes, and the necessary assumptions and criteria for an efficient property tax system. Taxes on immovable property in Australia consist of two types, municipal rates and land taxes.

Municipal rates are those property taxes collected by local councils throughout Australia and account for about 68 per cent of the total taxes on immovable property. The next largest are land taxes, which represent taxes at state level based on land values. These account for about 27 per cent of the total taxes on immovable property.

Origins and evolution

Australia and New Zealand are among the few countries in the world to employ a land value system for property tax purposes whereas most other western countries use an improved value system (either lump sum or annual value). Improved value is the market or present value of land including all improvements thereon but subject to certain assumptions necessary for mass valuation purposes, for example, the premises are assumed to be not subject to a lease agreement. Australia and New Zealand have embraced a land value system largely through the ideas of Henry George (1929) who advocated a tax on the unearned increment.

313

George argued that there was only a need for one tax; a land tax, as it compensates the government/society for the unearned increment in land value. The unearned increment as opposed to the earned increment is that part of land value caused by the expenditure of government and/or the general expansion of the economy. For example, if the government builds a school near residential lands then generally, those lands will increase in value as a result. Such capital gains enjoyed by the owners should be taxed by the government as they have been caused by public expenditure and therefore, are unearned. Compare such a windfall profit with a land owner who builds a house on his/her land that is, the land has increased in value because of his/her expenditure (earned increment). The earned increment should not be taxed to encourage development.

According to George and a number of researchers, a tax on the unearned increment alone, if sufficiently large, will force landowners to develop vacant land, thus reducing speculation and the price of land because of the increase in supply. Further, by not taxing improvements, such a tax encourages the development of land, and the improvement and upkeep of buildings. Australia, being a federation of states includes many local options and different state laws. Local governments throughout Australia levy a property tax on either the unimproved value, land value or site value, improved value, assessed annual (improved) value or a combination thereof. However, because of the influence of Henry George, the trend has been towards land values, a logical and necessary development of the unimproved value concept. The allegiance to the land value system in Australia is particularly strong in the Eastern States. For example, in an intensive examination of the land value system in Australia, Bronson-Cowan (1958) made the following comments:

> Special attention was paid to this subject during the field investigations on which these studies were based. No case was found where a municipality had reverted to the taxation of improvements, even in part, as the result of a depression. During the course of 60 years of experience with site value taxation, Australia and New Zealand passed through several depressions. These included the world wide depression of 1929-1934. While land values underwent considerable declines during these periods, their tendency has been to show continuous increases. These increases have been such as to indicate that, given sound municipal administrations, they tend to provide a constantly expanding source of municipal revenue.

Australia and New Zealand have developed the land value system to a greater extent than other countries. This has been under the influence of a court system that has laid down the proper use of sale prices, defined market value, and methods of valuation for over 80 years. For example, the 'definitive' statement on the most suitable sale evidence for the determination of market value is still the High Court decision; *Spencer v The Commonwealth* (1907) 5 CLR 418 (this is known as the willing buyer willing seller theory).

Tasmania was the first state to levy a tax on land values in 1857. Tasmania's current legislation was passed in 1952 and the land value base is the assessed annual value, i.e. annual rental value.

Queensland introduced the land value (unimproved value) system in 1887 for rural areas and in 1890, despite a nationwide and international depression, it was extended to urban areas. It is the only system used in Queensland as it is also used by the Metropolitan Water Sewerage and Drainage Board in Brisbane and other water supply authorities.

In 1893, South Australian municipalities were given the choice of adopting a land value system but with severe restrictions that hindered its general adoption. Today, only four councils have opted to tax on land values and the remainder prefer improved values.

In Western Australia, the Roads Act 1902 gave Road Boards permission to use either a site value or annual value system to raise revenue. The majority opted for the site value system. Urban municipalities were given the same power in 1945.

In Victoria, enabling rating legislation was passed in 1920 and within the next ten years, nine of the 28 municipalities in greater Melbourne adopted the new system including the choice of site values. Each municipality is allowed to choose its own rating base. The number of councils in Victoria have recently been reduced to just 78 from the previous 210. Following government pressure to adopt the capital improved value system 61 of the 78 have opted for that system, 11 for the net annual value system and only 6 for the site value system.

NSW's first land tax legislation was the Land and Income Tax Assessment Act 1895 using unimproved values. In 1906, NSW abolished the annual rental value system and made it compulsory for municipal councils both urban and rural, to use the unimproved value for a minimum rate. However, the balance could be raised by a tax on both land and buildings. The Sydney Harbour Bridge Act 1922 enabled the unimproved value taxation of land in the City of Sydney, municipalities and shires that came within the influence of the bridge. The Local Government Acts of 1905 and 1906 allowed local authorities to impose rates based on unimproved values.

The Local Government Act 1919, replaced the previous local government acts and provided for the assessment of a general rate on unimproved value. This has been replaced by the Local Government Act 1993 under which the main sources of finance for councils are rates, charges, fees, grants, borrowings and income from investments. The Act allows for categories of ordinary rates based on whether the land is residential, farmland, business or mining. There are also special rates for council services or special purposes such as water, sewerage or drainage,

The Commonwealth Government introduced the Land Tax Assessment Act in 1910. This Act was designed to break up large land holdings based on unimproved values. It was repealed in 1952 when its legality was threatened as being unconstitutional. However the contention was never viable as the High Court had decided in *Osborne v The Commonwealth* [1911] 12 CLR 321 that although the tax was progressive and designed to break up large holdings, it was within the taxing powers of the Commonwealth.

The Commonwealth tax was replaced by various state acts for example, the Land Tax Act 1956, and Land Tax (Management) Act 1956 in NSW. The NSW tax was a progressive tax until 1986 when it was reduced to a flat two cents in the dollar rate. The monies derived from state land taxes go into the state coffers alone.

Important inquiries into the property tax system include:

1   The Committee of Enquiry (1960) (The Bridge Report) recommended no major change in the use of unimproved values in the property tax system but rather, fine tuning of the statutory definition. However, the Committee did recognize the following problems with the concept of unimproved value:

> It would be futile for valuation purposes in England or the European Continent, to speculate whether land was marsh or forest or open country at some long past period.... It is important that the concept of value should be capable of reasonably precise determination .... It can readily be appreciated that in determining Unimproved Values of pastoral and agricultural lands, the most contentious are those relating to the amounts allowed for treatment of timber, scrub and undergrowth.

> Therefore, although recognizing anomalies in the definition of unimproved value particularly for rural lands, the Committee was not prepared to embrace the more modern land value concept.

2   The Queensland Committee of Inquiry (1967) also recognized problems with the valuation of timber treatment of rural land:

> This requirement introduces unnecessary uncertainty and complexity in the valuation process and provides differences, disputes and litigation between the valuation authority and the owner.

316

3   The NSW Royal Commission (1967) made specific recommendations on
     the problems recognized in the Bridge Report:

> The theory behind the recommendation made by the Bridge
> Committee was that the owner of the land would recoup himself for
> the cost of such invisible improvements through increased
> productivity due to the performance of the work, or when the land
> is sold ... by the price received for the land.

The Commission recommended important changes to the valuation base
particularly, the introduction of land values to overcome a number of
anomalies in the use of unimproved values.

With regard to rating in the Australian Capital Territory (ACT), a
Commonwealth Grants Commission Report was prepared in 1984 under the
chairmanship of Justice Rae Else-Mitchell. Another important report concerning
the system in the ACT was The Task Force on Self Government. The Task
Force recognized the likely need for an ACT Valuer General and a valuation
office when the Territories gained self government (Else-Mitchell, 1985).
However, despite having self government, this has not happened and property
tax values in both the ACT and Northern Territory are carried out by the
Commonwealth's Australian Valuation Office (AVO).

The Office of Local Government (Victoria) in August 1993 recommended
that capital improved value 'should be the only basis for municipal valuations,
and site value and net annual value (NAV) should no longer be used' (Rating
Review Paper). This is a valid recommendation as the degree of difficulty and
cost in determining an improved rental value is the same as that for determining
a lump sum improved value. However, the Paper went further, recommending
that capital improved value (CIV) should be the sole valuation base for the
purpose of assessing local government rates. There were three main reasons
advanced for this recommendation (Blackwell, 1994):

1   Capital improved value, while not perfect, meets the equity criteria
     considerably better than either site value or net annual value.

2   The concept of capital improved value is far more easily understood by
     ratepayers than either site value or net annual value.

3   There are advantages in having all councils use the same valuation base -
     arguments relating to widely differing rates for similar properties on either
     side of a municipal boundary caused by a different valuation base being
     adopted will tend to disappear.

The first reason advanced by the Office of Local Government, although initially attractive, does not apply in practice. Adding the third dimension (improvements) to the fiscal cadastre makes the improved valuation much more complex and subject to larger error. Therefore, equity is lost through larger error and the necessary longer lead time between general valuations.

With regard the second reason, there is no valid reason why taxpayers cannot understand the concept of site value. Not all valuations cover commercial areas and in rural, semi-rural and residential areas, site value is a common and typical term supported by a great deal of sales evidence such as for vacant lots. The word capital is superfluous as value necessarily implies a monetary measure. The resultant capital improved value (CIV) definition is still a statutory definition with all the complexities necessary for mass valuation purposes. For example, it assumes an unencumbered fee simple in possession and therefore, in many cases, the resultant value would be quite different from the more natural concept of market value.

The third reason ignores the situation described above where different councils have different typical land uses. For example, site value is easily the better value for rural councils. The advocates of the improved value system have to prove substantial superiority to the site value system as it is at least twice the cost of a site value base to prepare and maintain.

Another important Victorian report was the Land Tax Review, Victoria, 1991. The following are two important Western Australian reports.

1   The Keall Report - Western Australia

An investigative Committee was appointed to investigate the rating and taxing system so as to overcome a number of anomalies caused through the multitude of acts and bodies then concerned with rating and taxing. The principal recommendations of the Report were the creation of a central valuation body, consolidation of the various acts; that the new Act should include definitions of site value, annual rental value, assessed value, and capital value; the assessed value to be a certain percentage of capital value; the period between valuations be shortened and the methods for objections and appeals be streamlined.

2   McCusker Report - Western Australia

The McCusker Inquiry was established in 1980 to examine general problems of the rating and taxing system. The Committee recommended:

Where contributions are needed to meet the cost of more generalised services and a rating procedure is adopted, only one valuation base

318

should be used. The base should be capital value for improved properties and its equivalent, namely site value, for unimproved properties ... .

As yet these recommendations have not been implemented.

The place of the tax within the central tax system

The relative importance of property taxation in Australia can be gauged by comparing taxation revenues for Australia in 1994/95. Income tax dominated with about 51.8 per cent of the total, and goods and services with about 27.9 per cent. Taxes on immovable property accounted for only about 4.9 per cent and all property at about 11 per cent - see Figure 15.1

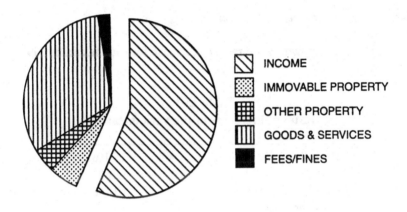

INCOME

IMMOVABLE PROPERTY

OTHER PROPERTY

GOODS & SERVICES

FEES/FINES

Figure 15.1   Australian taxes: all levels of government 1994/95

Source: Australia Bureau of Statistics

Figure 15.2 shows the dominance of income taxes as a ratio of total taxes of the Commonwealth. However, there has been a trend in recent years of the Commonwealth in increasing taxes other than income in an attempt to reduce the reliance on one tax system. Since scrapping Commonwealth land taxes, the Commonwealth has been forced to rely particularly on goods and services taxes as the main single alternative to income taxes.

Goods and services includes two taxes under Australian Bureau of Statistics classification; on the provision of goods and services, and on the use of goods and performance of activities.

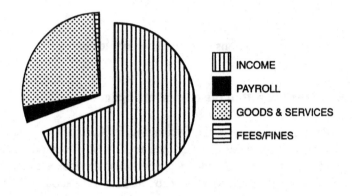

INCOME

PAYROLL

GOODS & SERVICES

FEES/FINES

Figure 15.2   Commonwealth taxes 1994/95

Source: Australia Bureau of Statistics

Recent trends are shown by the rates of increase for each tax from 1993/94 to 1994/95.

Table 15.1
Rates of increases in the various taxes

Payroll	25.1%
Income	11.6%
Goods and services	10.1%
Fees and fines	6.1%
Taxes on immovable property	0.9%
Other property taxes	-1.5%

Source: Australia Bureau of Statistics

Figure 15.1 clearly shows the dominance of income tax in Australia. As a ratio of total taxes, taxes on immovable property are very small being only about 1.64 per cent of Gross Domestic Product (GDP) in 1994/95. However, this does show a large increase in recent years over the historical mean of about 1.29 per cent (1969/1970 to 1989/1990). Since 1982 the ratio has remained remarkably level at about 1.4 per cent. Over the same period there has been a good correlation between taxes on immovable property and the Gross State Product (GSP). However, in recent years taxes on immovable property have outstripped the GSP.

320

Although the Commonwealth is not dependent on property taxes, local government is. About 93 per cent of local governments' total tax revenue was derived from property taxes in 1994/95. Australian Bureau of Statistics data shows a rapid increase in local property taxes from a base year of 1994/95, significantly outstripping other local taxes over this period.

NSW has a high ratio (43.5 per cent) of Goods and Services tax compared to the other states with Land and Other Immovable taxes accounting for only about 8.3 per cent of total taxation. However, all property taxes account for about 31 per cent because of the large amount of stamp duty obtained from property transfers (22.66 per cent). On the other hand, municipal rates are less than the national average at 61.17 per cent of the total - see Figure 15.3.

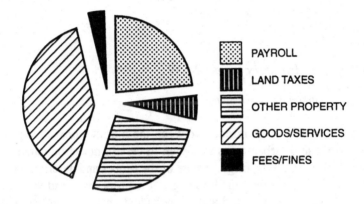

Figure 15.3   Taxation revenue - NSW 1994/95

Source: Australia Bureau of Statistics

Figure 15.4 shows the trend in taxes on Immovable Property against total taxes on property, total taxes, fees and fines. It can be seen that the tax on immovable property is not large as a ratio of total taxes and has dropped off in recent years.

Basis of assessment (the example of NSW)

As can be seen from the brief history outlined there is great diversity in the bases of valuation throughout Australia. However in this chapter, New South Wales (NSW) is used as a typical model for the total land tax system in Australia. The tax bases for NSW are land value replacing unimproved value in 1978 and assessed annual value (AAV) for non residential properties only.

321

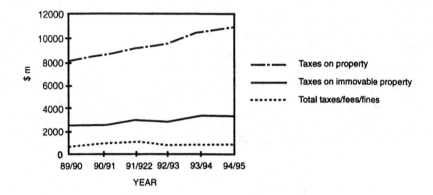

Figure 15.4   Property taxes - NSW

Source: Australia Bureau of Statistics

There is virtually no difference between the old unimproved value and the newer land value in urban areas however, in certain non-urban areas it allows the valuer to disregard the original state of the timber and determine land value based on the existing economic clearing of the property. Land values are now the compulsory value base for local councils and on all residential land for the Waterboard.

Land value

Land value is a statutory value subject to a number of statutory conditions and assumptions necessary for an efficient mass valuation system. It is the present value of the land excluding man-made structural improvements such as houses, fencing and driveways but including ground improvements. Land value is defined in the Valuation of Land Act 1916 as follows:

6A.   (1)   The land value of land is the capital sum which the fee-simple of the land might be expected to realise if offered for sale on such reasonable terms and conditions as a bona-fide seller would require, assuming that the improvements, if any, thereon or appertaining thereto, other than land improvements, and made or acquired by the owner or his predecessor in title had not been made.

322

(2)   Notwithstanding anything in subsection (1), in determining the land value of any land it shall be assumed that:

>   (a)   the land may be used, or may continue to be used, for any purpose for which it was being used, or for which it could be used, at the date to which the valuation relates; and

>   (b)   such improvements may be continued or made on the land as may be required in order to enable the land to continue to be so used,

but nothing in this subsection prevents regard being had, in determining that value, to any other purpose for which the land may be used on the assumption that the improvements, if any, other than land improvements, referred to in subsection (1) had not been made.

(3)   Notwithstanding anything in subsection (1), in determining the land value of any land, being land in relation to which, at the date to which the valuation relates, there was a water right:

>   (a)   the land value shall include the value of the right; and

>   (b)   it shall be assumed that the right shall continue to apply in relation to the land.

The assumptions in the statutory definition and the necessary system for an efficient mass appraisal system can be summarized as follows:

1   An unencumbered fee simple in possession (FSIP) is assumed and the effect of 'public' (as opposed to 'private') controls on land value are taken into account.

2   It is assumed that the improvements have never been made.

3   Improved sales can be used to determine land value.

4   'Special adaptability' is taken into account when determining the highest and best use.

5   Land value cannot be 'prairie value' and detriments are taken into account.

6   The need for rating relief or circuit breakers.

All of the above have been largely clarified by the courts so that the valuer and consumer can determine land value with a high level of confidence. The courts have interpreted the necessary assumptions as follows:

1   Unencumbered fee simple in possession

The subject land is assumed to have 'lean' title. This assumption was considered by the NSW Royal Commission as follows:

> ... if the submissions were conceded it would be necessary to value every estate or interest. This would create difficulties in valuation far greater than any which may now apply in the determination of the hypothetical fee simple - para 73.

The owner is assumed to have full freehold title without any encumbrance and is entitled to vacant possession for example, without the encumbrance of a mortgage (*Langford v WLC* (1959) 15 The Valuer 374). Although private restrictions on title are ignored, any general or public control is taken into account (*Royal Sydney Golf Club v The Commissioner of Tax* (1957) 91 CLR 610). Therefore, town planning controls are taken into account as well as general government policy.

2   That the improvements had never been made

Land value is determined 'assuming that the improvements, if any, thereon or pertaining thereto, and made or acquired by the owner or his predecessor in title had not been made' - s6A(1) Valuation of Land Act, 1916, NSW.

> What the Act requires is really quite simple. Here is a plot of land; assume that there is nothing on it in the way of improvements, what would it fetch in the market? - *Tooheys v Valuer General* [1925] AC439.

Therefore, when applying this criterion to licensed premises such as a hotel, the licence cannot be part of the land value as the hotel premises is necessary to obtain a hotelier's licence. Under the Queensland legislation the licence is expressly excluded in the definition of improvements.

3   Analysing improved sales to obtain land value

Although the improvements are considered never to have existed it is proper to determine the land value from improved sales by subtracting the value of the improvements from those sales (*James v Valuer General* [1942] 7 The Valuer 132). This method is expressly allowed in the Queensland legislation. However, the improvements must represent the highest and best use of the land otherwise an erroneous answer will result (*Horn v Sunderland Corporation* [1941] 2 KB 26). If the improvements are not the highest and best use, the sale price represents land value after an appropriate reduction for the cost of removal of the uneconomic buildings. Such sales are important evidence of value in the highly developed and expanding areas in most Australian cities.

4   Special adaptability

It was stated above that the licence component of the market value of licensed premises is ignored when determining land value. However, the land may have some special quality or adaptability for the licensed use, in which case, it becomes part of the land value. For example, the drive-in theatre site in *Peelmont v Valuer General* [1965] 19 The Valuer 384.

5   Prairie value

Prairie value is the value assuming that not only is the subject land vacant but also the surrounding infrastructure. However, this is the wrong approach as only the subject site should be considered as vacant and therefore, all of the external services such as roads, electricity, water, and sewerage are 'as is' and available to the land (*McGeoch v Fed Comm* [1929] 43 CLR 277; *Tetzner v CSR* [1956] 14 The Valuer 477 [1958] AC 50; *Comm of Rail v Valuer General* [1962] 10 LGRA 20, 16 The Valuer 512).

6   Detriments to the land ('worsements')

Not all of man's activities result in an improvement to the land. In some cases the land may deteriorate from its original condition for example, by erosion. Such detriments should be taken into account when determining land value (*Kiddle v Dep Fed Comm of Tax* [1920] 27 CLR 316).

Exemptions, reliefs and concessions

In 1986, in order to overcome problems of a long lead time between general valuations, NSW introduced the concept of equalization factors. Between general valuations an adjusted value is determined by applying the relevant equalization factor to the base date land value. The Valuer General determines the equalization factor each year for each zone in each local government area. The factor is multiplied by the nominal land value to approximate a value that would have been applicable if a general valuation had been made at the equalization date or common base date.

Assessed annual value (AAV)

The New South Wales statutory definition of assessed annual value is as follows:

7.(1) The assessed annual value of land is:

(a) nine-tenths of the fair average annual value of the land, with the improvements (if any) thereon; or

(b) $10,

whichever is the greater.

(2) In determining the assessed annual value of any land being premises occupied for trade, business, or manufacturing purposes such value shall not include the value of any plant, machines, tools, or other appliances which are not fixed to the premises or which are only so fixed that they may be removed from the premises without structural damage thereto.

(3) In determining the assessed annual value of any land it shall be assumed that the land, with the improvements, if any, thereon is not subject to the provisions of the Landlord and Tenant (Amendment) Act 1948.

Assessed annual value is similar to the definition used in most countries that tax on rental values. As with land value a number of assumptions are made to make the system work. For example, the subject premises is assumed to be vacant and therefore, no allowance is made for an existing tenancy. One unusual aspect of the NSW definition is the one-tenth deduction from gross rental value to arrive at net annual value. This is deemed to be a proxy for outgoings.

There are equivalent definitions for the land value (s7B) and AAV of strata (s7C). These are much longer than the definitions above in an attempt to overcome the special problems that the valuation of strata attracts.

326

Land improvements

Under the definition of land value above, land improvements become part of the land value. The definition of land improvements are as follows:

S4: 'and improvements' means:

(a) the clearing of land by the removal or thinning out of timber, scrub or other vegetable growths;

(b) the picking up and removal of stone;

(c) the improvement of soil fertility or the structure of soil;

(d) the restoration or improvement of land surface by excavation, filling, grading or levelling, not being works of irrigation or conservation;

(e) the reclamation of land by draining or filling together with any retaining walls or other works appurtenant to the reclamation; and

(f) underground drains.

The definition is an important adjunct to the definition of land value as it defines those improvements to be ignored when determining land value. They are ignored because:

1 they are hard to discover having merged with the land (for example, old filling and drainage);

2 it is usually very difficult to ascertain the value of such improvements because the only available sale evidence is land similarly improved. For example, if all neighbouring lands have been drained, there will no sale evidence of undrained land available to ascertain the value of the drainage.

Vacant lands

Under the land value system it is fundamental that vacant lands pay the same rates as improved lands. This is an attribute that:

1 does not tax the earned increment.

2 forces undeveloped land into development.

327

3   reduces speculation and therefore, reduces overall land values.

Therefore, there is no differentiation in property taxes paid on otherwise comparable vacant sites.

Rates charged and rates differentiation

Both land taxes and local rates are flat taxes and therefore, in this regard regressive. However, the regressive effect of local council rates are mitigated somewhat by being able to charge different rates for different land uses. This is particularly important in areas with a large commercial or CBD component as the local council invariably tries to reduce the effect of high rates on residential properties nearby.

It is common for large local council areas (such as Hornsby Shire north of Sydney) to reduce the rates payable on agricultural land. This is at the discretion of the local council. For example in Hornsby, primary producers pay half the rates payable by non-primary producers for equivalent land. This has had the effect of encouraging land speculation by profitable rural enterprises such as market gardens and nurseries who still enjoy windfall profits when eventually, with urban expansion the land is rezoned to a higher use.

In a number of inner suburbs of Sydney it is common for the local council to allow either rate rebates or rate reductions for pensioners. For example, in Leichhardt Council area pensioners pay no rates but the outstanding rates are taken out of the proceeds on the sale of the property or become a charge on the land if the pensioner dies.

Water and sewerage rates

The rates assessed by the various authorities for water and sewerage rates have historically been on a different premise to that applicable to property taxes at both local and state levels of government. Waterboard rates have generally been based on improved values (both lump sum and annual) and the trend is towards a 'user pays' system.

Case study - New South Wales

In Sydney the relevant authority is the Sydney Waterboard. The Board has two charges - Water Usage Charge and Service Availability Charges. In addition, there is a Special Environmental Levy that assists in funding a number of special environmental projects in the Board's area of operations. This Levy does not apply to pensioners eligible for a pensioner rebate. These charges are generally for a three month period.

Water Usage Charge

Water usage attracts an increasing price level according to the amount of water used. The total charge can only be determined after the meter has been read. Since water meters cannot always be read for exactly the same period at each reading, the Water Usage Charge is calculated on the basis of average daily usage (that is, the water usage is divided by the number of days in the meter reading period).

Service Availability Charges

Properties attract quarterly Service Availability Charges for each service available from the Board and are payable whether or not the service is used. It is made up of from the following two components for each service;

1   Base Charge, plus a Property Tax Charge where the land value of the property exceeds $33,000.

2   Property tax charge where the amount of the land value exceeds $33,000.

Maximum charge levels

All residential and vacant land properties have an upper limit for each Service Availability Charge that is payable for a property.

Special Environmental Levy

A Special Environmental Levy of $20 per quarter is payable where a property (including each home unit or flat in the case of multiple dwellings) has water and sewerage services available. Where only a water service is available the levy payable is $6.25 per quarter. Funds collected by way of the Special Environmental Levy are being kept separate from the other sources of revenue of the Board. These funds are specifically used to undertake a range of environment protection and enhancement works.

Sewerage Usage Charge

Where the volume of sewage discharged from a non-residential property exceeds 1,370 litres per day (125 kilolitres per quarter), a Sewerage Usage Charge is applicable.

Land tax in NSW

Land Tax is a state government tax using land values as the tax base. The following summarizes the tax system. The relative level of land tax against other taxes is shown in Figure 15.4.

Property used as an owner's place of residence

An owner's principal place of residence is exempt provided it does not exceed 2,100 m² (about twice the size of an average building block); or two hectares, where subdivision is prevented by planning regulations. Where the land exceeds these areas, land tax is payable on the excess. Any excess up to a value of $320,000 will not attract tax.

Property not used as an owner's principal place of residence

Tax is payable on land with an adjusted value of $160,000 or more. Tax payable is $100 plus 1.5 per cent of the value of land exceeding $160,000.

Equalization factors

All properties are increased by 17 per cent on the 1990 factors. This is a proxy for falling land prices.

Responsibility for making assessments

The current valuation act is the Valuation of Land Act 1916 (as amended). Under this act, the central valuation authority, the Valuer General, was created with the objectives of achieving continuity, uniformity, and stability of land valuations for property tax purposes.

> The object of the Valuation of Land Act, 1916, as gathered from its provisions, was to have one value for a block of land whether for taxation or for resumption purposes, Pike J., in *Mobbs v Valuer General* 6 LGR 79.

The Valuation of Land Act of 1916 is not a taxing act as many people seem to think. The object of that Act was to bring into line the serious differences that used to exist between the valuation of land for taxing purposes and the value of land for compensation and mortgage purposes; under the Act the one value applies in every case. It applies for compensation as well as for rating - Pike J, *Alison v Valuer General* 6 LGR 25.

These idealistic aims soon dissipated as the cost of upkeep of a proper improved value tax system was too prohibitive. The shortage of qualified and experienced staff meant that assumptions and qualifications in the definition of market value were necessary to maintain an efficient tax system. These controlling factors still apply today.

Critical analysis

The following are the necessary criteria for a good tax (Musgrave and Musgrave, 1980):

1   The distribution of the tax burden is equitable. Everyone is made to pay a 'fair share'.

2   The tax minimizes interference with economic decisions in otherwise efficient markets. Such interferences impose 'excess burdens' and therefore, should be minimized.

3   Where the tax is used to achieve other objectives, such as to grant investment incentives, this should be done so as to minimize interference with the equity of the system.

4   The tax should facilitate the use of fiscal policy for stabilization and growth objectives.

5   The tax should permit fair and non-arbitrary administration and be easily understandable by the taxpayer.

6   The administration and compliance costs should be as low as is compatible with the other objectives.

These criteria were also supported by the Commonwealth's Draft White Paper (June 1983) Reform of the Australian Tax System, 14. Current research shows the following conclusions about property taxes:

331

1   The distribution of the tax burden should be equitable

Compared with the income tax, property taxes are more equitable because somebody will pay the tax and therefore there is virtually no evasion and evasion of the income tax is carried out more by wealthy persons.

The 'modern' view is that the property tax is progressive because the incidence falls on the owner of the property rather than the tenant (Miezkowski, 1969). From an equity point of view, the land value system is favoured over the improved value system because greater equity is achieved through the shorter lead time between general valuations and a more up-to-date and easily maintained fiscal cadastre.

2   The tax should minimize interference with economic decisions

Generally, the Australian property tax system does not unnecessarily interfere with economic decisions in otherwise efficient markets. However, there is evidence that the land tax system does force development, particularly in CBD areas (Archer, 1973). This is considered an advantage as such 'forcing' increases the land and building stock, increases employment and discourages speculation.

The basic concept of the property tax system is also undermined by the liberal use of exemptions and allowances. Generally, except for the circuit breakers covered later, there should be no exemptions and allowances. If this norm is followed, the property tax system will not interfere with land markets.

3   Minimize interference with the equity of the system

The use of allowances and the delay in updating values (particularly in the improved value system) undermines the equity of the property tax system in Australia. The use of circuit breakers (for example, deferred rates following an increase in value caused by an upward change in zoning) can be justified on equity grounds when the taxpayer cannot afford to pay the increase. However, if the taxpayer is reasonably wealthy, inequity results and such allowances encourage speculation. Therefore, the taxpayer should be means tested before such allowances are granted.

There should be no exemptions from a property tax including government departments as otherwise the tax ideal of 'universality' is undermined, leading to inequities. For example, some local government areas with a large proportion of government departments or government owned land (for example, educational sites) have a much lower tax base than otherwise comparable areas. Where tax exemptions are granted to non-profit organizations such as charities, the Victorian system should be adopted whereby taxes owing or saved are paid back upon the sale of the land.

Property taxation in its basic form is a simple and progressive tax. However, when vested interests distort the system for their own ends, the tax becomes regressive and complex. This is particularly the case in America where the basic system has been corrupted by the special allowances and valuation waivers for vested interest groups. A good example of the tax becoming unwieldy and regressive is shown by the passing of Proposition 13 in California favouring existing homeowners against new homeowners. Such distortions and complexities are more difficult to introduce under the land value system as they are more obvious and less transparent.

4   Facilitate the use of fiscal policy for stabilization and growth objectives

Based on available data, taxes on immovable property have been as buoyant as the income tax with the exception of taxes on immovable property against household income that is a little below unity. Further, taxes on immovable property have shown a high association with Gross Domestic Product. Therefore, taxes on immovable property are generally buoyant taxes.

Although high buoyancy is often promoted as an attribute there are arguments against it. For example, a non-buoyant tax requires the taxing authority to publicly announce a new rate in the dollar more frequently whereas a buoyant tax system (such as land tax in an expanding economy) can surreptitiously increase tax revenue. Therefore, from the point of view of accountability, a non-buoyant tax is a better tax.

This is shown by work done by Reece and Brown (1994) using affordability indexes derived from land taxes and commercial rents. The index shows a steady erosion of affordability over the period 1984 to 1993 - see Figure 15.5. It is submitted that this is caused by the land tax system being buoyant in the sense that the rate in the dollar is not publicly changed each year to derive budgeted income.

This situation can be compared to local rates where the process is most public and commonly the local council announces a lower rate in the dollar to achieve the budgeted amount. Table 15.2 shows that because of this, the variability of land taxes is much higher than that for municipal rates even though the same property value base is being used.

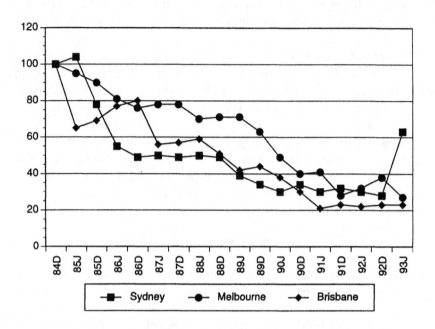

Figure 15.5   Affordability indices of land tax with BOMA rental data, CBD office space, 1984-1993

Source: Reece and Brown, 1994

5   An important part of the basket of taxes

Property taxes are an important part of the 'basket of taxes' in Australia and, at state and local levels, complement the federal government's large collection of revenue through income tax. It is also an important tax as it is the only tax that directly taxes wealth as measured by assets.

6   The tax should be easily understood

Land taxes are relatively simple compared to income taxes. The income tax has grown into an unwieldy and complex creature requiring experts for interpretation and preparation of the assessment. Simplicity of the tax system and assessment base is an important feature of a good tax system. On this criterion, the property tax system is a much better tax than the income tax system as currently applied in Australia.

The importance of simplicity is an important attribute of a good tax system and has been underestimated by a number of commentators on taxation. There is a hidden cost in income tax assessments as more and more income taxpayers employ professional tax consultants to prepare their tax returns. Because the income tax laws are so complex, the cost of determination is much higher than for a land tax system.

Table 15. 2
Coefficients of variation of taxation revenue (Real Terms)
1972/73-1991/92

State	Land Tax	State Payroll	Municipal Rates	Total
NSW	0.40	0.18	0.10	0.26
Victoria	0.32	0.20	0.16	0.22
Queensland	0.82	0.18	0.22	0.32
South Australia	0.22	0.16	0.17	0.21
Western Australia	0.38	0.23	0.24	0.34
Tasmania	0.30	0.17	0.11	0.30
All States	0.39	0.18	0.16	0.27

Source: Reece and Brown, 1994

7   Administration and compliance costs should be low

The extensive use of sales evidence in Australian valuation practice reinforced by a number of court decisions has made the 'proof component' of the property tax system extremely reliable. This has led to fair administration by valuation authorities and a better understanding of the system by taxpayers. However, there is room for improvement particularly in allowing 'class' and 'group' actions and greater public input in the valuation system at the early stages such as during the preparation of the fiscal cadastre and valuation roll.

The last two necessary attributes undermine the use of computers in mass valuations. A mass valuation must be endorsed by a 'human' if a dissatisfied taxpayer appeals against the assessment. The court will not accept a computer valuation per se.

Appeal process (NSW)

The appeal process in NSW is indicative of the appeal process throughout Australia. It has two components: objection to the Valuer General and an appeal to the courts.

There are a number of legal grounds for objection (s34 of the Act) but the most common one is that the assessment is too high. The Notice of Valuation is returned to the nearest Valuation Office with the objection section filled out and signed before the objection date expires (42 days). It is necessary to show on the objection or by way of a letter, the preferred value and reasons to support it.

If the Valuer General decides not to alter the valuation the objector can appeal to the Land and Environment Court. The Court requires a lodgment fee. Once in the court system the appellant can continue the appeal right up to the High Court. Always in the legal arena, the onus of proving the valuation wrong is on the appellant, and it may not be necessary for the Valuer General to prove the valuation correct.

References

Archer, R. (1973), *Site value taxation in CBD redevelopment, Sydney*, Urban Land Institute, Washington, Research Report 19.

Blackwell, F.M. (1994), *The future of local government valuations in Victoria*, Paper delivered at the 4th Australian Real Estate Educators Conference, Auckland, New Zealand.

Bronson Cowan, H. (1958), *Municipal improvements and finance*, International Research Commission on Real Estate Taxation, Harper & Bros., New York.

Else-Mitchell, R. (1985), Committee of inquiry on financing the Australian Capital Territory, *The Valuer*, January.

Miezkowski, P.M. (1969), Tax incidence theory, *Journal of Economic Literature*, Vol. 7.

Musgrave, R.A. and Musgrave, P. (1980), *Public finance in theory and practice*, 3rd. ed, McGraw-Hill, New York.

NSW, (1967), *Valuation and local government finance NSW*, Government Printer.

Reece, B.F. and Brown, D. (1994), *Measuring the affordability and volatility of Australian State land taxation to monitor government performance*, a paper delivered at the 4th Australasian Real Estate Educators Conference, Auckland, New Zealand.

Western Australia (1980), McCusker Report.

16 Property taxation in South Africa

Riël Franzsen

Introduction

Property tax, in a South African context, refers to a tax called a 'general rate' or an 'assessment rate'. It is levied by local government structures on the owners of immovable property on an annual basis. Property tax is presently levied in terms of provincial legislation in all nine South African provinces by primary local authorities within urban areas - be it small rural villages, towns, cities or metropolitan areas.

In recent years South Africa has seen dramatic and far-reaching political and constitutional changes at all three levels of government. These changes were especially far-reaching at local government level. Despite the changes that have already taken place at this level of government, local government will be in a state of transition until at least 1999. In order to understand the intricacies of and problems concerning the property tax, a brief historic background of local government structures and property taxation in South Africa is necessary.

Historical development of local government

Pre 27 April 1994: the Apartheid Era

The Union of South Africa was established under the South Africa Act of 1909 when four of the southern-most British colonies in Africa became a unitary state with four provinces in 1910. With the gradual enactment of apartheid legislation, such as the infamous Land Acts (of 1913 and 1936) and successive Group Areas Acts, South African society became stringently structured along racial lines. The result of South Africa's apartheid policies was that by the mid 1980s the

337

country was constitutionally divided into four (white) provinces (Cape of Good Hope, Natal, Orange Free State and Transvaal), four independent black homelands (Transkei, Bophuthatswana, Venda and Ciskei) and six self-governing (black) territories (Lebowa, Kwandebele, Gazankulu, Qwa-Qwa, Kangwane and KwaZulu).

Racial segregation was most evident at local government level. Within the four provinces, 'white' local authorities would typically boast a strong fiscal base of which property tax would be a major component. 'Black' local authorities (i.e. black townships in 'white' South Africa), on the other hand, would have a weak fiscal base with no property tax at all - relying primarily on central government grants. The lack of a property tax base within the black local authorities was a direct result of apartheid policies that prohibited black land ownership outside the homelands and also effectively ruled out commerce and industries from the black townships. In the independent homelands and self-governing territories, where the lifestyle was predominantly rural, local government was largely nonexistent. In many of these areas traditional authorities provided rudimentary services. In principle and practice levying a property tax in these areas made little if any sense. (In Bophuthatswana the Application of Municipal Laws Act (Act 24 of 1978) decreed that the Cape of Good Hope's local government ordinances would apply in that independent homeland.)

Post 27 April 1994: the new South Africa

When the Constitution of the Republic of South Africa Act (Act 200 of 1993) became the supreme law of the reconstituted South Africa on 27 April 1994, a new, nonracial democracy became a reality. The previous four provinces, independent homelands and self-governing territories were reunited and simultaneously divided into nine new provinces (KwaZulu-Natal, Free State, Western Cape, Northern Cape, Eastern Cape, Gauteng, Mpumalanga, Northern Province and North West).

Table 16.1 shows how the old provinces (Transvaal, Orange Free State, Natal and the Cape of Good Hope), independent homelands (Transkei, Bophuthatswana, Venda and Ciskei) and self-governing territories (KwaZulu, Kangwane, Qwa-Qwa, Kwandebele, Lebowa and Gazankulu) were reconstituted into the nine new provinces.

Although a nonracial, democratic order was established, the legacies of the apartheid era will remain a problem for South Africans - probably for generations to come. It is particularly evident within the sphere of local government. Outside the former homelands, the amalgamation of former white and black local authorities into local government structures based on historic and economic realities rather than race, is presently under way. This is an extremely cumbersome process - especially from an economic and fiscal point of view.

Table 16.1
Reorganization of provinces

Post 27 April 1994	Pre 27 April 1994
KwaZulu-Natal	Natal KwaZulu
Free State	Orange Free State A part of Bophuthatswana Qwa-Qwa
Western Cape	Part of the Cape of Good Hope
Eastern Cape	Part of the Cape of Good Hope Transkei Ciskei
Northern Cape	Part of the Cape of Good Hope
North West	Part of the Cape of Good Hope Part of the Transvaal Parts of Bophuthatswana
Gauteng	Part of the Transvaal
Mpumalanga	Part of the Transvaal Part of Bophuthatswana Part of Lebowa Kangwane Kwandebele
Northern Province	Part of the Transvaal Venda Part of Lebowa Gazankulu

The transformation of local government is taking place in terms of the Local Government Transition Act (Act 209 of 1993) which was enacted on 2 February 1994. This is indeed confirmed by the 1993-Constitution (section 245) and the 1996 Constitution (Schedule 6).

Table 16.2 sets out the various (transitional) local government structures in terms of the Local Government Transition Act.

In a metropolitan area the two-tier structure operates as follows: each transitional metropolitan council consists of, at the primary level, a number of

Table 16.2
Transitional local government structures

Metropolitan areas	Non-metropolitan areas
Transitional Metropolitan Councils	District Councils
Primary level	**Primary level**
Transitional Metropolitan Substructures (TMSS's)	Transitional Local Councils (TLC's)
	Transitional Representative Councils
	Transitional Rural Councils
	Local Area Committees, Health Committees, Local Councils

transitional metropolitan substructures. Non-metropolitan areas consist of district councils. Within a district council, primary local government structures exist in the form of transitional local councils (cities, towns and/or villages), transitional representative councils (commercial farms and smallholdings), transitional rural councils (small villages and smallholdings) and/or local area committees, health committees or local councils (small villages and smallholdings). Some of the smaller councils or committees provide only the most rudimentary services and have a limited capacity to raise taxes (e.g. property tax) and other service charges. Within many district councils there are still so-called 'remaining areas' for which no primary local structures exist at present. Within such areas the district councils are in the interim responsible for the provision of services and infrastructure. In many rural areas, especially in the former homelands, primary local government structures have not yet been set up in a satisfactory manner and revenue sources for these structures are limited. To the extent that these areas become more developed their tax bases will also develop.

Tables 16.3 and 16.4 summarize the revenue sources in metropolitan and non-metropolitan areas respectively.

Historical development of the property tax in South Africa

Although various property-related taxes were levied in early-colonial times (as early as 1677), property tax in its present guise was introduced to the Colony of the Cape of Good Hope by the Cape Municipal Ordinance in 1836.

Table 16.3
Revenue sources for metropolitan local government

Transitional Metropolitan Councils	- Taxes:
	  • Turnover tax
	  • Payroll tax
	- Levies or tariffs from substructures in respect of service or function rendered within their jurisdictions
	- Intergovernmental grants
	- An equitable contribution from substructures' gross or property rates income

Transitional Metropolitan substructures	- Taxes:
	  • Profits on trading services (implicit excise taxes on e.g. sale of electricity and water)
	  • Rates (property tax)
	  • Minor taxes (e.g. dog tax, bicycle tax)
	- User charges
	- Intergovernmental grants

As local government was primarily a provincial government function in the apartheid era, each of the former four provinces levied property tax in terms of its own ordinances. These ordinances made provision for property taxes to be levied only within the boundaries of municipal (urban) areas. All colonial land taxes (on primarily rural land) in the various provinces were abolished by national legislation by 1936. The only recent form of property tax on land outside primary local authority boundaries (levied only in the former Cape of Good Hope) was phased out by the end of 1989 as a result of the Abolition of Development Bodies Act (Act 75 of 1986).

Within former white local authorities, property tax was a very important tax. It has been in operation for many years and was generally well accepted. Generous rebates were granted to residential ratepayers, shifting much of the tax burden to commercial and industrial properties. Many local government councils could also afford to set low property tax rates. Substantial profits (an implicit excise tax) on certain trading services (e.g. delivery of electricity and

Table 16.4
Revenue sources for non-metropolitan local government

District Councils	- Taxes:
	  • Turnover tax
	  • Payroll tax
	- Levies or tariffs from primary structures in respect of service rendered or functions performed on their behalf within their jurisdictions
	- Intergovernmental grants

Transitional Local Councils	- Taxes:
	  • Profits on trading services (implicit excise taxes on e.g. sale of electricity and water)
	  • Rates (property tax)
	  • Minor taxes (e.g. dog tax, bicycle tax)
	- User charges
	- Intergovernmental grants

Transitional Rural Councils Transitional Representative Councils Local Area Committees, Local Boards, Health Committees	- Taxes: • Rates (property tax) - Service charges (e.g. sewage disposal) - Intergovernmental grants

water) allowed councils to 'cross-subsidize' the general rates account. Rates were set annually, after the revenue from all other sources were considered - in essence making up the shortfall.

With the demise of racially-segregated local authorities in terms of the Local Government Transition Act, the difficult process of amalgamating tax bases within the new, transitional local structures began. In terms of the 1993 Constitution, the property tax bases of former white local authorities had to be extended to former black local authorities in order to comply with a constitutional requirement of a 'uniform structure' for all taxes, tariffs and duties levied throughout the jurisdiction of any local government council. The process of extending the property tax base to the former black local authority areas (i.e. black townships) in the newly-amalgamated transitional councils have been completed in many areas. Within some jurisdictions, however, phasing-in the property tax in the black township areas is still to be completed.

As the extension of the property tax base is not yet complete throughout South Africa, data on the present size of the tax base and the total revenue to be raised from this source nationally is not available. It is clear, however, that property tax will remain a major source of own revenue for nonracial local councils.

Despite the many difficulties encountered in the interim (e.g. assessing all the new properties within the townships, addressing the culture of nonpayment which was rife during the apartheid era, especially since 1986), property tax remains a major source of revenue for the new, amalgamated local government councils.

In terms of section 229 of the 1993 Constitution (the so-called Interim Constitution) all laws which were in force immediately before 27 April 1994 in any area which forms part of the national territory, would continue to be in force in such area, subject to any repeal or amendment of such laws by a competent authority. This resulted in existing local government and property tax legislation of the former provinces and homelands (where applicable) remaining in force. Since April 1994 only minor amendments have been enacted by the new provincial legislatures.

In order to ascertain which provincial legislation applies in respect of a specific local government council, one needs to establish within which former province, independent homeland or self-governing territory that council was situated before 27 April 1994. This is especially problematic in Mpumalanga, Eastern Cape, Northern Province and North West.

Table 16.5 lists the most important statutes presently applicable to the charging, assessment and collection of property tax in the various provinces in South Africa.

For the remainder of this chapter it is accepted that property taxes are levied by and the revenue therefrom collected exclusively for the benefit of urban local government structures formally constituted at primary level (ranging from large metropolitan substructures to small local area committees). No property tax or land tax is currently levied at any level of government on rural land - i.e. land outside the boundaries of primary municipalities. The possibility has been mooted to extend the property tax to rural areas outside the boundaries of existing urban primary local government structures, although the introduction of a rural land tax at some stage in the future is more likely.

The remainder of this chapter will be devoted to the present status and future prospects of the property tax. The emphasis will be placed on the property tax as charged, assessed and collected in Gauteng province (in terms of the Local Authorities Rating Ordinance 11 of 1977 (Transvaal)). Although the smallest of the nine provinces (approximately 2 per cent of the total surface area), Gauteng is the most densely populated. Significant amendments to the former Cape of Good Hope and Orange Free State property tax legislation in 1993/94, had the

Table 16.5
Provincial property tax legislation

PROVINCE	STATUTES
Gauteng	Local Government Ordinance 17 of 1939 (Transvaal) sections 48 and 50 Local Authorities Rating Ordinance 11 of 1977 (Transvaal)
Mpumalanga	Local Government Ordinance 17 of 1939 (Transvaal) sections 48 and 50 Local Authorities Rating Ordinance 11 of 1977 (Transvaal)
Northern Province	Local Government Ordinance 17 of 1939 (Transvaal) sections 48 and 50 Local Authorities Rating Ordinance 11 of 1977 (Transvaal)
North West (Transvaal part)	Local Government Ordinance 17 of 1939 (Transvaal) sections 48 and 50 Local Authorities Rating Ordinance 11 of 1977 (Transvaal)
North West (Cape part)	Municipal Ordinance 20 of 1974 (Cape) sections 78-96 Property Valuation Ordinance, 1993 (Cape)
North West (Bophuthatswana part)	Municipal Ordinance 20 of 1974 (Cape) sections 78-96 Valuation Ordinance 26 of 1944 (Cape)
KwaZulu-Natal	Local Authorities Ordinance 25 of 1974 (Natal) sections 148-175
Free State	Local Government Ordinance 8 of 1962 (OFS) sections 113-119
Western Cape	Municipal Ordinance 20 of 1974 (Cape) sections 78-96 Property Valuation Ordinance, 1993 (Cape)
Northern Cape	Municipal Ordinance 20 of 1974 (Cape) sections 78-96 Property Valuation Ordinance, 1993 (Cape)
Eastern Cape	Municipal Ordinance 20 of 1974 (Cape) sections 78-96 Property Valuation Ordinance, 1993 (Cape)

result that the property tax systems in the Western Cape, Eastern Cape, Northern Cape, North West (Cape) and the Free State are very similar to the system operative in Gauteng (and Mpumalanga, Northern Province and North West (Transvaal)). Where there are material differences, it will be noted explicitly. The only province not in step with the uniformity drive and which retained its quite different property tax system, is KwaZulu-Natal.

Rateable property

Generally all land, be it zoned for residential, commercial, industrial or agricultural purposes, as well as any right in land and any improvements pertaining to land are rateable. It includes land owned by the local government council as well as vacant land. Two reasons for taxing vacant land are prevalent: the availability of public services and infrastructure also benefit (the owner of) vacant land and a tax on such land should stimulate the development thereof.

In the Local Authorities Rating Ordinance 11 of 1977 (Transvaal), which applies in Gauteng, Mpumalanga, Northern Province and part of North West the following relevant definitions are given (section 1):

'Land' means:

> any land registered under separate title and includes dominium therein, whether in full or diminished form, and any improvements in, or under such land.

'Improvements' in relation to land or any right in land means:

> any building, whether movable or immovable, or any other immovable structure in, on or under such land or pertaining to such right excluding-

> (a)   a structure constructed solely for the purposes of rendering the land concerned suitable for the erection of any immovable structure thereon; and

> (b)   any underground building, whether movable or immovable, or any other immovable underground structure on land which is the subject matter of any mining authorization or mining right as defined in the Minerals Act, 1991 (Act No. 50 of 1991).

The tax base

The applicable legislation in each province prescribes a particular basis for valuation which must be followed. In all nine provinces capital value is used for purposes of property rating.

Local government councils generally have the option to choose between at least two of the following three tax bases:

1   site rating, i.e. rating the unimproved value of the land only;

2   flat rating, i.e. rating the improved value of the land; and

3   composite (differential) rating, i.e. rating both land and improvements, but at different rate levels.

In terms of section 9(1) of the Local Authorities Rating Ordinance 11 of 1977 (Transvaal), which applies in Gauteng, Mpumalanga, Northern Province and part of North West the 'improved value of land' or the 'improved value of a right in land' is defined as:

> the amount which such land or right in land would have realized if sold on the date of valuation in the open market by a willing seller to a willing buyer.

The 'site value of land' or the 'site value of a right in land' is arrived at in a like manner to that referred to with reference to improved value, 'but on the assumption that the improvements, if any, had not been made'.

The value of improvements 'shall be arrived at by subtracting the site value of land or the site value of a right in land from the improved value thereof'.

In Gauteng, Mpumalanga and the Northern Province the majority of local government councils make use of site rating. In the Western Cape, Eastern Cape and Northern Cape as well as in the Free State many councils use flat rating, whilst in KwaZulu-Natal composite rating is favoured.

Ratepayer

The person responsible for rates is the 'owner' of the rateable property. 'Owner' would normally be defined to include the following:

1   the person in whose name the land concerned is registered;

2   the holder or lessee of a right in land; and

3   in the case of land which is the property of the local government council concerned, the lessee of such land.

Where the owner is insolvent or deceased, or has been placed under curatorship in terms of an order of court, or is a close corporation or company being wound up, the ratepayer will be the person in whom the administration of such rateable property is vested as executor, administrator, trustee, curator or liquidator.

Assessment

Methods of assessment

The value of land in all the provinces is assessed in terms of the comparable sales method, i.e. the estimated amount that the land would fetch if sold on the date of the valuation by a willing seller to a willing buyer in the open market.

Various methods for assessing improvements are used. In all the provinces except KwaZulu-Natal and the Bophuthatswana parts of North West, Mpumalanga and the Free State the value of improvements is arrived at by subtracting the site value from the improved land value. In KwaZulu-Natal (where composite rating is predominant) buildings (improvements) are valued at replacement cost (cost of erection at the date of valuation) less depreciation. In the former Bophuthatswana parts of North West, Mpumalanga and the Free State, improvements are also valued at replacement cost less depreciation (in terms of the Valuation Ordinance, 26 of 1944 (Cape) still applicable in these areas). The Property Valuation Ordinance, 1993 (Cape) (applicable in Western Cape, Eastern Cape, Northern Cape and North West (Cape)) states that if no open market value exists for an improved property, improvements could be valued at replacement cost (less depreciation) or in any other suitable manner.

In determining the value of rateable property in Gauteng, the valuer shall:

1   include any value due to the existence of a licence or privilege relating to the land or right in land concerned;

2   include the value of improvements that exist which are prohibited by law, conditions of title or any town-planning scheme;

3   exclude the value accruing to land or a right in land due to the presence of minerals in, on or under the land concerned;

4   not take into account any lease which is not a registered lease of a period less than 10 years or for the natural life of the lessee or another person mentioned in such lease.

Responsibility for valuations

In all the provinces a valuer employed by any local government council must be registered in terms of the Valuers' Act (Act 23 of 1982). The South African Council for Valuers, a statutory body established in terms of the Valuers' Act, supervises the conduct of all valuers or associated valuers in South Africa.

In Gauteng, Mpumalanga, Northern Province and part of North West (Transvaal) assessments are undertaken by valuers appointed by the local government councils. Larger councils (e.g. city councils) normally employ valuers within a specific department to undertake municipal valuations. Councillors or any officer of the local council (other than one employed in the valuation department) may not serve as valuers. Some councils appoint private firms to frame their valuation rolls. This diversity is well illustrated by the practice in the former primary authorities that were transformed into the four metropolitan substructures in the new Greater Johannesburg Transitional Metropolitan Council:

1   Johannesburg, Randburg and Sandton had their own valuation departments;

2   Roodepoort and Ennerdale made use of private valuers;

3   Lenasia South-East made use of the valuation department of the now dissolved Local Government Affairs Council;

4   Soweto, Dobsonville, Diepmeadows and Alexandra, the four black townships, had no valuations done before because no rates were levied by the former black local authorities.

In the Western Cape, Northern Cape, Eastern Cape and part of North West (Cape) the local council appoint a valuer. At the request of a particular local council, however, the Premier of the province may appoint a provincial service employee as valuer at the cost of the local council concerned.

In KwaZulu-Natal a valuer shall, as far as possible, be appointed from the staff of the local council's own valuation or estate department, if any. In the Free State the services of a valuer is terminated if he/she becomes a councillor or a full-time employee of the council which appointed him/her.

Valuation roll

The result of a valuation or revaluation is reflected in a comprehensive document, the valuation roll. As it is a certain and definite record of all rateable properties within its jurisdiction, a local government council relies on the valuation roll for the imposition of rates and framing its annual budget. Any addition, amendment or correction of the valuation roll can only affect future rights and obligations.

In all nine provinces the valuation roll must show at least the following:

1   the name of the owner;

2   a description of the property valued;

3   the size of the property;

4   the value of the land; and

5   the value of improvements (except in KwaZulu-Natal - if site rating applies).

In most of the provinces the improved value must also be shown. In KwaZulu-Natal the valuation roll must also show all non-rateable properties. In order to prepare the valuation roll, valuers are authorized to enter and inspect properties and to request information pertaining to properties from owners and/or occupiers.

The procedure for framing a valuation roll, is briefly as follows:

1   After all rateable properties have been valued, the valuer prepares a provisional roll which is sent, depending on the province concerned, to the council or town clerk.

2   A notice is published in the Provincial Gazette (except in KwaZulu-Natal) and also in the press (in all provinces), informing the public that a provisional roll has been prepared and is open for inspection free of charge.

3   Those who wish to submit written objections within a period stipulated in the notice, are invited to do so.

4   After an adjudicating body (e.g. valuation board or valuation court) has heard all objections and taken its decision, its chairperson signs and thereby certifies the roll.

5   The valuation roll becomes final and binding, in most provinces after a notice in the *Provincial Gazette* (e.g. Gauteng, Mpumalanga, Northern Province), all objections have been heard (KwaZulu-Natal), or on a date determined by the council (Free State).

Revaluation periods

In Gauteng, Mpumalanga, Northern Province, North West (Transvaal and Cape parts), Western Cape, Eastern Cape and Northern Cape general revaluations must be undertaken at least once in a four year period. The Premier of the province may extend the period for a further financial year. In the Free State and KwaZulu-Natal the period is five years.

In the former Cape of Good Hope province, before the Valuation Ordinance 26 of 1944 (Cape) was repealed by the Property Valuation Ordinance, 1993 (Cape), the period between valuations was 10 years. The untenability of such a lengthy period between valuations was strikingly borne out by the major problems experienced by the Cape Town City Council in the early 1990s. The rapid increase in especially residential property values within the 10 year period between reassessments in Cape Town resulted in a dramatic shift in the incidence of the property tax from commercial and industrial properties to residential properties. This consequently led to a property tax revolt by many residential ratepayers in 1993 which resulted in the council reinstating the previous 1979 valuation roll.

In the former Bophuthatswana parts of North West, the Free State and Mpumalanga the Valuation Ordinance 26 of 1944 (Cape) is still applicable - in terms of which a 10 year period between valuations applies.

In order to address errors, or at the request of the owner, or when new properties are added to the valuation roll (e.g. new towns established; properties are subdivided), interim valuations may be performed.

Objection and appeal procedures

Objection and appeal procedures exist in each of the nine provinces. After the provisional roll has been completed, it is open to the public to inspect. Property owners may then object against valuations within a statutory prescribed period. In some of the provinces (e.g. Gauteng, Free State) the council may also object against valuations.

In all the provinces provision is made for the appointment of quasi-judicial bodies to determine valuation rolls and/or to deal with objections and appeals against valuations. In all provinces (except the Free State and KwaZulu-Natal) valuation boards are constituted by the Premier of the province to consider and decide objections. The chairperson of a valuation board must be a retired magistrate, an advocate or attorney or any other person judged to be suitable for appointment as chairperson. The board must consist of not less than two or more than four members who must have sufficient knowledge and experience of the valuation of immovable property. A member of the local council concerned may not be appointed to such a board.

In the Free State a valuation court is appointed by the council to adjudicate objections. The chairperson must be a magistrate, retired magistrate or a legal practitioner with at least five years' practical experience. In KwaZulu-Natal the council determines the valuation roll but a right of appeal lies to a board of between three and five people, appointed by the council. None of the members may be employees or officials of the council. The chairperson must be a retired judge, a retired magistrate, or a person who has practised as an advocate, attorney or public accountant for at least seven years.

In all the provinces (except the Free State and KwaZulu-Natal) a valuation appeal board may be constituted to hear appeals against the decision of the valuation board. A valuation appeal board may be constituted for more than one local council. The chairperson shall be a retired judge of the Supreme Court or a person who has practised as an advocate for at least 10 years or a person in possession of legal qualifications and experience considered by the province's Premier to be sufficient. The valuation appeal board consists of the chairperson and two further members - with sufficient knowledge and experience of the valuation of immovable property. The valuation appeal board re-hears the matter which is the subject of the appeal and shall give written reasons for its decision.

Apart from appeal procedures a property owner may also use the common-law review procedure - where applicable (i.e. where the procedural steps could be faulted). In the Free State the Local Government Ordinance stipulates that the High Court may review a decision of an appeal board if a review action notice is lodged within 21 days of receipt of the board's decision.

Tax rates

Only flat (uniform) rates are used. Tax rates (normally expressed as x cent in the Rand) vary widely among the various councils, even within the different provinces. Although a maximum rate is still prescribed in some of the provinces (e.g. Free State, Western Cape), in others it has recently been abolished (e.g. Gauteng). The annual variation of property tax rates within councils could be ascribed to the fact that the revenue from rates is normally calculated to make up the shortfall from a council's other sources of revenue.

Table 16.6 sets out the flat (uniform) tax rates and applicable rebates for residential properties in some of the metropolitan substructures (MSSs) and transitional local councils (TLCs) in Gauteng for the 1996/97 financial year. All these councils use site rating.

Although these rates may seem very high, the following has to be kept in mind that these local councils all make use of site rating (i.e. the tax base excludes improvements); a generous rebate assists residential ratepayers (shifting much of the burden to commercial and industrial property owners); commercial and industrial property owners are allowed to deduct their property tax expenses for purposes of calculating their taxable income in terms of the Income Tax Act 58 of 1962 (shifting some of the burden to the general body of income taxpayers).

Table 16.6
1996/97 tax rates in some of Gauteng MSSs and TLCs

Transitional Council	Tax rate (cent/R)	Residential Rebate (%)
Pretoria City Council (MSS)	5.724	40%
Centurion (MSS)	8.25	30%
Northern Pretoria MSS	4.2	40%
Johannesburg (All 4 MSSs)	6.45	60%
Krugersdorp TLC	7.2842	27.75%
Heidelberg Town Council (TLC)	11.00	15%
Midrand MSS	6.86	40%
Springs City Council (TLC)	8.22	40%
Boksburg TLC	4.75	30%
Kemptonpark/Tembisa MSS	5.20982	40%

Exemptions, tax relief and rebates

In all nine provinces legislation provides for exemptions and other specific tax relief measures. As exemptions erode the tax base, efforts were made to limit these to the absolute minimum. For example, religious institutions are only exempt from rates to the extent that property is used exclusively for these purposes, (e.g., should a house belonging to a church be let commercially, that property will be rateable). It is noteworthy that not even state-owned properties are exempt. In terms of the Rating of State Property Act (Act 79 of 1984) state-owned properties lost their property tax-exempt status. In other words the national and provincial governments are liable for property rates, although a rebate generally applies.

Tax relief is generally granted through grants-in-aid, rebates differential tax rates or even a remission (in whole or in part) of tax payable.

During 1994 almost all exemptions were repealed and replaced by a system whereby classes of properties that formerly enjoyed a tax exempt status became rateable, but could, by majority decision of the relevant local government council, be granted a so-called grant-in-aid. Grants-in-aid may not exceed the amount of rates which may be levied in respect of the rateable property concerned.

Rebates are generally granted to specific categories (classes) of properties. The most widely utilized rebate is the rebate granted to residential properties (effectively shifting much of the burden to commercial and industrial properties).

Residential property rebates in the order of 40 per cent (see Table 16.6) are not uncommon. Additional rebates may be granted to ratepayers who are disabled, pensioners and/or have annual or monthly incomes below a set minimum. It is noteworthy that, in order to stimulate the development of residential areas, many councils do not allow a rebate on vacant land zoned for residential purposes.

Differential rates are normally only available for land held for very specific land uses, such as agricultural land holdings or land held under a mining authorization or mining right on which an approved township is situated, if such land is not used for business purposes.

Collection

The property tax is an annual tax. However, for the sake of convenience, it is normally collected in monthly instalments. This holds advantages for both ratepayers and councils as it negates the hardship which may be encountered with a once-off payment (e.g. cash flow problems) and ensures a relatively constant flow of revenue into the councils' coffers throughout the financial year. Joint owners of rateable property are jointly and severally liable for the amount due for rates. Local government councils may charge and collect interest on arrear rates.

A pending objection or appeal does not entitle a ratepayer to defer payment of rates. Should the amount due for rates be increased or decreased as a result of an objection or appeal, the difference shall be payable by or to the ratepayer. (However, the amount constituting the increase or decrease shall be deferred pending the outcome of an appeal.)

In all provinces the transfer of ownership of a rateable property in the office of the Registrar of Deeds is prohibited unless a 'clearance certificate' - stating that all rates with respect to that property is paid up - has been issued by the relevant local council.

Should rates be in arrears for a period exceeding three years, the property could be seized and sold by the local council at a public auction.

Other taxes on land and buildings

National taxes

The acquisition of immovable property is taxed by central government. Either value-added tax (VAT), levied in terms of the Value-Added Tax Act (Act 89 of 1991), or transfer duty, levied in terms of the Transfer Duty Act (Act 40 of

1949) is payable. VAT is charged at a standard rate of 14 per cent by registered vendors making taxable supplies of 'fixed property'. Fixed property is defined to include land and buildings, sectional title units, shares in a share block company and any time-sharing interest. Transactions attracting VAT are exempt from transfer duty (section 9(15) of the Transfer Duty Act). The letting of residential properties is exempt from VAT.

Where VAT is not payable, transfer duty is payable by the person who acquires 'property'. Natural persons pay transfer duty on a progressive scale, namely 1 per cent (on the first R60,000 of value), 5 per cent (on the value between R60,000 and R250,000) and 8 per cent (on the value exceeding R250,000). Persons other than natural persons (e.g. companies and trusts) pay transfer duty at a uniform rate of 10 per cent. Transfer duty is not payable when property is acquired by inheritance (section 9(1)(e) of the Transfer Duty Act).

Donations tax, levied in terms of sections 54 to 64 of the Income Tax Act (Act 58 of 1962), or estate duty, levied in terms of the Estate Duty Act (Act 45 of 1955), may be applicable where immovable property is alienated/acquired in terms of a donation or an inheritance.

Local taxes

Apart from general rates (i.e. property tax), the various provincial statutes in terms of which property tax is levied also provide for the following (minor) taxes which may be raised on the value of rateable property, i.e. the property tax base (in some cases as a percentage of the general rate):

1   an extraordinary rate (Western Cape, Eastern Cape, Northern Cape, North West (Cape));

2   a health rate (Western Cape, Eastern Cape, Northern Cape, North West (Cape));

3   a water rate (KwaZulu-Natal);

4   a sewerage rate (KwaZulu-Natal);

2   a sanitary rate (Gauteng, Northern Province, Mpumalanga, North West (Transvaal) and Free State);

6   a special rate (Gauteng, Northern Province, Mpumalanga, North West (Transvaal and Cape), Western Cape, Eastern Cape and Northern Cape) - which is really a kind of betterment levy.

In some of the very small villages or smallholding areas within the jurisdiction of district councils, the district council (on an agency basis) may administer or in some cases the primary councils themselves may impose local area rates (e.g. Western Cape), a local rate (Free State) or a land rate (e.g. Gauteng). These rates are indeed a form of property tax, however calculated with reference to property size rather than value.

Conclusion

Transitional local government structures in South Africa are presently facing various policy issues and practical problems which have a material impact on the property tax base. Some of these problems are legacies from the apartheid era. For purposes of this chapter the following brief remarks should suffice.

1   Although local government is constitutionally a provincial function, national framework legislation should at least aim to bring about uniformity concerning the charging, assessment and collection of rates where it is not yet the case. Structural uniformity does not undermine local autonomy.

2   Keeping property tax rates at politically acceptable or at least tolerable levels, despite increasing revenue needs to extend infrastructure and services in disadvantaged areas, will require extreme caution and responsible budgeting by local councils. The extent to which property tax could contribute towards cross-subsidization within the boundaries of a local council, even within metropolitan areas, is limited. Regard must be had to the ability of ratepayers to pay their taxes.

3   The legitimacy of the property tax system must not be compromised. Sound assessment and collection procedures must be applied throughout the area of jurisdiction of a local council. The culture of non-payment for municipal services (used as a political tool during the apartheid struggle) in the black township areas to which many 'new' ratepayers still subscribe, must be addressed speedily. The concerns and perceptions of the 'old' (predominantly white) ratepayers in this regard should not be ignored. Local councils can ill afford successful attacks under the 'equal protection' clause (section 9 of the 1996-Constitution).

4   The interaction between land and tax policies need to be kept in mind. For example, pending land restitution claims, illegal land invasion and squatting in urban areas, as well as government's response (or the lack thereof) to land invasions, may impact negatively on land values, and therefore, the property tax base.

5   Many newly-amalgamated local councils are struggling to extend the property tax base to former black township areas. Thousands of new properties are rateable and need to be added to the valuation roll and many new ratepayers need to be billed - stretching their limited administrative capabilities. In some provinces *in loco* valuations and revaluations of all rateable properties are required.

Despite these policy issues and practical problems alluded to above, the future of property tax in South Africa, as an important own source of local government revenue, seems secure. Many of the problems transitional councils are presently facing are associated with the process of transition and should only be of a temporary nature.

Property tax is a guaranteed source of revenue for local government (section 229 of the 1996 Constitution) and provinces are prohibited from introducing such a tax at provincial level (section 228 of the 1996 Constitution). Despite the fact that it is a local tax in terms of which local councils retain all the revenue, national and especially provincial framework legislation will - to a large extent - continue to regulate how it is charged, assessed and collected.

References

Statutes

The Constitution of the Republic of South Africa Act 200 of 1993 (the 1993 Constitution).
The Constitution of the Republic of South Africa Act 108 of 1996 (the 1996 Constitution).
Local Authorities Ordinance 25 of 1974 (Natal).
The Local Authorities Rating Ordinance 11 of 1977 (Transvaal).
Local Government Ordinance 8 of 1962 (Orange Free State).
Local Government Ordinance 17 of 1939 (Transvaal).
The Local Government Transition Act 209 of 1993.
Municipal Ordinance 20 of 1974 (Cape).
Property Valuation Ordinance, 1993 (Cape).
Valuation Ordinance 26 of 1944 (Cape).

Books and Articles

Cloete, J.J.N. (1993), *South African Local Government and Administration* (2nd ed.), J.L. van Schaick, Pretoria.

Craythorne, D.L. (1993), *Municipal Administration: A Handbook* (3rd ed.), Juta & Co, Kenwyn, Cape Town.

Franzsen, R.C.D. (1996), 'Property Tax: Alive and Well and Levied in South Africa?', *SA Mercantile Law Journal*, Vol. 8, No. 3, pp. 348-365.

Joubert, W.A. (ed.) (1986), *The Law of South Africa* (Vol. 23: Rating), Butterworths, Durban.

Kotzé, H.J.N. (1980), *Munisipale Eiendomsbelastings*, P.J. de Villiers, Bloemfontein.

Nel, G.A. (1995), 'Valuation for Rating Purposes: A New Challenge', *The SA Treasurer*, Vol. 67, No. 38, pp. 24-26.

Reddy, P.S. (ed.) (1996), *Readings in Local Government Management and Development: A South African Perspective*, Juta & Co, Kenwyn, Cape Town.

17 Real property taxation in Kenya

Washington Olima

Introduction

This chapter is concerned with the taxation of real property in Kenya. Real property taxation (land rate) is one of the local taxes in Kenya, and is commonly referred to as rating. It is a local charge levied by the local authorities on landed property owned by an individual, group of individuals, company, or public authority with or without improvements for the purposes of collecting revenue (Olima and Syagga, 1996). The property tax is a potentially attractive means of financing local government services in developing countries. Rating on the other hand is the process of valuing real property for the purpose of assessing the land rate with the objective of raising revenue for a particular local authority. Rating as a process of landed property taxation has an ancient origin. It goes back to the feudal era in England when the Anglo-Saxon kings delegated to the villages and towns the duties of watching over their local affairs (Emeny and Wilks, 1984).

Evolution of rating in Kenya

Rating is a relatively recent tax in Kenya, introduced in the first quarter of this century during the British Colonial rule when local governments were created and given responsibilities to provide and maintain public services, such as, primary education and public health (Syagga, 1994). During the formative stage of colonial rule, once an ordinance or law had worked in one colony, it was plausible to adopt it in another colony without environmental adjustments (Aritho, 1980). Evident from literature is the fact that Kenya's rating system was based on rating laws from other countries. According to Hicks (1961), the campaign for taxing land spread from South Africa into Rhodesia and later to the three British East African territories of Kenya, Uganda, and Tanganyika (now Tanzania). The Kenyan rating law was based on the 1916 Rating Ordinance of the Transvaal province of South Africa (Syagga, 1994). The first type of rating to be applied in Kenya was the annual rental value of occupied premises in Mombasa, the second largest city in Kenya. The rate was charged under the 1900 Street Cleaning and Lighting Regulations and in a sense was primarily for refuse removal. Annual value rating is based on the annual income earned from the property. The sum to be taxed is arrived at after a certain percentage has been deducted from the gross income as outgoings. In 1923, annual value rating was considered inappropriate as only few properties had been developed. The Mombasa District Committee therefore recommended unimproved site value (i.e. rating based on value of undeveloped site), although the annual value rating continued to be levied until 1928 (Syagga, 1994).

In Nairobi, the capital city of Kenya, rating based on annual rental value was introduced in 1901 but was also found inadequate (as in Mombasa), and in 1920 unimproved site value (USV) rating was to be introduced 'in accordance with the systems in force in Australia, New Zealand and West Canada' since 'the English Rating is unsuitable for introduction into the new growing townships' (NCC, 1950). The Nairobi (rating of unimproved site value) Ordinance was enacted in 1921; the valuation roll was prepared, confirmed and remained in force for five years. It was not until 1956, however, that a single rating law was enacted for the whole country.

Rating as a source of revenue

Local authorities in Kenya are empowered by the Local Government Act Cap 265 of the laws of Kenya to raise their revenue from a variety of sources including indirect taxes, income from property, sales of goods and services, and loans. The authorities therefore levy rates in order to raise revenue to meet expenses in the provision of public services in their areas of jurisdiction. These public services which are paid for out of rates include street lighting, maintenance of the streets, refuse collection and disposal, sewerage disposal, fire fighting services, and provision of public amenities such as parks, community halls and the like. The level of public services to be provided through local authorities revenue depend on the size of the authority. Since its inception, property tax has been an important component of the local authorities tax base. This source of revenue has greatly contributed in financing the operations of local authorities in Kenya. As a source of local authority revenue, in 1956 rates from site values contributed about 61 per cent of the annual revenue in Mombasa, 41 per cent in Nairobi, and 39 per cent in Nakuru (Hicks, 1961). At present, however, yields of urban property taxes in Kenya are relatively low (Kenya Economic Survey, 1995). For instance, the contribution of rating to the total income in Nairobi City Council (NCC) has continued to decline. Table 17.1 shows the estimated contribution of rates to the income of Nairobi City Council *viz a viz* other major sources of revenue from 1991/92 to 1995/96 financial years.

Table 17.1

Rates as a percentage of the Nairobi City Council total income, in million units of Kenya currency (pounds): 1991/92-1995/96

Current Revenue	1991/92	1992/93	1993/94	1994/95	1995/96
Property Rates	29.20	30.00	40.00	40.00	45.90
Indirect Taxes (Licences)	2.25	4.82	9.60	24.00	29.00
Service Charge	8.40	15.00	15.00	15.00	17.40
Other Sources (Sale of Goods, Transfer of Properties, Water Charges)	22.41	60.41	9.19	6.42	7.81
Total	62.26	110.23	73.79	85.42	100.11
Rates as % of Total Income	46.90	27.20	54.20	46.80	45.80

Source: *Printed Financial Estimates and Budgets of the Nairobi City Council 1991/92 - 1995/96 Financial years.*

The analysis reveals that rating is the largest source of revenue for the Nairobi City Council in comparison to other sources of revenue. It should however be noted that in 1992/93 financial year, the estimated contribution of rates to the total income was as low as 27.2 per cent. This was attributed to the increase in income from estimated service charge from Kenya Pounds 8,354,500 in 1991/92 to Kenya Pounds 15 million in 1992/93 and also due to an increase in estimated income from 'other sources' (sale and transfer of goods, water and sewerage charges) from Kenya Pounds 22,406,000 in 1991/92 to Kenya Pounds 60,414,000 in 1992/93 financial years (Kich, 1996). According to City Hall sources, the reason for the low level of rates collected could, perhaps have been due to the confusion and uncertainty that occurred during 1992 when general elections were held. This ultimately affected the collection efficiency. As a source of revenue for municipal councils in Kenya (including Nairobi city) the contribution has been declining from 32.7 per cent in 1990/91 financial year to 24.8 per cent in 1994/95 financial year as shown in Table 17.2. In comparison to other urban centres, the city of Nairobi receives a higher contribution in terms of percentage from rates than the rest. This can be attributed to the physical size as well the level of development of Nairobi which is the capital city of Kenya.

Table 17.2
Municipal councils: economic analysis of recurrent revenue, in million units of Kenya currency (pounds): 1990/91-1994/95

Current Revenue	1991/92	1992/93	1993/94	1994/95	1995/96
Property Rates	32.83	43.55	51.57	58.96	60.24
Indirect Taxes (Licences & Cesses)	2.17	9.82	10.76	18.00	7.47
Property Rents	9.16	9.84	12.92	16.01	23.08
Current Transfers	0.19	0.01	0.01	0.03	0.03
Sale of Goods, and Services	56.16	73.08	89.89	139.16	152.23
Total	100.51	136.30	165.15	232.16	243.05
Rates as % of Total Income	32.70	32.00	31.20	25.40	24.80

Source: Kenya Economic Survey, 1995

Similarly, Table 17.3 shows that the contribution of rates to current revenue being collected by the town, urban and county councils over the same period varied between 4.5 per cent and 8.5 per cent

Table 17.3
Town, urban and county councils: economic analysis of recurrent revenue, in million units of Kenya currency (pounds) for the period 1990/91-1994/95

Current Revenue	1991/92	1992/93	1993/94	1994/95	1995/96
Property Rates	1.78	1.68	1.68	3.95	5.12
Indirect Taxes (Licences & Cesses)	6.13	6.19	7.76	10.72	15.20
Property Rents	0.23	0.34	1.78	0.63	2.22
Current Transfers	0.10	0.05	0.15	0.11	0.18
Sale of Goods, and Services	26.73	27.57	25.97	38.90	37.41
Total	34.97	35.83	37.34	54.31	60.13
Rates as % of Total Income	5.1	4.70	4.50	7.30	8.50

Source: Kenya Economic Survey, 1995

361

Basis of valuation

Laws relating to administration and forms of rating in Kenya are contained in two Acts of Parliament which were passed to enable local authorities throughout the country to rate land and buildings. The two pieces of legislation that form the basis of rating in Kenya are Valuation for Rating Act 1956 (Chapter 266) and the Rating Act 1963 (Chapter 267) of the laws of Kenya. Valuation for Rating Act 1956, provides for valuation of land for the purposes of levying rates. Essentially this Act deals with methods of valuation for purposes of rating and the procedures to be followed in the preparation of valuation rolls. On the other hand, the Rating Act 1963 is supplementary to Valuation for Rating Act, and simply empowers urban and rural authorities to be rating authorities under the Valuation for Rating Act. Local authorities derive the power to levy rates from section 3 of the Rating Act which states that 'Rates shall be levied by the rating authority to meet all liabilities falling to be discharged out of the general rates fund'.

Section 4 (1) of the Rating Act stipulates the forms of rating that the rating authority may adopt for the purposes of levying rates. They include:

1   an area rate in urban areas in accordance with section 5;

2   an agricultural rental value rate in rural areas;

3   a site value rate or a site value rate in combination with an improvement rate in accordance with section 6.

The form of rating and the area to which it is to be applied is subject to approval by the Minister of Local Government. For instance, section 5 provides that the rating authority may, with the approval of the Minister, adopt one or more of the following methods of area rating:

1   a flat rate upon the area of land;

2   a graduated rate upon the area of land;

3   a differential flat rate or a differential graduated rate upon the area of land according to the use to which the land is put, or capable of being put, or for which it is reserved;

4   an industrial rate upon the area of land used for other than agricultural or residential purposes;

5   a residential rate upon the area of land used for residential purposes;

6   such other method of rating upon the area of land or buildings or other immovable property as the rating authority may resolve.

The rating authority may adopt different methods of area rating for different parts of a rating authority area and may from time to time vary the method or methods adopted. The percentage rate charged using the various forms of rating as mentioned above should not exceed 4 per cent of the unimproved value of land unless consented to by the Minister for Local Government. The two systems, unimproved site value rating and improvement rating can apply to urban areas whereas area rating was to be applied to agricultural land. For urban authorities, however, they primarily use the unimproved site value rating although the law does allow improvement rating as well. This was largely because at the time of the enactment large parcels of land within urban boundaries were undeveloped. The other persuasive argument was that site value rating is more amenable to mass appraisal and hence easier to carry out when compared to other methods.

The basis of assessment of land for purposes of levying rates are provided in section 8 of the Valuation for Rating Act as the value of unimproved land. Sections 8 (1) and 8 (2) state that:

> ... the value of land/the value of unimproved land shall for the purposes of a valuation roll or supplementary valuation roll, be the sum which the freehold in possession free from encumbrances therein might be expected to realize at the time of valuation if offered for sale to a willing buyer by a willing seller in an arms length kind of transaction.

> ... 'improvement' - in relation to land, means all work done or material used on, in or under such land by the expenditure of money or labour in so far as the effect of such work done or material used is to increase the value of the land, but does not include machinery, whether fixed to the soil or not.

Sections 25 (1) and 26 (1) of the Valuation for Rating Act 1956 stipulate that both public land and community land should be for the purposes of assessing the contribution in lieu of rates payable be valued in accordance with the principles laid down in this act. In arriving at the value of land, the valuer is empowered to use any suitable method of valuation since the act does not specify methods of valuation to be used. This has however given rise to several conflicting interpretations in valuation methods which in turn introduces uncertainty and complexity in valuations. For instance, a petrol service station with ancillary buildings is for purposes of rating based on throughput method of valuation, while adjacent plots are based on the general area zoning and plot sizes. It is a contention that although the valuation courts in Kenya have upheld the use of the throughput method, it is essentially a measure of annual value and not capital value. The Kenyan experience is that these uncertainties in valuations introduce unnecessary disputes and costly litigation between the rateable owners and rating authorities.

Responsibility for making the assessments

It is the responsibility of the respective local authority to coordinate the valuation of their properties for rating purposes, preparation of valuation rolls, and collection of the approved rates. The assessment departments are locally based within the jurisdiction of a given local authority. The practice however, varies from one local authority to another. For instance, in the case of Nairobi City Council and other big municipalities including Mombasa, Kisumu and Nakuru, the assessment departments are within the authorities. For example in Nairobi City Council the assessment of rateable properties is carried out by their employed valuers with the assistance of technicians in the Department of Valuation. In 1996, for instance, the number of staff involved in the assessment of rateable properties and preparation of valuation roll within Nairobi City Council is 23 of which 10 are valuers, 12 are technicians and 1 is a valuation assistant (Kich, 1996). On the other hand, the local authorities with no valuers in their direct employment have to rely on either the services of valuers employed by the central government or valuers employed by private valuation firms. For instance, Nyeri County Council initially relied on government valuers but have since stopped and currently hire private valuation firms (Githinji, 1990). Valuers in Kenya, however, whether or not working in public or private sectors are at least graduates in Land Economics from either the University of Nairobi or other recognized universities. In addition, they must be members of the Institution of Surveyors of Kenya and registered by the Valuers Registration Board.

Procedure for preparing the valuation roll

It is the obligation of the rating authority to ensure that a valuation roll is prepared at least once in every five years or such longer period as the Minister for Local Government may approve, in accordance with section 3 of the Valuation for Rating Act 1956. Before the beginning of the work, the rating authority is required to pass a number of resolutions and obtain the Minister's approval. The resolutions to be passed include the appointment of the valuer, adoption of the form of rating to be applied (whether improvement, site value or area rating) and declaration of an area within the council boundary to be rateable area. It is stipulated that only one form of rating can be adopted by a rating authority at any time.

364

The preparation of the valuation roll by valuers begins with the collection of all relevant development plans from the planning department. The sales figures available are marked on a map to give the valuer a picture of the land values in the town. Section 5 of the Valuation for Rating Act 1956 gives the valuers power to enter and inspect properties or call for any data that they may require to enable them to carry out thorough analysis so as to arrive at the appropriate site values. The valuation roll when completed will show all the rateable properties in terms of:

1   the description, situation and area of the land valued;

2   name and address of rateable owner;

3   the value of the land;

4   the value of the unimproved land;

5   the assessment for improvement rate.

Many local authorities still do not prepare the valuation rolls every five years as statutorily required. Apart from lack of adequate valuers, the absence of recent registered property sales has also led to the application of outdated valuation roll. In many cases the life of a valuation roll is 15 years or more. For instance, the last valuation for rating in Nairobi was carried out in 1980. Since 1980 the valuers have been preparing supplementary valuation rolls based on changes in ownership, user and possible cases of subdivision. The problem is not peculiar to the city of Nairobi only. The Municipal Council of Mombasa which is the second largest urban authority in Kenya sent out rate demands for 1995 based on values of all land appearing in the 1981 valuation rolls. Other towns which rely on government valuers for assessment of rates are in difficult situations.

Section (4) of the Valuation for Rating Act gives a local authority the power to amend the valuation roll and to cause supplementary valuation rolls to be prepared at least once in each of the years following the year of valuation. The reasons for such action may include the following situations:

1   any rateable property omitted from the valuation roll;

2   any new ratable property;

3   any rateable property which is subdivided or consolidated with other rateable property; or

4   any rateable property which, from any cause particular to such rateable property arising since the time of valuation, has materially increased or decreased in value.

A supplementary valuation roll shall include only those alterations and additions to the valuation roll which are permitted by subsection (1) or subsection (2) of section (4).

Before the adoption of the main or supplementary valuation roll, the valuer is expected to sign the roll and date its completion, and then transmit it to the town clerk in compliance with section 9 (1) of the Act. The town clerk shall then present the roll before a meeting of the local authority, after which it shall be available for public inspection at the local authority offices. A percentage rate to be applied to the value of unimproved land is determined by the resolution of the council and approved, by the Minister for Local Government if it exceeds 4 per cent. For instance, the highest rate of 13 per cent is levied by Mombasa Municipal Council, albeit on 1981 values. Nairobi City Council for 1996 levies a rate of 12 per cent on residential land and 13 per cent on commercial/industrial land, respectively, although again, on 1982 site values. Any person may during ordinary business hours inspect the draft main or supplementary roll and take copies or extracts from it.

The process of objection

Once the draft valuation roll or the draft supplementary valuation roll is completed, it is gazetted for public information to enable rateable owners not satisfied with the assessment to lodge their objections. The objections may arise either from inclusion of any rateable property in, or omission of any rateable property from the valuation roll, and value ascribed in any valuation roll to any rateable property. As in many countries, this is a critical part of the tax system where property owners should avail of the opportunity to be convinced that the assessment is fair and reasonable. The statutory period for lodging objections with the town clerk is 28 days from the date of publication of notice in the Kenya Gazette.

The town clerk shall, within 21 days after the date on which a notice of objection is lodged with him, send a copy to the rateable owner of the rateable property to which the objection relates, if such person is not the maker of the objection. If, on the expiration of the period of 28 days no objections have been received, or, if all objections duly received have been withdrawn before the day fixed for the first sitting of the valuation court, the town clerk shall endorse the draft valuation roll or draft supplementary valuation roll and sign a certificate to that effect. Section (12) of the Valuation for Rating Act, establishes a valuation court, consisting of a chairman who may be a magistrate having power to hold a subordinate court of the first class, or an advocate of not less than five years experience, and not less that two additional members appointed with the approval of the Minister for Local Government. The valuation court is appointed for the purposes of hearing objections and determining appropriate values.

The town clerk or any other person appointed by the local authority acts as clerk to the valuation court. At every sitting of a valuation court three members present constitute a quorum, and all the decisions are arrived at by a majority decision. After hearing all the objections, the valuation court confirms or amends the draft valuation roll or draft supplementary roll by way of reduction, increase, addition or omission. The chairman of the valuation court then endorses and signs a certificate confirming the completion of the exercise. The town clerk will then publish a notice that the draft valuation or draft supplementary valuation roll has been signed and certified. Section 18 (2) of the Valuation for Rating Act provides that a valuation roll duly signed by either the chairman of a valuation court or the town clerk shall remain in force until it is wholly superseded by a new valuation roll.

Any person who has appeared before a valuation court, and is aggrieved by the decision of the valuation court on the determination of objection, may appeal against the decision of the valuation court within one month from the date of the notice to:

1   the High Court, if such valuation court was appointed under section (12) of this Act;

2   a subordinate court held by a Senior Resident Magistrate or a Resident Magistrate, if such valuation court was appointed under section (13) of the Act.

The appeal to the High Court after the valuation court is final in the determination of rateable values.

Exemptions, reliefs and concessions

There are certain properties which are exempted from valuation for rating purposes. The nature of properties exempted are provided under section 27 (1) of the Valuation for Rating Act, and include:

1   places for public religious worship;

2   cemeteries, crematoria and burial or burning grounds;

3   hospitals or other institutions for the treatment of the sick;

4   educational institutions (including public schools within the meaning of the Education Act), and including the residence of students provided directly by educational institutions or forming part of, or being ancillary to, educational institutions;

5   charitable institutions and libraries;

6   outdoor sports; and

7   National Parks within the meaning of the National Parks of Kenya Act.

However, the listed properties are exempt from rating in as much as they are not used for profit making or for residential purposes other than for the residence of students. Section 22 (1) of the Rating Act points out that no area rate or agricultural rental value rate shall be imposed on any land which would be land in respect of which no valuation for the purposes of any rate may be made under the Valuation for Rating Act. The rating authority, however, can provide reliefs and concessions in the determination of rates payable by the prospective rateable owners. For instance, Nairobi City Council for 1996 levies a general rate of 13 per cent of the unimproved site value of land as appearing in the 1982 valuation roll. In accordance with section 22 (2) of the Rating Act, Nairobi City Council effected a reduction or remission of payment of the rates levied as follows:

1   rates equivalent to 1 per cent of the unimproved site value on land designated for residential purposes;

2   rates equivalent to 3 per cent of the unimproved site value on land designated for agricultural purposes.

In addition, section 16 (2) of the Rating Act empowers the rating authority with the approval of the Minister to allow a discount of not more than 5 per cent or such other discount on any rate paid on or before the day on which such rate becomes payable. Subsequently, the Nairobi City Council in 1996 resolved that the discounts ranging between 1 per cent and 5 per cent be applied on full payments of rates in 1996 as follows: full payments received by January - 5 per cent; February - 4 per cent; March - 3 per cent; April - 2 per cent; and May - 1 per cent. However, rate accounts with outstanding balances as at 31 December, 1995 do not qualify for the discount. If any rates remain unpaid after the 31 May 1996 interest at the rate of 2 per cent per month or part thereof to be paid to the Nairobi City Council on the amount unpaid. The concessions rarely benefit the ratepayers. Due to the bureaucratic procedures within the local authorities, the demand notices often reach the ratepayers late.

Collection procedures

The law is very explicit on the collection procedures. Section 15 (1) of the Rating Act, Chapter 267 provides that every rate levied by the rating authority shall become due on the first day of January in the financial year for which it is levied and shall become payable on such day in the same financial year as shall be fixed by the rating authority. The payment day and the amount of rate are to be made public by the rating authority by giving at least 30 days' notice.

Section 16 (1) of the same Act provides that when the rating authority has given notice under section 15 of the day on which any rate levied will become payable, it shall be the duty of every person liable for such rate to pay the amount of such rate at the offices of the rating authority or at any place. The Nairobi City Council and all other rating authorities in Kenya have accounts offices that deal with collection of all forms of rates.

Section 17 deals with procedures for enforcing rate payment by defaulters. When a rateable owner fails to pay rates due within the stipulated time period, plus any interest on any such unpaid rate, the rating authority may make a written demand notice on the rateable owner requiring him or her to make rate payment plus any interest that has accrued thereto within 14 days after service of the written demand notice. Failure to comply means the rating authority is empowered to take proceedings in a subordinate court of the first class to secure the payment of such rate and interest. A decree granted by a subordinate court in favour of the rating authority may be enforced by any rules made under the Civil Procedure Act, Chapter 22 of the laws of Kenya. In those situations where the sum due from the rateable owner is secured by a charge over the landed property by virtue of section 19, the decree-holder may apply to the High Court by originating summons to order the sale of such land to recover the amount of rate plus any interest due. The proceedings to recover unpaid rates may be commenced at any time within 12 years of the day upon which the rate became due and payable. In addition, section 18 of the Rating Act empowers the rating authority to recover unpaid rates from tenants or occupiers of the rateable property by issuing a notice requiring them to make all future payments of the rent directly to the rating authority until such a time that all the unpaid rates plus any accrued interest have been paid.

The actual collection of rates in the local authorities have experienced several problems. The methods adopted are themselves inefficient and ineffective. Frequently local authorities place advertisements in local newspapers appealing to ratepayers to remit their payments. This is an indication that local authorities are unable to collect all the rates due. The ineffective administration has resulted in a high rate of defaulting. For example, in the period between 1976 and 1979 the Kenya Railways Corporation owed the Nairobi City Council about Kshs 1.8

million in rates (Ogero, 1981). In 1990 a total of about Kshs 300 million in rates was owed to Nairobi City Council, representing about 40 per cent of rates due. As at 31 October 1991 private individuals owed the Nairobi City Council a sum of Kenya Pounds 35,563,485 in unpaid rates whereas government institutions owed the City Council a sum of Kenya Pounds 25,504,488 (Kich, 1996).

A recent study on Nairobi City Council by Kich (1996) revealed that there is a high rate of defaulting in rates payments by the ratepayers. Table 17.4 shows the estimated amount of rates due for collection and the actual amount collected for Nairobi City Council between 1991/92 and 1994/95 financial years.

Table 17.4
The amount of rates collected viz-à-viz the estimated amount due in million units of Kenya currency (pounds) 1991/92-1994/95

Financial Year	Estimated Amount of Rates Due	Actual Amount of Rates Collected	Amount of Rates Uncollected	Uncollected rates as % of Estimated Total
1991/92	29.20	13.14	16.06	55.00
1992/93	30.00	18.16	11.84	39.50
1993/94	40.00	12.82	27.18	70.00
1994/95	40.00	28.38	11.62	29.10

Source: Adopted from Kich, 1996:71

It is evident from Table 17.4 that although rating is regarded as the largest source of revenue for Nairobi City Council, in real terms the collection of rates has not provided the expected amount of revenue. There is a significant disparity between the amount billed as due for payment and the amount actually collected. Again, this situation is not peculiar to Nairobi alone. For instance, a recent notice in a daily newspaper showed that the Municipal Council of Mombasa is owed a total of about Kshs 20 million in rates (Daily Nation, March 14, 1995). Between 1982 and 1985, the municipality of Kisii recorded an average of 4 per cent defaulting rate in revenue to be collected from unimproved site value rating (Momanyi, 1986). Smaller local authorities with weaker administrative structures have proportionately larger arrears in rates revenue.

Despite of the legal framework, the lack of specific machinery to enforce rate collection has been identified as a problem in the administration of rating system in Kenya (Olima and Syagga, 1996). According to Olima and Syagga (1996), the problem may be attributed to lax collection methods as aggravated by the administrative bureaucracy in local government. In addition, there is poor response by the ratepayers and long legal process involved when dealing with defaulters (Kich, 1996). For instance, in the case of Nairobi City Council there have been about 2,000 cases filed in court since the middle of 1990 against defaulters, out of which only 500 cases had been determined by the end of 1991. The situation is further complicated because, unlike water or electricity where services are denied as soon as a consumer defaults, rate defaulting has no immediate remedies, except where the owner decides to transfer the property.

Critical analysis

Rating is viewed with mixed feelings, both from a policy objective and from its implementation. As a tax system, rating has both its advantages and disadvantages which have been the subject of debate. This section of the chapter will however, be devoted to the discussion of the merits and problems of the unimproved site value rating as practised in Kenya.

Advantages of unimproved site value rating

1   The unimproved site value rating system is certain in terms of revenue generation because all the parcels of land are rated whether or not they are developed. Rates are certain both to the taxpayer and the tax collector and hence can be planned for well in advance. This is because a rate is a predetermined form of taxation and is always fixed with the aim of raising a known sum of money for a given rating authority within a given time frame.

2   Rating is flexible in the sense that exemptions and reliefs can readily be granted by a rating authority to certain categories of property.

3   The unimproved site value rating system discourages land speculation because it increases the cost of holding such land. Anybody buying land for speculative purposes finds it a disadvantage to hold such land.

4   It may encourage land development by speeding up the development process for residential, commercial, and industrial purposes. This is because unimproved site value rating ignores income receivable from property, and hence reduces the tax burden on the developed property.

5   Rates are difficult to avoid or evade. This is because landed property is fixed in location and thus can neither be hidden from the rating authority nor be moved away from rate assessors.

6   Rates are relatively easy to collect. Should a rateable owner delay in paying or refuse to pay, the rating authority in question is empowered under section (17) of the Rating Act to distrain upon the personal goods and chattels of rateable owner to the value of the rates owed. The same section empowers the rating authority to occupy the landed property in question and take profits accruing until such a time when all the rates owed to them plus any interest thereto has been recovered.

Disadvantages of unimproved site value rating

1   Rating does not totally conform to the principles of ability to pay and benefits received. This is because rating, especially, the unimproved site value rating system is regressive in terms of the rateable owner's income from the rateable property. It may be considered unjust because it fails to tax the ability to pay by placing equal burdens on landowners who may have unequal income structures. Even where rating is based on the income received from landed property, it still falls short of meeting the characteristics of equity since income is not a perfect indicator of the ability of the rateable owner to pay. This is because however much income is received from a landed property, the expenditure pattern may reduce the rateable owner's ability to pay (Kich, 1996; Ndeleki, 1991).

2   The unimproved site value rating system provides for a minimal tax base because in areas where developments are substantial, for example, in Nairobi's Central Business District the unimproved site value rating system applied on its own cannot provide sufficient sizeable tax potentials, which is required to service the numerous facilities and amenities provided. In addition, it is difficult to assess, quantify and apportion benefits received by individual rateable owners and to charge them appropriately. This has largely contributed to the inequality in rating.

With better management of property administration it is possible that the contribution of this tax to local authorities can be enhanced. The current practice is for local authorities to strike different rates of tax on the assessed site values. Assuming the rates are reasonable, since they must be approved by the Minister for Local Government in the case of each local authority, if the site values had been current, the taxes levied could be equally substantial. What is then required to be improved is the methods of collection. This, however, assumes that Kenya does not wish to change the rating system from the unimproved site value. Other countries in the region, notably Tanzania, Uganda and Zambia have adopted different systems of rating.

Conclusions

The current low yield from urban property taxes reflect failures in the administration of the tax. In Kenya, a large proportion of properties are missing from the valuation rolls, properties on the valuation rolls are inaccurately valued and collection efficiency is extremely poor. These administrative failures can be adequately addressed through procedural reforms including adaptation of a different systems of rating, valuation accuracy, and improved collection efficiency. Adopting different system of rating could involve using unimproved site value rating for undeveloped land and improvement rating for developed sites.

It has to be noted that all land reforms are fundamentally political in nature, as are all tax reforms (Bird, 1974). Inefficient administration and low rates, however, are political liabilities inherent in the property tax. Inappropriate policy and poor tax administration affect the attainment of a sustained increase in yields (Olima and Syagga, 1996). Any reform therefore needs to be targeted at the two aspects identified. A suitable rating tax must be evaluated using the following general criteria, i.e. yield, equity, economic efficiency and ability to implement. An equitable way of collecting socially created land values must be devised. While rate increases offer the prospect of quick revenue increases, taken individually they exaggerate the inequities in the incidence of the tax. An increase in the effective tax rate places the burden of the increase on those few individuals whose properties are on the tax rolls, accurately valued, and from whom taxes are actually collected.

There is therefore an urgent need for improvements in administration to institute efficient machinery for appropriate land inventory, including geographical information systems (GIS). This should be followed with a more appropriate rating system and efficient collection system.

In Kenya, the Valuation for Rating Act 1956 provides for improvement as well as unimproved site value rating. It is recommended here that both systems should be applied. Developed properties should be valued to include land and improvements, and an appropriate tax rate levied. Undeveloped land should be valued appropriately and a tax rate levied accordingly. Thus instead of separating the two systems, Kenya's rating laws should simply provide for rating assessments based on 'market value of the rateable property'.

References

Aritho-Gitonga, G.M. (1980), Rating: Local Property Taxation in Kenya, *Tropical Environment Journal*, University of Nigeria.

Bird, R.M. (1974), *Taxing Agricultural Land in Developing Countries*, Harvard University Press, Cambridge.

Emeny, R. and Wilks, H.M. (1984), *Principles and Practice of Rating Valuation*, Estates Gazette Limited, London.

Githinji, L.G.W. (1990), *The Rating System in Kenya and the Need to Improve on it*, Department of Land Development, University of Nairobi.

Government of Kenya, (1956), Valuation for Rating Act Chapter 266, Laws of Kenya.

Government of Kenya, (1964), The Rating Act Chapter 267, Laws of Kenya.

Government of Kenya, (1995), Kenya Economic Survey, Government Printer, Nairobi.

Hicks, V.K. (1961), *Development from Below*, Oxford University Press, London.

Kich, J.A. (1996), *An Evaluation of Rating System in Kenya: A Case Study of Nairobi City Council*, Department of Land Development, University of Nairobi.

Momanyi, E.O. (1986), *A Study on the Administration of the Unimproved Site Value Rating in Kisii Municipality During the Period 1982-1985*, Department of Land Development, University of Nairobi.

Nairobi City Council, (1950), Nairobi Jubilee History 1900-1950, Nairobi, City Hall, Nairobi.

Ndeleki, D. (1991), *Rating in Zambia*, Diploma Project, Ardhi Institute, Dar-es-Salam.

Ogero, B.B. (1981), *Financial Problems of Urban Authorities: A case study of Nairobi City Council*, M.A. Thesis, University of Nairobi.

Olima, W.H.A. and Syagga, P.M. (1996), Rating System in Kenya: Evolution, Constraints and Potentials, *Journal of Property Tax Assessment & Administration*, Vol. 2, No. 1.

Syagga, P.M. (1994), *Real Estate Valuation Handbook: With Special Reference to Kenya*, Nairobi University Press.

Woolery, A. (1989), *Property Tax Principles and Practice*, Land Reform Training Institute, Taoyuan, Taiwan.

18 Land value taxation in Estonia

Tambet Tiits and Aivar Tomson

Introduction

Estonia, one of the Baltic States, gained its independence from the Soviet Union in 1991 and very quickly carried out monetary and fiscal reforms and established rights to private ownership. The country has a land area of approximately 45,200 square kilometres and a population in the region of 1.46 million. Tallinn is the capital city and has a resident population of 440,000.

In 1993, Estonia introduced a new land tax based on the market value of land only. The law on Land Tax was passed by Parliament in May 1993 and came into force on 1 July 1993. Buildings, improvements and growing plants are not included within the tax base. The Land Tax was introduced as part of the government's general tax reform carried out during the period 1991-1993.

The main features of Estonian land tax are as follows:

1   the tax is paid by the owners of privately held land and also by the users and occupiers of land which is still in public ownership;

2   tax rates are set annually by the local councils and vary between 0.5-2.0 per cent;

3   the tax represents a national tax however, 100 per cent of the collected revenue is allocated to local municipality budgets;

4   tax can be paid in equal quarterly instalments;

5   only limited groups of properties are entitled to exemption; and

6   the National Land Board is responsible for assessment, with the National Tax Board being responsible for collection.

Origins and evolution

In August 1991 Estonia regained independence and in June 1992 a monetary reform programme was initiated which introduced a national currency, the kroon. Prior to the reform, Estonia used the rouble and had an inflation rate in 1991 of 1,087 per cent. It was considered unrealistic to attempt the introduction of a property tax based on the market value real estate at that particular time. As a consequence of the monetary reform, inflation has now been brought under control and whilst still high, has declined each year, in 1996 it was 14.8 per cent (the Estonian kroon in 1996 had a fixed rate to German Mark: 8 EEK = 1 DEM).

Land tax was initially introduced as a shared tax between local government and central government and for the years 1993 and 1994 the tax rate was 0.5 per cent to both local and central governments. In 1995 local government was given responsibility to determine annual rates within the prescribed limits of 0.3-0.7 per cent whilst the rate of tax for central government remained at 0.5 per cent. Agricultural land has been treated preferentially, however, after 1997 will be fully taxable. In 1996 the decision was taken to allocate 100 per cent of tax revenues to local government (tax rates 0.8-1.2 per cent in 1996 and 0.5-2.0 per cent thereafter). There are separate rules for agricultural land; up to the end of 2000 the tax rate is 0.3-1.0 per cent (0.3-0.7 per cent in 1996 -1997). From 1 January 2000 the tax paid by owners will be allocated to local budgets, and tax paid by users will be allocated to central government.

Legislation and regulations for the assessment of land were adopted in 1992 with the assessments being undertaken in 1993. The idea of implementing a land only tax is also related to the institutions of land reform. As land was politically excluded from civil transactions during the Soviet period this had the detrimental effect of land being used uneconomically.

Revenue

Tax revenues from land tax are continuing to increase; 118 million EEK in 1994, 264 million EEK in 1997. Land tax represents 1-2 per cent of all tax revenue and 0.5 per cent of Estonia's gross domestic product. This increase in tax revenue is the result of higher tax rates, the revaluation in 1996 and collection efficiency.

Income tax is by far the most significant source of local government funds, providing the major part of municipal tax revenues. Sales tax has been introduced in only a few municipalities with a tax rate of 0.5-1.0 per cent. Whilst the sales tax represents an additional source of funds, the level of revenue raised is quite modest. Currently, there is quite high Value Added Tax (VAT) levied at 18 per cent on the majority of goods and services. VAT is a central government tax and represents an important revenue source.

Purpose of the tax

There is no special purpose designated for the land tax; it forms a part of the total tax revenue for local government and there are no special rules or criteria on how it is to be spent. The land tax, as previously mentioned is allocated totally to the local (municipal) budget.

Importance of the tax

From the perspective of a revenue raising tool the land tax is of relatively minor importance. However, it should be appreciated that the share of land tax revenue to local budgets varies from municipality to municipality. Generally, in urban areas it constitutes approximately 1-5 per cent of a municipality's revenue source, whereas, in the more rural areas and especially in the peripheral regions it can represent in the region of 20-30 per cent.

The land tax is essentially an instrument of local land policy and is recognized as being important for the establishment of strong local democracy (it is the responsibility of municipalities to decide the specific tax rate thereby effectively increasing local accountability).

Basis of assessment

The tax represents a tax on land only. The basis of the tax is the open market capital value of the land. In 1996 there were approximately 253,450 taxable units.

Responsibility for making the assessment

The National Land Board has primary responsibility for the valuation and assessment of all parcels of land. The National Land Board has local cadastral offices located in each county and its central headquarters has a responsibility to undertake valuations, prepare the methodology, support education and training, coordinate valuations and generally ensure a country-wide uniform approach. The central administration also has the authority to revise valuations periodically. The National Land Board therefore has the following duties:

1   preparation of assessment schedules;

2   provide advice and determine assessment methodology;

3   approves assessors; and

4   coordinate and control the process of assessment.

County cadastral offices carry out the actual valuations and for the valuation of each municipality, a county valuer works in association with municipal authorities. It is only in the large cities that sales information is systematically recorded. Thus, in most municipalities the gathering of sales information and other data required for the assessment is a matter for some concern, given that it is the municipalities' function to calculate the taxable value for every land unit.

Qualification of the assessors

Assessors within Estonia are primarily graduate surveyors, though there are some exceptions and a programme of special education has recently been provided. Private assessors are used as consultants to valuers from county cadastral offices and in addition participate in the educational programs.

Frequency of valuations

The first general assessment was carried out in 1993 with the second one completed in 1996. The law however, does not stipulate the frequency of assessment and no decision has been reached on when the next revaluation should be undertaken. It has been suggested that a three year revaluation cycle would be optimal for Estonia. There are at present no provisions within the legislation stipulating the use of indexation of assessed values between general revaluations.

Notification of assessed value

Before the county cadastral office can approve the assessment results a valuation list, map and comments must be displayed in the municipal office for at least for 20 days. Taxpayers are informed in the local newspaper and in other mass media. After this period has elapsed the valuations are approved and taxpayers are notified of the assessed value together with the tax bill.

Appeal procedures

Municipal government is responsible for the organization relating to the public display of the assessments for a period of 20 days with the offices of the municipality. The valuation report, maps and assessments including the analysed information is also to be made available for inspection. In addition, the names of assessors and the times when taxpayers can meet with them must be given. Taxpayers are entitled to receive any further information and to appeal if they disagree with the valuation results. Appeals will only be accepted if the assessment did not follow the legislation, regulations and appropriate methodology or the assessment error exceeds 20 per cent.

Subsequently, taxpayers have the right to appeal only if they pay a bail of up to 500 EEK in advance. In this case the taxpayer can only appeal if it concerns his property. If the appeal is well founded the bail money is returned, whereas if the appeal is unjustified the money is used to cover the procedural costs. Appeals are made directly to municipalities and interestingly, there is no special valuation or land tax tribunal in Estonia.

Methods of assessment

Within Estonia it is acceptable to use all traditional valuation methods, including comparative, profits and residual techniques. The primary legal base for assessment is the law on Land Valuation (1994). There are in addition several government decrees regulating such matters as procedures and methodology of assessment.

Comparative method

The comparative method is the main method for the estimation of value in urban areas (the only exception being city centres, where the profits method and/or a combination of residual methods are used). In rural areas, where the estimated value levels are considerably lower, the impact of indirect market information is important. For example, if there are two similar regions in terms of population, land use, economy, etc., and there is limited or no sales information available for one of the regions, it might still be possible to consider those regions as comparable. In a way it represents a technique of market simulation and mass appraisal.

Profits method

The profits method is the basis normally applied to the valuation of forestry land, for the assessment of agricultural land and is also used in the central business districts of larger cities. The method as applied to the assessment of forestry land is complicated by virtue of the fact that it is difficult to measure the value of such land, whilst ignoring the growing timber. In Estonia the value of forestry land is in the region of 14-17 per cent of the total value. The profits method was the primary method used for valuation of agricultural land for the 1993 valuation. At that time there was no free market for agricultural land, however there was a free market for agricultural products. With hindsight, it would appear that the majority of agricultural land was overvalued due to two main reasons:

1   it was relatively straightforward to estimate the gross income, but considerably more complicated to determine the real level of costs and the relationship between the different factors of production (the percentage of land); and

2   it was difficult to determine the real capitalization factor in the unstable economic market conditions.

The profits method is not as widely used at present. The method as applied in urban areas is used in conjunction with the residual method, simply because there is a lack of open market evidence. The contractor's method is used as part of the residual method in urban areas. The possibility of the widespread use of this technique is severely limited due to the fact that land is assessed to market value as opposed to cost. The residual method has a wide application within the central business district of the larger cities. All methods can be applied and combined in order to estimate the value of 'vacant' land. However, there are some valuation problems within the city centre areas including the lack of vacant land and sales information.

The most useful approach, as one might expect, is the comparative method. There are no prescribed regulations as to which method should ideally be used in a given situation. The most common case for using different methods at the same time would be in the estimation of city centre land values. It is possible to use the profits method or the comparative method to estimate the value of property including land and buildings and then to apply the contractor's method to estimate the value of the buildings. The difference between the value of the land and buildings and the value of the buildings would represent the land value. It is also possible to use sale prices of similar properties in two different areas, which would give an indication of the differences in land values between those two areas.

380

Use of mass appraisal techniques

Given that in Estonia the only taxable property is land, this represents a realistic opportunity to apply mass appraisal techniques; usually land is more homogeneous and not as unique as the improvements on it. Therefore, it is possible to use for example, the average (not real) level of building rights (the Estonian under-developed planning system does afford the opportunity to apply the highest and best use principles across the whole country).

There are no precise rules concerning the generalization of valuation results. The application of value zones or regions with the same value level, are commonly used. It is more a question of professional practice, but it is generally evident, that in areas of low value, the zones are normally larger and therefore attempting to achieve relatively high valuation accuracy is not of primary importance. However, in areas of higher value the situation is the reverse due to the high sensitivity of the final results.

Exemptions

There are only a few tax-exempt properties as prescribed under the legislation they include the following:

1   properties on which economic activities are prohibited by law;

2   properties owned by foreign governments, including embassies;

3   cemeteries;

4   properties relating to religious worship (only churches, temples etc.); and

5   public land e.g. streets, squares, etc., by the decision of the municipality.

Municipal owned land is also entitled to tax exemptions.

Relief measures

It is difficult to give precise data on tax reliefs. There are a number of special relief measures targeted at areas with restricted economic activity, primarily forestry land and depending on the extent of restriction, the annual payment could be 25, 50 or 75 per cent of the usual tax level.

There are special reliefs aimed at those engaged in farming who were given an initial five year tax free period (from all taxes), as an incentive for starting their own business. Such exemptions are now coming to an end. In addition, there are other temporary concessions for agricultural land; the tax rate for agricultural land is 0.3-1.0 per cent of taxable value (until December, 2000).

There are special rules for old age pensioners and those with disabilities. The municipality has the authority to decide on the tax exemption, which could be up to a maximum of 200 EEK annually (until December, 2000). The basis for the decision is an application from the owner or user. However, there are a number of conditions to be considered:

1   land use rights established prior to 1 July 1993 (starting point of taxation);

2   area of the unit, i.e. 0.1 hectares in urban areas and 1.0 hectares in rural areas; and

3   no rental income derived from the taxable unit.

Collection procedures

Land tax is collected by the National Tax Board on the basis of the assessed values determined by the municipalities. The tax bill is mailed annually to all taxpayers by the local Tax Board. There are local Tax Boards in all 15 counties. The tax bill specifies the taxable value, the tax rates and the total tax due. The annual land tax is divided into four parts, with taxpayers being given the choice to pay either in one instalment or up to a maximum of four.

Taxpayers are entitled to appeal the assessment however, there is no justification for the taxpayer in withholding payment.

Liability for the tax

Owners are legally responsible for the payment of land tax. During the process of land reform, occupiers of state-owned land also have an obligation to pay the tax. The liability of land users is however seen as a temporary measure.

Computation of the tax

Tax records and the printing of tax bills is fully computerized. The main problem at present relates to the ineffective lines of communication between municipalities and the tax authorities. In most cases there is no on-line connection resulting in a rather laborious and complex situation for the tax administration.

Absence of cadastre

In this context the under-developed cadastral system is seen as a significant problem; approximately 25 per cent of the Estonian land area has been registered in the Cadastre and Title Book (currently there is no information regarding the total number of units). The cadastral system has been computerized. All other information concerning land use units and property parcels is held by municipalities, and given that there is no unified register for those units and no unified system of parcel identification, this results in a piecemeal and highly localized system of registration. Land information held by the municipalities is also computerized, but there are problems of system compatibility.

Enforcement procedures

Unpaid land tax is treated like any other tax debt, which affects the taxpayer personally and can result in the property being sold to ensure payment.

Critical analyses

The advantages of the present land tax are as follows:

1   convenience for the application of mass appraisal techniques;

2   ease of implementation;

3   the collection efficiency is high (96 per cent in 1997);

4   less of a harmful influence on the economy (if compared with other taxes such as taxes on buildings and other improvements);

5   suitability as a local tax which can be imposed by local governments with the potential to act as an instrument to effect land policy; and

6   encourages the more efficient and economic use of land.

The disadvantages of the land tax would be:

1   the total revenue potential remains at less than 2 per cent of the total tax revenue;

2   a major part of the revenue collected is in fact paid by the central

government, i.e. state-owned forestry land and state land without private occupiers represent approximately 33 per cent;

3   the collection efficiency could be improved;

4   the problem of estimating market value is affected by the limited availability of sales prices and other market information; and

5   a property tax based on the value of both land and buildings would be a more appropriate mechanism to reflect the concept of ability to pay than the present land tax.

Proposed changes

There are several important changes proposed by government, these are to include:

1   tax revenues are to be shared between local and central tiers of government; the tax paid by owners will be allocated to local government, and the tax paid by occupiers will be passed to central government (the starting point is to be January, 2000); and

2   ground rent will be paid by the occupiers of state land, which in effect will represent an amount equal to tax payment (starting point January, 1999).

References

Malme, J.H. and Youngman, J.M. (1997), *Property Tax Developments in Transition Economies*, paper presented at Fourth International Conference on Local Government Taxation, IRRV, Rome.

Tiits, T. (1996), *Property Market and Ownership Rights in Estonia*, paper presented at European Real Estate Society Conference, Belfast, Northern Ireland.

19 Unimproved land value taxation in Jamaica

Suzanne Lyons and William McCluskey

Introduction

The island of Jamaica is situated in the Caribbean Sea between 17⁰ 43' and 18⁰ 32' North latitude and 76⁰ 11' and 78⁰ 21' west longitude, approximately 161 kilometres west of Haiti and 149 kilometres south of Cuba. The island is divided into 3 counties - Cornwall, Middlesex and Surrey - and 14 parishes. The total area of the island is 4,411.21 square miles or about 2.8 million acres. From a tropical temperature of 80-86⁰ F at the sea coast to 40-50⁰ F on the tops of the highest mountains there is a dryness of atmosphere that renders the climate of the mountain particularly delightful and suitable to the most delicate constitution. The surface of the island is extremely mountainous and attains considerable altitude particularly in the eastern section where the central range which is known as the Blue Mountains attain an elevation of 7,402.4 feet above sea level at the Peak. From this range subordinate ridges and spurs run northerly and southerly with smaller ridges branching off in every direction with regularity. This results in a surface consisting of a series of ridges with intervening gullies. This terrain has been a source of consideration in the development of the property tax system of the island.

Everywhere in the western world the concept of taxation as a means of providing a budget for government is well known and is often an entity to avoid. In particular, property tax has had a long history. From the very birth of mankind there was a requirement to give to God in sacrifice 1/10th of the fruits, crops and animals produced each year from the land. An annual quit rent to retain ownership of land divested by the Crown to its loyal servants was required in Britain's history.

The maxims of taxation, as declared by Adam Smith in his book 'Wealth of Nations' of equity, certainty, convenience of payment and economy in collection has long governed the imposition and maintenance of property taxation. Jamaica has had a long, interesting and diverse history of property taxation. It was first introduced in the mid-17th century under British administration and has reflected the social, economic and political climate of the country at the various stages of its history and development. The first tax imposed on land and real property was the Quit Rent. This tax was a nominal payment of one penny per acre. Under the provisions of the 1901 Valuation Law property tax was based on capital values. In 1956 there was an attempt to have this base extended to include both capital and land values. However, after three years of valuation field operations and the lack of completion of the first parish this was abandoned. Capital value as the basis for property tax was proving too costly and time consuming an operation. The property tax base became the land value and all rates and charges on land would thereafter be levied on this basis.

By 1974 the entire island was revalued under the provision of the Land Valuation Act (1956) on the basis of the 'unimproved value' of the land. This saw another stage in the simplification of the Jamaican property tax system. This system has continued with a few changes to today. This chapter will examine the property tax system. It will document the historical background of the property tax system and travel through the diverse changes to the system as it exists presently, looking at the areas of the property tax rate, the base property tax, the collection of this tax. It will attempt to chronicle the rationale to the changes made and the present thinking with regards to the future of property tax, its uses and application.

Historical background

Prior to 1903 four taxes were imposed on land under the provision of the 1901 valuation law:

1   Quit Rent of one penny/acre per annum. This was a nominal tax acreage to maintain ownership of the land by the Crown. Non-payment led to forfeiture of the land but there was the provision for redemption on the payment of a lump sum usually related to the value of the land;

2   House Tax which was a tax on the value of each dwelling unit;

3   Crop Tax levied on cultivated land; and

4   Graduated Holding Tax on all parcels of land.

Quit Rent and the Graduated Holding Tax was paid to central government while the House Tax and the Crop Tax was paid to the Parochial Board (Parish Council/

Local Authority) in the relevant parishes. Tax collected on real property and land was shared 5/12 to central government and 7/12 to the local authorities. Property tax at this time amounted to as much as 64 per cent of direct tax in the island.

A review by a Select Committee of the Legislative Council on Real Property Tax in 1903 and the subsequent report of this committee resulted in the then existing land taxation law being repealed except for the Quit Rent Law. In 1903 a new Property Tax Law was enacted. This law imposed a single property tax rate of 8 pence in the £10 of capital value of all real property. Section 13 of the 1903 law was considered to allow within this rate the inclusion of the 1 penny per acre Quit Rent. Additionally, all taxes now went to central revenue, a situation which has continued until a recent change in legislation which will see property tax revenue now being directed in total to local authorities.

Funding of the local authorities was provided for under the new law by way of a general rate and a service rate. Service rates paid for the provision of services such as street lighting, fire protection, sanitation and the provision of sewers in Kingston and St Andrew. The general rate was a compensation to the local authorities used for infrastructure and economic development of the respective parishes. The law set the limits at which these rates could be charged.

The 1901 Valuation Law had asked for the establishment and maintenance of a valuation roll which remained the fiscal cadastre for the 1903 Law. This roll was created from 'ingivings'. The law required that all persons in possession of real property in the island needed to furnish the Collector of Taxes of the parish in which the property was located with a true and correct ingiving stating: the description of the property, the location, acreage, particulars of tenure, area under cultivation, type of cultivation, description of all buildings, dwelling houses, warehouses, factories, etc., on the property; stating the value against each item and finally giving a gross value for the entire property. There were three values required and asked of landowners under this law:

1   the annual gross present value of the real property;

2   the actual or presumable net annual rental of the real property; and

3   the presumable net value of the ground forming the site of the real property in its natural and unimproved condition in its then present surroundings.

Revisions to the valuation roll of 1901 subsequently took place in 1911, 1929 and 1937. These revisions constituted copying the previous roll with the exception of those properties which had changed hands or had been subdivided. In the late 1930s the property tax system came under attack as the questions of its obvious inequalities and weaknesses were exposed. The basis of the roll being landowners 'ingivings' meant that values varied with individuals' consciences or their ability to negotiate with the Collector of Taxes who approved the values stated. This was further compounded by the fact that the values on the rolls were long outdated and the valuation staff did not have the expertise to properly determine the value of large agricultural holdings and commercial properties being entered on the roll. It was these issues and anomalies which resulted in a Resolution being moved in the Legislative Council which called for the establishment of a Commission to investigate and make recommendations in dealing with the problems of land valuation in the island.

Reports on the property tax system in Jamaica

A Royal Commission with the Hon. Simon Bloomberg as Chairman was established in 1943 to examine and report on the problems as well as to make recommendations as to changes to be made and the means of effecting these recommended changes. The Bloomberg Committee's report was a comprehensive one and 'can surely be said to be the bow from which the arrow of a modern system of land valuation was sent forward'. The Commission further recommended the adoption of the unimproved value system (site value or value of the bare land) as the valuation basis for the assessment of property tax. This recommendation was further endorsed by four other teams of international experts mainly to discourage the holding of land in an idle or under-utilized state. Other recommendations included:

- A permanent central valuation department be set up to deal with all valuations for the purpose of taxation, and the collection of land taxes to remain the function of the Collector General's Department (now the Inland Revenue Department).

- Government obtain the services of a Valuation Commissioner who has had experience of the practical administration and application of the 'unimproved value' system.

- Revaluation should be quinquennial.

- Quit Rents be abolished.

- Property tax be abolished and that revenue from all rates and taxes on land should go to the local authorities.

- Ingivings be required from owners which should show the unimproved value and capital value of the real property.

These recommendations were accepted in principle but the government had great difficulty in obtaining the services of a qualified Valuation Commissioner and did not succeed in the endeavour until 1950 with the appointment of Mr Harris, a senior valuer from the Inland Revenue Department in London. He faced a situation of a lack of suitably qualified staff, the unavailability of maps to form the basis of his task of revaluation and the lethargy of the government to whom revaluation was just another name for higher taxation. He returned home before the end of the year.

Mr C.H. Hipgrave, MBE, Chartered Surveyor arrived in 1951 to deal with the problem of revaluation and to put the necessary framework in place for this exercise. His work on the revaluation was frustrated by much the same problems that confronted his predessor. He returned home after completion of his three year tour in the island. However, his report gave invaluable appreciation of the difficulties involved in undertaking a revaluation exercise. His suggestions formed the basis of the report by the Mission of the International Bank for Reconstruction and Development in 1952 following the hurricane which ravished the island in 1951. He recommended that large scale planimetric maps be produced from aerial photographs for the city of Kingston and the other principal towns of the island as well as cadastral maps, delineating boundaries for title purposes.

In 1954, Professor J.R. and Mrs Hicks were invited to visit Jamaica to investigate and report on the revenue system of the island and to make recommendations to enable the government to more efficiently use its revenue sources. The issue of property taxes was addressed under the section of the report dealing with local finance. They recommended the retention of capital value as the basis for property tax and further suggested that the progressive rates applied to property tax should be reconsidered in favour of a flat rate.

In 1955, the government sought, through the United Nations, the services of a qualified advisor practised in the 'unimproved value system'. This yielded the services of J.F.N. Murray, BA, FRICS of Australia whose report of his findings and recommendations presented in June 1956, 'served as the blueprint for the building of the structure of the system of land taxation based on unimproved values'. The report also contained the draft of a valuation law which was substantially the Bill which was presented to Parliament. This comprehensive report dealt with the incidence of land tax and rates together with the probable appreciation of the valuation problems in Jamaica and the method of solving them, the valuation of improvements, sales analyses and the collation of sales evidence, the work of revaluation, staff requirements and the legislation in detail necessary to give legal effect to the recommendations.

Mr J.M. Copes, also an Australian, was appointed the first Commissioner of Valuation with the responsibility of implementing Mr Murray's recommendations. He piloted, organized and established the Land Valuation Division, under the Ministry of Agriculture, and directed the programme of revaluation from 1956 to 1961. All this rested on the Land Valuation Law, 73 of 1956.

The legal framework of property valuation and taxation

The Land Valuation Act 1956

The Land Valuation Act currently in existence today has only been slightly amended from its original drafting and passage into law. This is primarily because from its initial inception the existing legislation has served the purpose of those who gave birth to its existence. From a study of the proceedings of the House of Representatives as recorded in the Jamaica Hansard (Session 1956-57 No. 3) the following were the two major objectives in introducing the Land Valuation Bill. Firstly, it was considered desirable to introduce a tax base which:

1   did not tax a person in the efforts he put into the land;

2   provided a means of taxing values created by the community at large; and

3   discouraged the withholding of land from use.

Secondly, the system of valuation was unsatisfactory for the following reasons:

1   it placed too great a reliance on the voluntary declaration of value by the owner as a basis for preparing the valuation rolls;

2   it was pointed out that by and large individual inspections of land were not made under the system;

3   it was not difficult to see that the system would lead to competitive under-assessment on the part of landowners with the inevitable result that the rolls would lack uniformity - a feature which is generally regarded as a *sine qua non* for a rational system of land taxation; and

4   anomalies and inequalities were widespread due not only to the basic defects of the system but also to the failure to undertake a general revaluation.

The Land Valuation Act of 1956 made provision for the administration of the Act by the Commissioner of Valuation, under the direction of the Minister. The

Commissioner is required to make a valuation of the unimproved and improved value of every parcel of land in each district. The parishes formed district boundaries for the purpose of the Act. The Commissioner is required to set the date at which each parcel of land is to be valued but the Minister brings a valuation roll into effect. The Act makes provision for a process of appeal for persons not agreeing with the valuation of the Commissioner initially to a Valuation Board, now to the Revenue Court, with further appeal to the Court of Appeal.

Although the Act provided for the determination of two bases of value, i.e., unimproved and improved value, the rolls were published with only one set, the unimproved values. The following extract from Ministry Paper No. 4 (1959) - Revaluation of Land Proposed System of Taxation explains why only one base was determined:

> The house will recall that is was intended that property tax and parish rates, the two principal forms of land tax, should be based on unimproved values as defined in the Land Valuation Law, that is to say, on the actual market value of the land exclusive of the values of any buildings, cultivations, or other improvements on/or attached to the land. On the other hand, it was intended that charges for particular services, such as water and fire, should be based on improved values.
>
> It was found, however, that to attempt to compile two sets of valuation rolls would take so long that it might well have taken more than ten years to complete the valuations of the whole island. Moreover, it was thought that there was no important reason for insisting that special rates should be charged on improved values. The availability of special services in a given area in itself enhances the unimproved value of the land and the removal of all elements that discourage improvement of the land was though to be better secured by having a simple uninformed system applicable to every type of rate. It was therefore decided that only one valuation roll should be prepared, that is to say, a roll based on unimproved values and the property tax, parish rates and service charges would all be based on that roll. It will be necessary to amend the Land Valuation Law, 1956 to provide for this matter.

The Law was subsequently amended by deleting the improved value of the land as one of the particulars required to set forth in the valuation roll in respect of each and every valuation. If, however, at some future time, it is decided to revert to the two bases, the Act provided for the Minister to prescribe by regulation that the improved value of the land is an additional particular to be shown on the valuation roll.

Developing the cadastre and property inspections

It was however, to take Jamaica approximately 18 years from the passing of the 1956 legislation to complete the first revaluation of the entire island. This meant that some parishes were being revalued for the first time since the 1937 revision. The programme commenced in 1956 as a Division under the then Ministry of Agriculture and Lands. The office was structured with a very small nucleus of trained professional valuers who directed operations together with a workforce of 'para-valuers' who were trained locally to carry out certain of the mass valuation functions and to be responsible for the bulk of the valuations which were mainly rural and comprised of relatively low value parcels having little complexity. They were also responsible for the referencing and identification of parcels for the valuation roll and would sketch these on a map to allow for the ascribing of the unique geo-code map based reference numbers given to these parcels. This exercise was based on the development of an 11 digit reference number comprising a map, grid, enclosure and parcel number called the 'Valuation Number' which uniquely identifies parcels by virtue of ownership and use.

It had been widely held prior to 1956 that a cadastral survey was a prerequisite for the establishment of a fiscal cadastre. However, in his report Mr Murray not only disagreed with this view but offered an alternative to the matter of valuation and the cadastre. He wrote:

> A detailed cadastral survey is not essential for the valuation purposes but its existence would make the task of approval easier and would ensure, with certainty, the identification of each parcel and the location of its boundaries.

> The cost of production of such a map would not, in my opinion, be justified, and the additional information obtained from precise surveys would not warrant the huge cost involved because most of the difficulties of location and identification are referable to small properties which yield little in revenue, further, a detailed survey would take many years to complete while the valuation is urgently needed.

> There is available, in Jamaica, a considerable volume of information which might be used for or adapted to valuation purposes and, as the valuation proceeds, a sketch map, with admitted imperfections, might be compiled and would show the mosaic of ownerships. The preparation of the valuation map would proceed, *pari passu*, with the work of appraisal and the new valuations might be applied to parishes without waiting for the completion of the whole survey.

However, in undertaking the revaluation programme which commenced in 1957 after the establishment of the Land Valuation Division it was necessary to have some sort of map based identification of the parcels forming the valuation roll and the subject of the valuations. Again the suggestion of Mr Murray cited in the last paragraph above was to be fully adopted. The change in the methodology of preparing the new valuation rolls was fundamental. At the time of the establishment of the land valuation division the maps, plans and aerial photographs available included:

1   topographical sheets covering the whole island at a scale of 1:50,000;

2   general map of Jamaica at a scale of 1:250,000;

3   aerial photographs taken in 1941 covering the whole island, at a scale of 1:50,000;

4   aerial photographs taken between 1951 and 1953 covering the whole island to a scale of 1:12,5000;

5   aerial photographs of urban areas taken in 1954 to a scale of 1:6,000;

6   cadastral sheets to a scale of 1:15,840 covering several parishes;

7   plans at Titles Office; and

8   estate plans and maps.

The number of holdings to be valued at this time was estimated to be approximately 350,000 and over 60 per cent were estimated to be small low value rural holdings with no well defined boundaries which were expected to yield low tax revenues. Additionally, registered titles existed for only approximately 45 per cent of the total number of parcels islandwide. The majority of these registrations further existed in the urban centres where, the requirements of loan financing, mortgages, etc., made such registration a prerequisite. However, in many of the more rugged areas of rural Jamaica this did not apply. It was against this background that the revaluation programme was executed. The mapping and valuation strategies were then developed to produce a fiscal cadastre capable of justifying the revenue yield.

The valuation base maps were produced at a scale of 1:12,500 using the various aerial photographs. This produced 248 maps with grid lines extending 30,000 feet in easting and 20,000 in northings. All available survey plans and estate maps in respect of properties in excess of 8 hectares (20 acres) were plotted on the base map to produce field sheets showing the mosaic of ownership. The blank spaces were completed by investigations and surveys in the field. These surveys were not very precise though adequate enough to establish ownership and values of these 'missing holdings'. For example, field investigators usually with the assistance of a local 'guide', - an older man with knowledge of the land ownership pattern in the area - were able to increase the number of parcels in St Catherine from 39,481 on the old roll to 41,404 on the new roll. St Catherine was the first parish in which field work was undertaken. Ownership for unregistered parcels were established by the field exercise using 'owners' return forms', similar to ingivings previously used in the preparation of the 1901 valuation roll.

The change was from a system where property tax records were handwritten in leather bound volumes to a partly computerized system. Each of the larger properties had to be inspected in detail and inventories of soil type, slope categories and land use capabilities documented. This record is still available and utilized in revaluation and valuation exercises. The smaller parcels were grouped in classes and each class was inspected and analysed. Valuations were then made on the basis of value standards arrived at after careful analysis of recent transactions, topography, land use, etc.

The data gathered on parcel characteristics and environmental factors in addition to those on ownership and values during this and subsequent programmes are essential ingredienst of a land information system and form the basis of the development of the geographic information system which is currently being developed.

The islandwide revaluation of 1974

However, as previously stated it took almost two decades for the first islandwide revaluation programme to be completed. With the programme beginning in 1957, various shift in political emphasis resulted in the rise and fall of the fortunes and priorities of the office. The situation as existed by 1972 is adequately described in the speech of the then Minister of Finance, the Hon. David Coore, at the Budget Debate where he stated:

> The first obvious area in which the tax burden is not being equitably borne is the area of property tax. We propose this year to make substantial increases in property tax. At the moment, we have been collecting $1.7 million in straight property tax under the Property Tax Law and some $4.3 million in rates. This total of $6 million paid by way of tax on all the land in Jamaica represents less than the amount collected by way of excise duty on consumption. We propose therefore this year to abolish the

distinction between property tax and rates. You will have no rates as such this year but we will charge one simple tax on land which will be fixed at an amount sufficient to include what the Parish Councils would have collected by way of rates and which will be distributed to them. The $1.7 million which would normally come in under property tax and an additional $10 million towards the requirement of $17.9 million.

Now, Mr Speaker, the problem that you face with imposing property tax on a rational basis is that the valuation of land in Jamaica at the present is not uniform. In Kingston, St Andrew, St James and Hanover, property values are on the old property valuation system, are hopelessly out of date and bear no relation to reality.

In the parishes of Manchester, Clarendon and Westmoreland, they are also valued on the unimproved value basis but are 1972 values.

Obviously, if you impose a uniform rate throughout the whole country people will pay very different amounts of tax, depending upon the parish in which they happen to be, and this in face is what it is right now.

We had hoped it would have been possible to complete the valuation to 1972 values of the whole island before we brought in a new property tax rate structure but it will not be possible for that exercise to be completed until the Budget month next year. In the course of this year the whole island will be revalued and we will have one uniform valuation roll and we can then impose a uniform tax. We will be imposing property tax on a much more logical basis and setting up proper de-rating procedures for agricultural land and so on. But for the time being in order to obtain reasonable revenues from property tax we have had to do a temporary exercise.

What we have done is to establish in effect three separate rate structures for the three different categories of land. One rate structure has been set up for Kingston, St Andrew, St James and Hanover, another for Portland, St Thomas, St Mary, St Ann, Trelawny, St Elizabeth and St Catherine, and a third rate structure has been set up for Manchester, Clarendon and Westmoreland.

What we have sought to achieve is to ensure that everybody will pay the same amount in actual cash of rates regardless of where his holding happens to be. This has to be so because some values are up to date, some are ten years out of date and some are thirty-five out of date. So obviously the values bear no relation to each other so we have to set up new rate structures.

He further stated:

> ... there have been increases, I increased the structure in such a way that they fall heavily, as is only right, upon those who are able to bear it. Naturally, the great bulk of the increased revenue from the property tax will come from the parishes of Kingston and St Andrew because this is where the most of the property in terms of value is to be found.

> By and large the increases range between increases of 40 per cent to 226 per cent. The increase in the higher echelons of property, extremely valuable property which are on the tax roll for little or nothing - there are buildings on Duke Street worth more that $1 million that are on the tax roll for $20,000 or $30,000 and the property tax rates in fact which are going to be charged are very reasonable compared with what is paid by way of property tax in other countries. This is a long overdue tax reform.

> ... it may be that there will be anomalous situations and it may be that in some instances of particular hardship these will have to be dealt with from time to time on an ad hoc basis, but by next year it is expected we will have the whole of Jamaica revalued on a uniform basis and we will be able to have one uniform rate based upon the proper percentage of value as the upper limit of our rates. We will then be able to set up proper rate procedures, but for the time being that is the position with regard to property tax.

The government's commitment to land tax reform policies ensured the eventual success of the revaluation programme of 1974. The programme called 'Land Val '74' received wide publicity and media coverage to advise landowners as to what to expect and to solicit their cooperation during the programme. The objective of this programme was to revalue for the first time in nearly 50 years the parishes of Kingston and St Andrew which together contained nearly 80,000 parcels and more than half the real estate value in Jamaica as well as the parishes of Hanover and St James (with the famous tourist resort of Montego Bay) which similarly has not been valued since the 'revaluation' of 1937. Additionally, the programme would see the revaluation of those parishes already valued using the unimproved value system. All this was expected to be completed within one year. This was in fact completed within the time frame with only minor works being done in St Catherine and St Ann in April 1974 when the new valuation roll was declared. A new era of property tax was launched with a single rate structure being applied to a single base of property value. Several lessons were learnt from the exercise but it produced positive results. The capital value of the tax base increased from $55 million in 1954 to $1.8 billion in 1974 and currently amounts to $87.24 billion (1998). Additionally, the number of holdings increased from 350,000 to 492,000 and currently there are 629,000 parcels on the valuation roll. The gross tax yield increased from $33 million in 1988 to $474 million.

Table 19.1 provides some information on gross property tax collections for the period 1986-1997. Of these figures approximately only 60 to 75 per cent was actually collected. This was a reflection of exemptions, relief, derating and noncompliance. The significant increase in 1994 relates to the revaluation which became effective in that year.

Table 19.1
Gross property tax collections 1986-1997

Year	Collections ($millions)
1987	33
1988	53
1989	59
1990	68
1991	67
1992	70
1993	88
1994	258
1995	461
1996	490
1997	474

Valuation

All land in Jamaica is valued in accordance with unimproved value as defined in the Land Valuation Act 1956. Valuations are based on the market value of the land, that is, the price you would expect to receive if you were selling the land alone. This disregards the value of any improvements on the land, such as buildings or crops. Within the valuation exercise the following factors are taken into account, area of parcel, location, use, land prices in the area, zoning, development potential, topography, land capabilities. The following statutory definitions prescribe the nature of the interest to be valued.

Unimproved value means:

1   in relation to unimproved land the capital sum which the fee simple of the land together with any licence or other right or privilege (if any) for the time being affecting the land, might be expected to realise if offered for sale on such reasonable terms and conditions as a bona fide seller would require;

2   in relation to improved land the capital sum which the fee simple of the land might be expected to realise if offered for sale on such reasonable terms and conditions as a bona fide seller would require, assuming that at the time as at which the value is required to be ascertained for the purposes of this Act the improvements as defined in this Act do not exist (Section 2, Land Valuation Act 1957).

Improvements in relation to land means physical additions to land and all works for the benefit of the land undertaken by the existing or previous owners, that have the effect of increasing the value of the land. However, the following are not to be considered as improvements:

1   the destruction or removal of timber or vegetable growth;

2   the draining, filling, excavation or reclamation of land;

3   the construction of retaining walls or similar works necessary to prevent the erosion or flooding of land; or

4   the grading or levelling of land.

In determining the unimproved value, the Commissioner may assume that:

1   the land may be used, or continue to be used, for any purpose for which it was being used or could have been used at the time as at which the value is required to be ascertained.

2   such improvements as may be required in order to enable the land to be so used or continue to be so used, will be made or continue to be made.

Therefore, unimproved value does not mean strict adherence to current use, but rather all the advantages which the land possesses, present or future, may be taken into consideration. In addition, the unimproved value shall be less than the sum obtained by deducting the value of the improvements from the improved value. The value of the improvements in relation to land is defined as that added value which the improvements give to the land, irrespective of the cost of the improvements.

Administration of property tax

With the introduction of a single rate for property tax and the completion of the revaluation exercise in 1974 which saw the entire island being valued on the unimproved value system at the same valuation date, the administration of property tax was also simplified. Prior to 1973 there existed property rates and taxes. The former was paid to the parish councils, while the latter was paid to central government. Now there existed a single tax which was paid to central government only. Funds were then dispersed to the parish councils for the provision of services within the parishes.

Valuation roll

Within the Land Valuation Act (section 11) revaluations should be prepared for each district on a quinquennial basis. However, the Minister may by order require that a revaluation be undertaken at intervals of less than five years. When a revaluation has taken place a valuation roll is prepared for each district and contained prescribed particulars to include the following:

•   the name, status and postal address of the owner;

•   the situation, description and measurement or area of the land;

•   the unimproved value of the land;

•   such additional particulars, including the improved value of the land, as may be prescribed.

Notwithstanding the statutory requirement to implement quinquennial revaluations, general islandwide revaluations have taken place in 1974, 1984 and 1993 all based on the unimproved value system.

Alteration of the roll

The valuation roll may be amended between revaluations, as necessary to reflect the following:

1   subdivision;

2   two or more parcels of unoccupied land adjoining each other are valued as one parcel, and one or more parcels has been sold or is occupied;

3   the value of the land has been altered due to the effect of public works or services;

4   the land has been permanently damaged by adverse natural causes, for example, flooding;

5   the unimproved value has been altered either by the loss or acquisition of a licence or other rights or privileges, that form part of the value of the land;

6   land used exclusively for residential purposes when valued, changes to industrial or other purposes which, in the opinion of the Commissioner, alters its value;

7   in the opinion of the Commissioner, circumstances affecting the valuation of the land render an alteration necessary or desirable for preserving or attaining uniformity in values between the subject valuation and those subsisting valuations of other comparable parcels of land.

Objection to assessments

If on receipt of a Notice of Valuation the landowner is dissatisfied, he may within a period of 60 days of service of the notice, serve a Notice of Objection on the Commissioner. The grounds for an objection are restricted to one or more of the following:

•   the assessed values are either too high or too low;

•   that lands which should be included in one valuation have been valued separately, or vice versa;

•   that the person named in the Notice is not the owner.

In considering the objection, the Commissioner may either disallow it, or allow it either wholly or in part. On receipt of the Notice of Decision of the Commissioner, if the landowner is still dissatisfied, he may within 60 days of that decision, or such longer period as may be permitted by rules of court, appeal to the Revenue Court. The Revenue Court has the power to confirm, reduce or indeed increase the assessment. If either the Commissioner or any person affected by the decision of the Revenue Court is dissatisfied with the decision of the Revenue Court, he may within 60 days of the decision, appeal to the Court of Appeal.

Collection

The Commissioner of Inland Revenue shall cause to be assessed a property tax payable by every person in possession of property liable to the property tax. A Notice of Assessment specifies the amount of property tax properly to be payable. The tax is payable by the owner, which means the person who, whether jointly or severally is in possession or entitled to any estate or interest in land. The due date for payment is 1 April in each year, however, payment can be made at any time during this month, made payable to the Collector of Taxes of the parish where the property is situate.

Where the tax has not been paid within the month of April a penalty of 10 per cent on the full amount of the tax is added to the debt. Interest of 15 per cent (or such other rate as the Minister may prescribe) per annum is levied on property tax unpaid for a period of 30 days after the collection date.

The tax may be payable by four equal quarterly instalments (April, July, October and January). If an instalment is not paid in the due month then all property tax becomes due, this in effect removes any future right to pay the debt by instalment. The Property Tax Act 1903 (as amended) provides for the forfeiture of property for nonpayment of property taxes.

The collection of the property tax is seen as one of the weaknesses of the system. Tax arrears has historically been a problem. Risden (1976) estimates that in the fiscal year 1977, the tax collected was only 61 per cent of the collectable amount. Holland and Follain (1990) for financial year 1984 estimated that collections levels were in the region of 50 per cent. A problem of tax compliance remains a significant one with compliance levels currently in the region of 60 per cent. Tax arrears is a more significant problem, particularly since property revenue has now been transferred from the Consolidated Fund to the parish councils. Given their own service responsibilities parishes will become increasingly conscious of the need to match the cost of services to the available revenue, therefore arrears and tax compliance will be high on the parish agenda.

There is a clear need to improve the relatively low levels of compliance which has resulted in the accumulation of significant unpaid property tax. The average level of property tax payment is annually in the region of 60 per cent. Given the fact that local government is to finance the cost of property related services, administrative and legal procedures for the collection of the property tax need to be strengthened. In this regard the following aspects are considered as imperative:

1   the Collector of Taxes to issue a certificate confirming that all outstanding property taxes have been paid as at the date of transfer and mortgage documents are submitted for stamping and registration;

2   legislation to provide for the sale of a property for non-payment of property taxes after two years have expired. This is considered as a remedy of last resort, but should have a positive effect of preventing delinquency by absentee owners;

3   the need to be able to collect arrears beyond the present six year limit;

4   all businesses seeking the renewal of licences will be required to submit evidence that property tax payments are up-to-date; and

5   an integrated computerization system which would make it possible to pay property taxes at any collectorate throughout the island.

Exemptions

The Property Tax Act specifies a number of properties which are exempt from the property tax, they include the following:

- all buildings held in trust exclusively for public religious worship including contiguous churchyards and burial grounds;

- all buildings and lands used solely for charitable or educational purposes;

- all buildings and lands belonging to and used by the University of the West Indies;

- all buildings and lands belonging to primary schools and secondary schools;

- all unoccupied property belonging to, and all property in the occupation of the Crown, the Government of the Island, or any parish council or the Kingston and St Andrew Corporation;

- all freehold property vested in the Commissioner of Lands and in the actual occupation of the Crown, the Government of the Island, or any parish council or the Kingston and St Andrew Corporation;

- all buildings belonging to any church including, rectories, halls and all land provided it does not exceed one acre;

- all buildings and lands belonging to and used solely for the purposes of a private hospital;

Land taxation relief

The Land Taxation Relief Act 1959 allows landowners to enjoy derating or relief from tax liability in the case of agricultural land and specified lands for which potential has been taken into account.

The Act is administered by the Land Taxation Relief Board (appointed by the Minister) comprising six members including the Commissioners of Land Valuation and Inland Revenue. The Board does not have the jurisdiction to change assessments, but simply adjudicate on the request for relief. Relief is granted to the current owner and ceases on the sale of the parcel or if he/she dies, relief is therefore personal and not transferable and must be reapplied for.

Agricultural land

Derating is provided for specified land uses, essentially agricultural land. A derating certificate, if approved, is effective for periods ranging from one to three years, as specified by the Board. The derating certificate ceases to have effect as soon as the land to which it relates or part thereof is subdivided or used for any purposes other than that purpose for which the certificate was granted. It must however be demonstrated that the land at the time of the valuation was being used bona fide as agricultural land and the valuation takes into account the potentials of the land for use other than agricultural land. The derating relief is currently 50 per cent of the tax assessment. Prior to 1993 the level of relief was 75 per cent. Agricultural land is defined in The Land Taxation (Relief) Act 1960 as being:

> ... land which for the time being is used exclusively or principally for agricultural, horticultural or pastoral purposes or for the keeping of bees, poultry or livestock.

In determining whether a derating certificate ought to be granted, the Board may take into account whether the land in respect of which the application is made is in substantial production. In determining this the Board may take the following into account:

1   whether the whole of the land is used exclusively for agricultural purposes;

2   the extent to which and the manner in which:

   (i)   arable land is being cropped (where the land has not been cropped for more than two or more years the land shall not be regarded as being in substantial agricultural production);

   (ii)   the land is stocked;

   (iii) pasture land is being maintained;

3   the capacity of the land;

4   any other factor which affects the development of the land.

Potential uses for dwellings

Statutory relief is granted in those cases where the valuation takes into account a potential use of the subject land which would give a higher assessed value than the current use. An example would be where the owner (occupier) of a dwelling is in a location where the character of the location has changed from predominately residential to commercial. In this case the valuation of the parcel will reflect commercial values of the potential uses. In this case the owner must show that the house is being used as a bona fide dwelling house and the valuation of the land takes into account the potentials of that land as suitable for any of the following types of development:

•   hotel or guest house;

•   shop, office or other commercial building;

•   an industrial building;

•   a block or residential flats; or

•   a type of residence which would necessitate redevelopment of the land and involve substantial capital expenditure. In this case the state of repair of the dwelling will be an important factor.

The Board in determining whether or not a relief certificate ought to be granted will have regard to all the circumstances and may take the following into account:

1   whether it is reasonable that the land should continue to be used for its existing purpose; and

2   whether the payment of the whole amount of land tax would, because of circumstances peculiar to the applicant, cause hardship.

In relation to the level of relief, it is at the discretion of the Board to determine by how much the tax assessment should be reduced.

Potential uses for approved purposes

Relief is also provided where land is in bona fide use at the time of valuation, for an approved purpose, and the valuation took into account the potential of that land being used as a suitable site for a subdivision or for any of the types of development noted above. Approved purpose covers the provision of playing fields for cricket, football and other outdoor games. An approved organization refers to Members' Club registered as such under the Registration of Clubs Act. Under the Property Tax Act the Minister of Finance is empowered to give approval for relief to any purpose or organization if he is satisfied that either the purpose or the organization is mainly of a social, cultural or educational nature. Therefore schools, churches, hospitals and certain charitable organizations may qualify for relief.

Hardship relief

Relief from property tax on the grounds of hardship may also be granted at the discretion of the Minister of Finance. In this case the Special Discretionary Relief is granted in genuine cases of hardship where the taxpayer finds it burdensome to pay the property tax. The typical relief recipient has been those on low fixed incomes including the elderly and pensioners. If, in spite of the level of relief, a taxpayer is still suffering hardship a case may be made to the Minister of Finance for the remission of the tax.

Tax rate structure

The tax rate structure in Jamaica is based on a progressive approach as shown in Table 19.2, the rationale being that the more valuable properties are taxed at the higher rates. Interestingly, however, the number of properties owned by an individual is not aggregated in terms of value which creates an anomly. For example, if someone owns two properties, each worth $500,000, the tax payable is $3,230 for each property making a total of $6,460. On the other hand if the same person owns only one property with a value of $1,000,000, the tax liability is $10,730.

Table 19.2
Property tax rate schedule

For first $20,000 of value	$50
For every $1 of the next £30,000 of value	0.10c
For every $1 of the next £50,000 of value	0.30c
For every $1 of the next £400,000 of value	0.75c
For every $1 of the next £500,000 of value	1.50c
For every $1 of the next £1,500,000 of value	2.00c
For every $1 of the next £2,500,000 of value	2.50c
For every $1 of remainder	3.00c

Table 19.3 illustrates the actual tax liability for a range of land values. Given the progressive nature of the tax, high valued properties effectively carry the highest burden.

Table 19.3
Tax liability for selected land values

Land value $	Tax payable $
60,000	110
200,000	980
500,000	3,230
1,000,000	10,730
5,000,000	103,230

Table 19.4 provides estimates of effective tax rates, i.e. the ratio of tax liability to assessed land value. The structure of the tax schedule is both cumulative and progressive, with the higher land values being the target of effective rates of tax in excess of 2 per cent. However, only land with a value over $1m would have an effective rate of over 1 per cent. The rationale for a progressive structure as opposed to a proportionate rate allows the lighter taxation of a greater number of parcels with the result that the highest percentage of total revenue is based on a smaller number of properties. By concentrating the revenue on the highest

valued properties, this has the positive effect of making collection easier and ensuring that arrears are proactively dealt with.

Table 19.4
Effective tax rates

Land Value Class	Tax		Tax Rate (%)	Effective Tax Rate (%)
Under 20,000	50			0.25
20,001-50,000	30	(80)	0.0010	0.16
50,001-100,000	150	(230)	0.0030	0.23
100,001-500,000	3,000	(3,230)	0.0075	0.64
500,001-1,000,000	7,500	(10,370)	0.0150	1.07
1,000,001-2,500,000	30,000	(40,730)	0.0200	1.63
2,500,001-5,000,000	62,500	(103,230)	0.0250	2.07
Over 5,000,001	103,230	+ 0.03%	0.0300	2.10

One of the important issues relating to the tax structure is the lack of buoyancy within the system. This is principally due to the inherent fixed nature of the progressive rates, which remain fixed between revaluations, therefore the only opportunity to change the rates is at a forthcoming general revaluation. As all land parcels are or should be included within the valuation roll, the amount of revenue raised each year is effectively fixed. This has the obvious disadvantage of being inflation prone in relation to escalating costs of service provision to be funded by a static revenue source. Clearly, this represents an aspect of future property tax reform which should address this lack of revenue buoyancy, by increasing the tax rates at least by the annual rate of inflation as an intra-revaluation measure.

The annual gross collectable revenue under the 1983 revaluation was in the region of $88 million. However, of this figure the actual revenue yield was in the region of $24m, the difference being a reflection of tax delinquency and tax reliefs. With regard to the latter it has been estimated that as much as 30 per cent is attributable to tax relief schemes. For the 1993 revaluation the gross collectable revenue increased to around $450 million. Table 19.5 gives an indication of the cost of services in comparison to the property tax revenue.

Table 19.5
Cost of services versus potential revenue

Year	Cost of Services	Property Tax Revenue
1992/93	$379m	$88m
1993/94	$474m	$450m

As shown in Table 19.6 after the 1993 revaluation some 77 per cent have an assessed value of up to $100,000; of this total of 462,000 parcels around 90,000 attracts the minimum property tax of $50. At the other end of the scale only approximately 2 per cent of parcels have a value in excess of $5m.

Table 19.6
Distribution of parcels by value category

Value Categories	Number of Parcels	J$Bn	% of Total Parcels
Under 20,000	90,480	1.0	15.07
20,001-50,000	213,705	6.7	35.60
50,001-100,000	157,949	10.6	26.31
100,001-500,000	115,391	22.8	19.22
500,001-1,000,000	14,392	8.9	2.40
1,000,001-2,500,000	5,453	8.0	0.91
2,500,001-5,000,000	1,880	6.3	0.31
Over 5,000,001	1,057	12.1	0.18
Total	600,307	76.4	100.00

Note: *The figures are exclusive of any form of relief.*

Critical review

In relation to resources available the unimproved value system is much more cost effective in comparison to improved value systems. Given the diversity in terms of improvements to land, the need to have a system which would continuously monitor changes and cause reassessments creates an incredible pressure on monetary and human resources. Having a tax basis which excludes improvements should provide for a more cost effective and efficient allocation of scarce resources.

It satisfies the canons of horizontal equity to the extent that market values are determined on the basis of highest and best use, and vertical equity can be achieved by structuring the rate of tax on a progressive rather than a proportional basis, so as to more effectively capture the taxable capacity of real property.

The system discourages speculation in land to the extent that the real cost of holding unproductive land is made prohibitive. In other words the level of tax would be the same notwithstanding that an actual income is being derived thus, in effect, 'forcing' the holders of idle land into either developing it or selling it. The converse argument is also true in that the system does not discourage development as improvements to the land are part of the tax base.

It is generally accepted that a site value approach should, in theory, at least result in the implementation of frequent and regular revaluations. In practice however, other factors adversely affect the implementing of regular revaluations such as political will, taxpayer lobbying, etc. The quality of the valuation roll is therefore adversely affected by the infrequent revaluation; since the implementation of site value in 1956, there have been three revaluations, the first in 1974, then in 1983 and the last being in 1993. A further revaluation is however planned to become operative from 1999.

There are a number of disadvantages of the site value system including penalizing the holding of accommodation land particularly when a change of use is not yet economic. In addition, it is also argued that it is insensitive to the taxpayer's ability to pay, for example where the present use is not the most valuable and where the tax is assessed on the latter value.

A considerable degree of wealth is tied up in buildings and other improvements to land which is effectively exempt for taxation. This creates a fairly restricted or narrow tax base with the result that tax rates on land need to be higher than they would normally be.

The property tax system is to some extent affected by the rather liberal exemptions particularly for agricultural land. This fact has in part been recognized by government as the rate of relief has been reduced from 75 per cent to 50 per cent. In addition, the previous relief granted to hotel land has been removed as from the date of the last general revaluation in 1993.

The level of collection efficiency has already been mentioned however, it is worth noting that the Collector of Taxes should have the power to seek the payment of arrears notwithstanding the time bar of six years imposed by the Statute of Limitations. Clearly, if action is taken prior to the six years, there should be no legal impediment in pursuing the claim for arrears. The problem would seem to occur in seeking to impose payment on arrears which have been outstanding for more than six years before collection action has been taken. To remedy this latter aspect legislation would need to be enacted to empower the Collector of Taxes.

Sales analysis and developing a sales data bank

In order to facilitate the possible implementation of a computer assisted mass appraisal system, a computerized land sales data bank is being set up. Information on sales contracts would be received from the Office of the Stamp Commissioner and the Registrar of Titles. This would include parcels of land which already have registered titles (under the Registration of Titles Act) as well as unregistered parcels, which currently number in the region of 300,000.

References

Holland, D. and Follain, J. (1990), The Property Tax in Jamaica, in Bahl, R. (ed.), *The Jamaican Tax Reform*, Lincoln Institute of Land Policy, Cambridge, United States.

Murray, J.F.N. (1956), *Valuation, Land Taxation and Rating: Report to the Government of Jamaica*, Kingston, Jamaica.

Risden, O. St Clare, (1976), A History of Jamaica's Experience with Site Value Taxation, in *The Taxation of Urban Property in Less Developed Countries*, TRED-10, University of Wisconsin Press, United States.

Risden, O. St Clare, (1980), *Site Value Taxation in Developing Countries*, paper presented at Caribbean Association of Tax Administrators, St Kitts.

20 Real property taxation in Poland

Jan Brzeski

Introduction

A programme of economic reforms were introduced in Poland during the Solidarity Revolution of 1980. This in essence was a gradual evolution culminating in a relinquishment of communist power in 1989. Further economic reforms were subsequently introduced in 1990-1991 leading to economic growth of 3 per cent in 1992 increasing to 6 per cent in 1996.

Real property tax as a source of revenue for local self-government has a long tradition in Poland. It existed prior to the Second World War during the period of market economy. In 1950 when the communists liquidated local self-governments and introduced central planning the property tax lost its significance. Various forms of levies related to the ownership of real assets as well as to remnants of private wealth however, did exist during the communist period. By the mid-1980s there was in existence three taxes related to real property:

1   a tax on urban properties;

2   a tax on agricultural land; and

3   a tax on forestry land and buildings.

Property taxes were imposed differently on public sector enterprises and on private sector entities (firms) and individuals. The tax base used prior to the Solidarity Revolution consisted of the so called 'obligatory insurable value' and applied to buildings only (land was deemed to have no value). This value was calculated on the basis of an administrative set of normative indicators.

The restitution of local self-government in Poland by the middle of 1990 resulted in the division of public finance into local and central budgets. By 1

411

January 1991 local governments obtained their own autonomous revenue sources and property tax became the chief generator of local revenue. Other local revenue sources in Poland included Transportation Vehicle Tax, Street Vendor Tax, Dog Tax, Local Business Tax, and a number of local administrative fees. Practice has shown that some 20 per cent of local self-government revenue was generated by property taxes. The larger cities have tended to exploit to a greater extent their property taxation powers, whilst smaller communities have not be able or chosen not to do so.

In 1990 the Solidarity-led government of Poland introduced sweeping economic reforms, including a discussion of the merits of a property tax based on market values. The desire to establish an ad valorem property tax base was quickly discounted due primarily to the general immaturity of real estate markets at that time. Instead, an area based property tax was instituted in 1991 as the tax base.

A major legislative change took place on 12 January 1991 when a new law relating to local taxes and fees was introduced. The new law provided that local taxes (including property tax) were to be the sole revenue source for local government. It, amongst other things, introduced equality among taxpayers, attempted to limit obligatory statutory exemptions and abatements, and gave powers to local self-governments to set tax rates subject to national ceilings. Local governments were also given the right to use discretionary tax exemption and abatement powers.

The law retained the distinction between the urban property tax and agricultural and forestry land taxes. Both agricultural and forestry taxes were related to soil and timber classifications and thus could be related indirectly to imputed values. The urban property tax applied to floor area and type of use with one exception to be mentioned later. The remainder of this chapter focuses on urban property taxation.

Tax liability

Property tax liability arises on ownership rights, perpetual land leaseholds and ownership of mobile homes. This pertains to lands not included in either the agricultural or forestry tax bases. One could say that whatever is not subject to agricultural and forestry tax becomes, by default, an urban property tax. The important principle is that property tax liability attaches always to the property and its owner, regardless of whether he is in possession or not. Property tax is imposed also on condominium flats, but not on cooperative proprietary flats (which are not considered to be a separate property).

Taxpayers are physical and legal persons as well as functional entities not having a separate legal status. In the case of public sector properties, owned by

412

the state or municipality, it is the users/occupiers of these properties who are liable for the property tax provided they are the direct parties holding user rights to the public sector properties. In the case of council housing properties the direct user of the property is the municipal housing management company, which is liable to pay property tax. In the case of perpetual land leaseholds, it is the land user who is liable to pay property tax (although the state or a municipality is the owner).

Tax base

The tax base consists either of the building area in case of buildings and of land area in case of land. Additional categories within the tax base include structures, such as bridges, tunnels, roads, railroad tracks, power lines, industrial installations, sport facilities, etc. In this case the tax base consists of the 'gross value' estimated by applying specific regulations used for capital depreciation purposes. Building area is measured on a net internal basis, excluding staircase areas and elevator shafts. If the storey height of a building is 1.4 m to 2.2 m high, only 50 per cent of the area is included in the tax base. If the storey measures less than 1.4 m in height, the area is not included in the tax base.

Tax rates

Tax rates are established by local municipal councils but within maximum levels determined by national legislation on an annual basis. Maximum allowable tax rates are set by the Ministry of Finance each year and have been increased by the application of officially published inflation rates for the preceding period (average for the three quarters). Property tax rates are differentiated by functional use categories:

1   residential; and

2   commercial and other (recreational, garages, used by non-profit organizations).

These categories apply both to land and building areas. Consequently, the amount of tax is dependent on area and use of the land and buildings. The highest rates are applied to commercial uses. This includes residential buildings used for commercial purposes such as hotels, motels, dormitories, pension homes, etc. Maximum tax rates vary substantially, in 1995 these were as follows based on a price per square metre:

residential use building area	- 0.09 US$
commercial use building area	- 3.32 US$
other use building area	- 1.11 US$
structures	- 2% of capital depreciation base
land under commercial use	- 0.11 US$
land under other non-commercial uses	- 0.01 US$

The tax collection system is different for physical and legal persons. Individuals are required to fill in tax questionnaires and receive payment forms to pay the tax in four instalments over the year (15 March, 15 May, 15 September and 15 November). Legal persons are obliged to calculate the tax themselves and make a tax declaration to that effect by 15 January each year. The tax is payable by 15th of each month. The administration of the tax collection is carried out by larger cities themselves. Smaller municipalities rely on state tax offices to perform these functions.

Exemptions

Tax exemptions can be divided into 3 groups:

- those granted by the law on local taxes and fees;

- those granted by separate legislation; and

- those granted locally by self-governments.

Tax exemptions granted by the law on local taxes and fees include:

- properties used for the administrative functions of a local self-government;

- properties owned by foreign countries and foreign institutions/organizations;

- public roads and rights of way;

- structures used exclusively for public transport (rail, air, river, sea);

- structures used for the generation and transmission of energy, gas, heat, fuel, water;

- sewage including their rights of way;

- land used by water reservoirs or by hydroelectric stations and land under flowing waters and sailing canals;

- buildings used for agricultural and forestry purposes;

- properties used by non-governmental organizations for statutory activities benefiting children and young people, but not having commercial purposes; and

- properties listed in the historic heritage registry provided they are in compliance with historic preservation regulations and not being used for commercial purposes.

Tax exemptions granted by other national laws:

- properties used by religious organizations for non-commercial purposes;

- enterprise garden plots;

- institutions related to the film-making sector;

- institutions of higher learning except properties used for commercial purposes;

- properties used by enterprises for handicapped persons;

- properties used by schools and public institutions; and

- properties used by research and development entities except for commercial purposes.

Tax exemptions granted by the City of Kraków:

- communal rental apartments;

- properties used by theatres, libraries, clubs, cultural centres, kindergartens, social assistance centres - all of these being financed through city budget; and

- properties used for charitable activities.

Some tax abatement schemes exist for new buildings, because tax liability arises only on 1 January of the following year. In mid-1996 a major amendment to the existing area based system was adopted by the Parliament with effect from 1997.

Major changes included the setting up of a minimum property tax rate of 50 per cent of the maximum (ceiling) rate.

Presently, the national land and building statistics provide evidence on numbers of taxable property; 28,712,000 land plots with the total area of 31,278,000 hectares. The number of plots is not the same as the number of properties and does not correspond to the number of buildings subject to property, agricultural or forestry taxes. This is because, one property may consist of several land plots; or on one plot there may be several objects being the subject of different taxes.

The total number of buildings in Poland is in the region of 4,554,000 of which some 4,319,000 are residential (1,483,000 in urban, and 2,836,000 in rural areas). The number of dwellings in Poland amounts to 10,875,000 of which 7,135,000 are in urban locations and 3,740,000 in rural areas. This data refers to the 1988 Census, the most recent available.

There are some 11 million ownership titles registered in perpetual (title) books administered by the court system. This figure does not fully reflect the number of real properties, since many still do not have clarified legal status. On the other hand the perpetual (title) books also include cooperative property rights (proprietary leasehold rights).

Tax revenues

In 1994 revenues from urban property, agricultural and forestry taxes amounted nationally to some 150 million US$ of which 18 per cent came from agricultural taxes, 2 per cent from forestry taxes and 80 per cent from the urban property tax.

The number of registered taxpayers by category was 2,162,000 agricultural taxpayers, 1,216,000 forestry taxpayers and 5,402,000 urban property taxpayers. The average annual tax bill per taxpayer for the 1994 financial year was 100 US$ for the agricultural tax, 16 US$ for forestry tax and 190 US$ for urban property tax.

This tax burden per taxpayer was calculated by using the total revenues for a given tax, and does not reflect significant differences in rate levels (maximum allowable rate for economic activity is 35 times the rate for residential uses).

Land records are being kept by a number of institutions, geographically spread throughout the country. Regional offices (sub-regional central government administration) covers 56 per cent of land plots, municipal offices (local government administration) covers 27 per cent, voivodship offices (regional central government administration) covers 10 per cent, and other entities cover 7 per cent of land plots.

While the existing area based system has been functioning during the 1990s, a substantial degree of effort has been put into reform work aimed at introducing an ad valorem system of property taxation. The initial major tax reform efforts focused on income taxation (January 1992) and indirect taxes such as the VAT and excise taxes (July 1993).

Attention began to shift towards examining possible reform options for the property tax, especially as a means of strengthening local government finance, that had been experiencing increasing difficulties. In this regard, the Polish Parliament passed a resolution on 5 March 1994 obliging the government to prepare a draft ad valorem property tax act. In June 1994, the Council of Ministers adopted a long-term economic development strategy called, 'Strategy for Poland', which empowered the Ministry of Finance to institute a comprehensive and complex fiscal cadastre of real properties, that could be used for mass assessment work on an ad valorem property tax to be introduced in Poland in 1999. In early 1995 an Inter-Ministerial Working Group was established under the chairmanship of the Ministry of Finance and composed of Ministry of Justice, Ministry of Construction, and Ministry of Agriculture.

The Working Group was to establish basic premises of the reform and to resolve institutional and jurisdictional issues, and disagreements among ministries over who will control various elements of property data registers and mass valuation. The Group during its work, had also to take into account the recently announced government intention to reorganize its structures by creating a new structure responsible for the economy. The Group in its brief statement of premises for the new property tax, did proclaim the need for an ad valorem tax and stressed that it supports the idea of creating a central agency called the National Office of Cadastre, Geodesy and Cartography, which would develop and run property information systems and registers, as well as performing national cadastral valuations. The Ministry of Finance has been working, since the autumn of 1994, on drafting new acts introducing the basic legal foundations for an ad valorem property tax system. Proposals for these laws incorporated recommendations of the Inter-Ministerial Working Group. After several rounds of discussions and strong pressure by local self-government lobby, several modifications of these proposals were made.

The revisions of the package, made by Ministry of Finance in 1996 go further towards giving local self-governments a larger role in administering the proposed ad valorem system. Management of the cadastre and full administration of local taxes including property tax, gift and inheritance taxes, as well as stamp duties would be transferred in the new draft law to local government entities, often composed of several municipalities in order to provide for 'economies of scale'. Only the largest cities will be allowed to have full autonomous control or independence. While administration of the above local taxes will be left wholly to local governments, subject only to general laws, the cadastral operations will be supervised and coordinated through two arrangements. Firstly, the management of the real property cadastre will officially take the form of a task assigned by central government administration to local government. The final responsibility will rest, therefore, with the central government administration. Secondly, cadastral operations including national valuation will be supervised by the National Office of Cadastre, Geodesy and Cartography, which will be a politically controlled central agency.

The momentum for ad valorem taxation reform in Poland has matured, but the legislative process hampered by political positioning and discussion over information control will need to run its course. Professional and political forces mobilized around land surveying, title registration and taxation, despite being in agreement as to principles (through the Inter-Ministerial Working Group) will need to see that mutual accommodation is the only way to go forward. The ambitious legislative package developed with so much dedication and international advice will finally see implementation requiring massive technical work yet to be completed despite many elements being already in place with the present property tax system.

The lesson to be learned is that institutional procedures in transitional countries is a protracted process, which has to address and resolve the problems of vested interests acquired and remaining from former times. The longer the transformation process lasts the more difficult it will be to overcome these interests for the higher good of economic development and the country.

21 Local property taxation in Hungary

Gábor Péteri and Mihály Lados

Introduction

A new system of local taxation was introduced in Hungary in 1991, with the development of political and administrative systems of local government. This was the final stage of the fiscal reform process, initiated in the late 1980s, which has drastically changed intergovernmental finances. A general grant system was developed in 1990, which eliminated the important influence of the central budget on local government revenues. Local discretion in using national grants and other transferred revenues created the potential for higher municipal revenue. Local taxes are essentially regarded as tools for developing local autonomy, where municipal services are adjusted to meet local needs.

Local taxes in Hungary

Local tax systems are not an entirely new feature of local government finance in Hungary. Several of the presently used local taxes originated in the last century. For example, the 'Land Tax' and 'Building Tax' were introduced by Habsburgs around 1850. After the Second World War, the newly imposed political era replaced those taxes. However, each element of the new system has extended the application of the previous taxes including user fees, with the exception of the 'Business Tax'.

'Act C' on Local Taxes (ALT) was adopted by the Parliament in December 1990 and has been in operation since 1 January 1991. This legislation removed all the previous local taxes (11 types), however, the new law has replaced 7 of them by 4 new forms of taxes. The basic distinction between the old and new systems is that to levy a local tax is now a basic constitutional right of local

419

municipalities. This was not true of the previous 40 years. To illustrate some of the main differences see Table 21.1. Old style local taxes were introduced by ministerial decrees; currently, local taxes are regulated and legislated for by Parliament, effectively removing the previous powers of the various ministries.

Historically, local government had little influence on local taxation. Municipal tax officers were simply empowered to comply with the then law. Within the new framework they have to implement the objectives of the municipality. In the old system, central government regulated incentives of local tax administration in an attempt to avoid corruption. Currently the elected body of the municipality has the discretion to introduce such incentives which can formally be incorporated within the local tax code.

Table 21.1
Comparison of the old and new local taxes in Hungary

	The Old System	The New System
Where is the tax defined?	Separate ministerial decrees	Frame-law
How are taxes used?	Mandatory	Local goverment can choose any or none of the taxes
Who is liable to be taxed?	Individuals (except 'user fee on plot')	Individuals and businesses
Who determines the rate?	Central government	Central government defines the upper limit
Who defines exemptions?	Central legislation	Several mandatory and specified in the legislation, however local government can permit additional exemptions
Who collects the taxes?	Local government	Local government
Tax administration?	Central government	By means of a local decree or local tax code

Historically the system of local taxation was more or less fixed, with the taxes imposed tending to yield relatively small amounts of revenue. As the new system is based on the discretion of local municipalities they have the choice to levy any, all or none of the taxes. Should a local municipality decide to levy taxes, it has the power to decide the type(s), base(s), what rate setting should be used and what, if any, additional exemptions should be granted. The choices adopted by any municipality largely depend on the financial position of the local budget and the opportunity to formulate local tax policy in an attempt to affect the local economy. Therefore, with an efficient tax structure and policy, fewer taxes need to be administered, with a higher potential revenue. In the past the rate of collection efficiency directly influenced the tax yield as opposed to the application of a particular budgetary requirement. In contrast, under the new system, local budget needs may or indeed should govern the size of local tax revenue within the given central regulatory framework and also take into consideration the tax capacity and the potential benefit from those taxes to the community.

The 'Act C' on Local Taxes defines five taxes specifically assigned to municipalities including:

1   property tax on buildings;

2   property tax on plots;

3   communal tax (poll tax);

4   tourism tax; and

5   business tax.

The bases of the taxes, rates and exemptions are detailed in Table 21.2. These taxes basically extend the range of pre-existing local taxes collected and administered by the local councils under the previous regime.

The introduction of local taxes was part of an experimental process, when the basic characteristics of local governance, public administration, local finances and municipal financial management were transformed. The first attempt at a modern local tax system was highly controlled, in order that any difficulties might be readily corrected by other elements of intergovernmental finance. The first version of the 1990 Act was based upon local government's power as a taxing authority, however, central government retained control by prescribing maximum tax rates and by the introduction of a great number of mandatory tax exemptions. High levels of local taxation were prevented by the legislation which did not permit double taxation. Local taxes paid by individuals (with the exception of taxes paid in 1995) are not deductible from the national personal income tax.

Table 21.2
Local taxes in Hungary

Tax Category	What is Taxable?	Basis of Tax	Maximum Tax Rate	Exemptions
Tax on buildings	Residential and non-residential	Area per m² or corrected value*	900 Ft/m² or 3%	- poor social housing; - properties of less than 100 m² in villages having fewer than 500 inhabitants - property owned by income tax exempt organizations - agricultural property
Tax on plots	Net unimproved area	Area per m² or corrected value	200 Ft/m² or 3%	- land owned by transport and telecommunication companies
Communal tax on private individuals	Owned or rented real estate	Object of the tax	12,000 Ft per annum per property	
Communal tax on entrepreneurs	Employed persons	Number of employees	2,000 Ft per annum per employee	
Tourism tax	Tourists	Number of nights or fee	300 Ft per person per night or 4%	- persons under 18 or above 70 years - students - employed relatives
Business tax	Profits	Gross income	1.2%	
	Temporary business	Gross income	5,000 Ft per day	

*   *Corrected value = 50 percent of government-determined 'assessed price', which corresponds to 50 per cent (on average) of actual observed market price.*

Source: 'Act C' of 1990, 'Act LXXVI' of 1992 and 'Act XCVIII' of 1995 on Local Taxes

Local property taxes within the general tax system

The basis of local tax administration is somewhat different from the national system given the philosophy of a strict separation of municipal and centrally provided functions. There is only one important shared tax within the Hungarian tax system, i.e. the personal income tax, however the trend is to finance the cost of local government services by locally collected revenue and grants. Local government is still highly dependent on central government transfers, since all the significant tax revenue sources are essentially central government controlled taxes. The personal income tax which represents a major revenue source is shared between national and local budgets, with around 20 per cent of the revenue being transferred to the local level. Table 21.3 illustrates the relative importance of local taxes, and in particular, the property tax in comparison to the GDP.

Table 21.3
Composition of the Hungarian National Tax System 1994

Tax	Taxpayer	Tax Rate	Tax Yield (Ft Billion)	Share of GDP (%)
Social Security	E I	44%[1] 10%	554.3	12.7
Value Added Tax	E;I	12%;25%[2]	349.2	8.0
Excise Tax	E;I	Individual	174.6	4.0
Personal Income Tax	I	20-44%[3]	309.9	7.1
Corporate Income Tax	E	18%;38%	91.7	2.1
Customs Duties	E;I	Individual	148.4	3.4
Local Taxes	E;I	-	34.0	0.8
Property Taxes	E;I	-	4.3	0.1

E - enterprises; I - individuals

1   *Reduced to 39 per cent from 1996*
2   *The lower rate of tax is for public services and basic foods.*
3   *Progressive tax. Parliament has reviewed the tax rates every year since 1988.*

Source: World Bank, 1995

Any change in the tax structure will ultimately lead to a major reallocation of public service functions between central government and local government. No increase in local taxes is feasible, without a consequent reduction in national taxes. In Hungary, both firms and individuals are taxed at quite high rates from the centre which has the effect of reducing the potential significance for local property taxation.

Central government has assumed that the maximum rates as currently set are sufficiently high enough so as not to require any increases in them for several years. The projected potential local tax yields for the various local taxes is illustrated in Table 21.4.

Table 21.4
Estimated local tax yield in Hungary 1991

Tax burden on	Households		Entrepreneurs		Potential
Tax	Tax base (million m²)	Tax yield (Ft Billion)	Tax base (million m²)	Tax yield (Ft Billion)	Maximum yield (Ft Billion)
Tax on buildings:					
- Houses	10.0	3.0	-	-	-
- Other	20.0	9.0	120.0	36.0	45.0
Tax on plots	60.0	6.0	705.0	7.0	13.0
Communal tax:					
- Social flats	1.0	3.0	-	7.0	10.0
- Employees	-	-	3.5	-	-
Tourism tax	-	0.8	-	-	0.8
Business tax	-	-	-	27.0	27.0
Sub-total	-	21.8	-	77.0	95.8

Tax base: Tax on Buildings - data is estimated from the CSO census of property. This shows that there are 2.5 million housing units, with an average size of 67m²; of the 167 million m² of tax base, 10 million m² are assumed to be taxable as housing, and 20 million m² taxable as other property (garages, etc.). Tax on Plots - based on CSO census of property data showing land owned by individuals and entrepreneurs. Communal Tax - data on number of social flats is taken from CSO census of property.

Tax Yields: Tax base multiplied by maximum rate. In the case of Tourism Tax, it is assumed that all municipalities levy this tax permitted under the previous regime.

Source: Ministry of Finance

The central administration expects that each of the 3,100 municipalities will levy the new authorized taxes at rates equivalent to 20 per cent of the maximum rates during the first year. This will result in a total estimated yield of Ft 21 billion. This expectation was, at least, three times higher than the level realized by the previous system in 1990. Therefore, it is realistic for central government to assume that local government will gradually increase the potential of local taxes. As local tax rates continue to increase annually the maximum tax rates set by the centre will need to be reviewed at least to reflect inflation which has been in the region of 20 per cent per annum since 1990.

Local property taxes and municipal finances

In Hungary, local public expenditure is approximately 14 per cent of GDP, which represents a relatively high ratio in terms of international comparison. Local government is responsible for a wide range of services including, education, health care and several welfare services, for a list of the various services provided see Table 21.5. The cost of providing these welfare based services is in the region of two-thirds of all local expenditure. As user charges are collected directly by the service providers, only local grants and subsidies are shown in the budgets.

Table 21.5
Local government expenditure by sector

Sector	1991	1995
Education	36.5	28.8
Health Care	23.0	19.0
Administration	6.5	13.3
Communal Services	4.4	6.7
Social Services	6.1	5.7
Culture, Sport	4.7	3.8
Water Management	2.6	3.6
Industry, Commerce	4.6	2.8
Transportation	5.9	2.2
Housing	1.9	1.5
Others	3.8	12.6
Total	100.0	100.0

Source: Ministry of Finance

The structure of local government revenue

The local government revenue structure is defined by the services required to be provided by the local sector. Education, health care, social services should be made available to every citizen, therefore a stable revenue base is required to finance these activities. Approximately two-thirds of local government revenues are transfers from the national budget taking the form of grants (general, matching, earmarked, etc.), direct transfers to service institutions (e.g. the health sector) or shared revenues (personal income tax and vehicle tax). Table 21.6 illustrates the various sources of revenue to local government. Autonomous revenue sources are primarily recurrent revenue, however, one-third of revenue is of a capital nature resulting from the privatization and sale of assets, which as one might expect is a declining revenue potential for local government.

Table 21.6
Local government revenues (%)

Revenue	1991	1995
Local taxes	2.4	5.5
Other current revenue	15.2	15.6
Capital revenue	3.3	10.1
PIT	11.5	11.1
Other shared revenue	0.3	0.3
Grants	48.1	34.1
Health care fund transfers	16.9	9.4
Other revenue	1.1	7.2
Loans	1.2	6.7
Total	100.0	100.0

Source: Ministry of Finance

Local tax revenue

The history of modern local taxation shows that municipalities have had to increasingly rely on independent revenue sources, see Table 21.7. During 1991 central government projections were rather optimistic, assuming that local taxes would increase threefold. However, during the first year the application of the new local taxes was at the discretion of municipalities since the 'old' local taxes were also in operation resulting in a total tax yield significantly different from the target yield.

Table 21.7
Realized local tax revenue plans 1991-1996

Years	Tax Revenue		Actual (Local)	Actual (%)	
	Central	Local	Tax Revenue	Central	Local
	(Ft Billion)			(%)	
1991	21.0	-	9.5	45	-
1992	25.0	13.9	17.2	69	124
1993	22.0	17.4	27.1	123	156
1994	25.0	27.0	34.0	136	107
1995	29.0	-	46.4	160	-
1996*	42.0	-	73.0	174	-

*   *Expected*

Source: *Ministry of Finance*

Municipal property taxes including, the tax on buildings, tax on plots and tax on tourism represent a small proportion of total local tax revenue. Figure 21.1 shows the relative importance of the main local taxes. As can be seen the most significant local tax is the business tax, which represents 82 per cent of the total local tax yield. This tax is levied on local business activities, is based on the net turnover, and is therefore very similar to a 'municipal VAT'. As the tax represents a cost element, it is deductible from the corporate income tax.

Local property taxes tend to be applied in those regions of the country which are more highly developed. Table 21.8 gives an indication of the levels of tax across several regions. More than half of the property taxes were collected from the central region, where only 29 per cent of the population lives. In the economically distressed eastern regions of the country the local property tax potential is significantly lower (only 18 per cent of property taxes were collected here, while 41 per cent of population lives in this region).

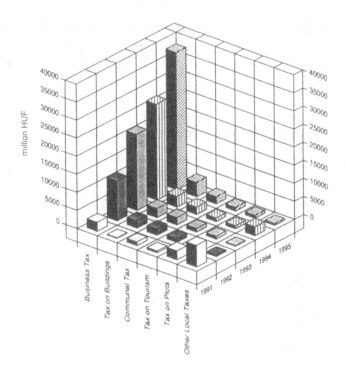

Figure 21.1   Local tax revenues 1991-1995 (Ft million)

Source: Lados (1995) and Ministry of Finance

These figures illustrate that the property tax base is relatively weak in Hungary, however, the introduction of taxes levied and administered by local government was nonetheless essential. This was in effect the last remaining potential revenue source for local government, which had not been utilized. Within the group of municipal taxes available to local government, the preference would appear to be for the business tax, which does not have a direct influence on the local electorate. Therefore, under the present tax system the property tax is still not widely utilized nor efficiently implemented.

Property taxes

There are three types of real property taxes, including the Tax on Buildings, the Tax on Plots and Tax on Tourism (real property). Regarding the measures taken during the transitional period it would appear that the Tax on Buildings replaced the previous Housing Tax and the tax on nonresidential buildings; in addition,

Table 21.8
Local taxes by regions 1995 (%)

Local Taxes	Total	Budapest	Pest County	Central Region	Trans- Danubia Region	Eastern Region
Tax on buildings	8.9	8.8	10.9	9.1	9.5	8.0
Tax on plots	1.8	1.9	6.5	2.6	1.1	0.6
Tourism tax (property)	0.8	0.0	0.8	0.1	2.5	0.4
Property tax	11.5	10.7	18.2	11.8	13.1	9.0
Communal tax	3.9	0.0	3.5	0.5	6.2	9.1
Tourism tax	1.7	1.1	0.2	1.0	3.9	0.8
Business tax	82.3	87.8	75.6	86.0	76.5	80.4
Other local taxes	0.6	0.4	2.5	0.7	0.3	0.7
Local tax, Total	100.0	100.0	100.0	100.0	100.0	100.0
Local tax by region	100.0	43.9	7.7	51.6	24.9	23.5
Property tax by region	100.0	40.9	12.3	53.2	28.4	18.4
Population	100.0	18.7	9.6	28.3	30.5	41.2

Source: *Ministry of Finance; Statistical Yearbook 1995 (CSO)*

the Tax on Plots replaced the earlier tax on plots and user fee on plots. In terms of official government projections the property taxes have the greatest potential across all the local taxes. Their share is some 64 per cent of the total estimated tax yields. The distribution of tax burden between residential and business property will be 30 and 70 per cent respectively. However, the share of tax on residential buildings represents only 5 per cent of the total property taxes. Local property taxes have accounted for a rather small proportion of total local revenues during the first part of this decade, see Table 21.9.

Table 21.9
The share of local property taxes

	1992	1993	1994	1995
Tax on buildings	2,119	2,598	3,255	4,144
Tax on plots	394	465	710	813
Tax on tourism	400	320	309	363
Total property taxes	2,913	3,383	4,274	5,320
Share of local revenue (%)	0.56	0.54	0.59	

Source: Ministry of Finance 1995

There are three general provisos of ALT which affect local property taxes:

1   Two taxes may not be levied on the same 'object', which means the same base cannot be taxed twice: for example, a summer cottage might be taxed as a property under the tourism tax or under the communal tax but not both.

2   The pre-existing centrally determined preferences and exemptions may not be restricted. This raises the practical question of whether residential property remains subject to tax under this proviso.

3   Locally set rates may not exceed the centrally defined maximum prescribed in the act.

Tax on buildings

Local governments can levy a property tax on all privately owned buildings located within the administrative area of a municipality. The plots (land) belonging to the building, which are less than the average (local) area, are also subject to taxation. The tax is payable by the owners of the buildings with the municipality having the right to choose between the two methods of assessment. These are an area based or unit tax per square metre or a value based, ad valorem approach. If a municipality selects assessment by value, there is a mandatory 50 per cent correction of the market value, with the corrected value known as the assessed value. It is reasoned by the legislators that to levy a tax based on full market price would be unfair, given that there have been relatively few market related transactions.

During the first four years of the new legislation central government defined a significant number of exemptions, many of which will remain in force well into the next century. Property types which are generally exempt from the property tax, are small apartments having basic public utilities, small village houses under 100 m² without utilities, buildings used for welfare services, churches, historic buildings and 25 m² for each resident.

Property tax office records show an almost exclusive reliance on the area basis rather than an ad valorem approach. The only exception is the municipality of Nyíregyháza, which introduced a value based property tax for non-residential buildings. Here, the tax administration has an unique administrative arrangement where the tax department and the Fee Office are part of the same organization sharing a common database system. This enables the municipality to be able to administer the ad valorem property tax because of the provision of adequate technical expertise.

Local governments prefer the unit or area based tax for two reasons, firstly, it resembles the earlier building and land tax and secondly, it is much easier to administer. It is an accepted fact amongst municipalities that the area based tax is more inflexible than one based on market values. The ad valorem approach requires more preliminary work to be undertaken by municipalities, a well maintained cadastre, valuation experts and well trained staff. In order to facilitate the widespread implementation of ad valorem property taxation a computerized cadastral system for all municipalities has been established.

Tax on plots

The tax on plots is essentially a property tax on the unimproved value of privately or publicly owned land (with the exception of land used for transport and telecommunication purposes) situated within the administrative area of a municipality. This tax is imposed on the owners of those plots, which are above the average area within a certain municipality. The average size of plots varies between local government regions and is normally defined in the current master plan of each city. The tax rates applied on these larger plots are normally lower than those applied to the buildings.

Tax on tourism property

Tax on tourism property is primarily aimed at summer cottages and holiday homes. The tax regulations are broadly similar to that of the tax on buildings.

Introduction of local property taxes

The estimated potential yield from property taxes is in the region of Ft 43 billion, approximately equal to the Personal Income Tax which was Ft 46.9 billion for 1991. The building tax is also applied to buildings not used for residential purposes including offices, shops, workshops and factory buildings. The land tax may also influence the entrepreneurial sector, because only plots used for public transport and telecommunication companies are exempt from tax.

The application of property taxes on enterprises can have two possible effects. The first is the opportunity for tax export (assignment of that cost to consumers). The second is that, property taxes, in principle, may influence the site selection of economic units. If the property tax is levied equally (the same tax burden per square metre) such as the poll tax, this has the virtue of being economically neutral or efficient in the sense of giving rise to no excess burden. In practice, however, differential local poll taxes are easy to evade by moving. Finally, it can be stated that the introduction of property taxes does not influence the utilization of agricultural land, as this type of land is not taxed.

As Table 21.9 shows, the building tax yield has almost doubled during the period 1992-1995. The basic reason for this growth has been the increasing number of local governments which have levied one or more of the local (property) taxes. By 1996 almost one-sixth of local governments levied the non-residential building tax, see Figure 21.2. Only one-sixteenth of the municipalities tax residential property simply because of the wide exemptions currently available, and the high rates of tax on personal incomes.

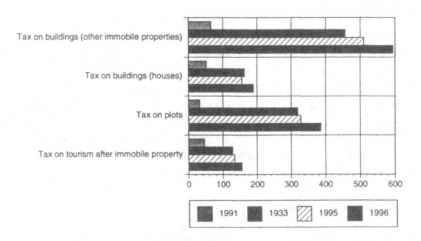

Figure 21.2   Number of local governments introducing property tax

Source: Lados (1995) and Ministry of Finance

432

Local tax revenues have become a major differentiating factor amongst local governments. A small group of local governments have no significant tax base, as 52 per cent of local governments in Hungary have a population of 1,000 or less. Immovable property is considered to be a good local tax base as such property exists in every municipality. However, there is a tendency within a number of small villages to have high numbers of elderly residents who are exempt from the tax. Notwithstanding some demographic problems (ability-to-pay) the regulation permits exemption for residential dwellings. Table 21.10 gives some statistics on the percentage of property entitled to exemption.

Table 21.10
Losses in taxable residential property in Győr 1991

	Number of houses	Taxable houses (%)
Total housing stock of Győr	48,335	100.0
Municipal stock[1]	14,843	30.7
Private housing stock	33,492	69.3
Housing stock[2] less than 80-110 m²	30,188	62.5
25m² exemption per family member	2,612	5.4
Taxable housing stock	672	1.4

1   *Exemption regulated by ALT*
2   *Exemption regulated by local decree*

Tax administration

An efficient local valuation system will only work with the proper information support. The legal cadastre is managed by the Land Offices (Földhivatal), which are part of the Ministry of Agriculture. Organized on a county basis, there are 109 local units under the county offices (plus 22 district offices in Prague). Property information comprises the identification of the owner, use of the property for both land and buildings, and legal information (such as rights and restrictions, e.g. mortgages). This information is categorized by parcel identification numbers and is detailed on maps. A digitization programme was recently launched in the Land Offices.

At local government level the Fee Offices (Illetikhivatal) maintain the records relating to transactions. The 19 county Fee Offices and the 22 offices in Prague operate within the local government administration, under the Notary. They also collect information on transaction prices relating to sales, inheritance and gifts. These offices have a particularly heavy workload which tends to result in delays in recording amendments. There is a short term proposal to establish a national statistical information system based on transactions for the Ministry of the Interior.

Within the local administration, the tax departments and technical departments have access to property information. Tax departments have the responsibility to collect information on residential property. Technical departments (sometimes covering several municipalities) have responsibility for the registration of building permits, local master plans (zoning) and public utility information. Currently, this information (residential and technical) is not integrated within most local government systems. However, efforts are in progress within some cities to establish a comprehensive, digitized physical infrastructural information system.

The information flow among the various offices should ideally be organized for property tax purposes. The Land Offices, as managers of the legal cadastre have to provide information for the Fee Offices and for the local tax departments. The Fee Offices who employ assessors and register fiscal information are able to transfer details on sales and other transaction data to local governments.

The necessary linkages between these important sources of information does not exist at present. However, the larger cities have the capability to build their own property register and valuation systems. Depending on the speed of computerization at the Land Offices and Fee Offices, city administrations will be able to integrate technical and legal (taxation) information. This process will be supported financially, as a larger proportion of property tax is raised in cities.

For the smaller municipalities a regional system of property registration and valuation is required which should be established at county level. The valuation function could be organized as a professional service, charging municipalities on a non-profit basis. Unlike the larger cities, the identification and the valuation processes within the smaller municipalities could be separated from the assessment, with collection and enforcement functions being implemented locally.

Cost of administration

The determination of the costs associated with the administration of a particular local tax are important and it is relatively straightforward to measure the costs of labour and the technical requirements of the tax administration. In a central government survey completed in 1992, property taxes were more costly than, for example, the 'Business Tax'. There is a significant difference between costs for each type of local tax in terms of the population size of the municipalities, see Table 21.11. Within the larger jurisdictions, these costs represent a smaller percentage of the tax revenue than in smaller villages.

Currently, local tax offices have two major tasks. Firstly, to administer the local taxes of the municipality, and secondly to collect the Motor Vehicle Tax, which is a shared tax. Presently when most local governments do not implement the tax on residential buildings, the ratio of tax proceeds is in the region of 1:3 between local taxes and the shared tax. This means that the Motor Vehicle Tax is more costly to administer, representing around 30 per cent of the tax yield. However, it should be stressed that only the revenue is shared, the municipality must bear the full cost of collection and administration.

Table 21.11
The share of administration costs of local taxes within different population groups 1991 (%)

Settlement Groups	less than 5,000	5,000 - 9,999	10,000 - 49,999	Greater than 50,000	Total
Tax on buildings	15.5	14.2	13.0	124.4	13.1
Communal tax	12.8	12.3	12.1	11.8	12.6
Business tax	12.1	11.6	11.4	10.6	11.0
Total of local taxes	13.2	12.5	12.0	11.9	12.0

Source: Based on Pitti (1992)

In Gyõr, administering the Motor Vehicle Tax involves employing at least four to six people on a permanent basis.   In comparison, the Business Tax only requires two officers, and yields approximately ten times more in revenue, than the Motor Vehicle Tax.

Problems and proposals

At present, as imposed the property tax is neither efficient nor equitable. Property tax usage is very limited because of the plethora of exemptions. The slow process of privatizing the municipal housing stock, uncertainty as to property ownership and the lack of a real estate cadastre have all contributed to reduce emphasis on property tax. Due to existing regulations, the property tax cannot be levied against residential property thereby reducing its potential revenue capacity.

ALT encourages local government to place a higher tax burden on firms. Firstly, the Business Tax is a form of income tax and is clearly a burden on enterprises. This tax yields approximately 75 per cent of the total local tax revenue. Secondly, large numbers of residential property are exempt from taxation. In total, firms bear more than 85 per cent of the total local tax burden. The gap between the respective tax burdens on individuals and firms is continuing to widen. One of the reasons for this relates to the fact that tax rates remained unchanged between 1991-1995. Annual increases in tax rates would not be acceptable politically. If local government does not change the tax rates, the effective tax rate will continue to decline each year. Consequently, the relative tax burden on individuals will decrease in real terms.

The potential for local taxation is to attempt to increase the role of property taxation. A number of objectives need to be established, firstly, the taxation of residential buildings and secondly, to change from unit based property tax system, to one based on market values. To prepare an action plan for this strategy two issues need to be addressed. The first relates to the existing regulatory system i.e. the ALT and the framework of the national tax system. The second issue refers to the ability of each municipality to undertake the necessary reforms and be able to implement the new property based taxes at the local level.

Under the new local tax system, all municipalities can choose one or more taxes that are adequate for their objectives (i.e. to increase or replace their previous tax revenue raising mechanisms). This is the principal reason as to why the tax on residential buildings and tax on plots are not favoured options. Given the general exemption of residential property it would be more appropriate if the act on local taxes could delegate the right of establishing exemptions to the local level. Without this change in the regulations the tax on real property will not become an adequate revenue source for municipalities.

A number of issues which relate to technical aspects need to be addressed that is the partial responsibility of central government. The local tax administration is currently computerized with the current software being a typical example of the previous centralized public administrative system. The application of the system was particularly relevant for the traditional (centrally planned) bottom-up data flow, i.e. to get all information that is needed for central planning. However, the system is not flexible enough for most local applications in terms of evaluating each tax and improving the efficiency of collection. The system cannot classify the tax yield by type of property (i.e. flat, garage, summer cottage, shop, office or factory building, etc.) nor can it separate taxpayers into specific categories. The problem of valuation also needs to be addressed by central government in terms of a requirement to regulate the valuation and assessment of property.

436

A further and potentially more difficult problem is the Motor Vehicle Tax whose revenue is presently shared between local and central government whilst the full cost of administration is borne at the local level. At present, the level of administration is in the region of 65 per cent of the local tax administration resources. This effectively results in municipalities having a limited opportunity to additionally administer other local taxes. Such administration requires the continuous development of the tax procedure from discovery, to billing and collection.

A weak issue of the local administration is the poor level of communication among municipal departments. There are many separate data bases all related to real estate whilst in practice there is little integration of these data bases. Local government has started to install their own computerized information systems, in several cases this is also supported by geographic information systems (GIS), however, it will be several years before these systems become fully operational.

As a matter of policy several issues need to be considered in designing an efficient and equitable local property tax system both at the local and central levels of government. Several of the suggested actions are detailed later in the chapter.

One of the most important aspects is that local government should determine the local tax policy or local tax code. Such a document would clearly establish for what purposes municipalities use local taxes. The following are some questions which would need to be addressed:

- What is the relationship between the taxes and city development, annual budgeting and the organizational relationships to the municipality?

- How should local government introduce a local tax?

- What form of research should be undertaken? What is the most appropriate valuation method (if not prescribed throughout the country); and what should be the revaluation cycle?

- How is the local tax administration to be organized?

Additional issues are coming to the fore as the tax reform proceeds, such as the need for a cadastral system. This could be computerized and regulated between the various offices including the Land Office, Duty Office, National Tax Office and some special departments of the City Hall (e.g. property management, housing construction approvals). What has to be established is an adequate information system within the municipality, within each department and amongst the departments of local government agencies. There is also a need for an economic and financial analysis of the locally employed taxes undertaken on an annual basis.

Action by central government

Short term

- complete the reform of local government finance;

- evaluate the performance of the present local tax system;

- decide on the implementation of market value based property taxation:

    - supporting research and surveys to establish an ad valorem approach;

    - support training activities in this field.

Medium term

- support higher education to introduce new undergraduate, graduate and postgraduate courses in public finance;

- make funds available for students and professionals to study public finance in foreign countries:

    - to join international training courses;

    - to support study trips;

    - to support student exchange;

    - to support the applications for postgraduate courses in this field.

Action by local government

Short term

- form a local tax policy or local tax code, including the identification of:

    - the purposes for new local taxes;

    - the relationship of the tax to city development, annual budgeting and organizational aspects within the municipality;

- the revaluation cycle of properties;

- what aspects of research should be undertaken for local tax purposes;

- organization of local tax administration;

- staff incentives for local tax administration;

• using economic and financial analysis for the local tax system on an annual basis;

• improving the publicity of local government activities;

• to build up an efficient partnership among municipal departments, municipal agencies and decentralized central government offices;

• introduce a residential property tax.

Medium term

• to develop procedures for property taxation:

- complete the computerized information system of the City Hall;

- completion of the real estate cadastre;

- undertake studies into the potential change from an area basis to a market value based system of property taxation.

22 Property taxation in the Czech Republic

Alena Rohlícková

Introduction

After the velvet revolution in 1989 the process of reform began in the Czech Republic, with the former communist regime being replaced by a democratic system of government. During the last six years the framework for a market economy has been successfully established. One of the most important steps taken in 1993 was the implementation of a completely new tax system. Within the context of this tax system the following property taxes were introduced: the Real Estate Property Tax, Inheritance Tax, Gift Tax and Immovables Transfer Tax. Other direct taxes currently in place are the Road Tax and taxes on income and profits, i.e. Personal Income Tax and Corporate Income Tax. Indirect taxes introduced include taxes on goods and services, i.e. Value-Added Taxes and Excise Duties.

Real Estate Property Tax

The Real Estate Property Tax was introduced in 1992 with the passing of the Property Tax Act by the Czech National Council. This tax is levied annually on the owners of real property including, individuals and corporations. However, there is one exception, that is where the property is owned by the state, the user or occupier is responsible for the tax. There are also problems relating to uncertainty in terms of the identification of every parcel of agricultural land in the cadastre, due primarily to the process of restitution of the real property to its previous owners. In cases where the ownership is difficult to prove, users are primarily liable to the tax.

The Real Estate Property Tax consists of two parts firstly, a tax on land and secondly, a tax on the structures. The source for this division is contained in the civil law which stipulates that immovable property is both land and immovable/ permanent structures.

Tax on land

For land to be taxable it must be located within the national territory of the Czech Republic and registered in the Real Property Cadastre (land register). For tax purposes the land is divided into a number of categories:

1   agricultural land, which means arable land, hop-fields, vineyards, gardens, orchards, meadow and pasture land;

2   woodland;

3   fish farms;

4   plots upon which buildings have been constructed including yards;

5   unimproved land as determined by landuse planning; and

6   other land.

Land used for special purpose forests, water surfaces and land for defence purposes are not included within the tax base.

Tax on structures

The tax on structures is imposed on buildings and other structures for which the appropriate building approval has been issued, or which are subject to such approval and are used, or have been finished in accordance with the building regulations. Structures belonging to dams, watercourse regulating facilities, water mains and water works facilities, utility distribution facilities and public thoroughfares used for transport (i.e. highways, airport facilities, railroads, waterways and ports) are not included.

Property transfer taxes

Property transfer taxes include Inheritance Tax, Gift Tax and Immovables Transfer Tax passed by the Czech National Council in 1992.

Inheritance Tax

The basis of this tax is the acquisition of property by inheritance. Included in the tax base are immovable objects, non-residential premises, movable objects, securities, money both in Czech and foreign currency, property rights and other valuable assets. No tax is levied on immovable property situated abroad.

Gift Tax

Included in this tax is the gratuitous acquisition of movable and immovable property and other property benefits, excluding the gratuitous transfer of property ensuing from an obligation stipulated by a legal requirement.

Immovables Transfer Tax

The subject of this tax is the transfer of real property on sale. The seller would normally be the taxpayer with the buyer being the guarantor. The buyer is liable to pay the tax in cases where the property is acquired by the enforcement of a legal ruling, expropriation and bankruptcy. Both transferor and transferee are liable to pay the tax in the case of the exchange of property.

Revenue

Revenue from property taxes in 1995 was in the region of 0.6 per cent of GDP. Table 22.1 shows the level of property tax during the period 1993-1995 as a percentage of GDP.

Table 22.1
Property tax for period 1993-1995

Year	1993	1994	1995
Property Taxes	0.4	0.6	0.60
Real Estate Property Tax	0.3	0.3	0.30
Inheritance and Gift Tax	NA	NA	0.02
Immovables Transfer Tax	NA	NA	0.20

Table 22.2 shows that the main revenue sources are VAT, excise and income taxes as a percentage of GDP.

Table 22.2
Main revenue sources as a percentage of GDP

Year	1993	1994	1995
Income Taxes	11.1	11.5	11.4
Taxes on goods and services	12.9	12.7	12.3
Other Taxes	3.3	1.5	1.3

Property taxes, similarly to all other taxes, are centrally administrated by tax offices known as Financial Offices. The revenue from transfer taxes is allocated as income for the state budget. Generally, the Real Estate Property Tax is considered as a local tax, the revenue of which is treated as income for local budgets, according to the location of the real estate. The revenue received from this tax is approximately 3.6 per cent of all local revenues, and 6.9 per cent of total tax revenues to the local budgets. Income taxes are shared by both central and local government. Expenditure of local budgets are geared primarily for the provision of local services. The Ministry of Finance establishes the methodology for local budgets though it does not directly specify how the Real Estate Property Tax revenue should be spent.

Notwithstanding the relatively low levels of revenue raised from the real estate tax an important factor is that all the taxpayers have fulfilled their duty by presenting their tax returns with the necessary data for taxation. This represented the first important step in introducing a system of property taxation within the context of a general tax reform.

Basis of the tax

Real Estate Property Tax

The property tax at present, is not based on the market value of the property, but rather it is based on the area of the property in square metres. The basis for the tax on structures is the area in square metres as indicated on the ground floor plan of the building as at 1 January for the given tax period.

The reason for choosing an area based approach was that in 1992 there was no suitable legal framework for the assessment of the market value of property. At the same time there were no value maps in existence for the whole of the Czech Republic.

The value assessed according to the Price Decree forms the basis of the tax on agricultural land, commercial forestry and fish farms. All remaining property is assessed on the area based system.

Transfer taxes

Immovable Transfer Tax is based on the market value referred to in the Act as 'current value'. The Price Decree issued by the Ministry of Finance represents a form of special legislation, which is used for assessing the property's official value for the purposes of the Inheritance Tax and Gift Tax. This Decree is also used by assessors for ad hoc transfers; however, if the sale price of the property is lower than the value assessed according to the Price Decree, the latter officially assessed value is taken as a base in assessing the Immovable Transfer Tax. The Price Decree is suitable only for an ad hoc assessment due to its rather complicated technique.

Tax bases and tax rates

Agricultural land

The Ministry of Agriculture in conjunction with the Ministry of Finance issued a decree which includes a list of cadastral regions showing average prices per square metre of agricultural land, as derived from soil classifications. This classification given for every parcel of agricultural land determines the soil quality. All agricultural land within the country is recorded on maps showing agricultural land quality. The list of average prices of land will only remain in force for a certain period of time. A project which attempted to match the cadastre with the quality of the soil on agricultural land commenced in 1994 and is due to be completed in late 1998. This should make it possible to tax every parcel of agricultural land according to its value. The annual tax rate applicable to agricultural land is 0.75 per cent. The Price Decree issued by the Ministry of Finance contains prices per square metre for certain soil classifications used for the ad hoc assessment of transfer taxes.

Forestry land

The Price Decree states that the value of the forests should take account of the type of forest and the quality of the soil. This results in approximately 180 prescribed values to reflect the different types of woodland and soil types. These prescribed values are used for all the property taxes. The annually tax rate is currently 0.25 per cent.

Fish farms

The Price Decree stipulates only one value per square metre for this type of land, and similarly for forestry land, it is used for all property taxes. Only intensive fish farms and those used for industrial fish breeding are taxable under the Real Estate Property Tax at an annual rate of 0.25 per cent.

Plots upon which buildings are constructed and yards

In this case the total area in square metres is taken as the basis for the Real Estate Property Tax with a fixed tax rate of 0.1 Kc per square metre.

Developed land for structures

Building plots suitable for development is taken to mean any unencumbered parcel of land upon which a building is to be constructed in accordance with official procedures. The basis of the property tax is also calculated on the footprint area of the building in square metres, at a fixed tax rate of 1 Kc multiplied by one of the following coefficients:

0.3   for municipalities with less than 300 inhabitants;

0.6   for municipalities with more than 300 and less than 600 inhabitants;

1.0   for municipalities with more than 600 and less than 1,000 inhabitants;

1.4   for municipalities with more than 1,000 and less than 6,000 inhabitants;

1.6   for municipalities with more than 6,000 and less than 10,000 inhabitants;

2.0   for municipalities with more than 10,000 and less than 25,000 inhabitants;

2.5   for municipalities with more than 25,000 and less than 50,000 inhabitants;

3.5   for municipalities with more than 50,000 inhabitants and spas;

4.5   for the capital Prague.

The above coefficients can be changed by municipalities and, in addition, they may choose to vary the coefficients applied in different parts of the municipality.

Structures and other buildings

There are different tax rates applicable to different buildings, such as:

445

1   residential houses/buildings - 1 Kc per square metre;

2   other buildings adjacent to residential houses - 1 Kc per square metre above 16m²;

3   buildings for individual recreation (i.e. weekend houses) and holiday dwellings - 3 Kc per square metre and 1 Kc per square metre for other adjacent structures except garages;

4   garages detached from residential buildings - 4 Kc per square metre;

5   buildings devoted to business activities such as:

    (a)   buildings for agricultural production, forestry and water management - 1 Kc per square metre;

    (b)   buildings used in industry, construction, transport, utilities and for other agricultural production - 5 Kc per square metre. With regard to multipurpose buildings the basic rate applied relates to the predominant business activity occupying the largest area; should the floor area of the premises used for different business purposes be the same, the rate to be applied is the highest relevant rate;

    (c)   buildings used for other business activities - 10 Kc per square metre;

6   other buildings - 3 kc per square metre.

The basic tax rate per square metre is increased by 0.75 Kc for each additional floor above ground floor level, provided the area of such a floor exceeds two-thirds of the area of the built-up property. In the case of buildings used for business purposes the basic tax rate per square metre is increased by 0.75 Kc for every floor above ground floor.

The basic tax rates which may be increased due to multi-floors, are multiplied by the coefficient attributable to the municipality. In the case of residential property the coefficients are the same as applied to developed land, in the case of other structures the coefficient to be applied is 1.5. The tax rate increases by 2 Kc per square metre of floor area for non-residential uses located within a residential building and used for business purposes, with the exception of buildings used for agricultural production or where such non-residential premises are subject to exemptions. With regard to dwellings located in national parks and other protected areas and devoted to individual occupation, family houses and in respect of buildings which fulfil an ancillary function to such houses, the rate is multiplied by a coefficient of 2.0. For all the taxpayers the Immovable

Transfer Tax rate is 5 per cent of the sale price or the assessed price, in event that the sale price is the lower.

Inheritance and gift taxes are progressive and take into account any family relationship between donor and donee. There are three groups of taxpayers; the first represents direct relatives, ancestors and descendants with a tax rate of 1 per cent to 5 per cent; the second group includes indirect relatives with a tax rate of 3 per cent to 12 per cent; the third group, which includes all other unrelated parties, the rate varies from 7 per cent to 40 per cent. The Inheritance Tax rate is then multiplied by a coefficient of 0.5, which effectively reduces the tax by one-half.

Responsibility for making the assessment

For the Real Estate Property Tax the assessment of a property's value by the authorities is not required. The tax including the values as required by the legislation are declared by taxpayers themselves, i.e. a form of self-assessment. The assessment of immovable property for Property Transfer Tax purposes is made by expert assessors. These experts are appointed by the head of the District Court and are required to provide official assessments in accordance with the Price Decree. The Price Decree is extremely comprehensive and detailed and requires all experts to adhere to it. The taxpayer has a duty to declare an expert assessment as part of the tax return and has to pay the associated costs.

Appeal procedures

Appeal procedures are implemented in accordance with the Administration and Collection of Taxes Act, which regulates the administration of all taxes. The appeal must be submitted within 30 days from the date of delivery of the tax assessment decision. If the appeal does not include particulars prescribed by law, the tax administrator must notify the taxpayer that amendments are required and what those amendments relate to, setting an appropriate time-limit of at least 15 days for compliance. An appeal has no delaying effect. During the appeal process the procedures can involve reassessment or a new assessment of the property prepared by another professional assessor. Within the system there is no committee of assessors or similar body to adjudicate on appeals as is common in most other countries.

The tax administrator, whose decision is challenged by an appeal, decides on the appeal, and if he is in agreement with the appeal no further appeal may be made against the decision. However, if he only agrees in part with the appeal, a further appeal is admissible. If the tax administrator does not decide the appeal he can refer the appeal, together with results of the completed proceedings, full documentation and his submission, to the appeal authority for decision. The appeal authority is superior to the tax administrator and its responsibility is to review the contested decision to the extent applied for in the appeal and is not in any way bound by the appellant's proposals. It can therefore amend the decision contested in the appeal to the appellant's disadvantage. No appeal is permissible against the decision of the appeal authority. If the taxpayer is not satisfied with the result of the tax proceedings, he can present his case against the decision of tax authorities to the Court.

Methods of assessment

For purposes of the Transfer Tax the methods of assessment used are only those specified in the Price Decree. For property taxation purposes only single property valuations techniques are applied and in essence, the cost approach is used for the assessment of buildings and other structures. This approach is based on predetermined values of the property according to the type of structure and further adjusted by applying coefficients. The most important coefficients are those relating to the materials of construction, i.e. brick, monolith concrete, metal, wood etc., height, location and depreciation and are used for the assessment of rental houses. In addition both the cost approach and the income approach (that is the annual rent divided by the capitalization rate which is prescribed by the Ministry of Finance) may also be applied.

Urban land is assessed according to value maps if any exist, or by fixed values per square metre, which are stated by the Price Decree, corresponding to the size of the municipality. The Price Decree contains the precise method of how to create value maps, referred to as Price Maps. To date only four municipalities have prepared comprehensive value maps.

Agricultural land is assessed according to the soil quality determined for every parcel of land. Every soil type has its own price stated within the Price Decree. The assessment of forestry land corresponds to a representative set of forest types on the land, which all have their own basic price stated in the Price Decree. There are also prices for overgrowth with regard to cost, area, age, quality, etc.

Exemptions

The number and extent of exemptions which are in keeping with the IT system represent approximately 16 per cent of the total level of collected real estate property taxes. The onus is on the taxpayer to apply for exemption from the tax on land in the appropriate tax return.

Exemption from land tax component

1   Land in possession of the state, unless it is used for business purposes or leased, except for leases granted to organizations financed from the state budget.

2   Land in the possession of a municipality.

3   Land used for foreign embassies.

4   Land administered by the Land Fund of the Czech Republic, or the land transferred to the National Property Fund, unless the land is subject to a lease.

5   Land constituting one functional unit together with a building or a part thereof used for the purposes of religion, conducted by churches or other religious societies recognized by the state; also buildings or parts thereof used as administrative buildings of such churches and other religious societies. 'Land constituting one functional unit with a building' means such land which is necessary for operating and proper functioning of the building.

6   Land constituting one functional unit with a building in possession of a citizen's association and other organizations acting in favour of public welfare.

7   Land constituting one functional unit with a building serving schools and school facilities, museums and galleries which are specified by a special regulation, libraries, state archives, health facilities, social care facilities, foundations and with buildings of listed monuments specified by a decree issued by the Ministry of Finance in conjunction with the Ministry of Culture.

8   Land constituting one functional unit with buildings serving exclusively for the improvement of the environment and specified by the appropriate decree of the Ministry of Finance in conjunction with the Ministry of the Environment.

9   Land used for cemeteries.

10   Land situated in protected areas which complies with legislation governing the protection of nature and countryside, with the exception of national parks and protected natural areas; land situated in national parks and protected natural areas which is classified as Zone I.

11   Land used for game reserves, groves, windbreaks, meadows and pasture land; land located in zones of hygienic water protection and land in other areas which cannot be used in any other way.

12   Land used for public parks, recreation areas and sport facilities.

13   Agricultural land is exempt for a period of 5 years and forestry land for a period of 25 years, commencing in the year following the year in which such land has been reclaimed and returned to agricultural or forestry production.

14   Land is exempt for a period of 5 years from the 1 January 1993, including any agricultural land and forestry land up to a maximum 10 hectares restituted to the original owners. This also applies to those cases where substitute land has been provided in lieu of the original land with the proviso that this land is exploited by the owners or related persons and rights to such land have not been transferred or assigned to other persons except related persons. Under this condition the taxpayer must prove that private agricultural business activities are carried out on the given agricultural land by an extract from the official records.

15   Land used for public transport.

Exemptions from the tax on structures

1   Buildings in the possession of the state, unless it is used for business purposes or leased, except for leases granted to organizations financed from the state budget.

2   Buildings in the possession of municipalities.

3   Buildings in the possession of another state used by diplomatic representatives.

4   Buildings administered by the Land Fund of the Czech Republic or transferred to the National Property Fund, unless such buildings are leased.

5   Buildings in the possession of churches and religious societies recognized by the state used for religious purposes and also administrative buildings of such churches and other religious societies.

6   Buildings in the possession of citizen's associations and other organizations acting for purposes of public welfare.

7   Buildings for a period of 15 years, commencing in the year following the year in which the building acceptance certificate was issued; new residential houses in the possession of individuals used for permanent housing of the owner or related persons and new apartment buildings in which the apartments are exclusively in the possession of individuals.

8   Buildings for a period of 15 years from 1 January 1993 including residential buildings restituted to individuals in accordance with legislation, unless the property right to such buildings has been transferred or assigned to persons other than related persons. Buildings in the possession of individuals subject to the proviso that such buildings were built prior to 1948 with the majority of flats being rented or occupied for at least 15 years by occupiers other than the owner and the owner's related persons in compliance with earlier legislation.

9   For a period of 10 years from 1 January 1993 including residential apartment buildings which were transferred to individuals by the state, municipalities or cooperatives, unless the property right has been subsequently transferred or assigned to persons other than related persons.

10   Buildings used as schools and school facilities, museums and galleries, state archives, libraries, health facilities, social care facilities, foundations, citizen's associations of disabled persons and public accessible listed buildings.

11   Buildings used for public transport.

12   Buildings used exclusively for improvement of the environment.

13   Residential houses and houses for recreational purposes in possession of individuals who receive social benefits and who are holders of disabled persons certificates to the extent that these houses are used as the permanent residence of such persons.

14   Historic buildings improved by the owner, for a period of eight years commencing the year following the year in which the construction permit was issued.

15   Buildings which were subject to improvements consisting of changing the heating system from solid fuel to gas, electricity or introducing systems which utilize solar, wind, geothermal or bio-mass energy to improve the thermal efficiency of the building.

Collection procedures

All property taxes are administered by Financial Offices organized on a district level. These authorities are responsible for tax administration including tax collection. Rules for the collection of tax and procedures are determined by the Administration and Collection of Taxes Act. According to this Act, details of tax proceedings are never made public.

A tax return has to be completed and submitted on a prescribed form issued by Ministry of Finance or on a computer printout whose data is identical with the Ministry's form. Each year the Ministry of Finance produces explanatory leaflets to assist taxpayers in how to complete the tax returns. Tax returns for the Real Estate Property Tax have to be filed no later than on 31 January of the year on which the tax will be assessed. If there have been no changes, taxpayers are not required to submit a tax return. Tax administrators deliver to the taxpayer the assessment notification with an appropriate payment record. In the event that the tax on a number of taxable properties is assessed collectively in the form of list, this is known as 'delivery by collective listing' and consists of displaying an announcement about the collective list on the municipality's official bulletin board. At the time of viewing, the taxpayer is informed of the tax obligation.

Real estate property tax can be paid in one lump sum or by instalments. The terms for payment are defined in the legislation. It is possible to pay by means of two equal instalments where the taxpayer is involved in agricultural production, or by four equal instalments in all other cases. Transfer taxes are however paid in one lump sum after assessment notification. Payments can be made by cash directly at the Financial Offices, by post or at banks, or by credit transfers. In some cases, at the taxpayer's request there is a provision for tax deferral.

Tax Offices systematically record tax liabilities and actual payments.

Computation of the tax

The taxpayer has to compute his own tax liability and must report any exemptions and deductions. Only in the case of Inheritance Tax is the tax liability computed by Financial Offices, this is because liability is dependant upon the inheritance procedures and is complicated by virtue of the many deductions and other issues involved.

Enforcement procedures

Where doubts arise, the tax administrator can ask the taxpayer for an explanation or additional information. In the event that a tax return or supplementary tax return was not submitted within the prescribed time limit, despite a request from the tax administrator, or to remedy incorrect information, the tax administrator is authorized to determine the tax base and estimate the tax liability by means of instruments of proof available at the time, without further collaboration with the taxpayer.

In the event that the taxpayer is in arrears, the tax administrator can determine a remedial time limit of at least eight days, after the expiry of which measures will be taken to collect the arrears without further notification. The process is realized by means of executory proceedings by Tax Offices or by the court. Tax execution proceedings are performed by an executory order to obtain directly the arrears from the taxpayer's bank accounts, orders for deduction from salary, sale of movable property or sale of real estate.

Penalties

The penalty for an overdue payment is computed beginning with the day following the day payment was due until the day the payment is made inclusively. The basic penalty is 0.1 per cent of the whole overdue amount. The penalty for an overdue payment additionally assessed on the basis of supplementary tax returns from the taxpayer who recognized the fault himself are subject only to one-half of the penalty rate. However, in the event that the tax default was ascertained by the tax administrator, the penalty is based on double the rate.

Critical analysis

The present property tax system is recognized as being simple and easy for taxpayers to fulfil their duties provided that all necessary documents are available. Computation of the tax is relatively straightforward and without significant problems. One of the most important advantages is the computerized tax administration by the Financial Offices which is linked with the State Information System, including the Real Property Cadastre and the Inhabitants Register.

One of the disadvantages of such a system is that the property tax does not reflect market values. The rates per square metre are far removed from this objective standard and the Price Decree used mainly for transfer tax assessments does not provide for market based assessments.

Proposed changes

Since 1993 there has been a project of Technical Assistance Mission on Property Taxes organised by the OECD. This project submitted to the Ministry of Finance a number of recommendations concerning tax administration and valuation methodologies which would be required if the system were to be changed to one based on the market value of land and buildings. New legislation is due to be passed in 1998 with the new property tax system likely to be introduced in 1999. Pilot studies have been implemented which have demonstrated the importance of involving municipalities in tax administration and possibly with the tax collection process.

References

Administration of Taxes and Fees, Act No 337/1992 Coll.

Inheritance Tax, Gift Tax and Immovables Transfer Tax, Act No 357/1992 Coll.

Property Tax, Act No 338/1992 Coll.

ECD (1995), Technical Assistance to the Czech Republic on Valuation Methodology for the Property Tax.

OECD (1996), Technical Assistance to the Czech Republic on Valuation Methodology for the Property Tax.

The Price Decree No 178/1994 Coll. on Values of Structures, Land and Permanent Vegetation, OECD Report for Czech Republic, (1993), Technical Assistance Mission on Property Tax Administration.

Rohlícková, A. (1996), *Transformation of the Czech Economy and New Conditions for the Application of a New Real Property Tax System,* paper presented at Institute of Revenues Rating and Valuation Third International Conference, Rome.

Index

Printed in the United States
by Baker & Taylor Publisher Services